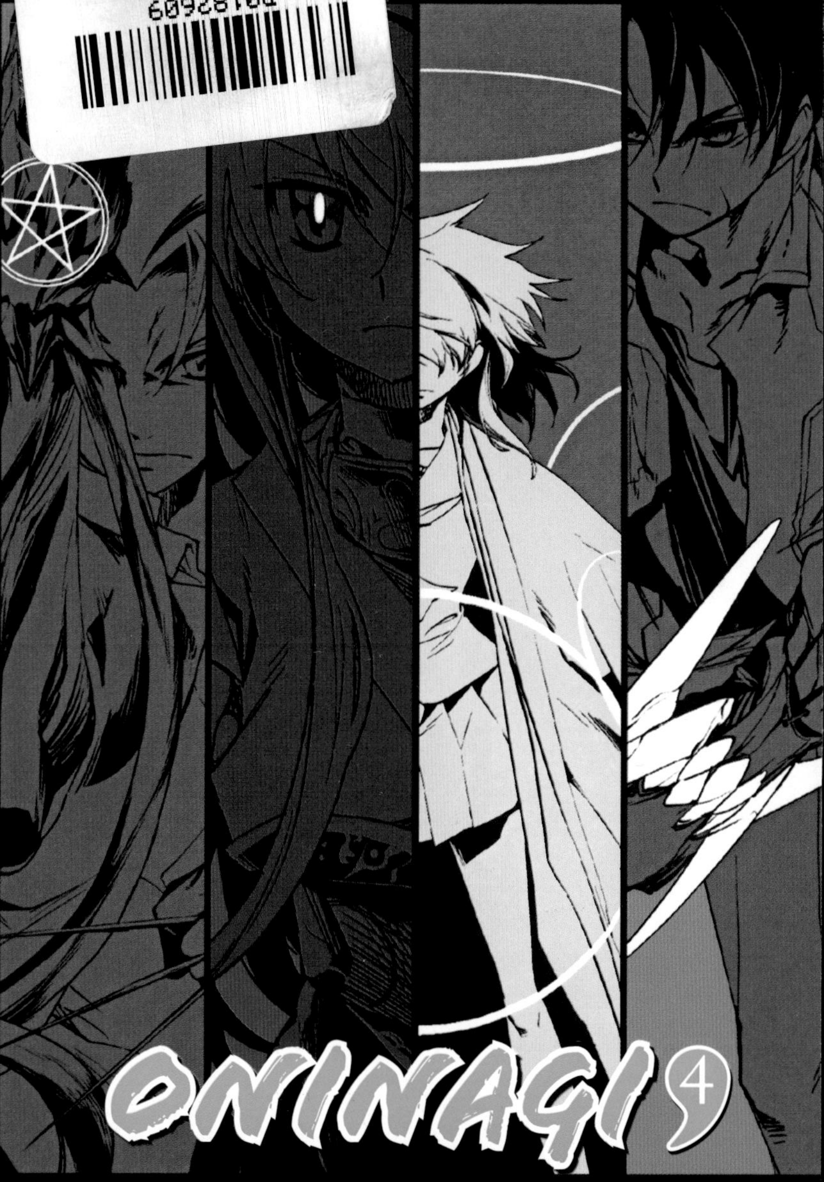
ONINAGI 4

A K I R A   I S H I D A

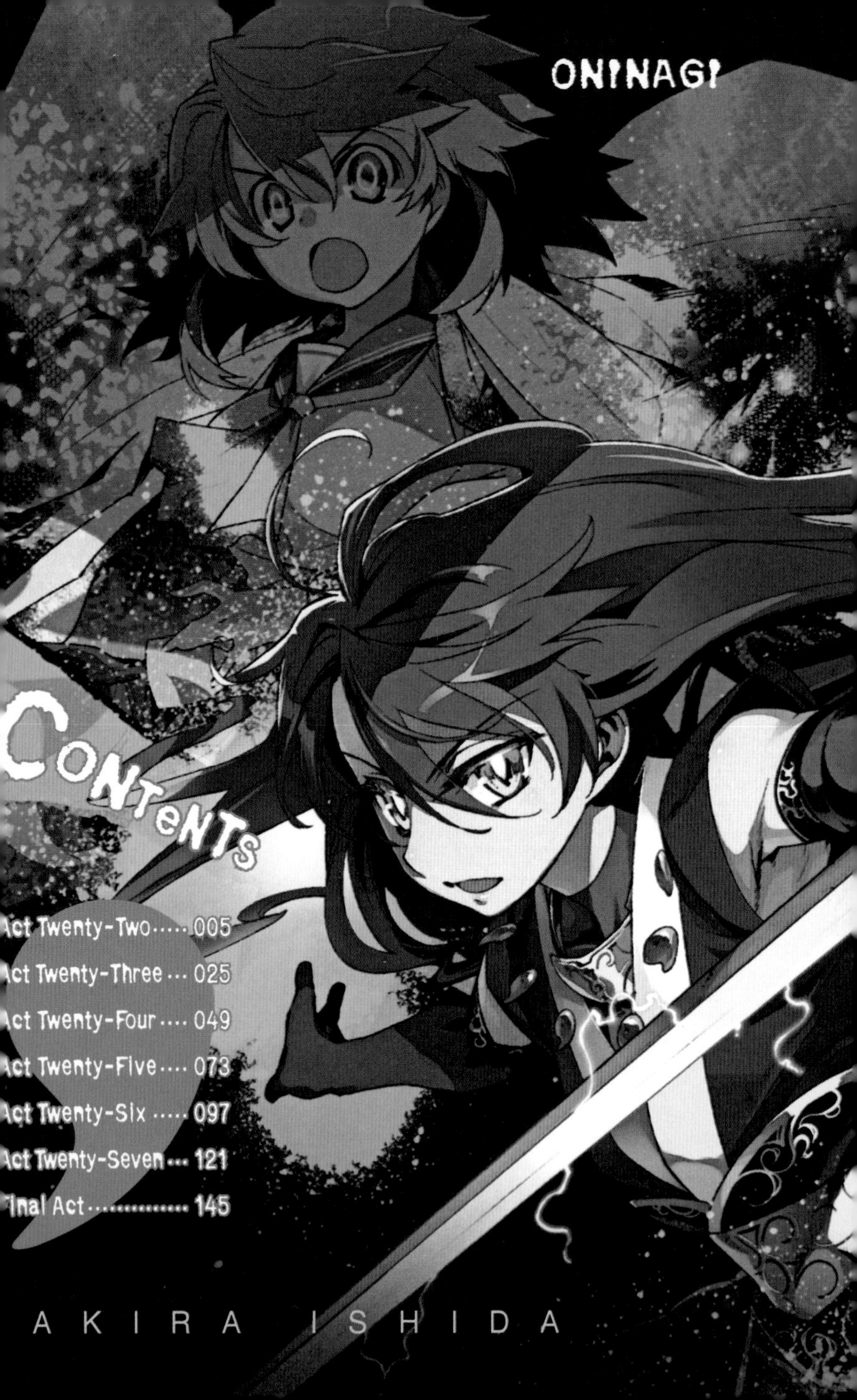

ONINAGI

Contents

A K I R A   I S H I D A

ONINAGI

Typical high school girl Nanami Kushimiya finds herself under suspicic of being a "demon." In order to harness the skills hidden within her, Nana begins training with Tomotaka's teacher. Meanwhile, the Arcana, the demo organization in pursuit of Nanami's powers, sustains a massive attack by Divine Enforcers, while an Arcana splinter group, having broken throug the shrine barrier, heads toward Nanami and company's location—

Nanami Kushimiya

rl with demon blood
r veins. She's usually
typical high school
but when her hidden
er powers appear,
does a completely
rent personality with
emonic abilities.

Tomotaka Onigoroshi

Slayer first class of
the Divine Enforcers.
As the legitimate heir
to the Onigoroshi House,
she has made the hunting
of demons her life's work.
She masterfully wields
the sword, "Oninagi."

Kazuto Sanjouin

Slayer second class of
the Divine Enforcers. Uses
animated needles created by
weaving collected "taint" into
needle form as weapons. Part
of a Sanjouin branch family,
he has complicated feelings
toward the head house.

Tsurug

A demonic pup
created for use
battle approxim:
four hundred year
by Nanami's anc
"Princess Kinkan."
allegiance to the pr
descendant, Nar

Demons
Those who harbor the "taint"
vithin their bodies. Once, they coexisted with
umans, but now are hunted targets. They are able
o morph into vicious forms and attack humans

Divine Enforcers
An organization that exists to hunt demons.
Tomotaka and Kazuto are members. They believe th
actively antagonistic dos ans will lead to disaster

鬼薙

オニナギ 4

ONINAGI

AKIRA ISHIDA

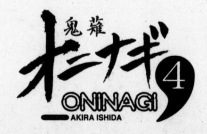

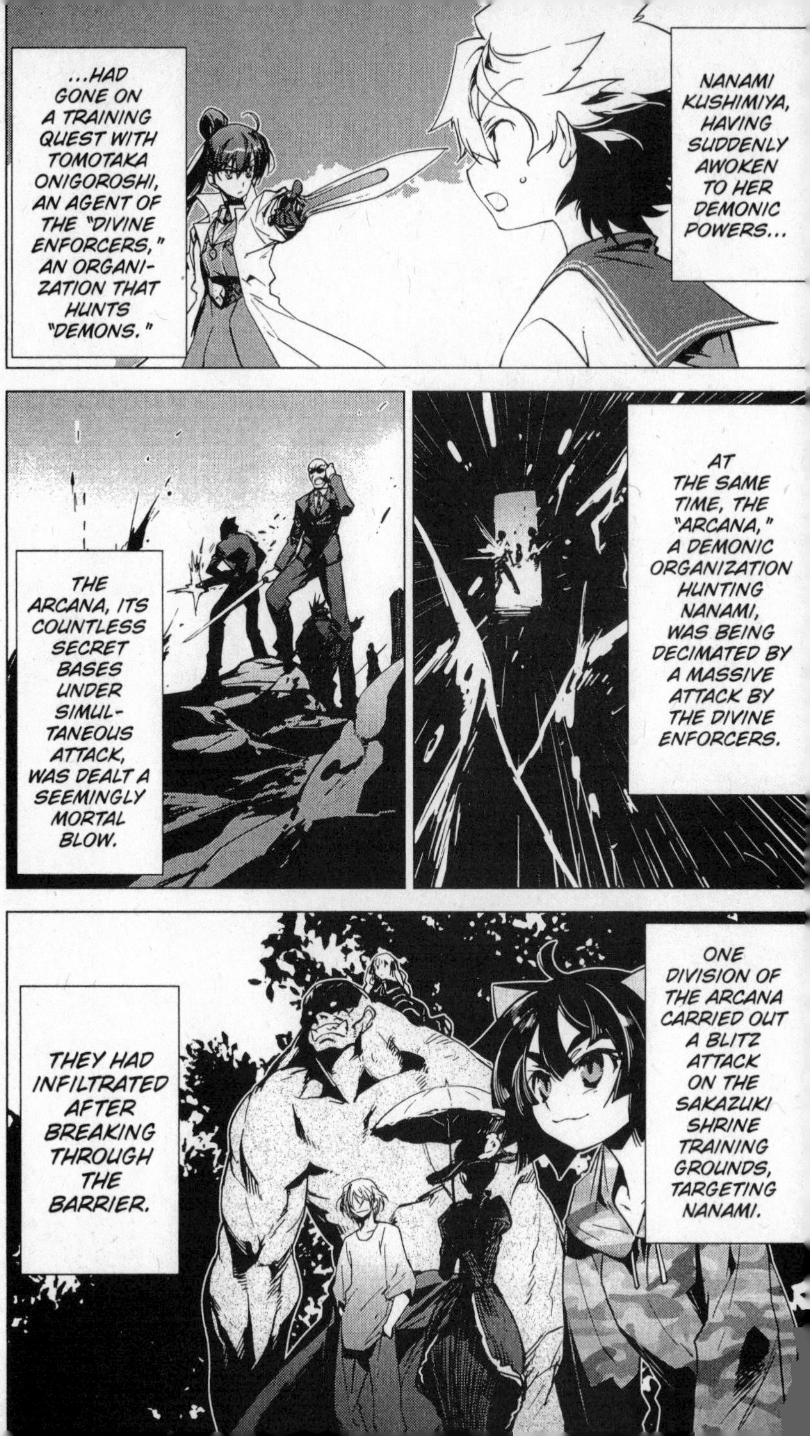
NANAMI KUSHIMIYA, HAVING SUDDENLY AWOKEN TO HER DEMONIC POWERS...
...HAD GONE ON A TRAINING QUEST WITH TOMOTAKA ONIGOROSHI, AN AGENT OF THE "DIVINE ENFORCERS," AN ORGANIZATION THAT HUNTS "DEMONS."
AT THE SAME TIME, THE "ARCANA," A DEMONIC ORGANIZATION HUNTING NANAMI, WAS BEING DECIMATED BY A MASSIVE ATTACK BY THE DIVINE ENFORCERS.
THE ARCANA, ITS COUNTLESS SECRET BASES UNDER SIMULTANEOUS ATTACK, WAS DEALT A SEEMINGLY MORTAL BLOW.
ONE DIVISION OF THE ARCANA CARRIED OUT A BLITZ ATTACK ON THE SAKAZUKI SHRINE TRAINING GROUNDS, TARGETING NANAMI.
THEY HAD INFILTRATED AFTER BREAKING THROUGH THE BARRIER.

ACT TWENTY-TWO.

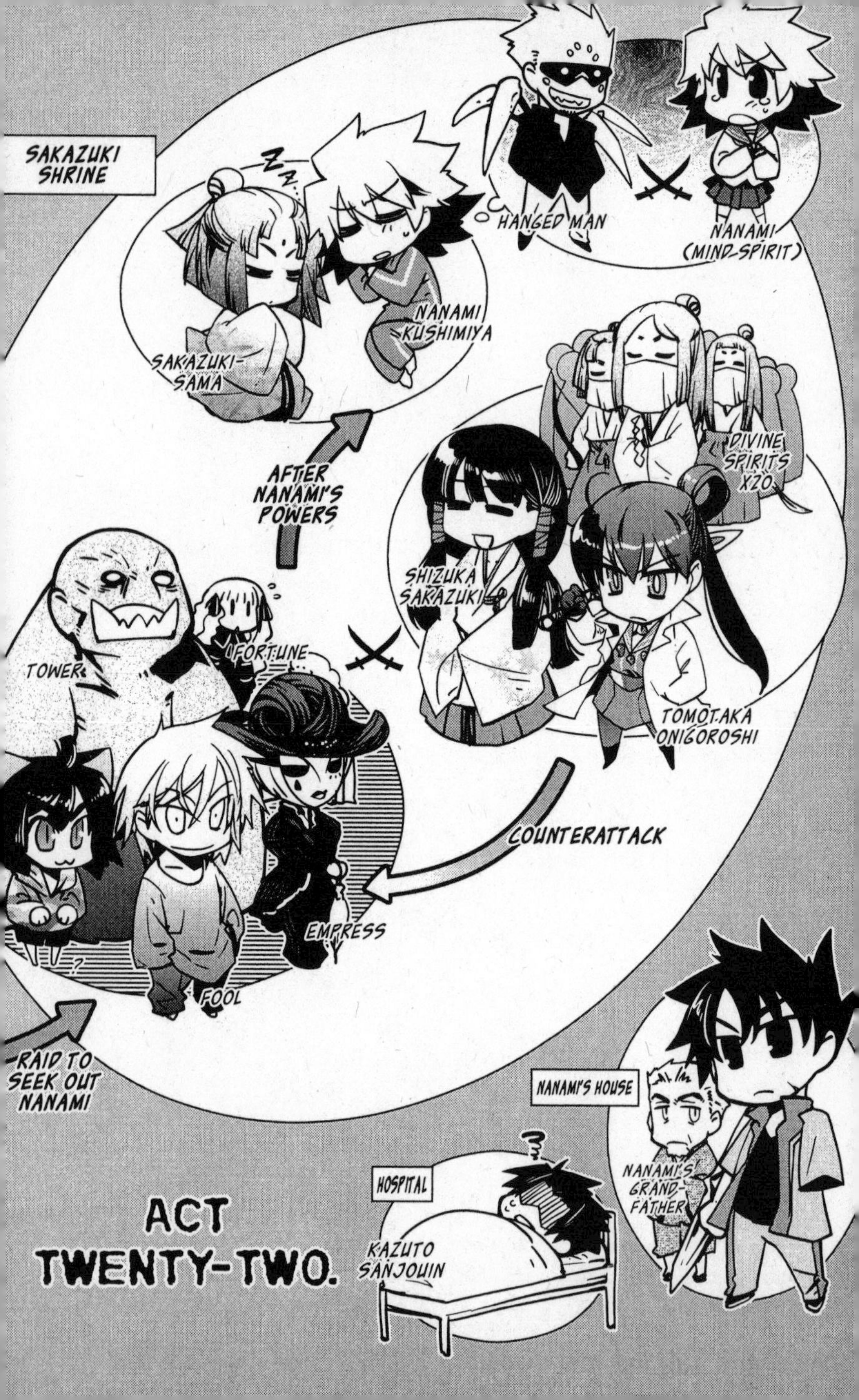
NANAMI (MIND-SPIRIT)
HANGED MAN
SAKAZUKI SHRINE
NANAMI KUSHIMIYA
SAKAZUKI-SAMA
AFTER NANAMI'S POWERS
DIVINE SPIRITS X20
SHIZUKA SAKAZUKI
TOMOTAKA ONIGOROSHI
COUNTERATTACK
FORTUNE
TOWER
EMPRESS
FOOL
RAID TO SEEK OUT NANAMI
NANAMI'S HOUSE
NANAMI'S GRAND-FATHER
HOSPITAL
KAZUTO SANJOUIN

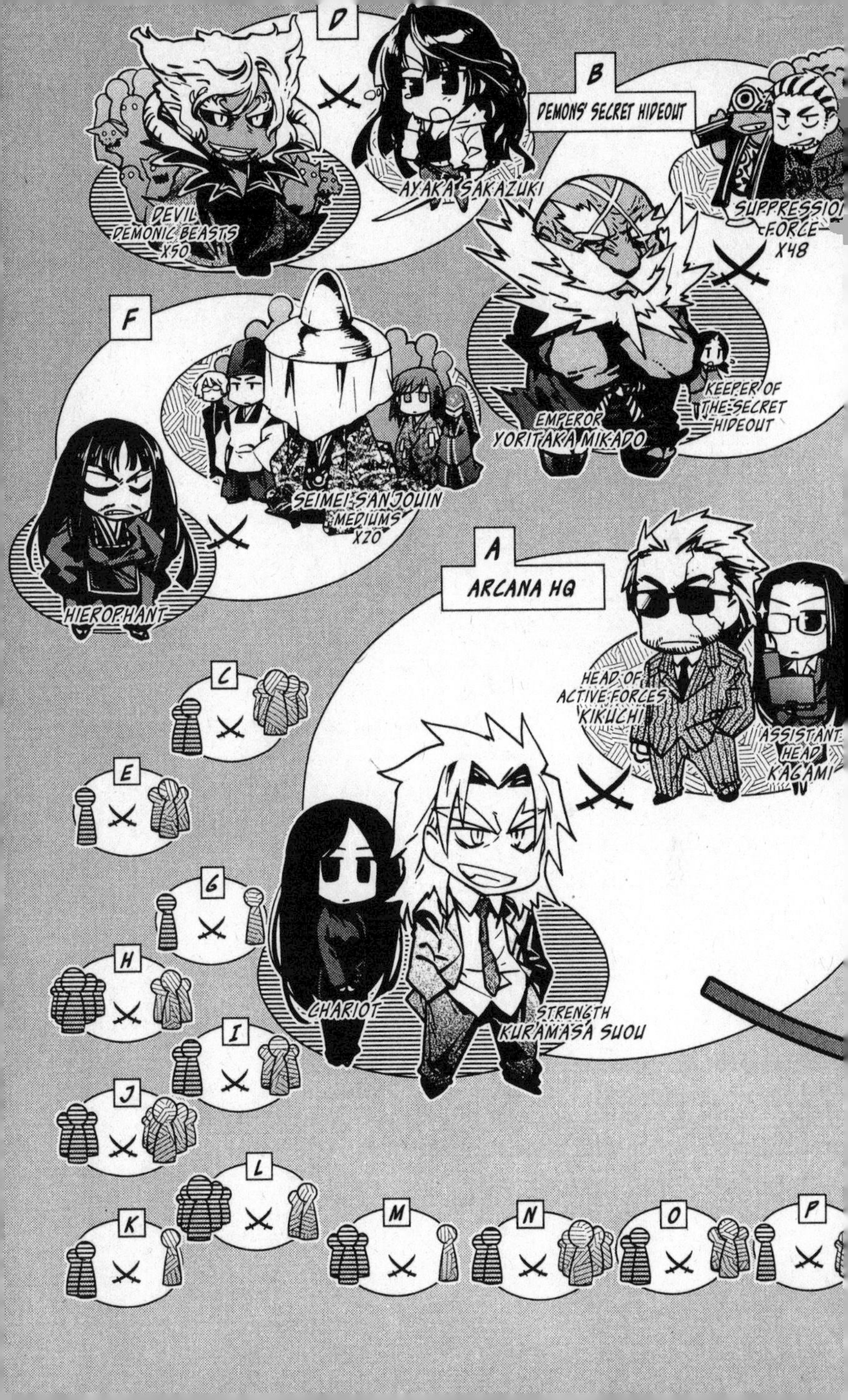
B
DEMONS' SECRET HIDEOUT
SUPPRESSIO
FORCE
X48
EMPEROR
YORITAKA MIKADO
KEEPER OF
THE SECRET
HIDEOUT
D
AYAKA SAKAZUKI
DEVIL
DEMONIC BEASTS
X50
F
SEIMEI SANJOUIN
MEDIUMS
X20
HIEROPHANT
A
ARCANA HQ
ASSISTANT
HEAD
KAGAMI
HEAD OF
ACTIVE FORCES
KIKUCHI
STRENGTH
KURAMASA SUOU
CHARIOT
C
E
G
H
I
J
L
P
O
N
M
K

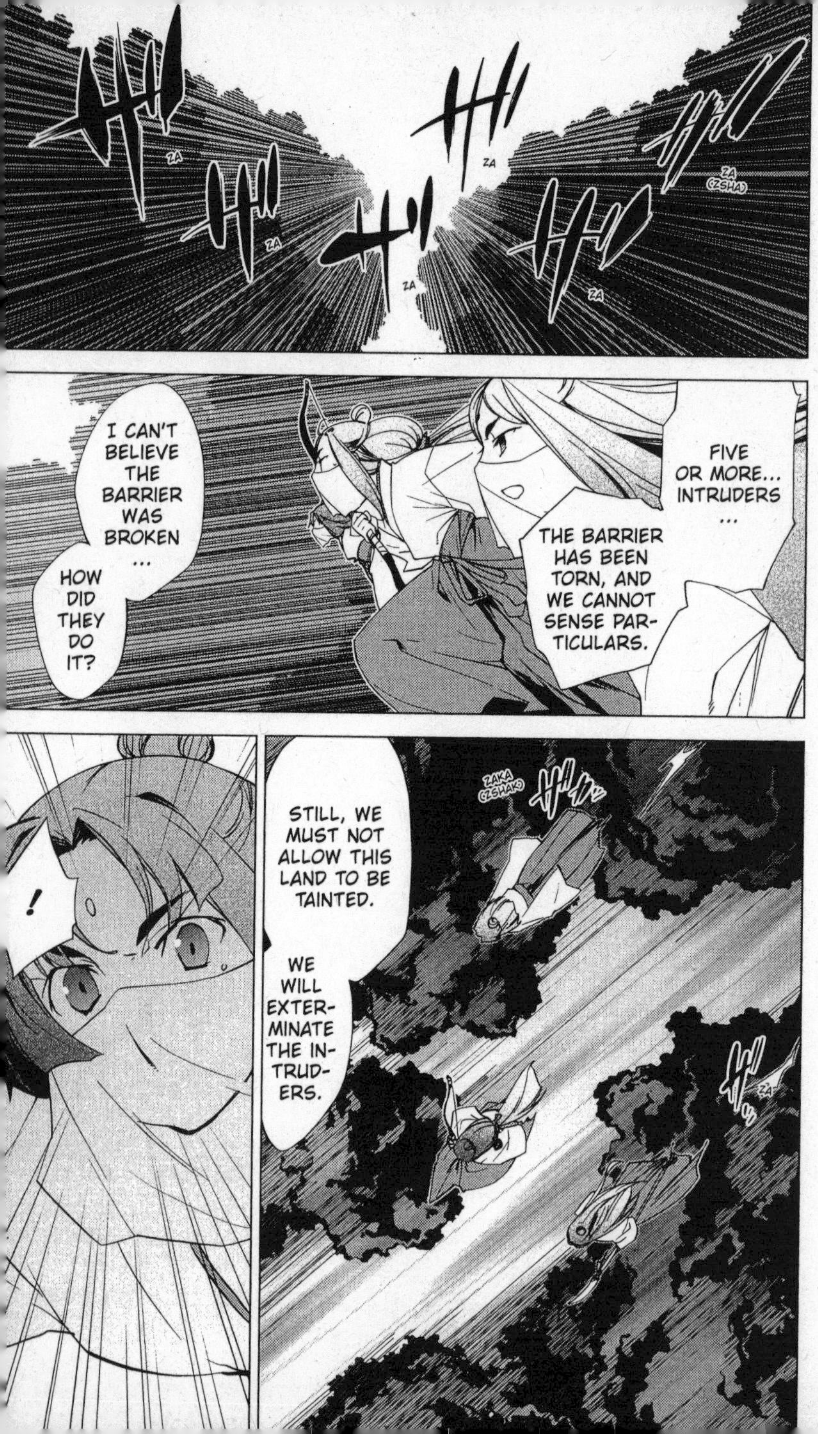
ZA (ZSHA)
ZA
ZA
ZA
ZA
ZA
FIVE OR MORE... INTRUDERS ...
THE BARRIER HAS BEEN TORN, AND WE CANNOT SENSE PAR-TICULARS.
I CAN'T BELIEVE THE BARRIER WAS BROKEN ...
HOW DID THEY DO IT?
ZAKA (ZSHAK)
STILL, WE MUST NOT ALLOW THIS LAND TO BE TAINTED.
WE WILL EXTER-MINATE THE IN-TRUD-ERS.
ZA
!

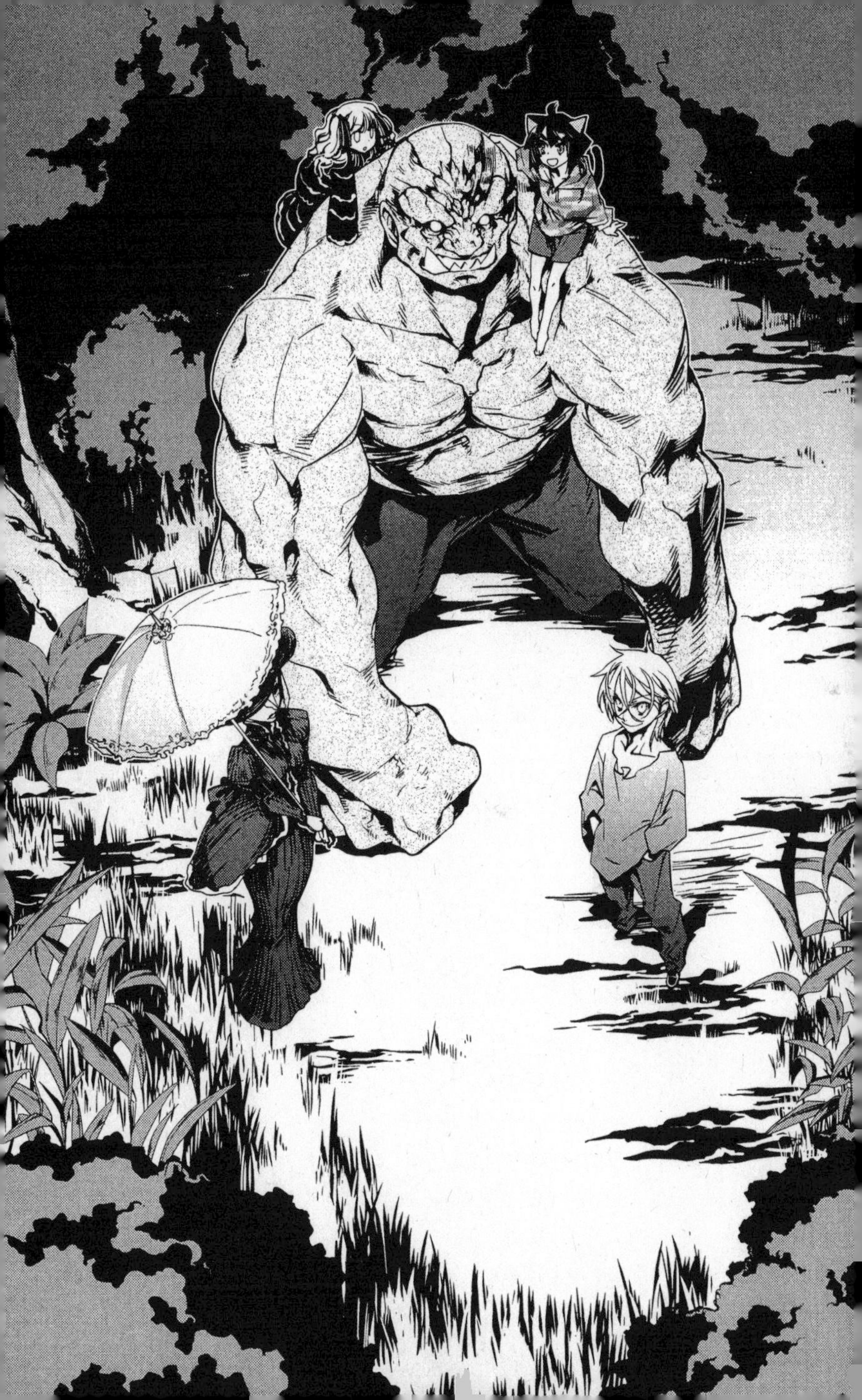

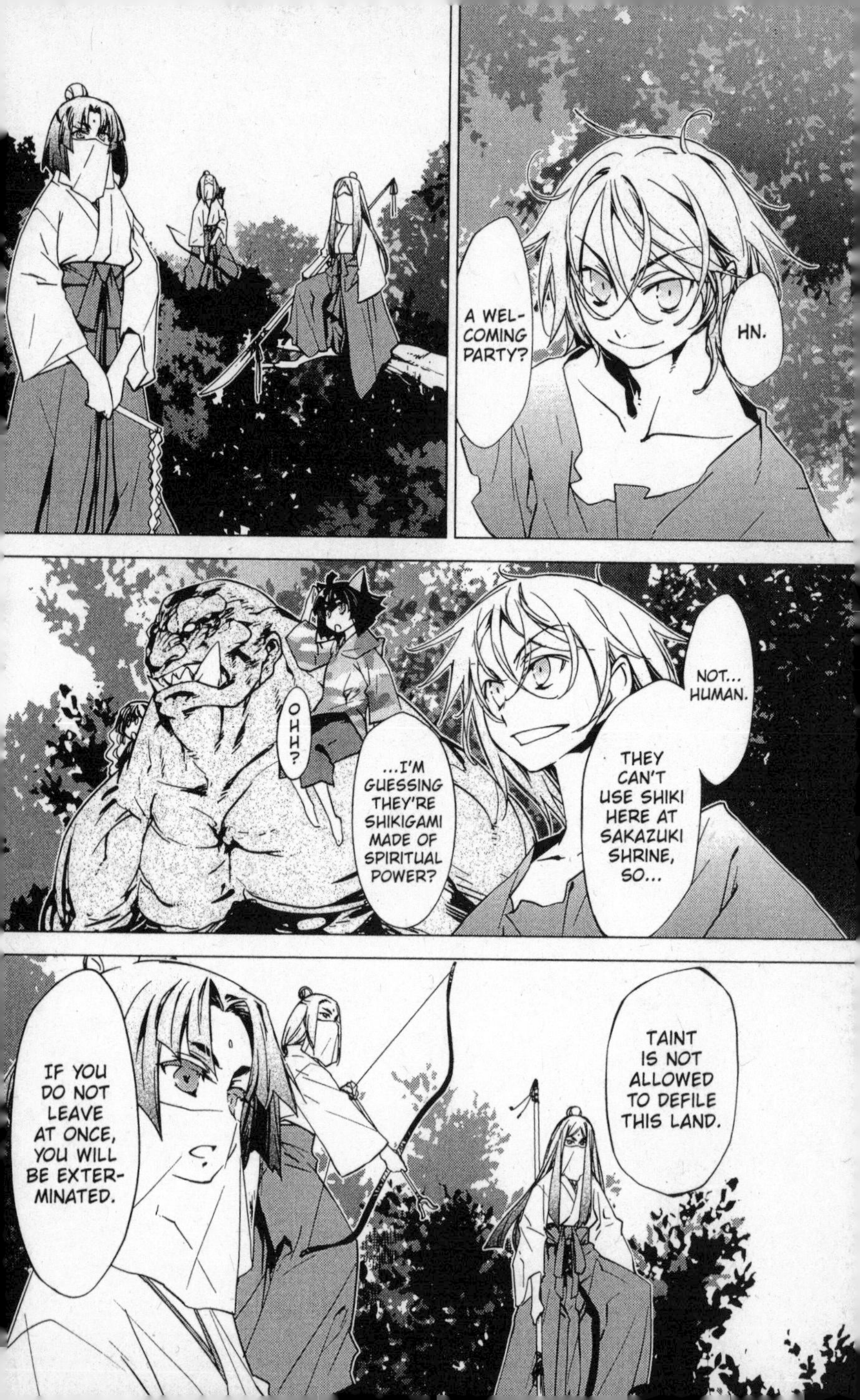
HN.
A WEL-COMING PARTY?
NOT... HUMAN.
THEY CAN'T USE SHIKI HERE AT SAKAZUKI SHRINE, SO...
...I'M GUESSING THEY'RE SHIKIGAMI MADE OF SPIRITUAL POWER?
OHH?
TAINT IS NOT ALLOWED TO DEFILE THIS LAND.
IF YOU DO NOT LEAVE AT ONCE, YOU WILL BE EXTER-MINATED.

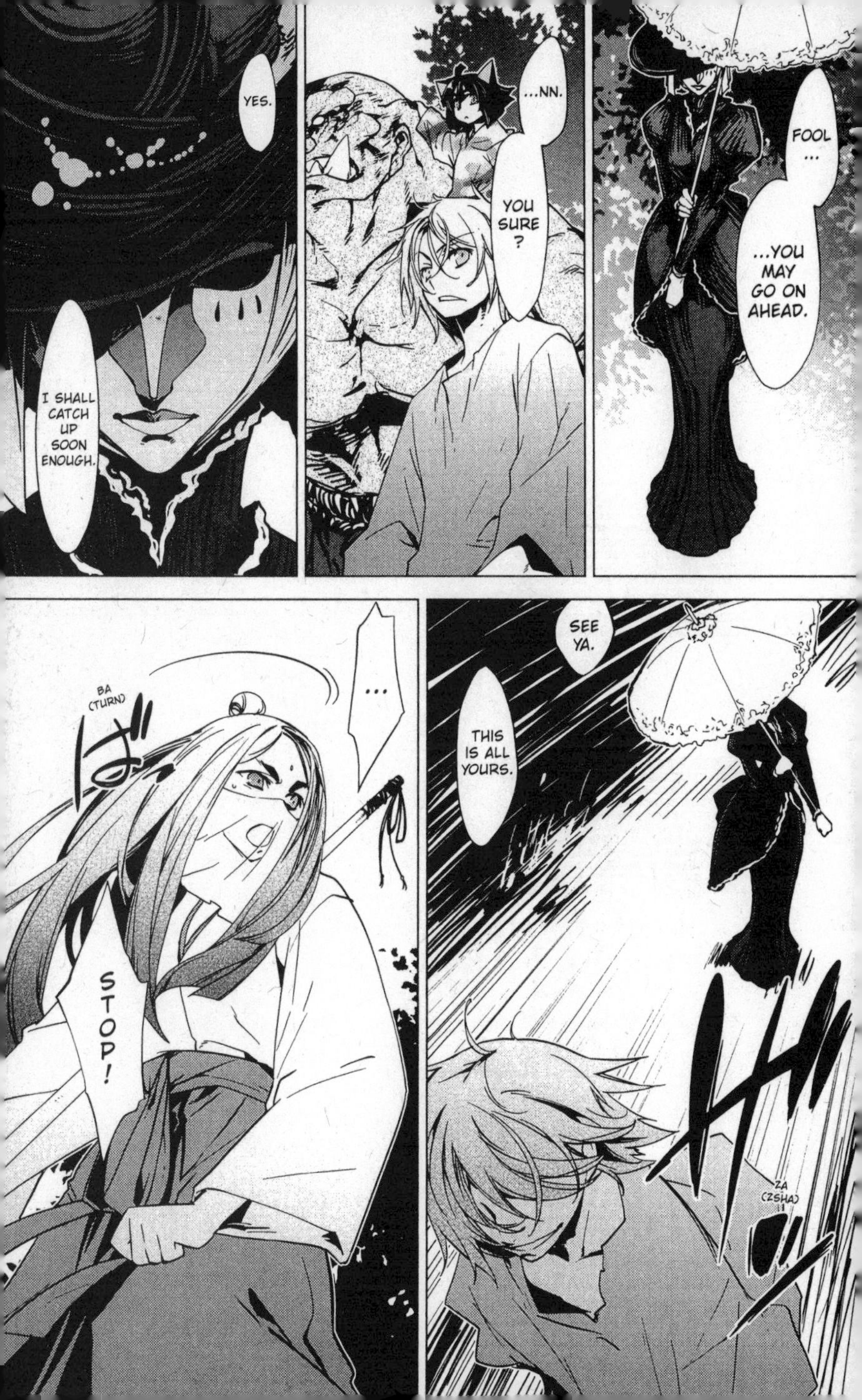
FOOL...
...YOU MAY GO ON AHEAD.
...NN.
YOU SURE?
YES.
I SHALL CATCH UP SOON ENOUGH.
SEE YA.
THIS IS ALL YOURS.
ZA (ZSHA)
...
BA (TURN)
STOP!

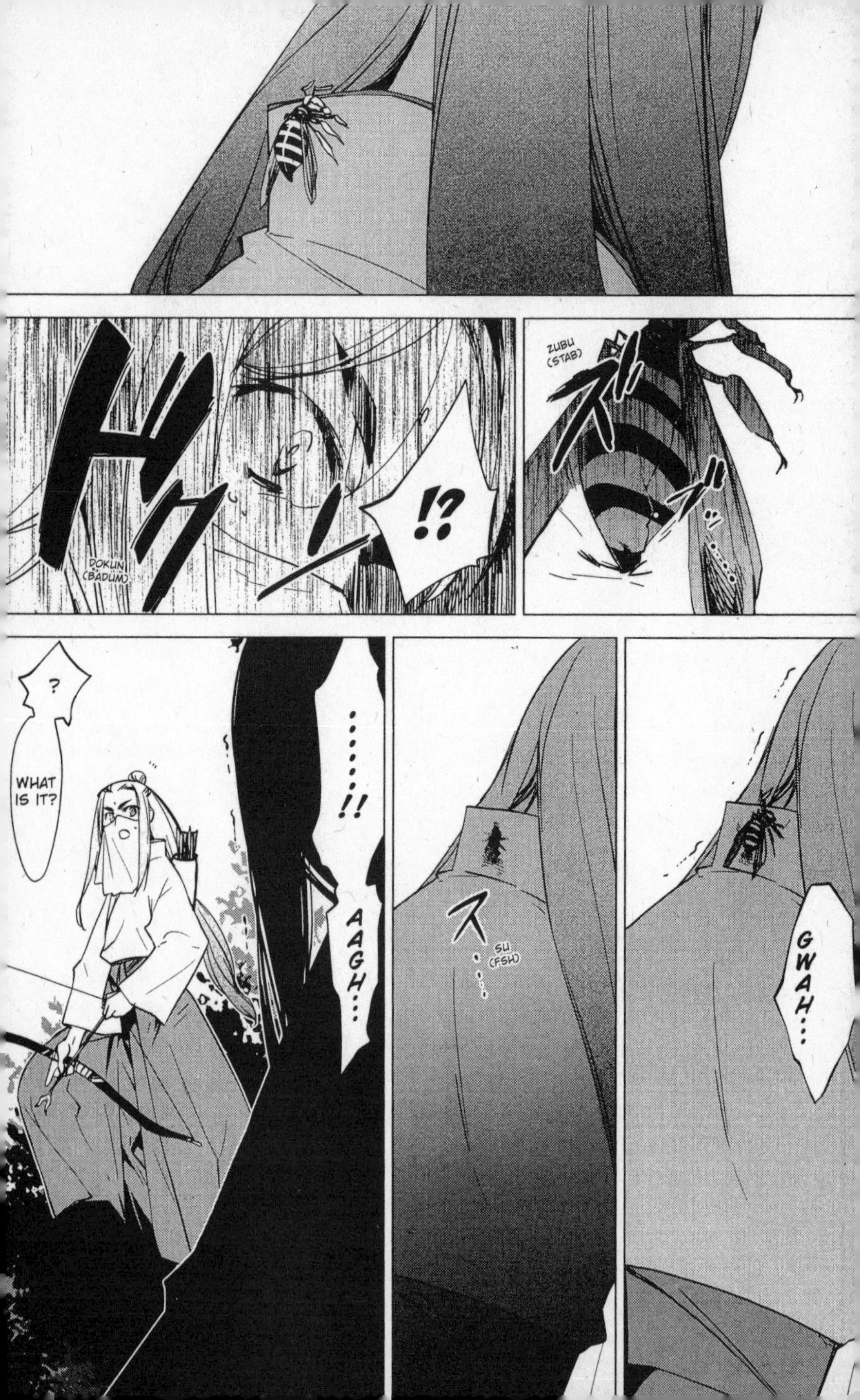
ZUBU (STAB)
!?
DOKUN (BADUM)
GWAH...
SU (FSH)
......!!
AAGH...
?
WHAT IS IT?

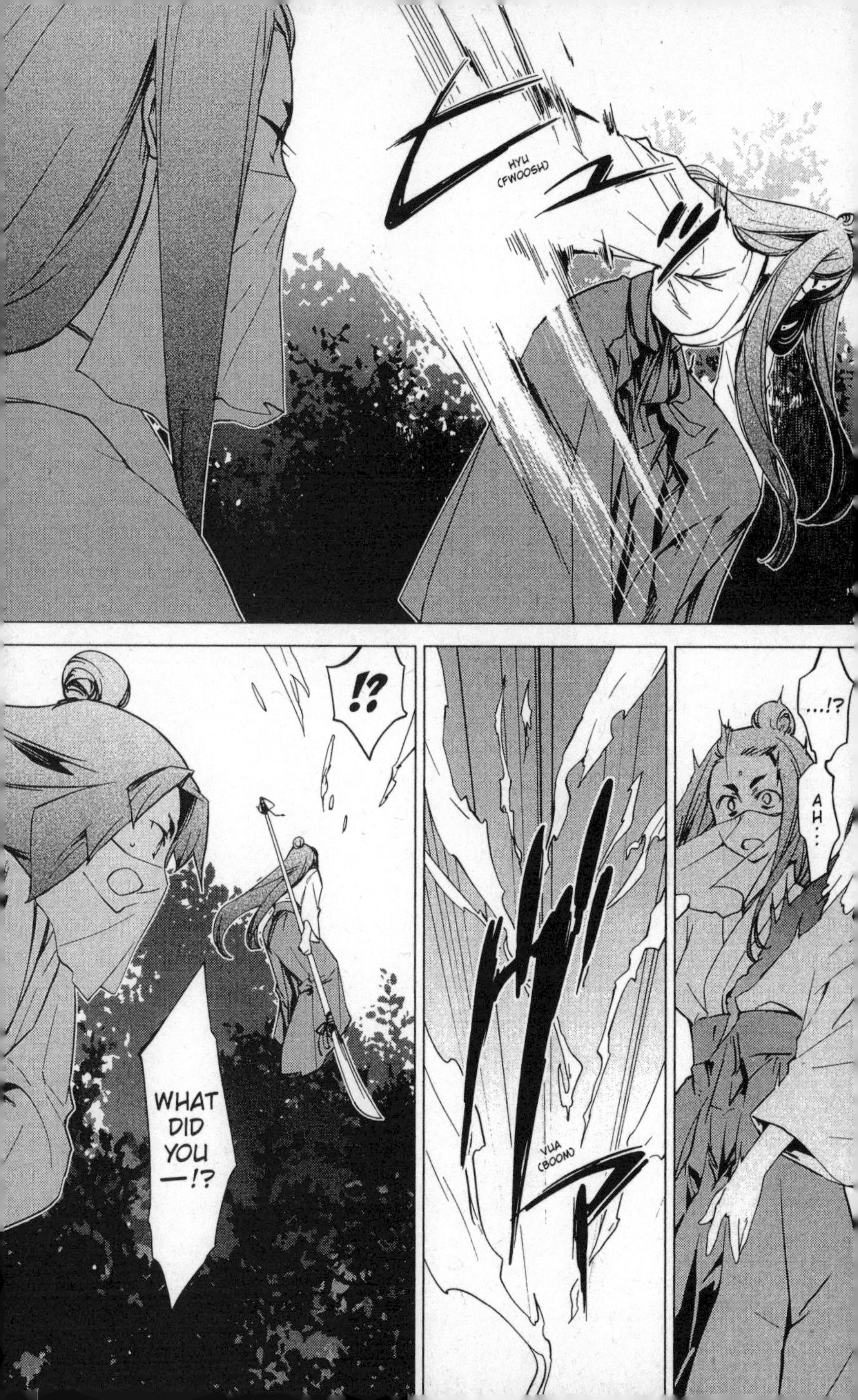
HYU
(FWOOSH)
...!?
AH...
VUA
(BOOM)
!?
WHAT DID YOU—!?

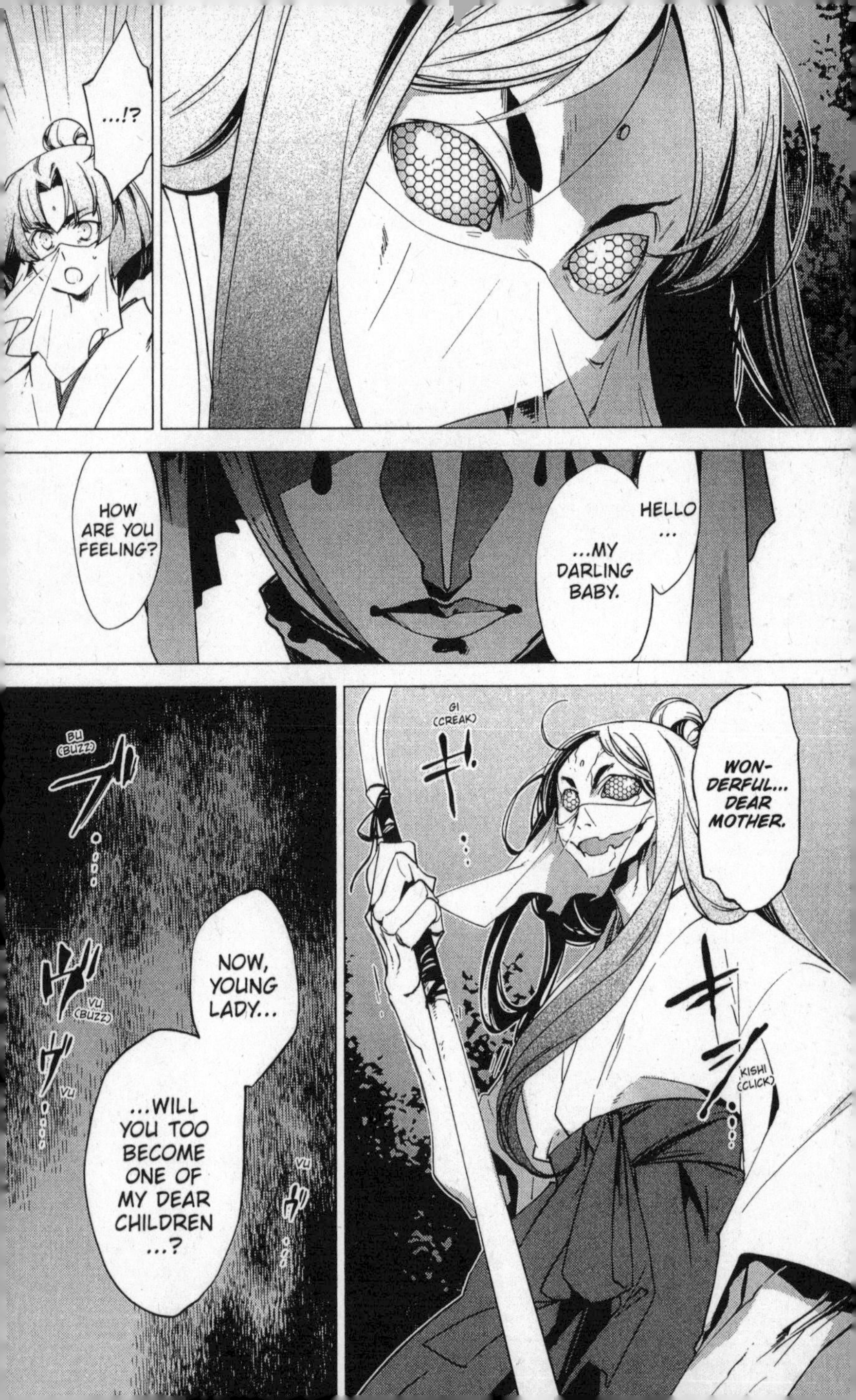

...!?
HELLO...
...MY DARLING BABY.
HOW ARE YOU FEELING?
GI (CREAK)
WON-DERFUL... DEAR MOTHER.
KISHI (CLICK)
BU (BUZZ)
NOW, YOUNG LADY...
VU (BUZZ)
VU
...WILL YOU TOO BECOME ONE OF MY DEAR CHILDREN ...?
VU

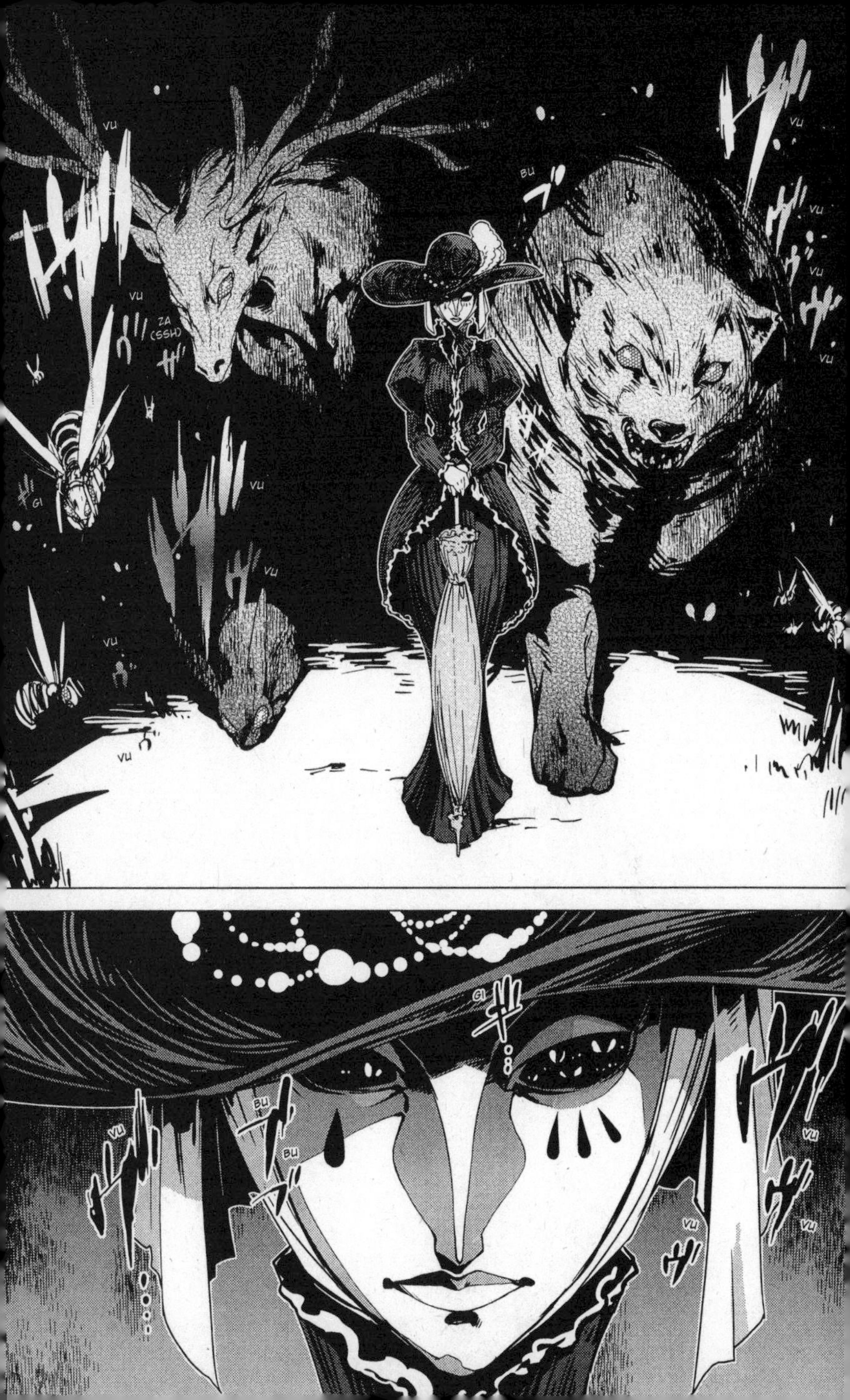
VU
BU
VU
VU
VU
VU
VU
ZA (SSH)
GI
VU
VU
VU
VU
GI
VU
VU
BU
BU
VU

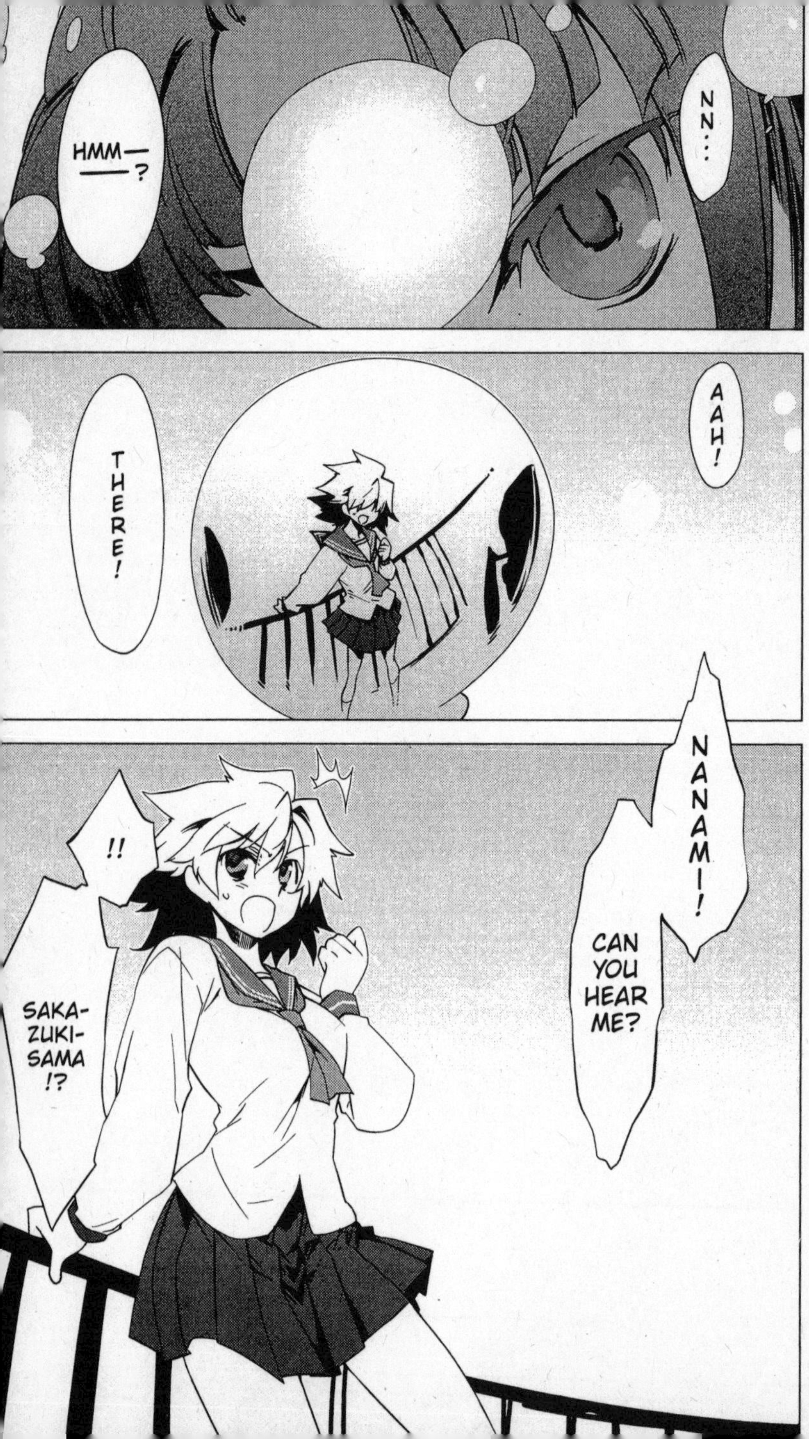
NN...
HMM— —?
AAH!
THERE!
NANAMI!
CAN YOU HEAR ME?
!!
SAKA-ZUKI-SAMA!?

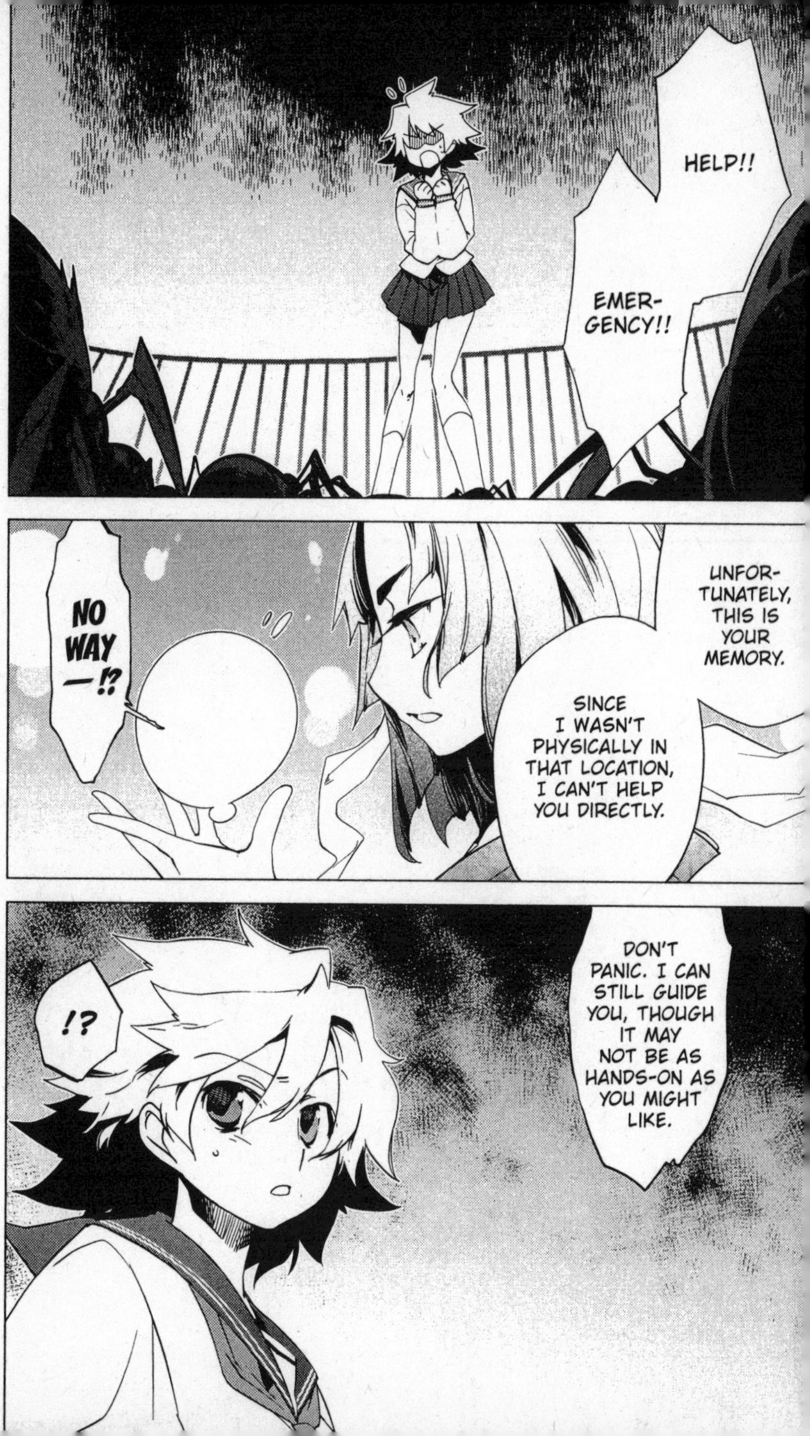
HELP!!
EMER-GENCY!!
UNFOR-TUNATELY, THIS IS YOUR MEMORY.
SINCE I WASN'T PHYSICALLY IN THAT LOCATION, I CAN'T HELP YOU DIRECTLY.
NO WAY —!?
DON'T PANIC. I CAN STILL GUIDE YOU, THOUGH IT MAY NOT BE AS HANDS-ON AS YOU MIGHT LIKE.
!?

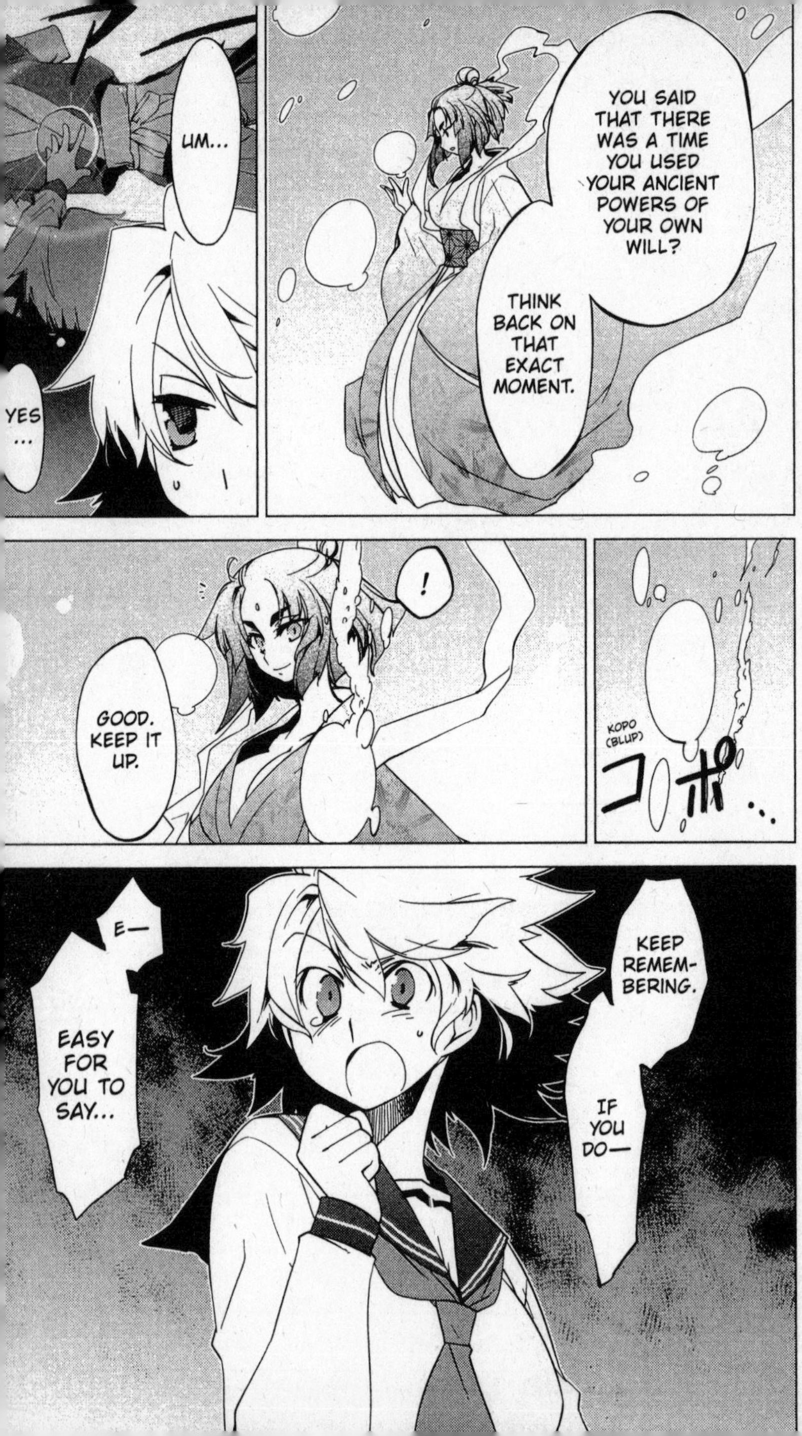
YOU SAID THAT THERE WAS A TIME YOU USED YOUR ANCIENT POWERS OF YOUR OWN WILL?
THINK BACK ON THAT EXACT MOMENT.
UM...
YES...
KOPO (BLUP)
コポ...
!
GOOD. KEEP IT UP.
KEEP REMEMBERING.
IF YOU DO—
E—
EASY FOR YOU TO SAY...

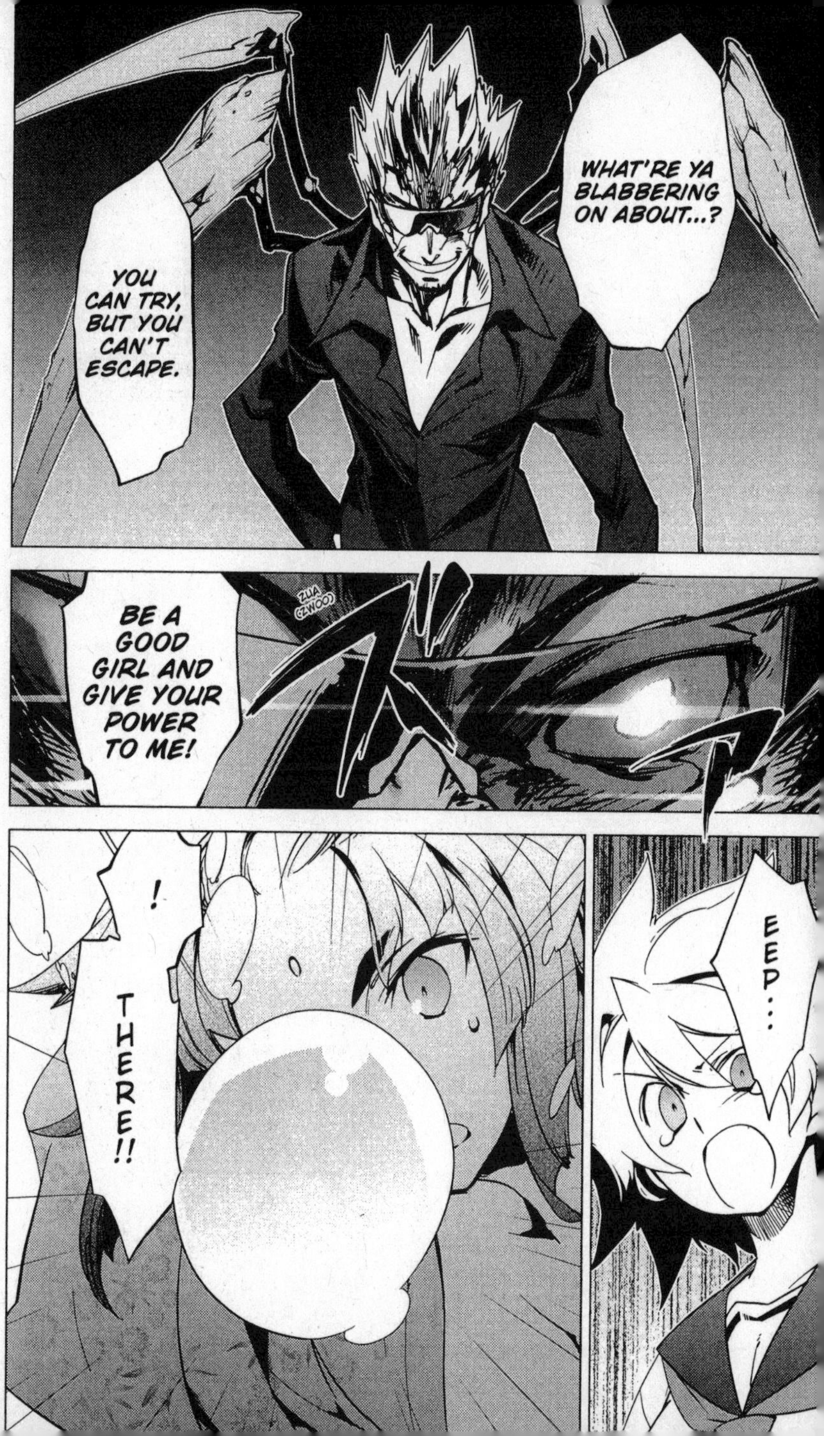
WHAT'RE YA BLABBERING ON ABOUT...?
YOU CAN TRY, BUT YOU CAN'T ESCAPE.
ZUA (ZWOO)
BE A GOOD GIRL AND GIVE YOUR POWER TO ME!
EEP...
!
THERE!!

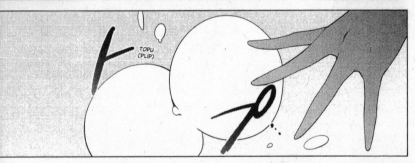

TOPU
(PLIP)

WHAT THE HELL ...

...IS THIS ...?

!?

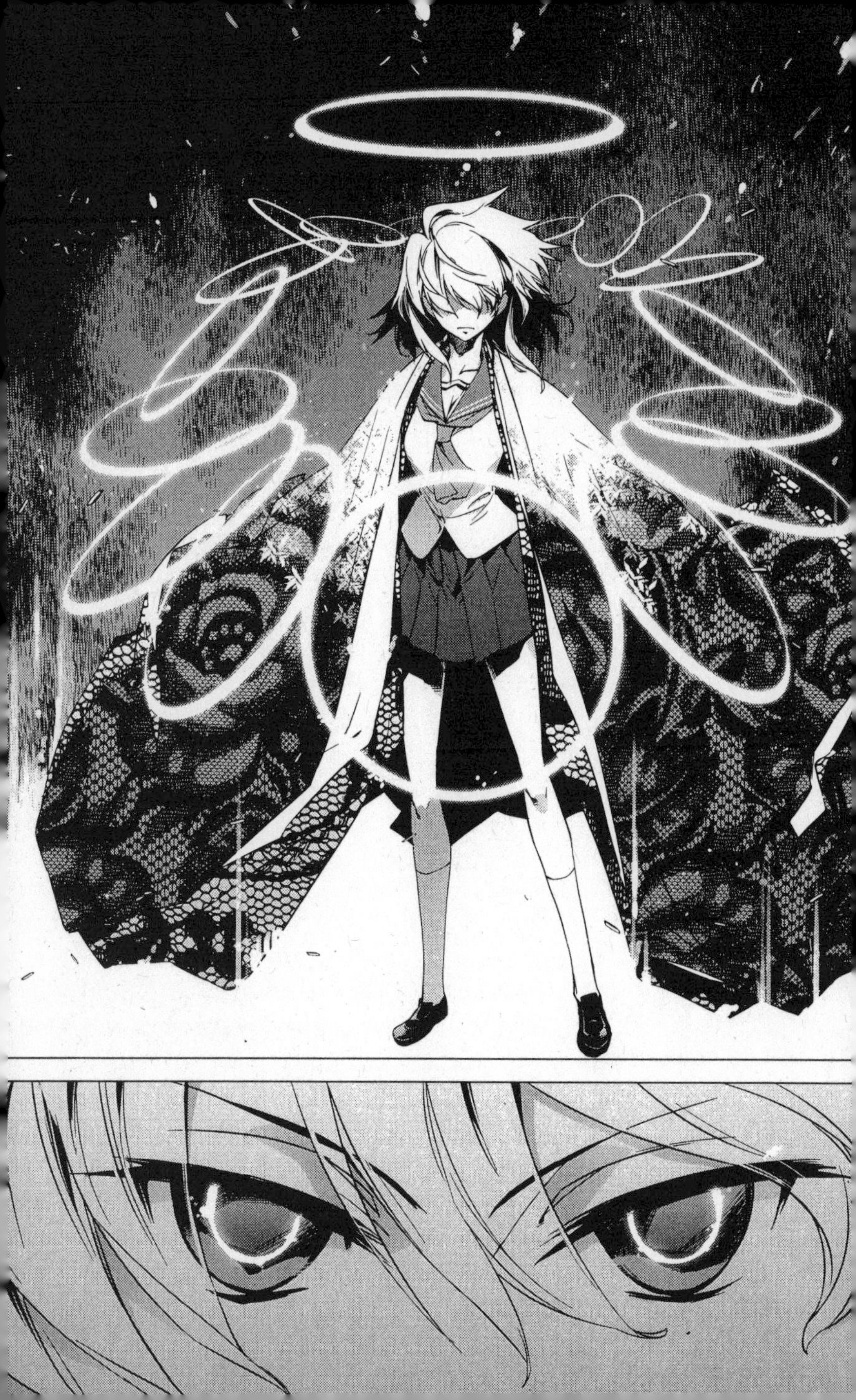

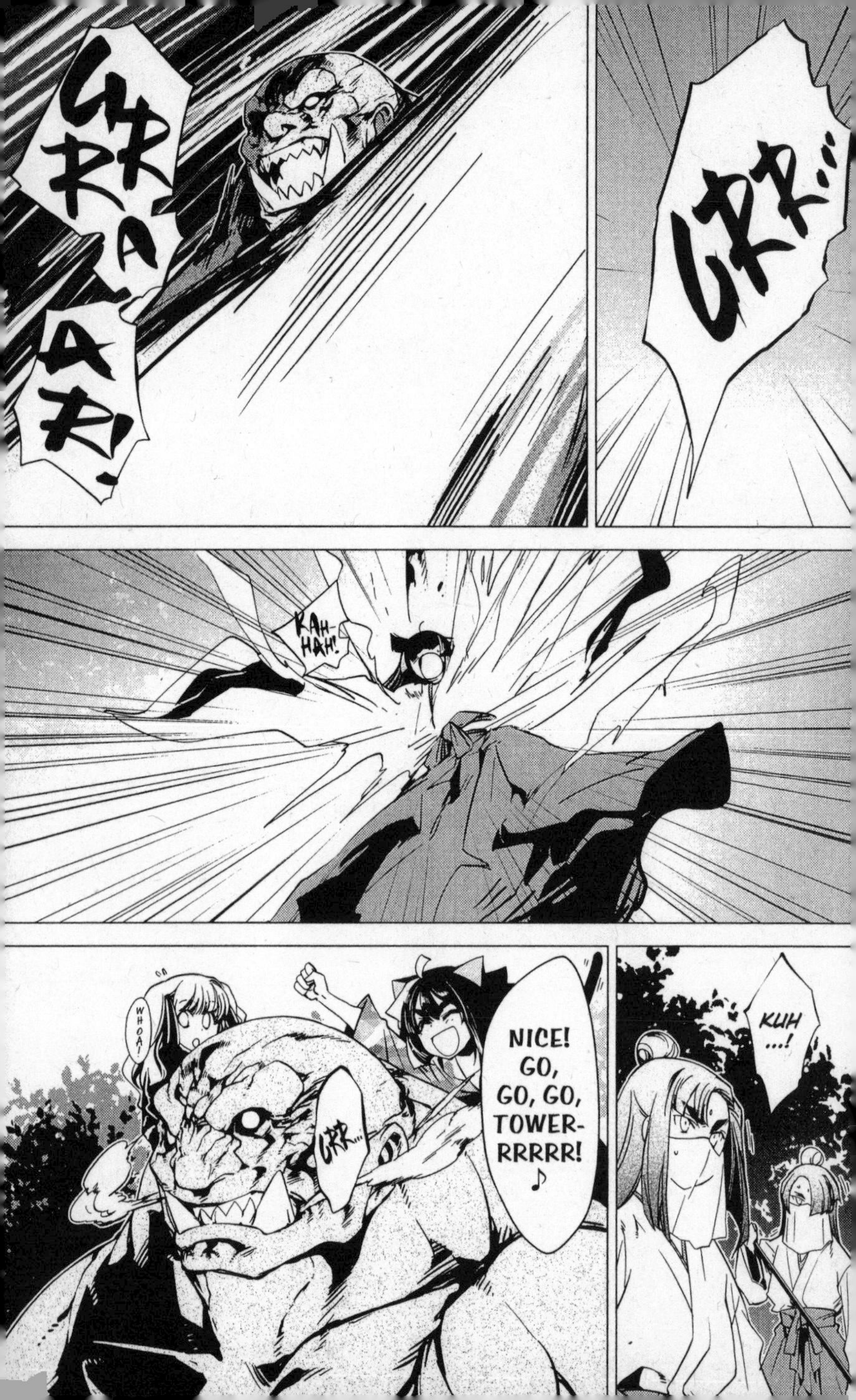
URR...
URRRAAAR!
KAH-HAH!
KUH...!
NICE! GO, GO, GO, TOWER-RRRRR! ♪
URR...
WHOA!

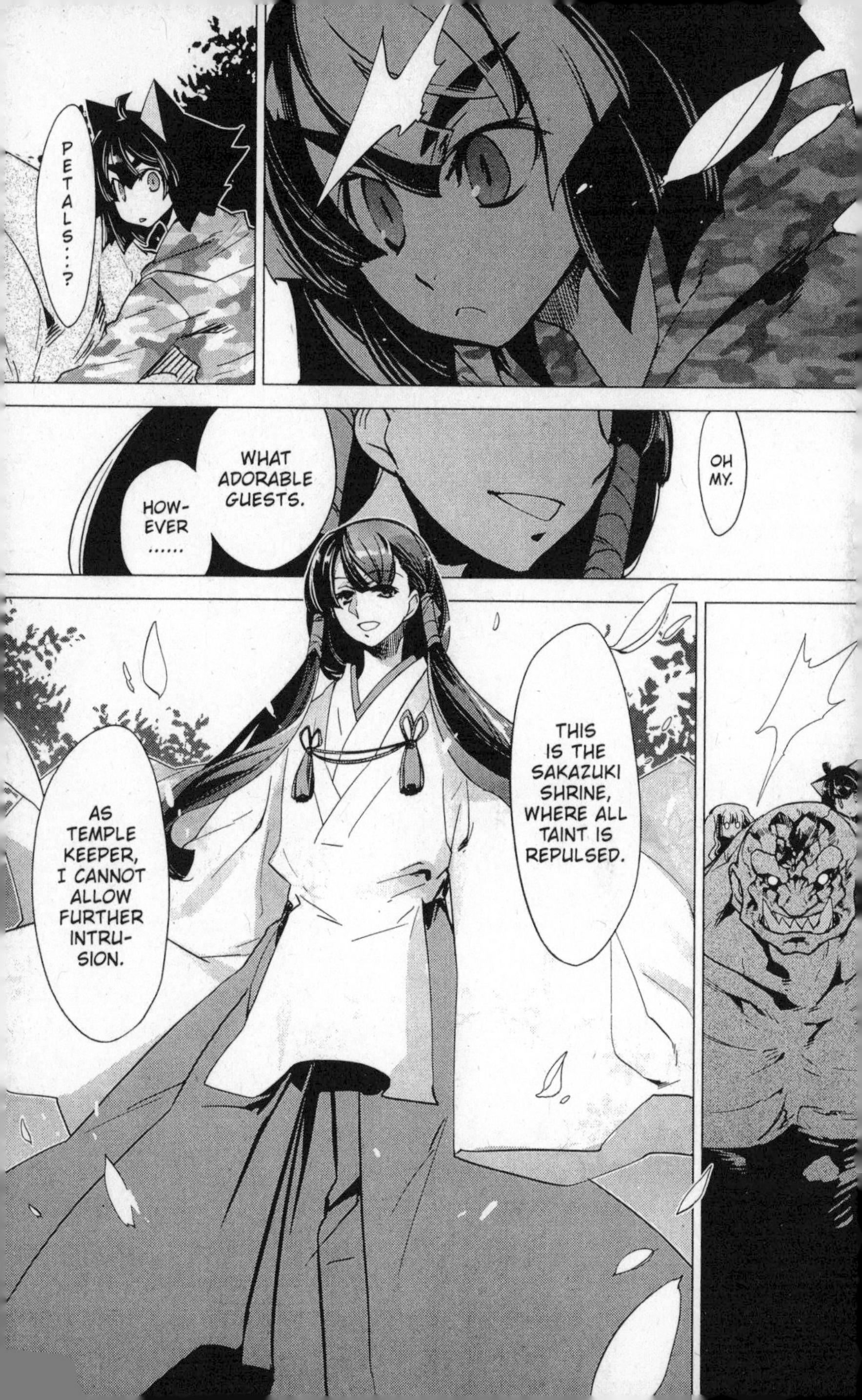
PETALS...?
OH MY.
WHAT ADORABLE GUESTS.
HOW-EVER ......
THIS IS THE SAKAZUKI SHRINE, WHERE ALL TAINT IS REPULSED.
AS TEMPLE KEEPER, I CANNOT ALLOW FURTHER INTRU-SION.

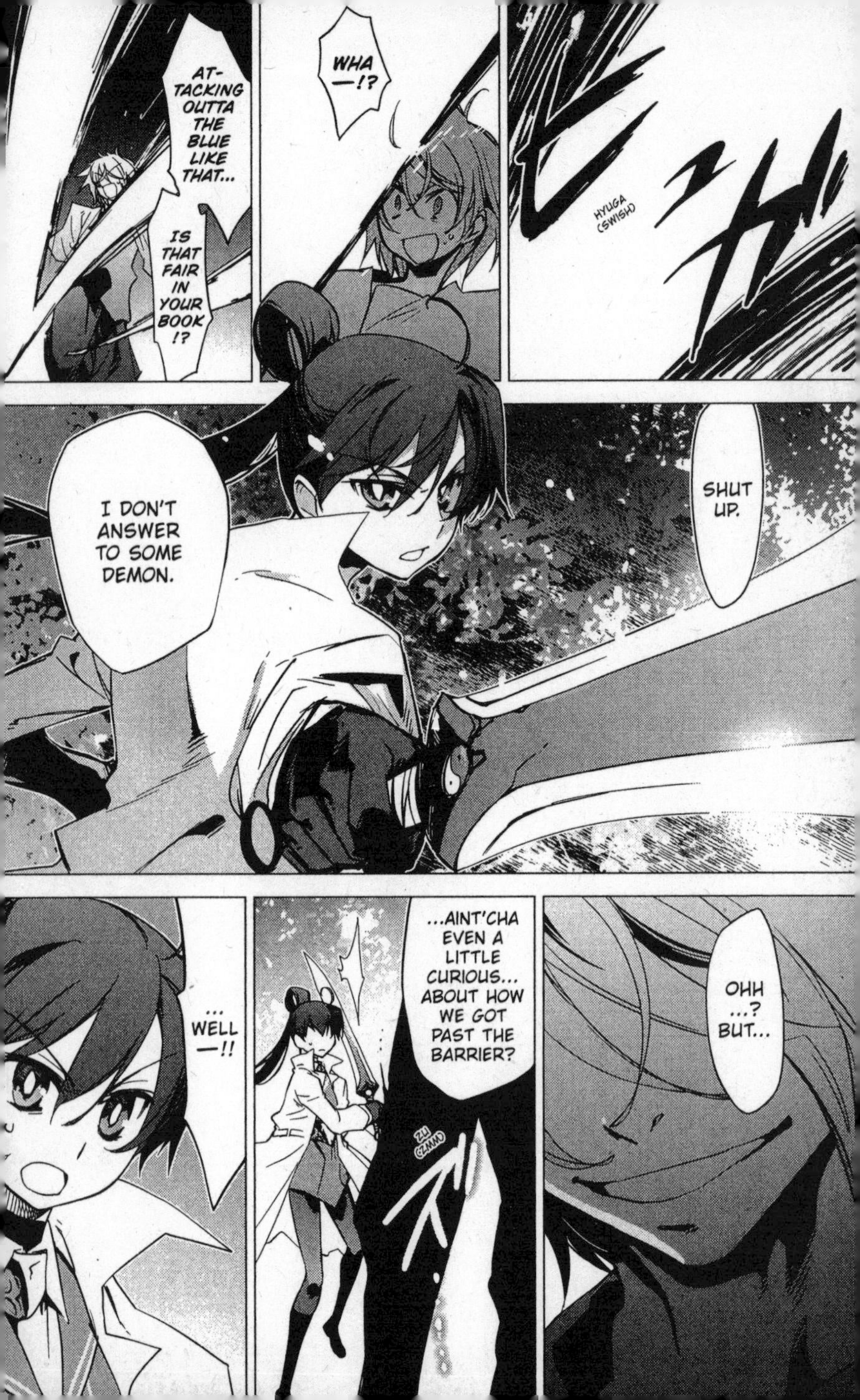
HYUGA (SWISH)
WHA—!?
AT-TACKING OUTTA THE BLUE LIKE THAT...
IS THAT FAIR IN YOUR BOOK!?
SHUT UP.
I DON'T ANSWER TO SOME DEMON.
OHH...? BUT...
...AINT'CHA EVEN A LITTLE CURIOUS... ABOUT HOW WE GOT PAST THE BARRIER?
ZU (ZMMM)
...WELL—!!

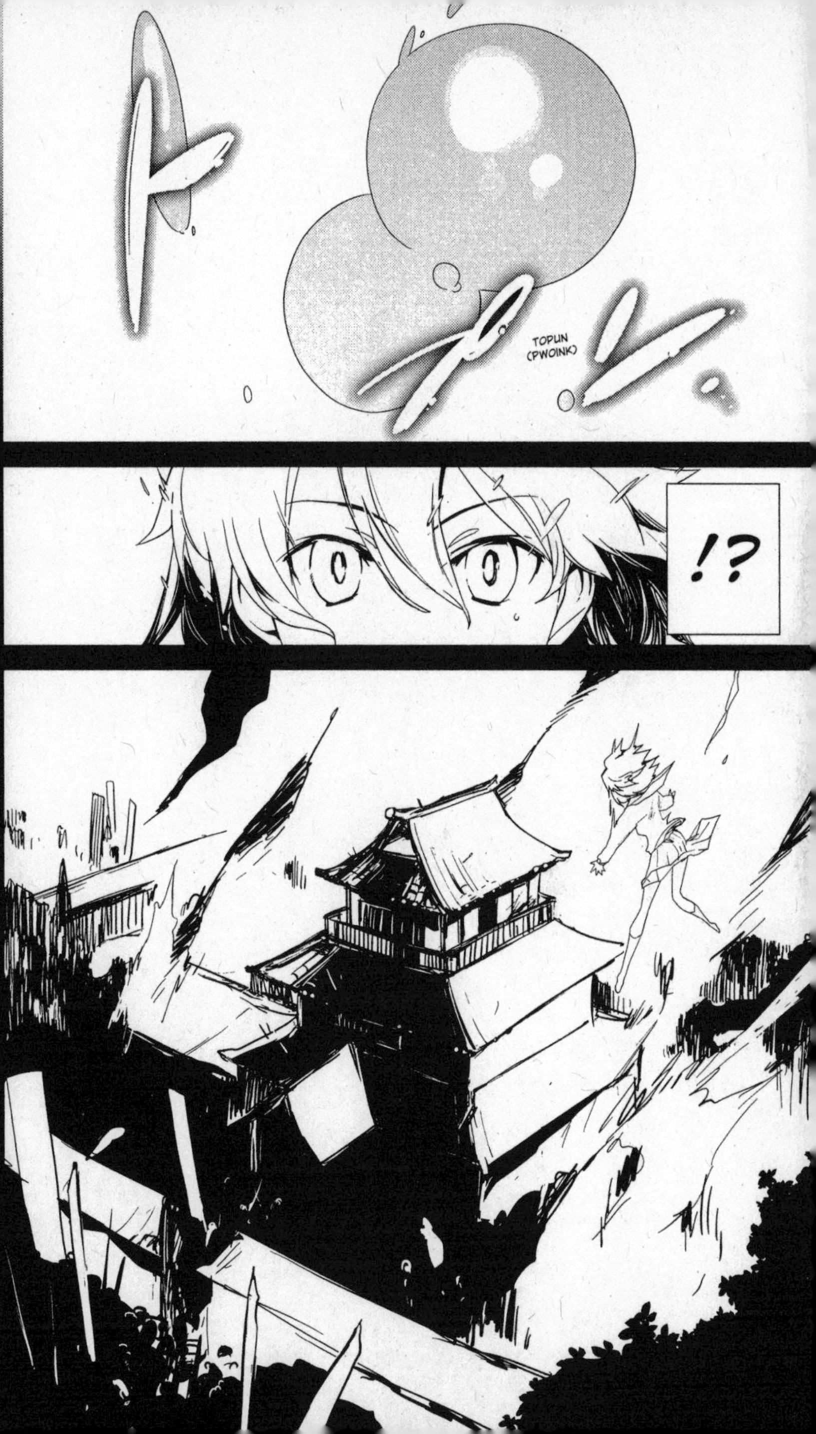
TOPUN
(PWOINK)
!?

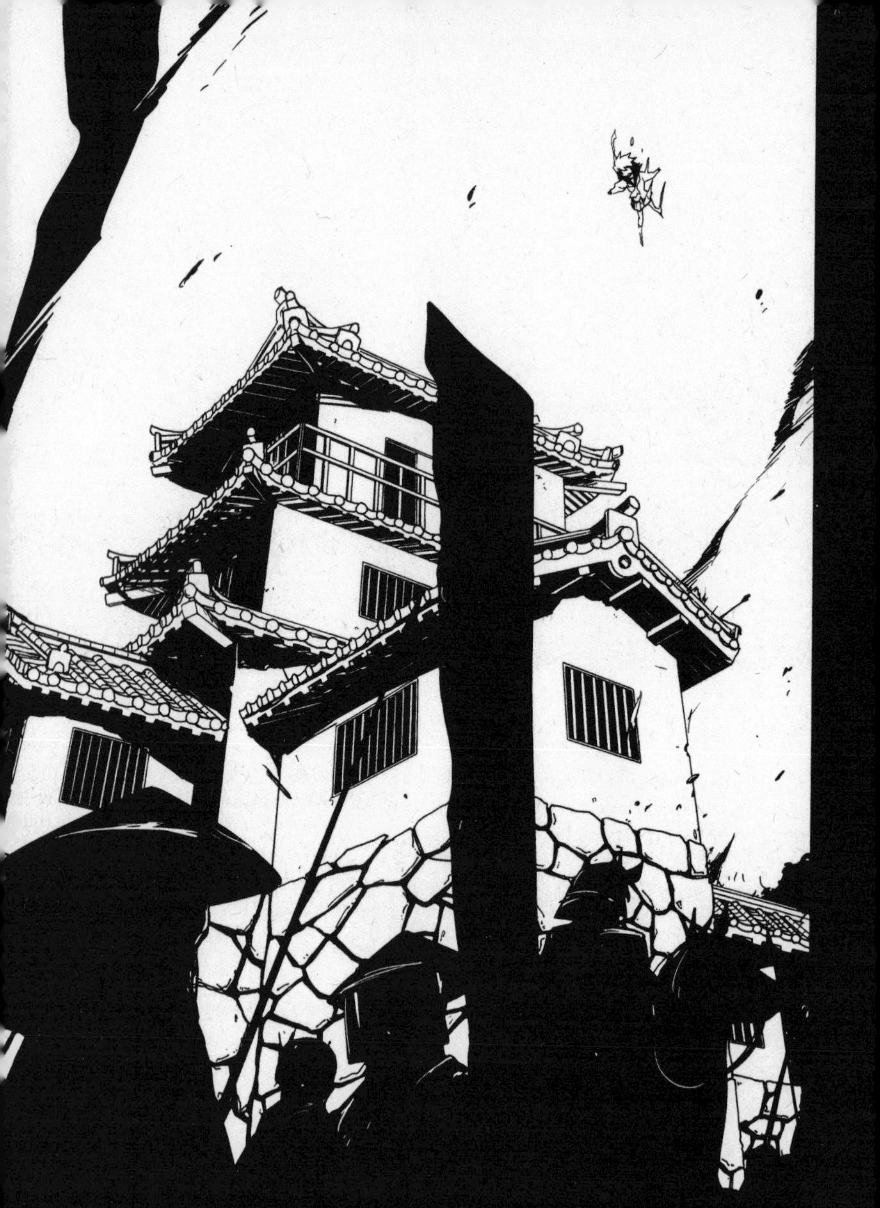

ACT TWENTY-THREE.

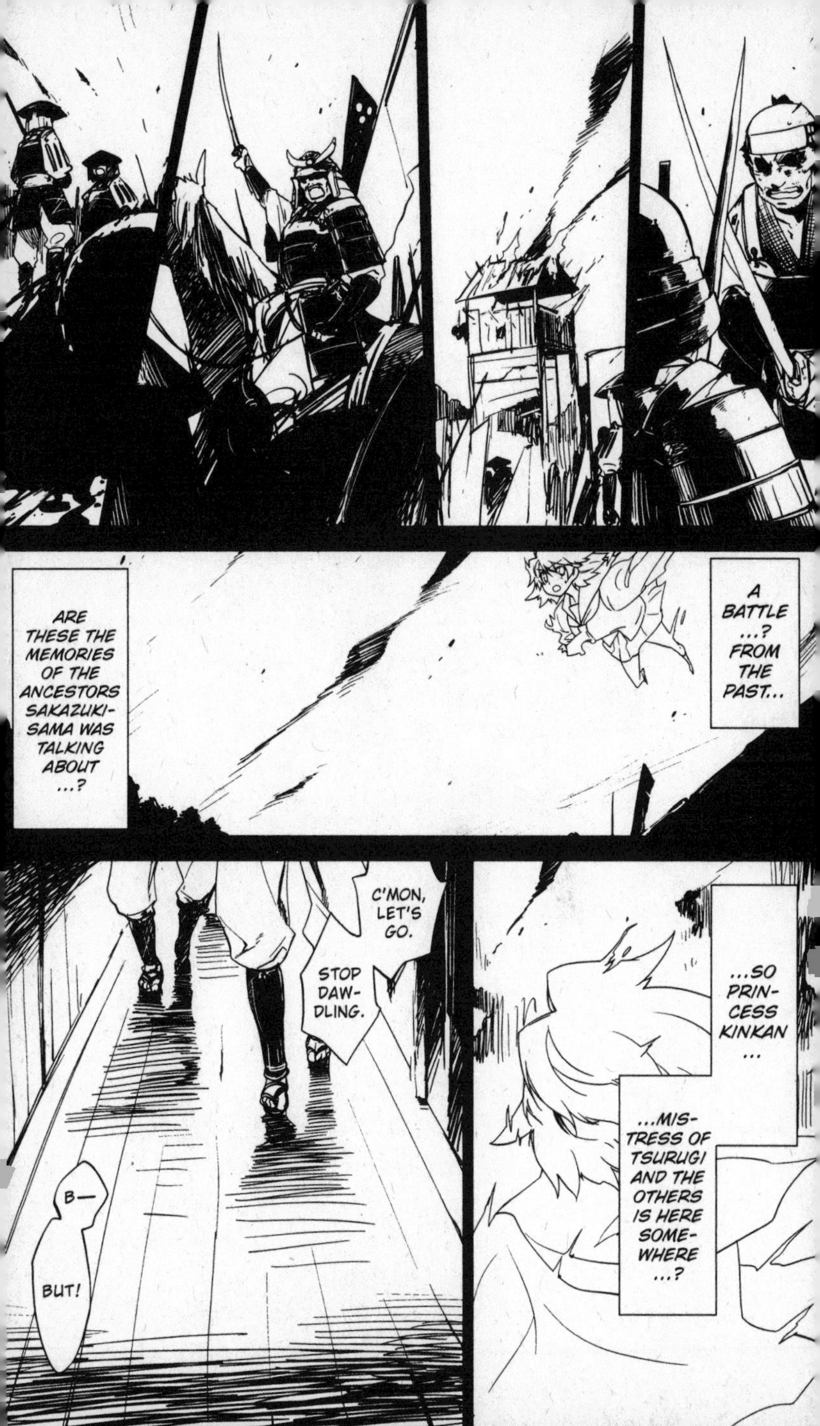
A BATTLE ...? FROM THE PAST...
ARE THESE THE MEMORIES OF THE ANCESTORS SAKAZUKI-SAMA WAS TALKING ABOUT ...?
...SO PRINCESS KINKAN ...
...MISTRESS OF TSURUGI AND THE OTHERS IS HERE SOMEWHERE ...?
C'MON, LET'S GO.
STOP DAWDLING.
B— BUT!

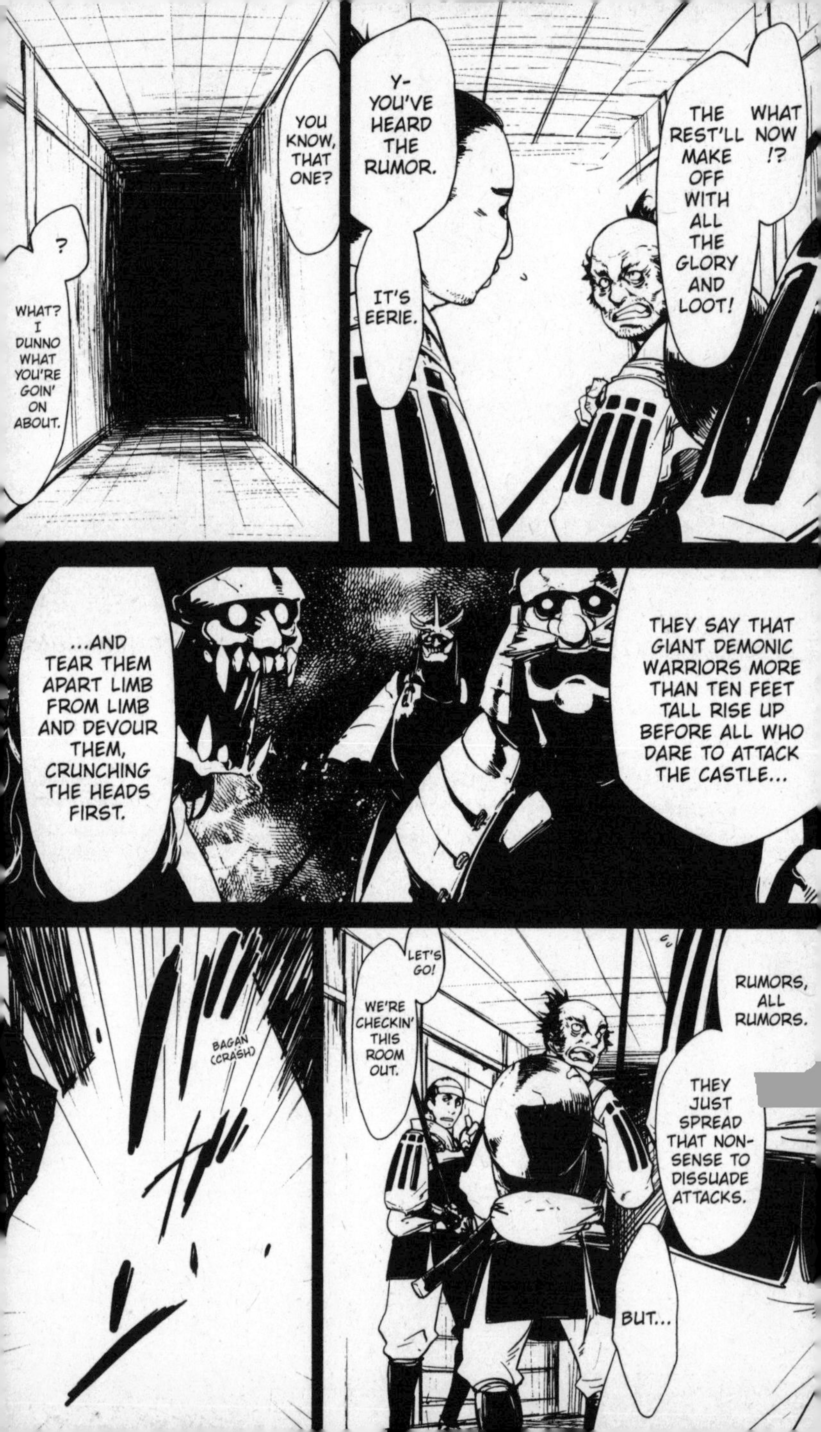
WHAT NOW!?
THE REST'LL MAKE OFF WITH ALL THE GLORY AND LOOT!
Y-YOU'VE HEARD THE RUMOR.
IT'S EERIE.
YOU KNOW, THAT ONE?
?
WHAT? I DUNNO WHAT YOU'RE GOIN' ON ABOUT.
THEY SAY THAT GIANT DEMONIC WARRIORS MORE THAN TEN FEET TALL RISE UP BEFORE ALL WHO DARE TO ATTACK THE CASTLE...
...AND TEAR THEM APART LIMB FROM LIMB AND DEVOUR THEM, CRUNCHING THE HEADS FIRST.
RUMORS, ALL RUMORS.
THEY JUST SPREAD THAT NON-SENSE TO DISSUADE ATTACKS.
BUT...
LET'S GO!
WE'RE CHECKIN' THIS ROOM OUT.
BAGAN (CRASH)

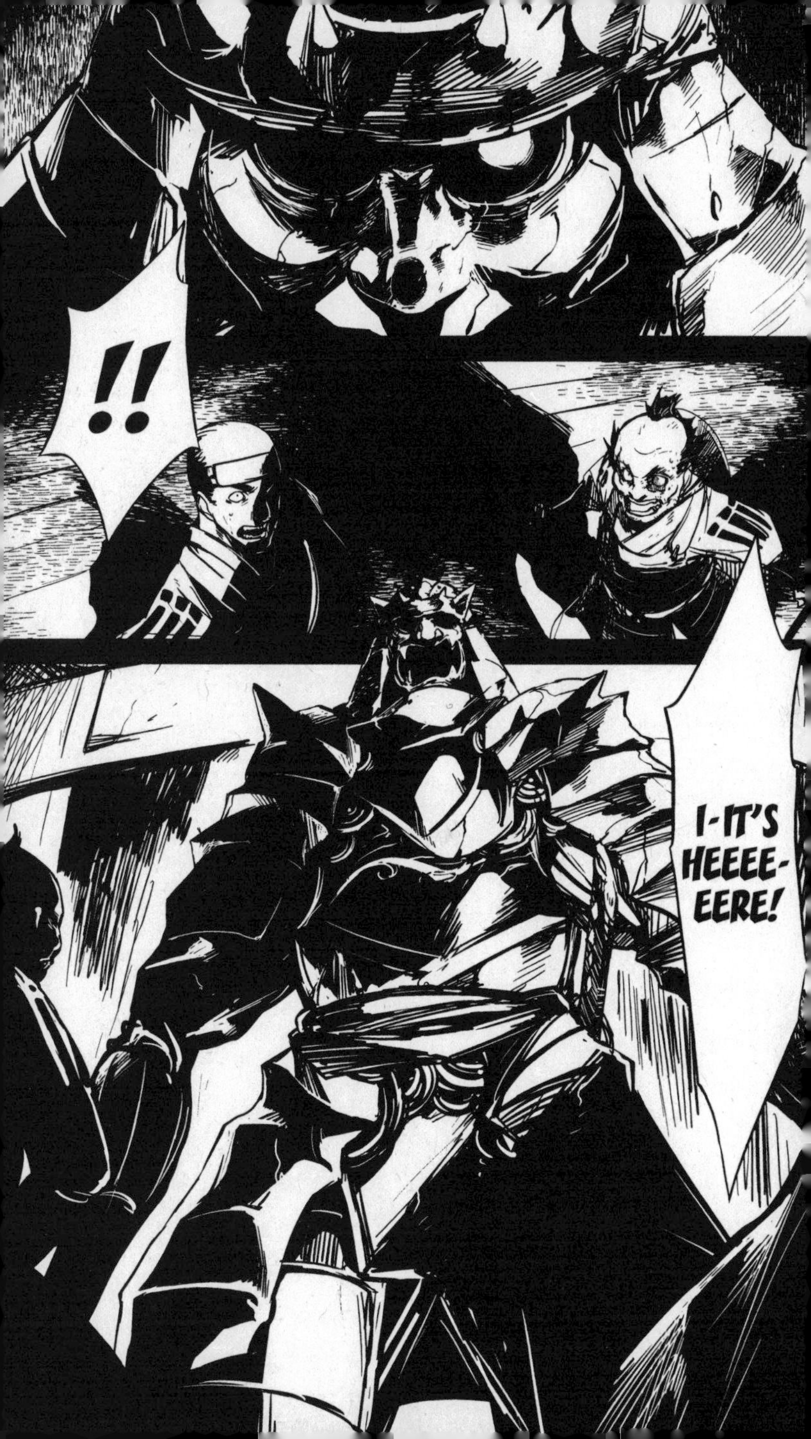
!!
I-IT'S HEEEE-EERE!

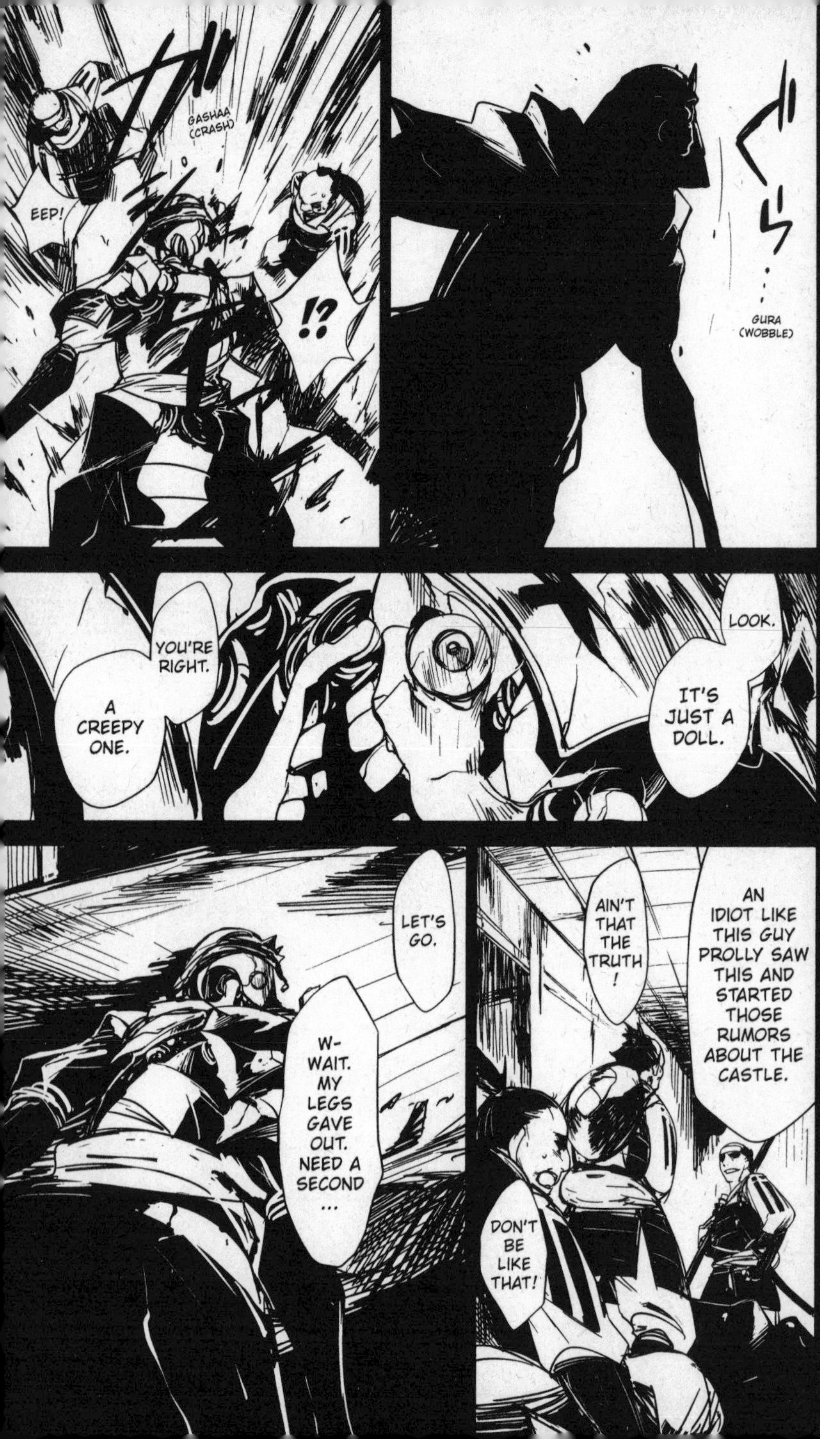
ぐら
GURA (WOBBLE)
GASHAA (CRASH)
EEP!
!?
LOOK.
IT'S JUST A DOLL.
YOU'RE RIGHT.
A CREEPY ONE.
AN IDIOT LIKE THIS GUY PROLLY SAW THIS AND STARTED THOSE RUMORS ABOUT THE CASTLE.
AIN'T THAT THE TRUTH!
DON'T BE LIKE THAT!
LET'S GO.
W-WAIT. MY LEGS GAVE OUT. NEED A SECOND...

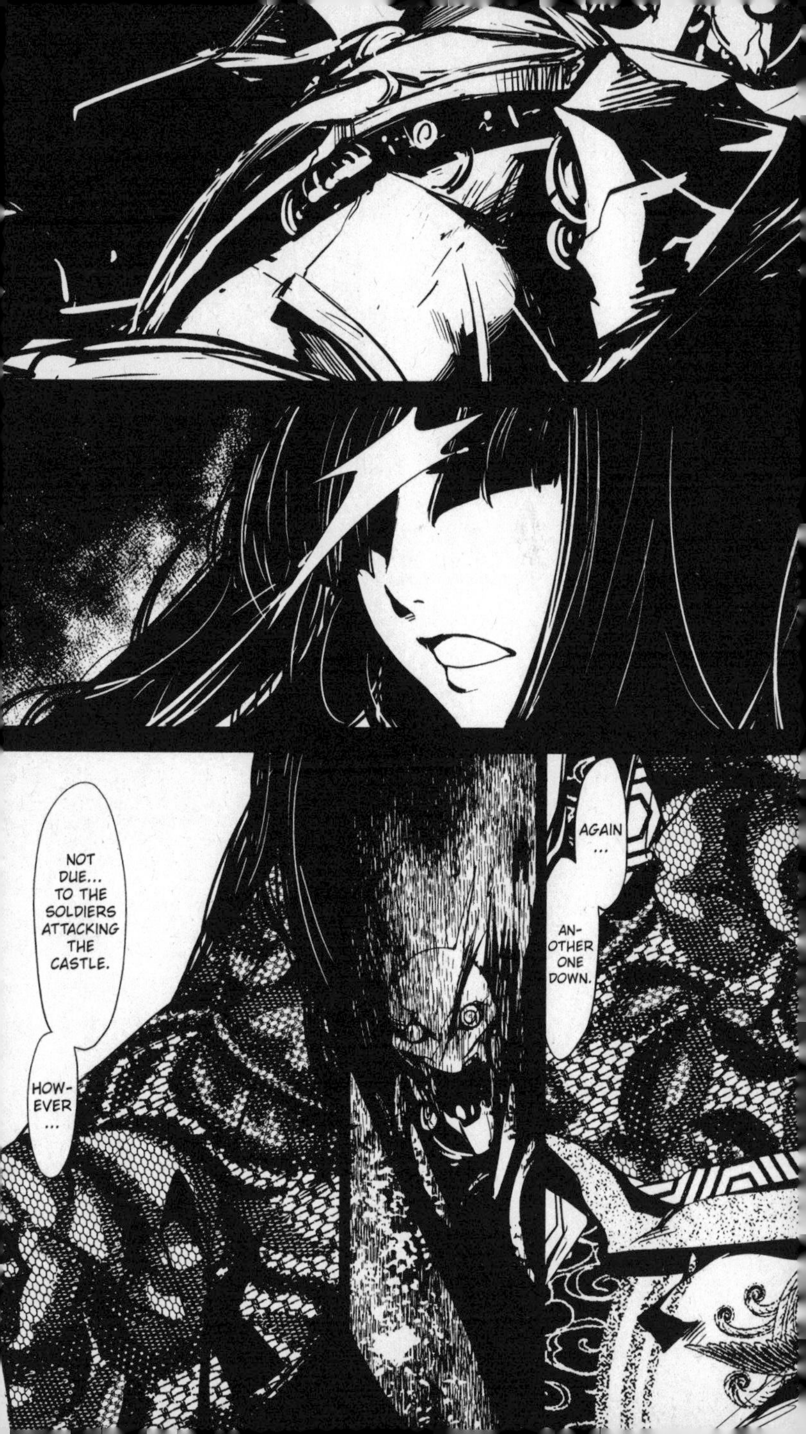
AGAIN...
AN-OTHER ONE DOWN.
NOT DUE... TO THE SOLDIERS ATTACKING THE CASTLE.
HOW-EVER...

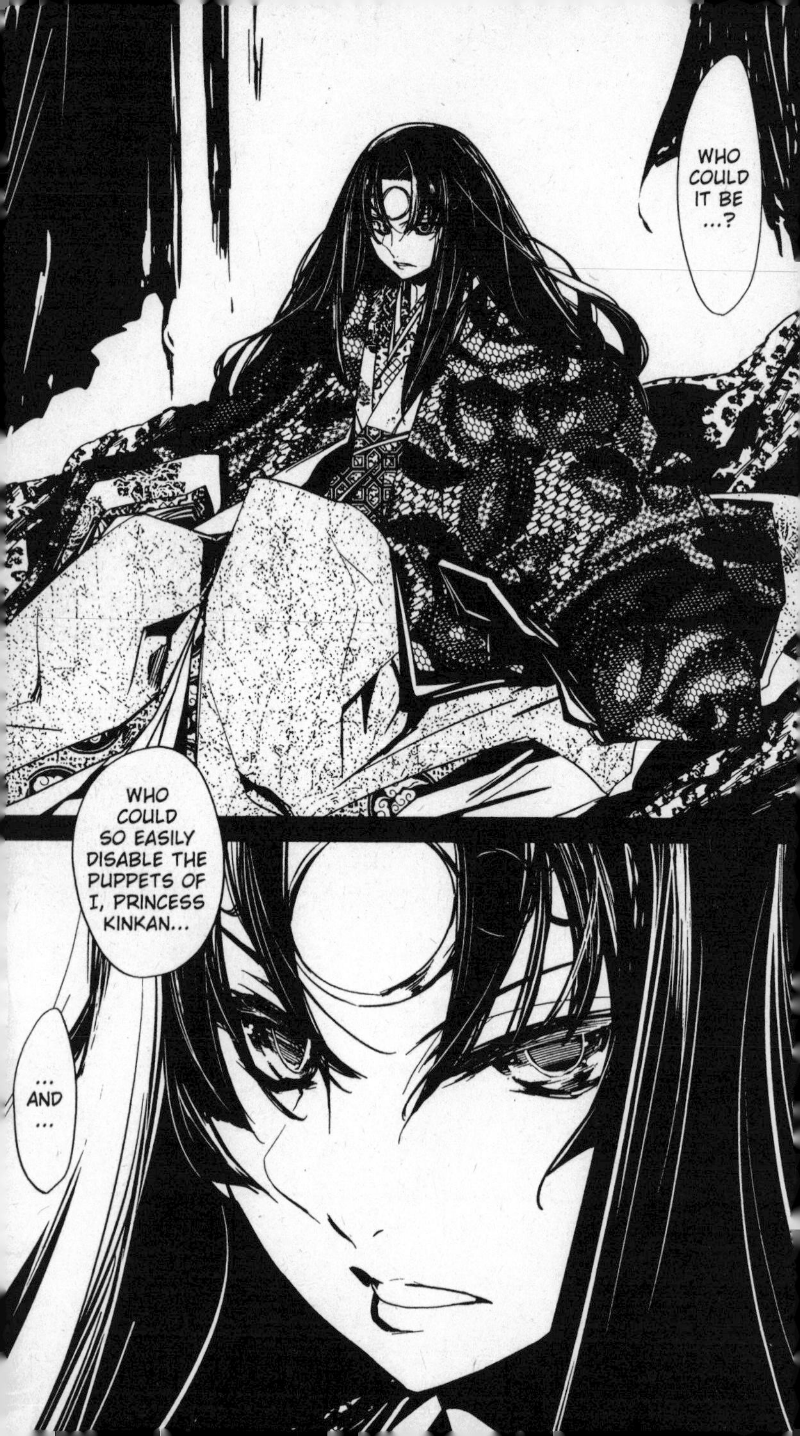
WHO COULD IT BE ...?
WHO COULD SO EASILY DISABLE THE PUPPETS OF I, PRINCESS KINKAN...
... AND ...

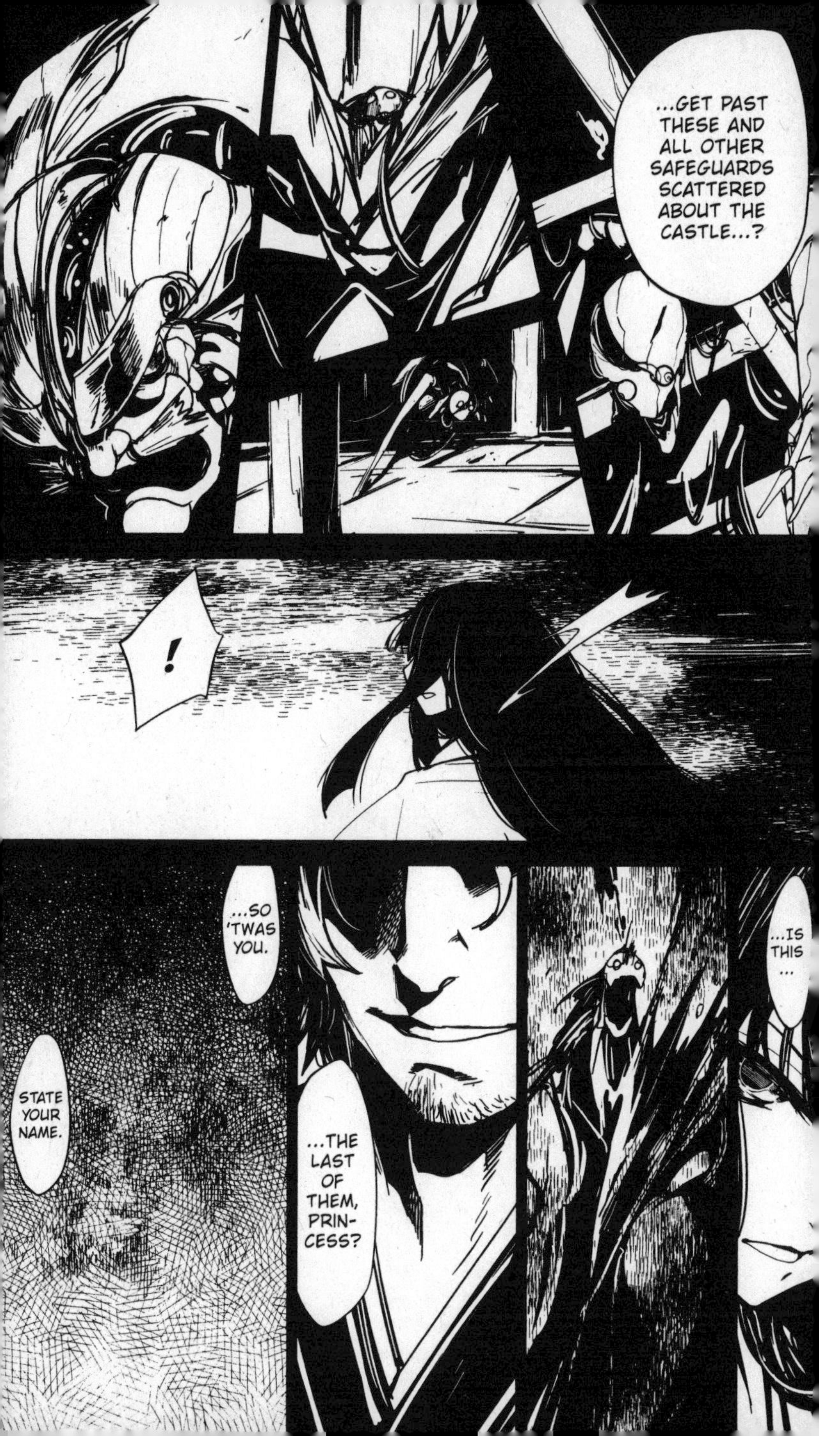
...GET PAST THESE AND ALL OTHER SAFEGUARDS SCATTERED ABOUT THE CASTLE...?
!
...IS THIS ...
...THE LAST OF THEM, PRIN- CESS?
...SO 'TWAS YOU.
STATE YOUR NAME.

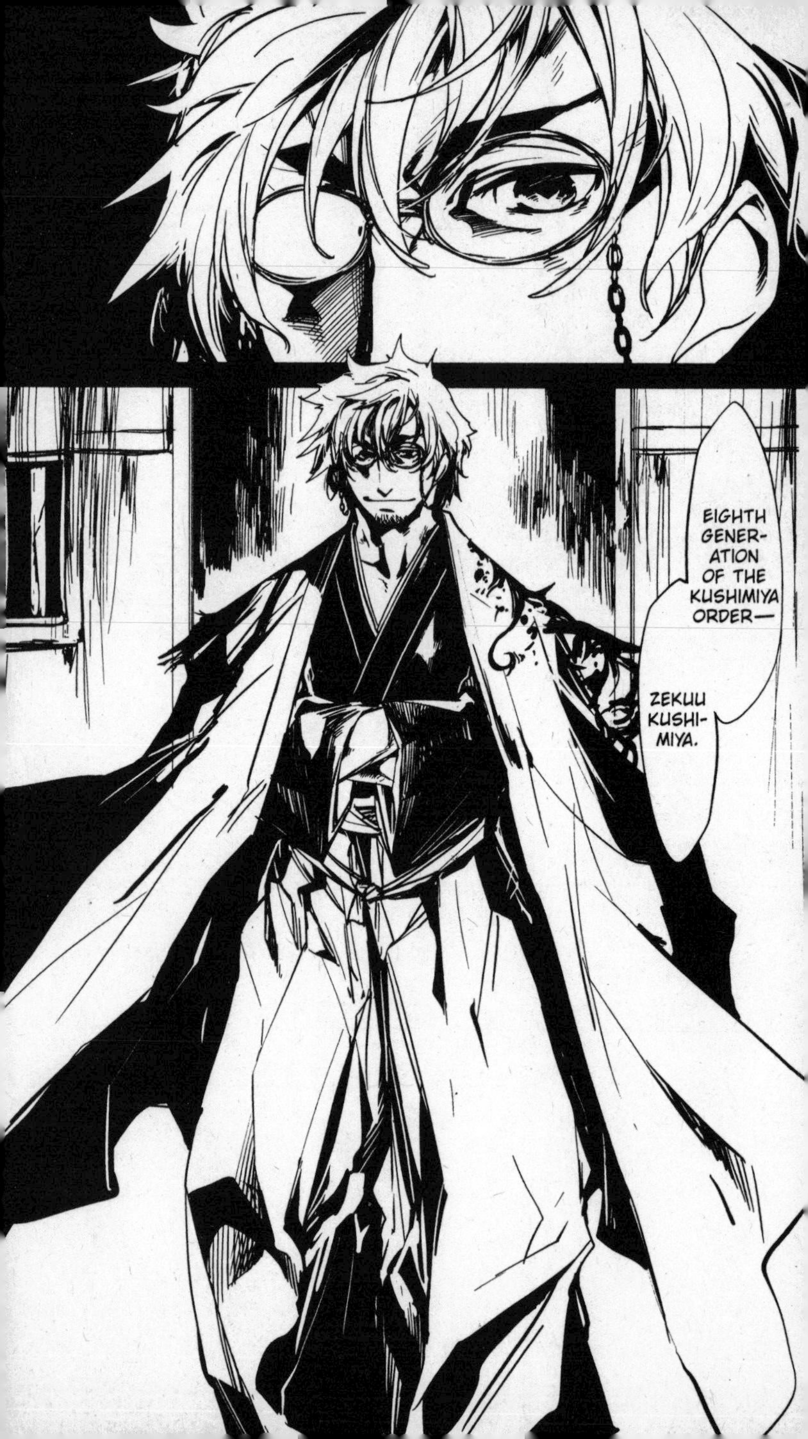
EIGHTH GENER-ATION OF THE KUSHIMIYA ORDER—
ZEKUU KUSHI-MIYA.

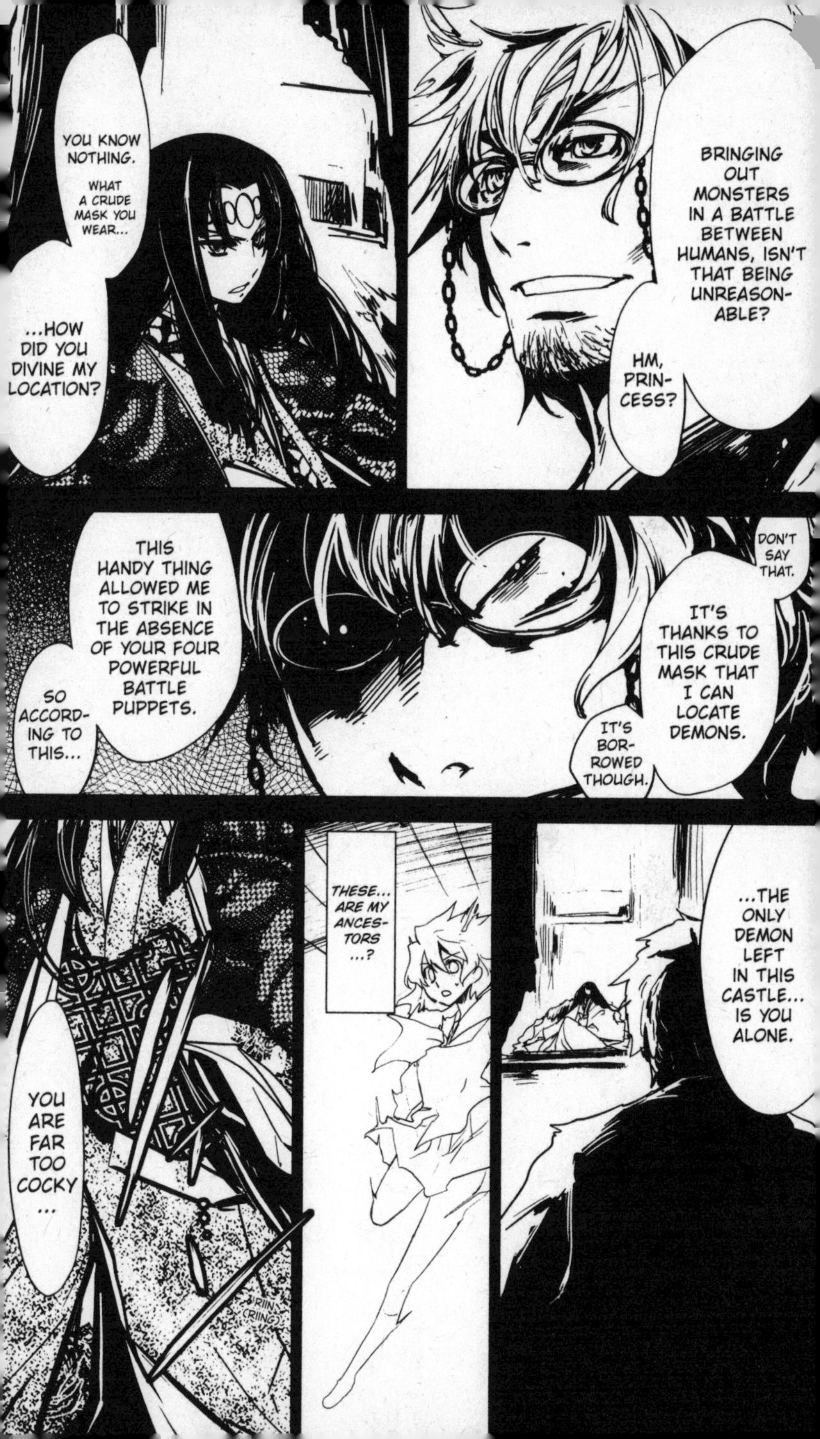
BRINGING OUT MONSTERS IN A BATTLE BETWEEN HUMANS, ISN'T THAT BEING UNREASONABLE?
HM, PRINCESS?
YOU KNOW NOTHING.
WHAT A CRUDE MASK YOU WEAR...
...HOW DID YOU DIVINE MY LOCATION?
DON'T SAY THAT.
IT'S THANKS TO THIS CRUDE MASK THAT I CAN LOCATE DEMONS.
IT'S BORROWED THOUGH.
THIS HANDY THING ALLOWED ME TO STRIKE IN THE ABSENCE OF YOUR FOUR POWERFUL BATTLE PUPPETS.
SO ACCORDING TO THIS...
...THE ONLY DEMON LEFT IN THIS CASTLE... IS YOU ALONE.
THESE... ARE MY ANCESTORS...?
YOU ARE FAR TOO COCKY...
RIIN (RIING)

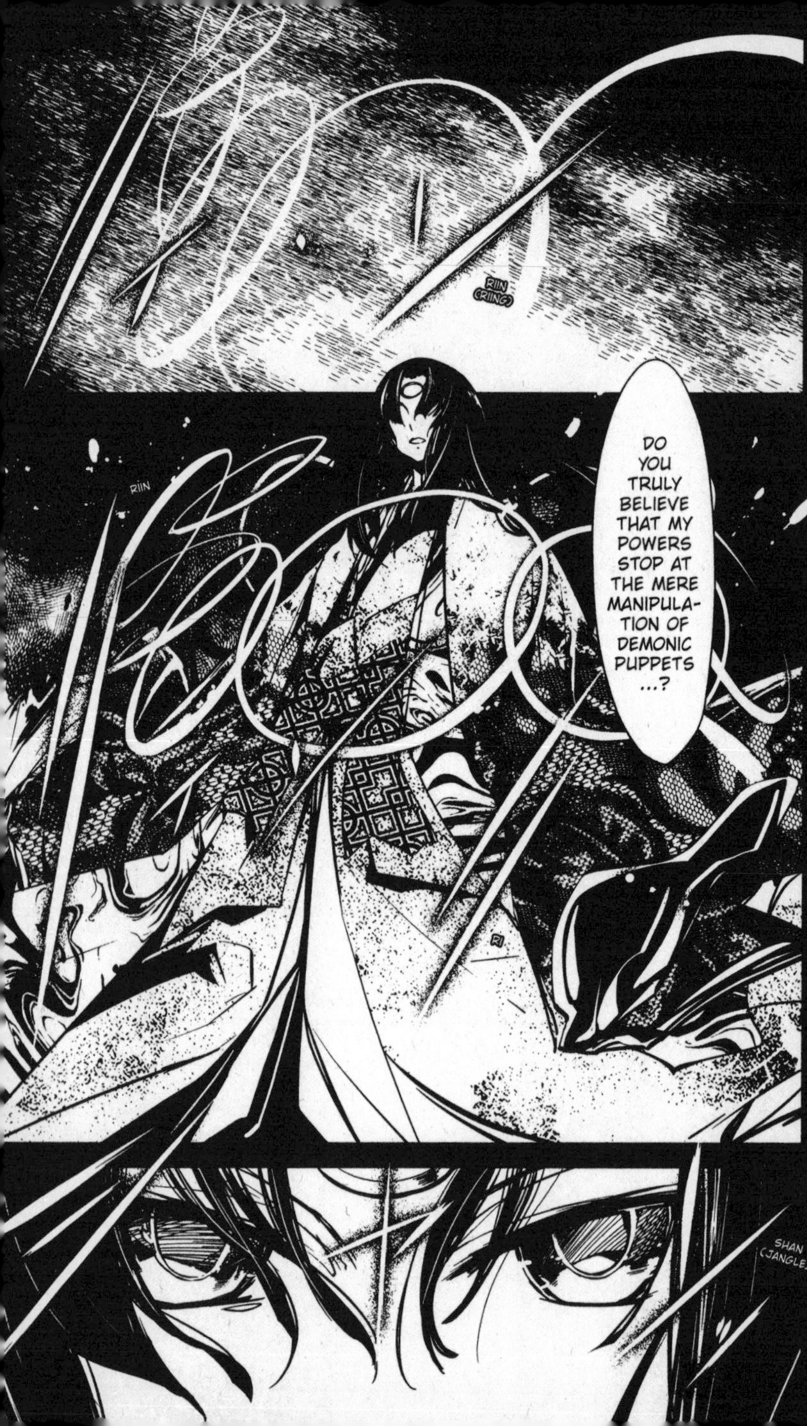
RIIN
(RIING)
DO YOU TRULY BELIEVE THAT MY POWERS STOP AT THE MERE MANIPULATION OF DEMONIC PUPPETS ...?
RIIN
RI
SHAN
(JANGLE)

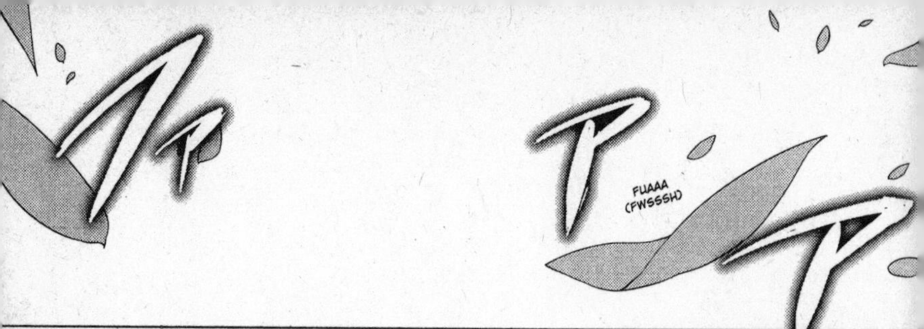
FUAAA
(FWSSSH)
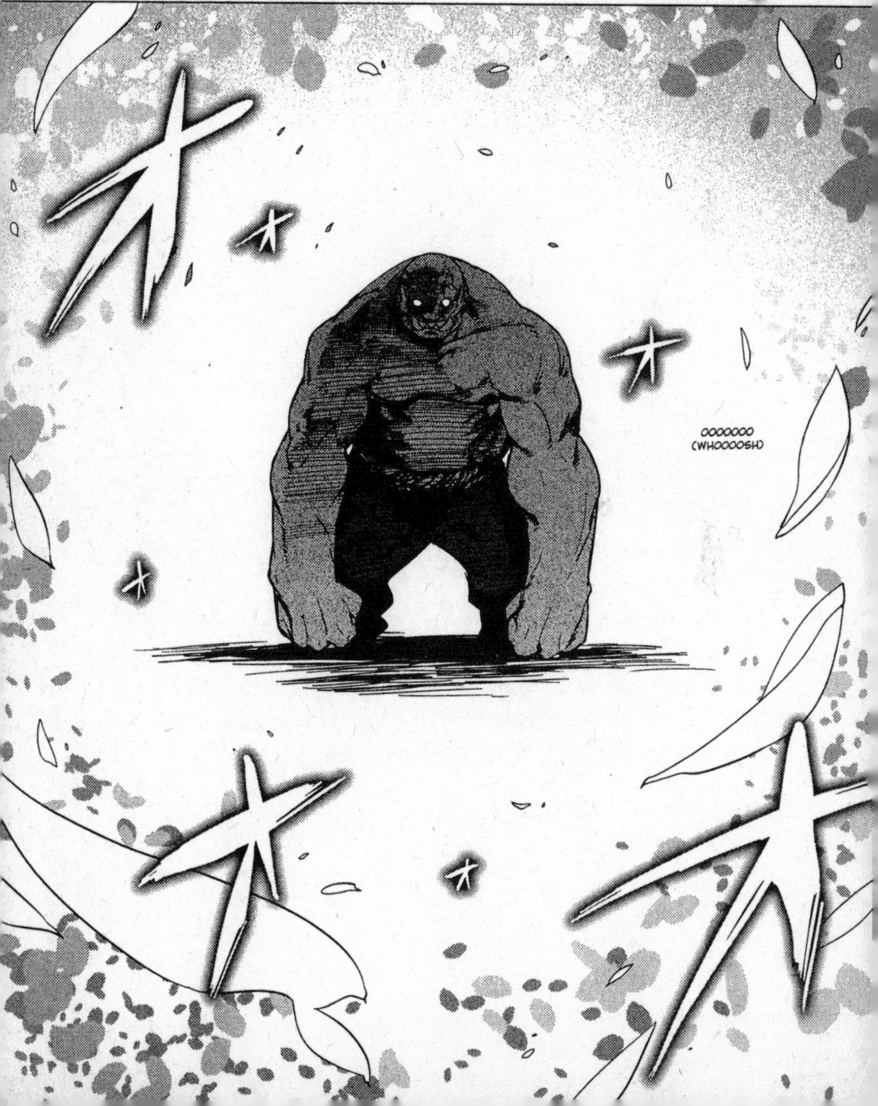
OOOOOOO
(WHOOOOSH)

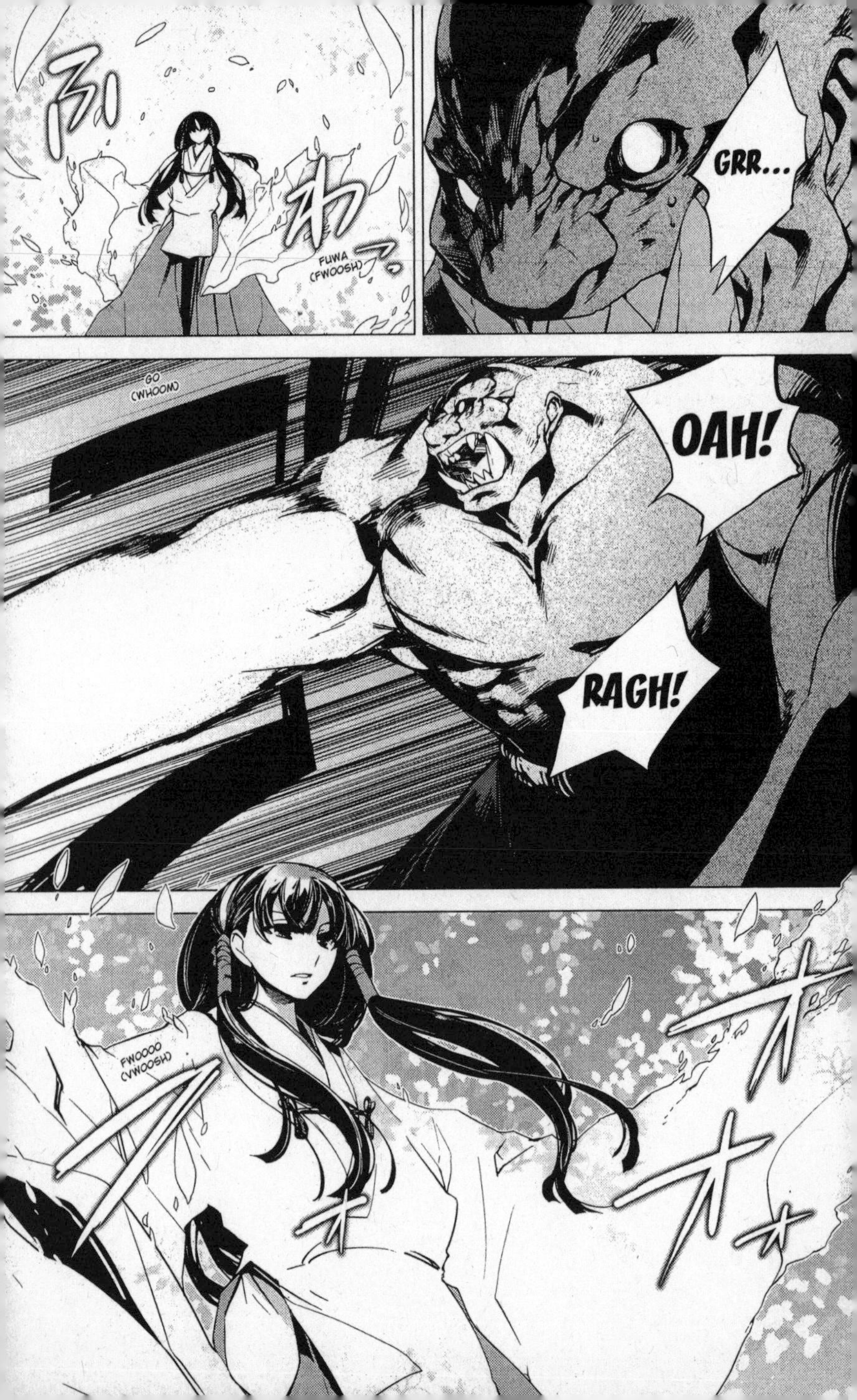
GRR...
FUWA (FWOOSH)
OAH!
RAGH!
GO (WHOOM)
FWOOOO (VWOOSH)

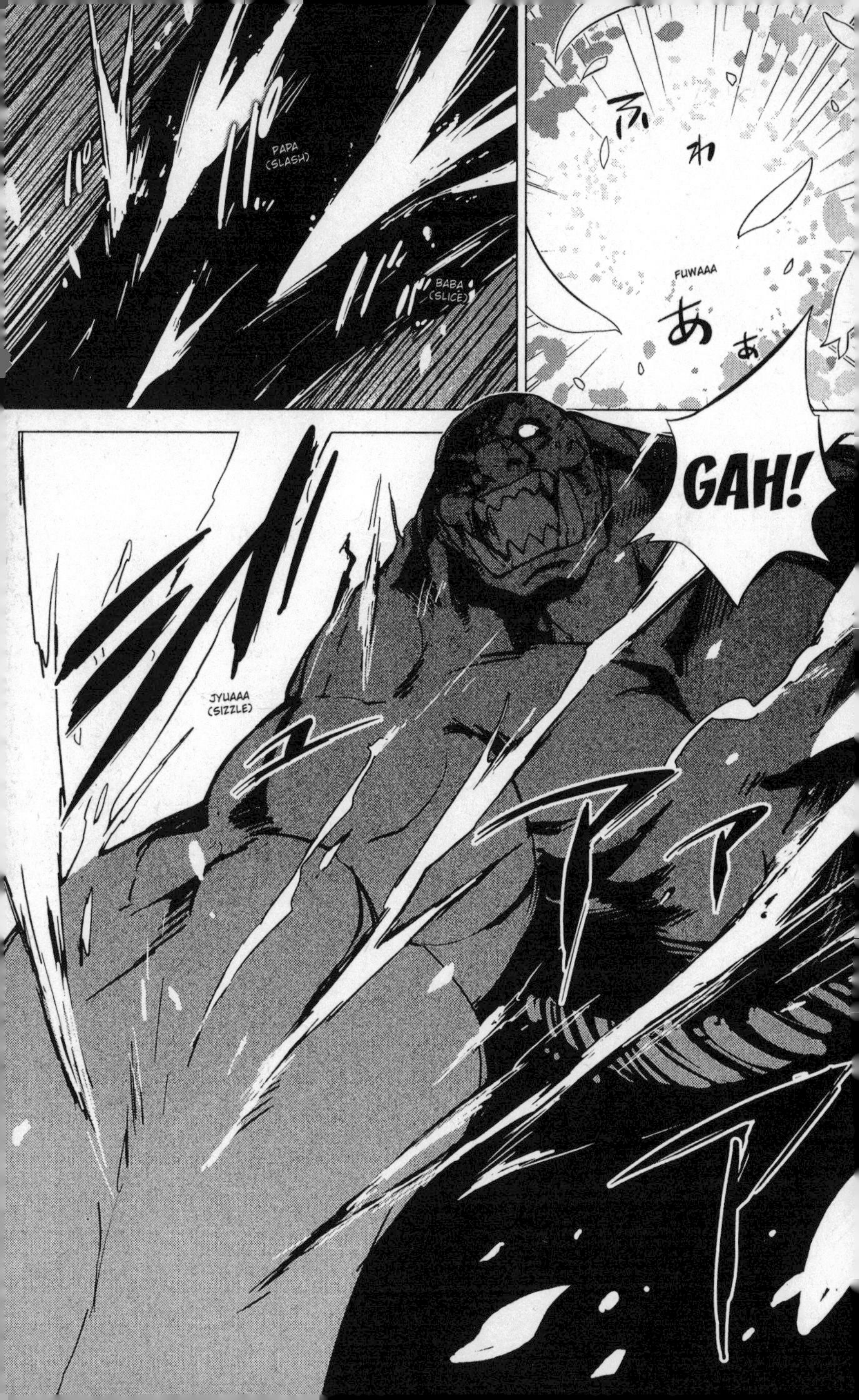
FUWAAA
PAPA (SLASH)
BABA (SLICE)
GAH!
JYUAAA (SIZZLE)

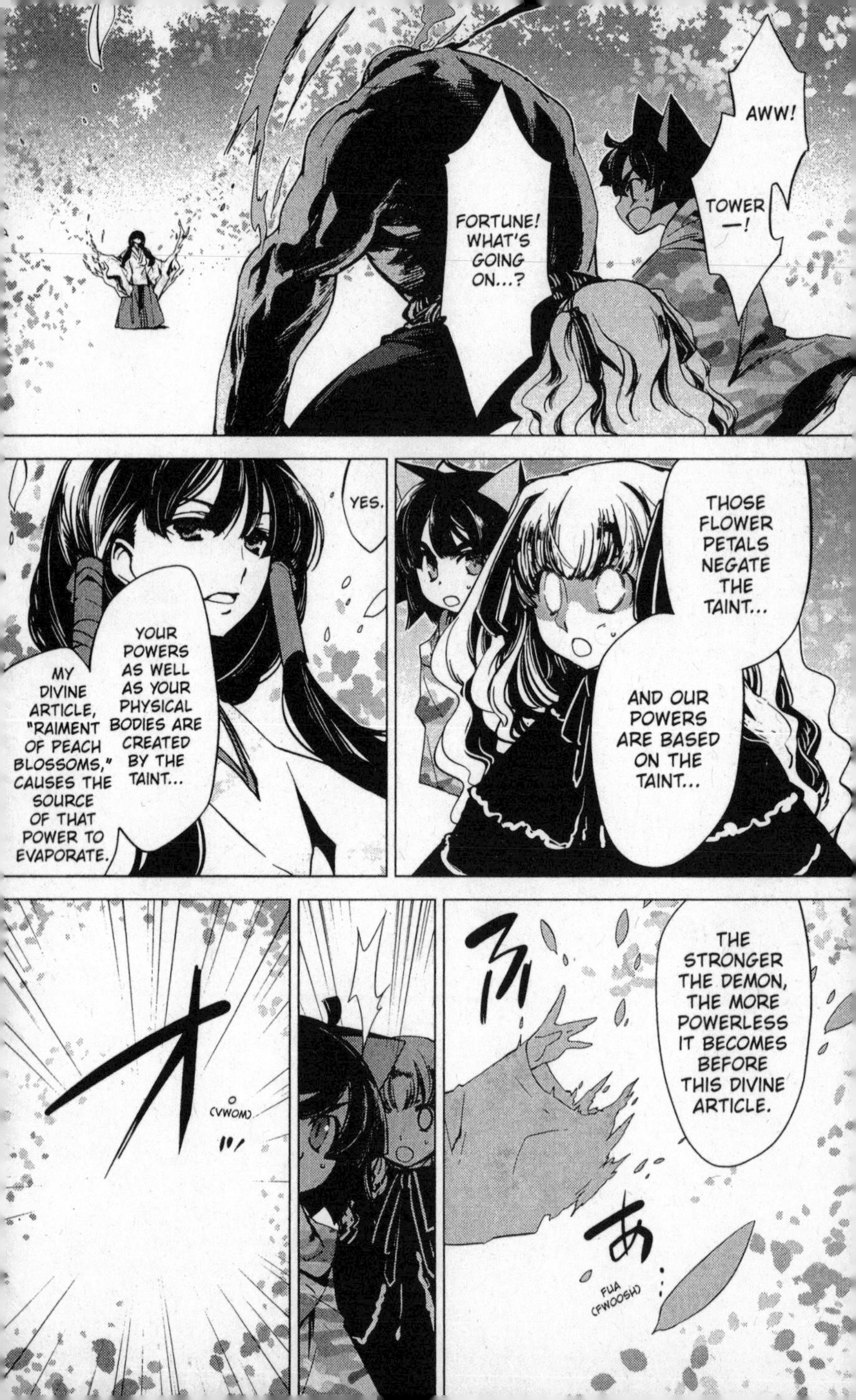
AWW!
TOWER—!
FORTUNE! WHAT'S GOING ON...?
THOSE FLOWER PETALS NEGATE THE TAINT...
AND OUR POWERS ARE BASED ON THE TAINT...
YES.
YOUR POWERS AS WELL AS YOUR PHYSICAL BODIES ARE CREATED BY THE TAINT...
MY DIVINE ARTICLE, "RAIMENT OF PEACH BLOSSOMS," CAUSES THE SOURCE OF THAT POWER TO EVAPORATE.
THE STRONGER THE DEMON, THE MORE POWERLESS IT BECOMES BEFORE THIS DIVINE ARTICLE.
FUA (FWOOSH)
(VWOM)

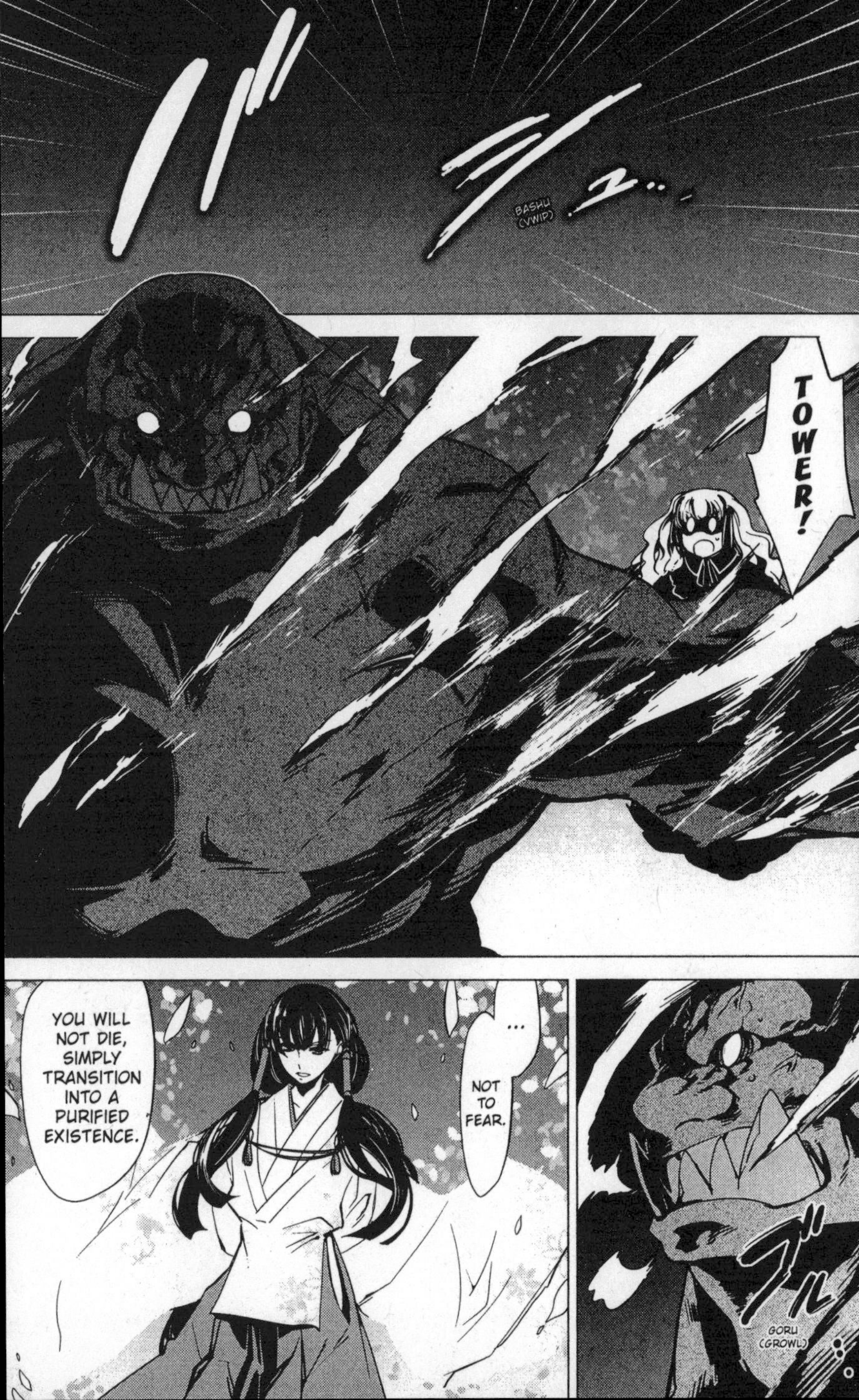
BASHU (VWIP)
TOWER!
...
NOT TO FEAR.
YOU WILL NOT DIE, SIMPLY TRANSITION INTO A PURIFIED EXISTENCE.
GORU (GROWL)

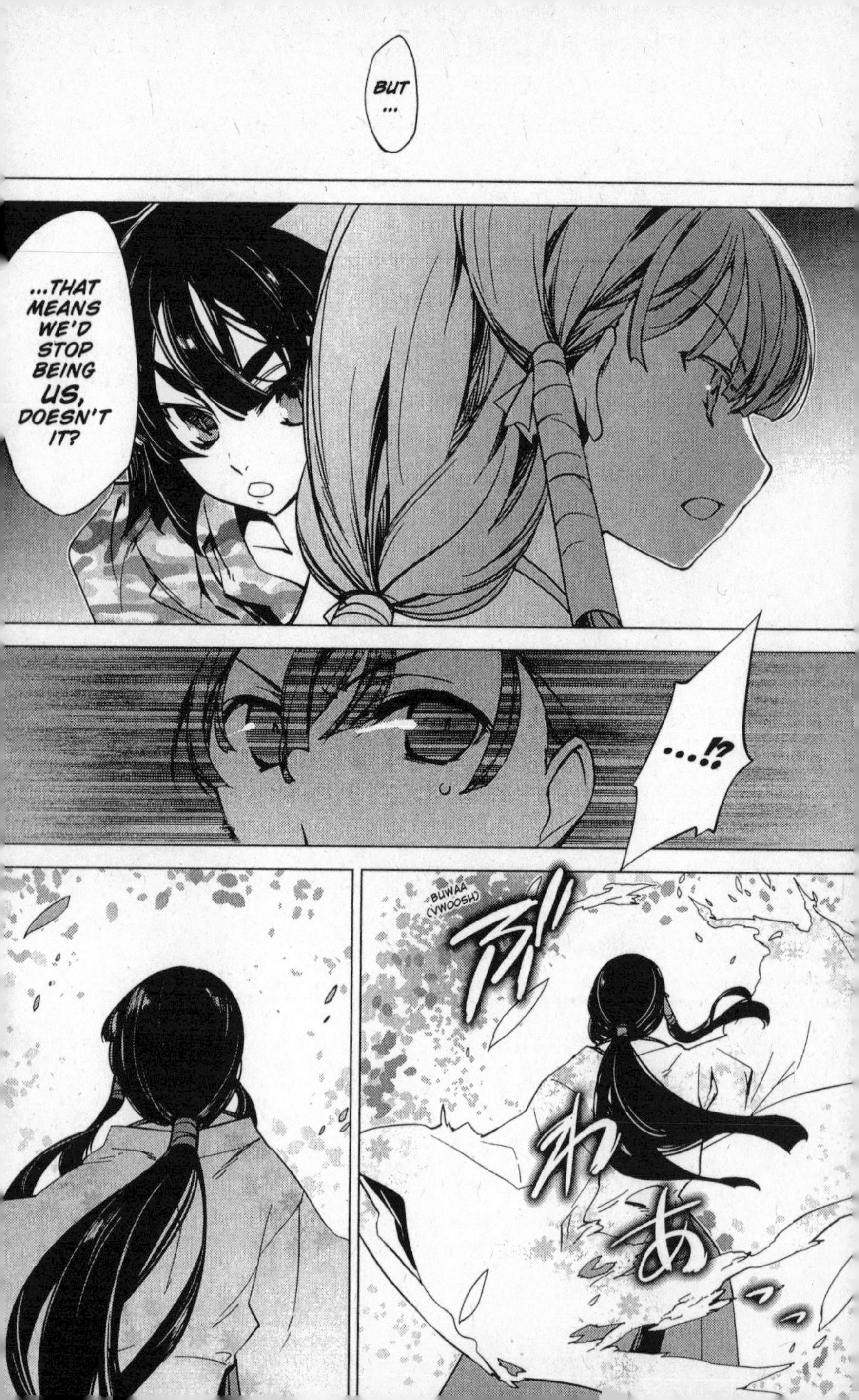
BUT ...
...THAT MEANS WE'D STOP BEING US, DOESN'T IT?
...!?
BUWAA (VWOOSH)

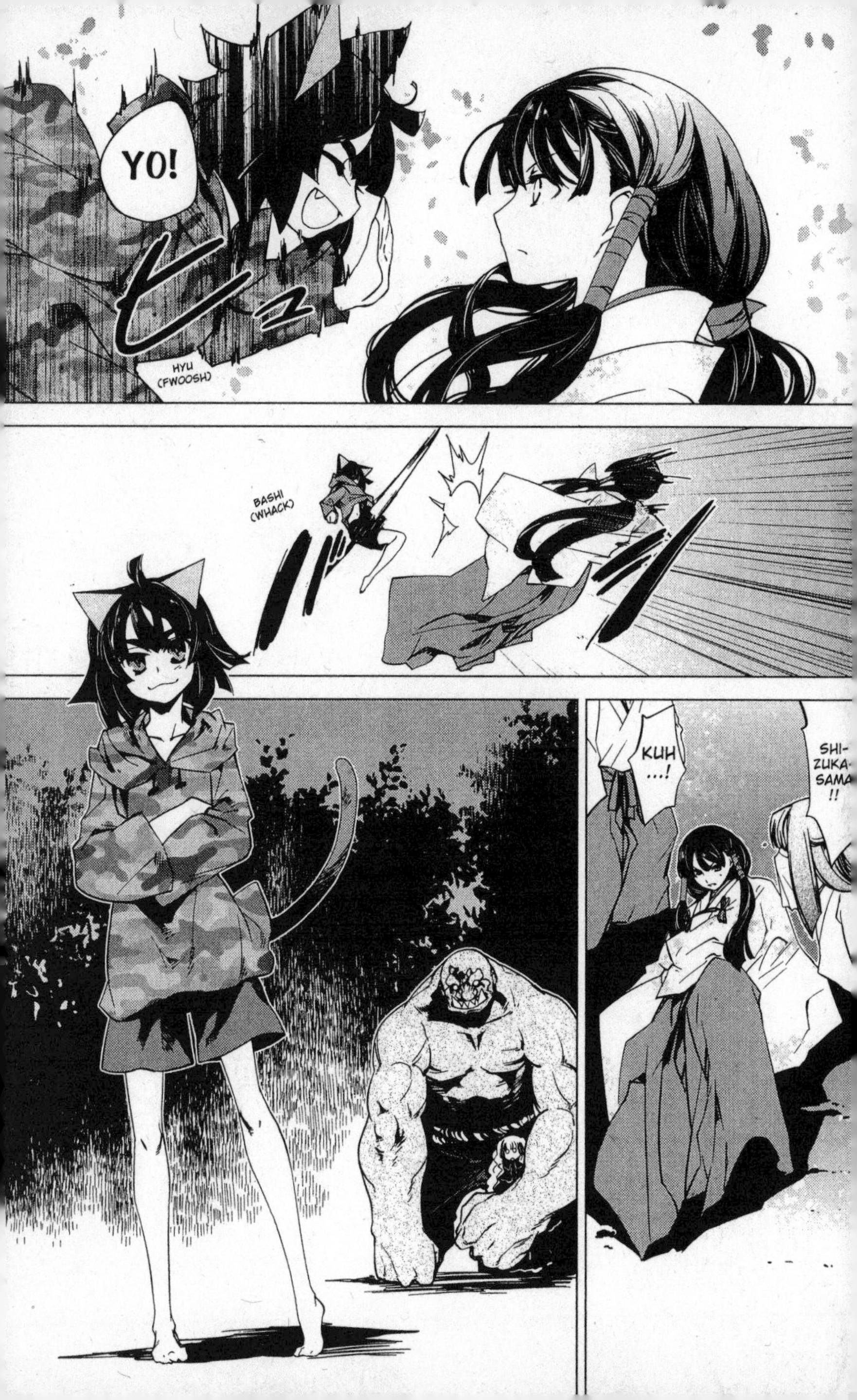
YO!
HYU (FWOOSH)
BASHI (WHACK)
SHI-ZUKA-SAMA!!
KUH ...!

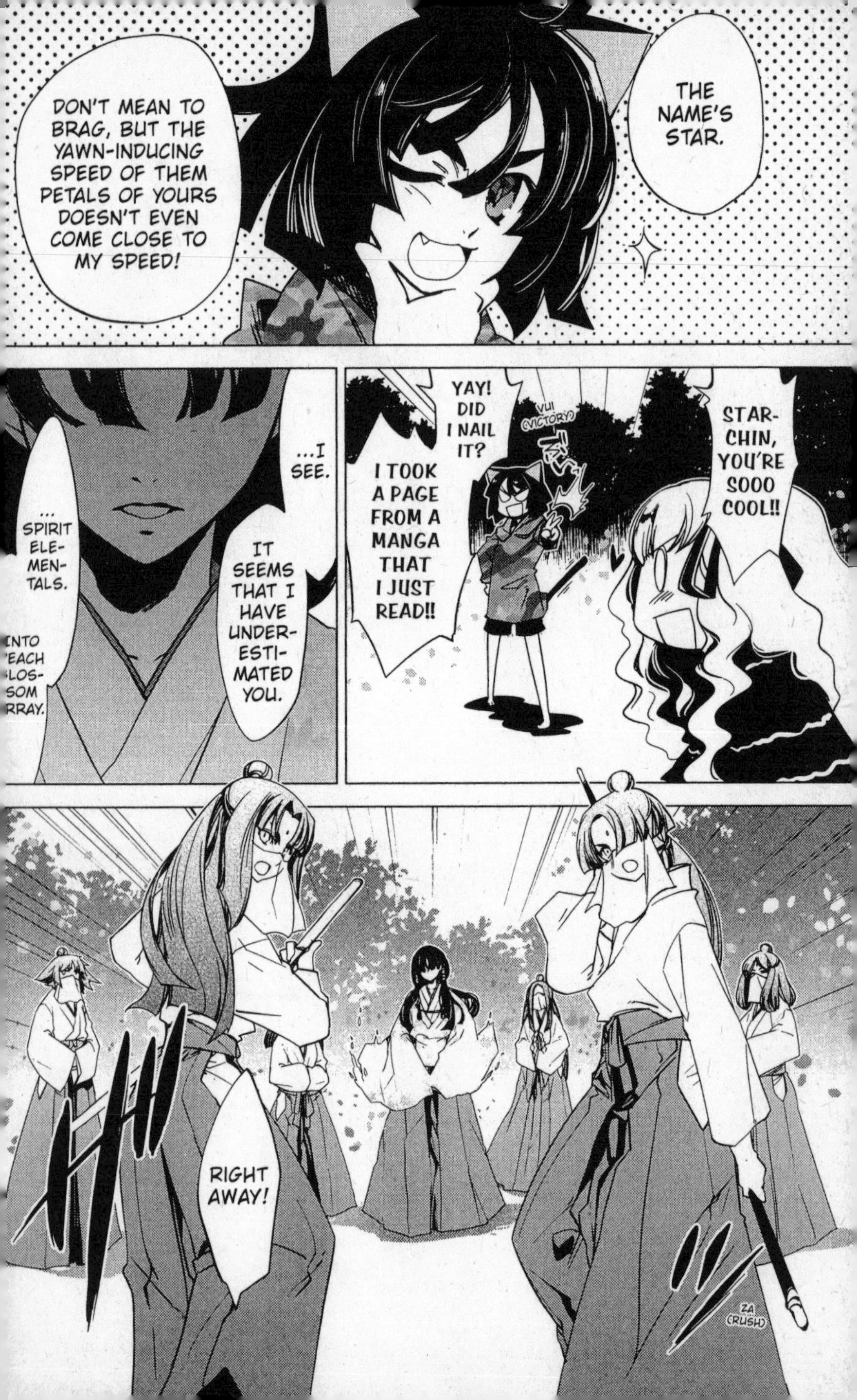
THE NAME'S STAR.
DON'T MEAN TO BRAG, BUT THE YAWN-INDUCING SPEED OF THEM PETALS OF YOURS DOESN'T EVEN COME CLOSE TO MY SPEED!
STAR-CHIN, YOU'RE SOOO COOL!!
VUI (VICTORY)
YAY! DID I NAIL IT?
I TOOK A PAGE FROM A MANGA THAT I JUST READ!!
...I SEE.
IT SEEMS THAT I HAVE UNDER-ESTI-MATED YOU.
... SPIRIT ELE-MEN-TALS.
INTO EACH LOS-SOM RRAY.
RIGHT AWAY!
ZA (CRUSH)

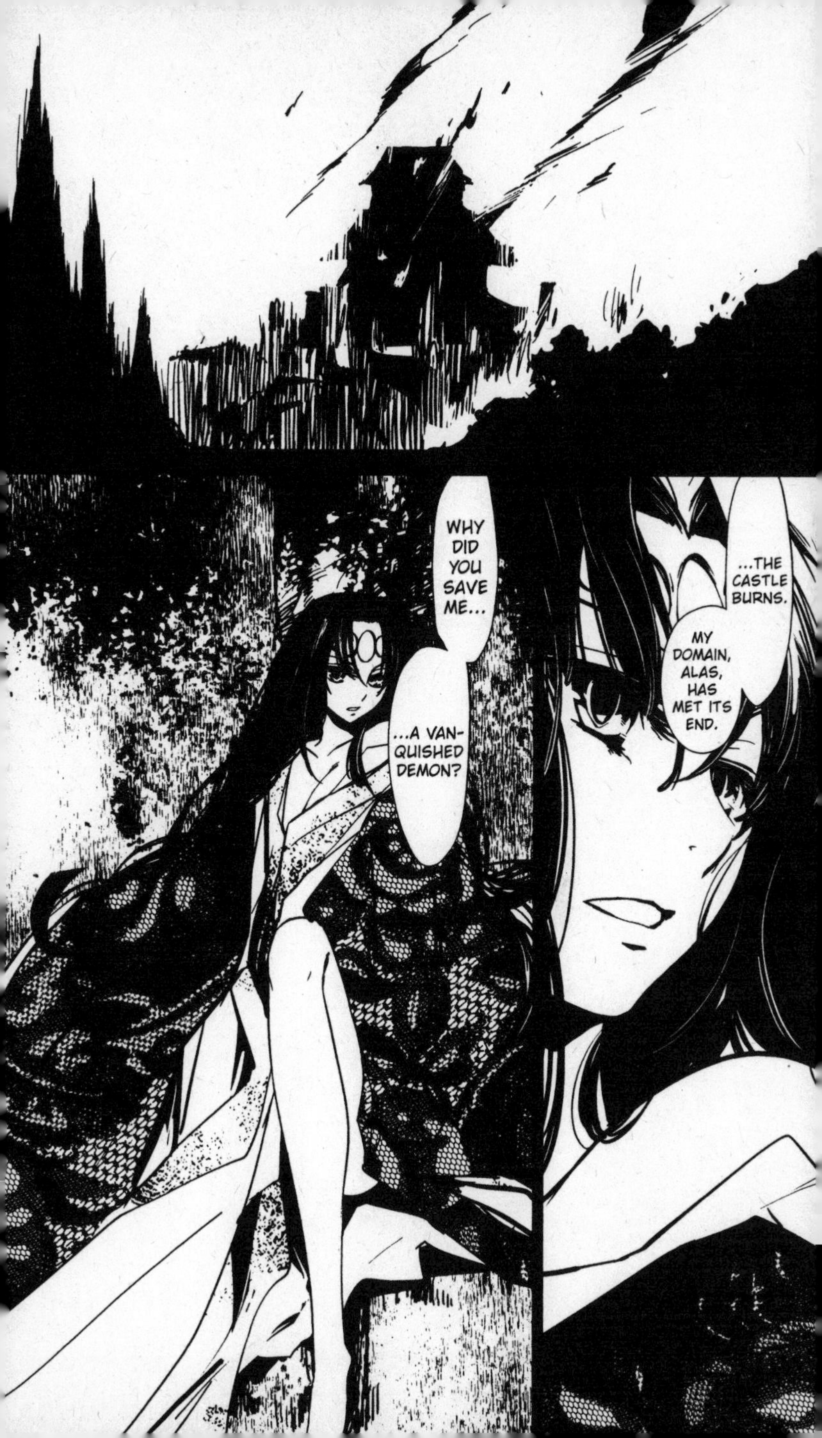
...THE CASTLE BURNS.
MY DOMAIN, ALAS, HAS MET ITS END.
WHY DID YOU SAVE ME...
...A VAN-QUISHED DEMON?

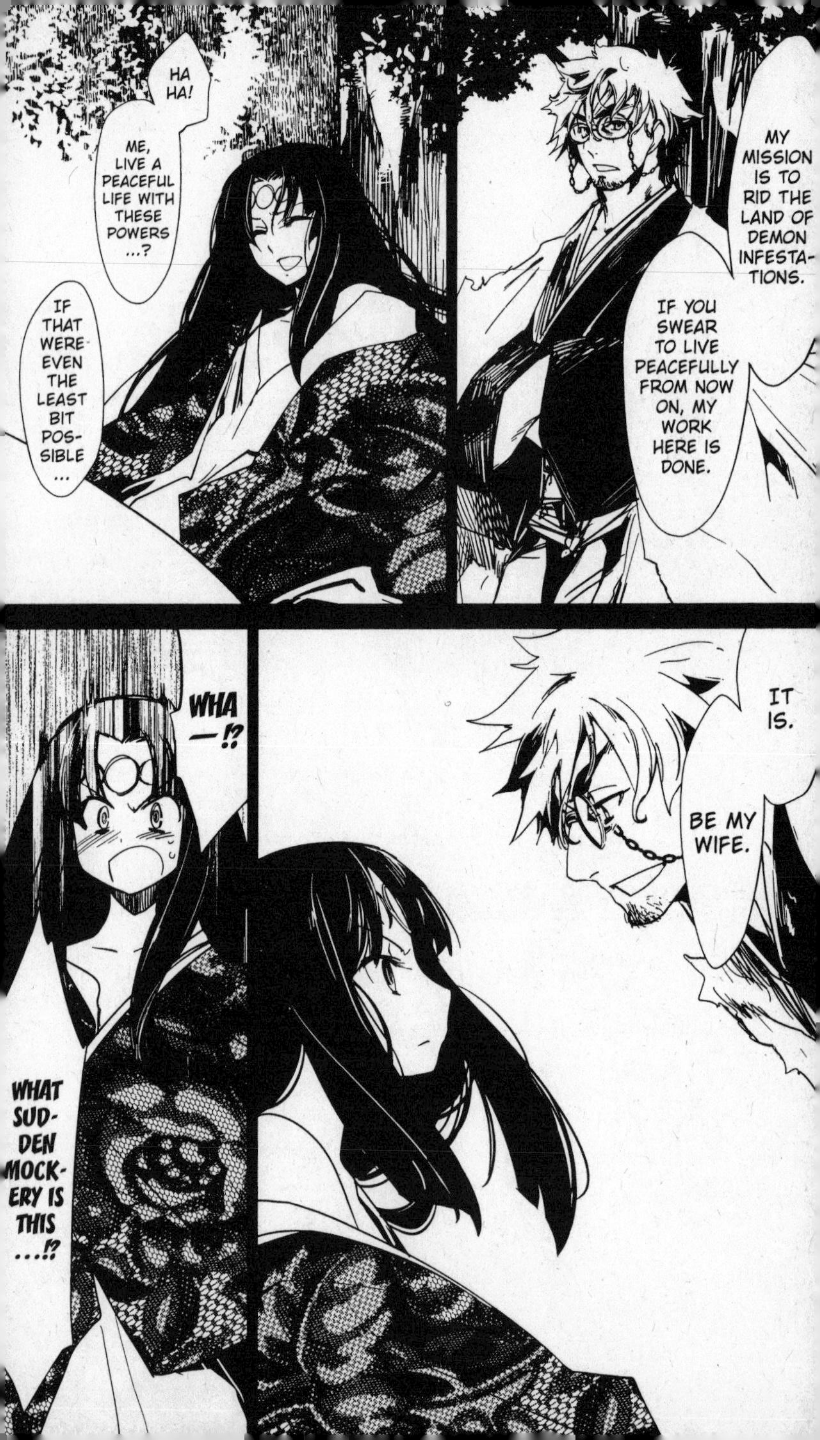
MY MISSION IS TO RID THE LAND OF DEMON INFESTATIONS.
IF YOU SWEAR TO LIVE PEACEFULLY FROM NOW ON, MY WORK HERE IS DONE.
HA HA!
ME, LIVE A PEACEFUL LIFE WITH THESE POWERS ...?
IF THAT WERE EVEN THE LEAST BIT POSSIBLE ...
IT IS.
BE MY WIFE.
WHA—!?
WHAT SUDDEN MOCKERY IS THIS ...!?

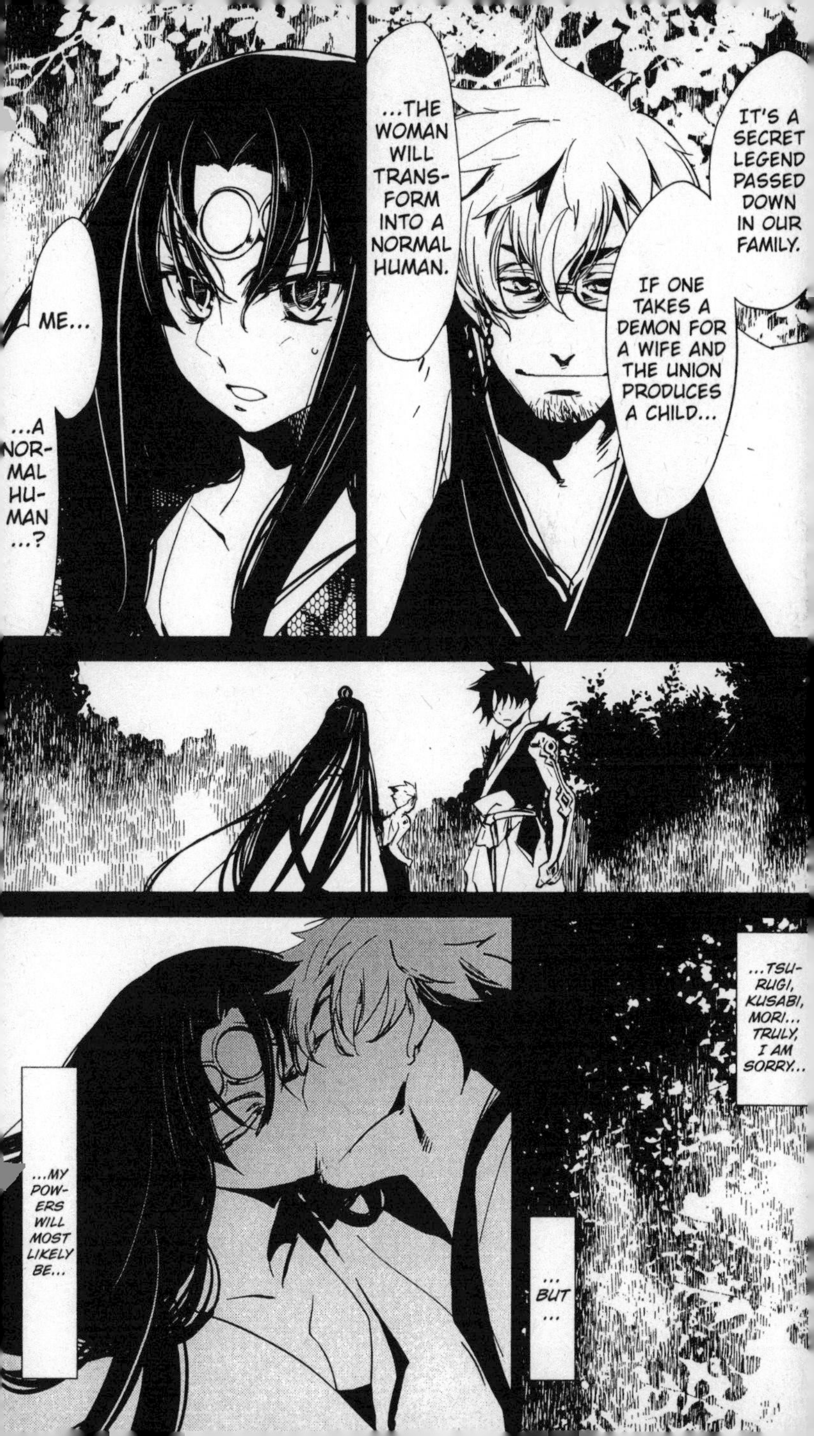
IT'S A SECRET LEGEND PASSED DOWN IN OUR FAMILY.
IF ONE TAKES A DEMON FOR A WIFE AND THE UNION PRODUCES A CHILD...
...THE WOMAN WILL TRANS-FORM INTO A NORMAL HUMAN.
ME...
...A NOR-MAL HU-MAN ...?
...TSU-RUGI, KUSABI, MORI... TRULY, I AM SORRY...
... BUT ...
...MY POW-ERS WILL MOST LIKELY BE...

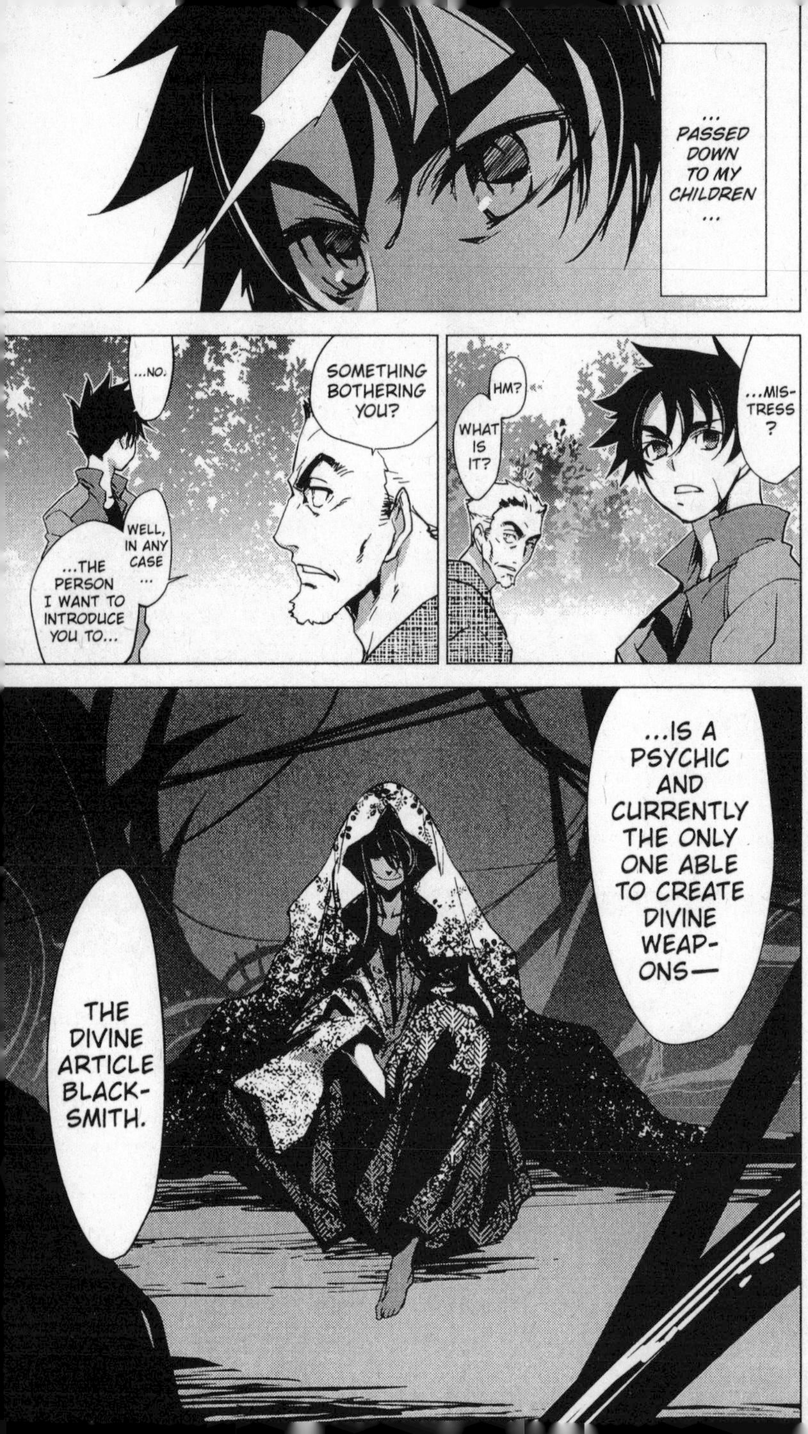
...PASSED DOWN TO MY CHILDREN ...
...MISTRESS?
HM?
WHAT IS IT?
SOMETHING BOTHERING YOU?
...NO.
WELL, IN ANY CASE...
...THE PERSON I WANT TO INTRODUCE YOU TO...
...IS A PSYCHIC AND CURRENTLY THE ONLY ONE ABLE TO CREATE DIVINE WEAPONS—
THE DIVINE ARTICLE BLACKSMITH.

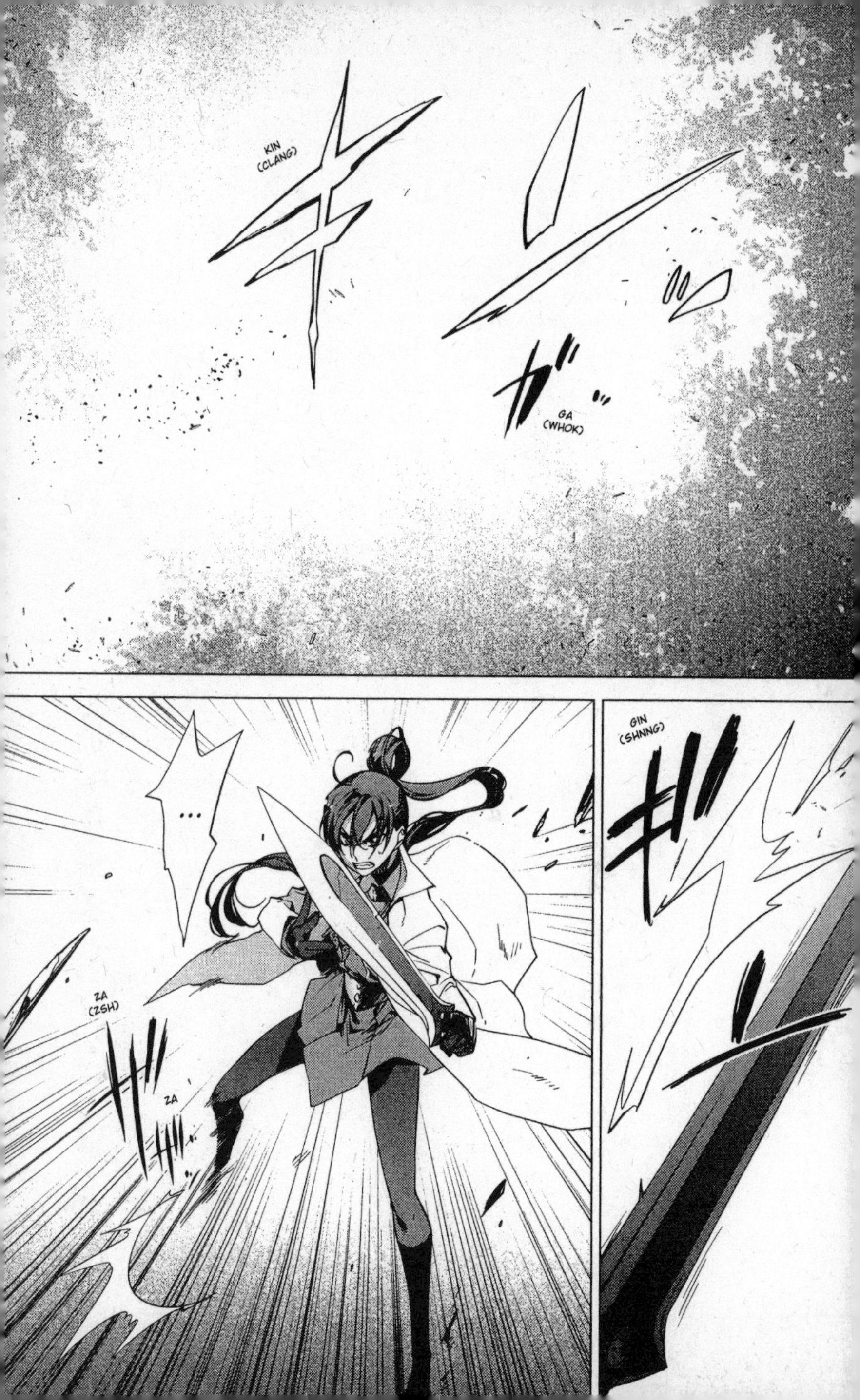
KIN (CLANG)
GA (WHOK)
GIN (SHNNG)
...
ZA (ZSH)
ZA

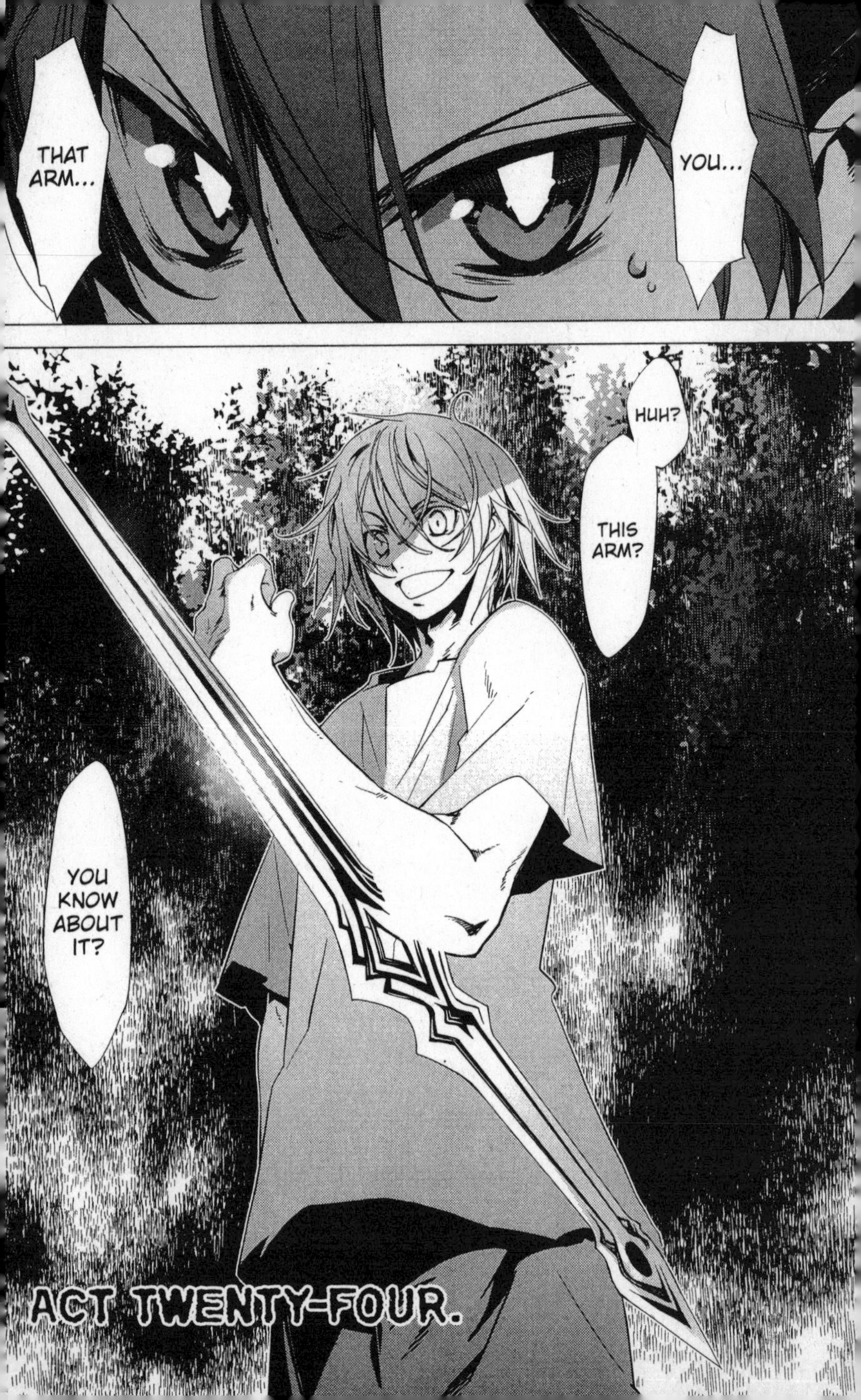
YOU...
THAT ARM...
HUH?
THIS ARM?
YOU KNOW ABOUT IT?
ACT TWENTY-FOUR.

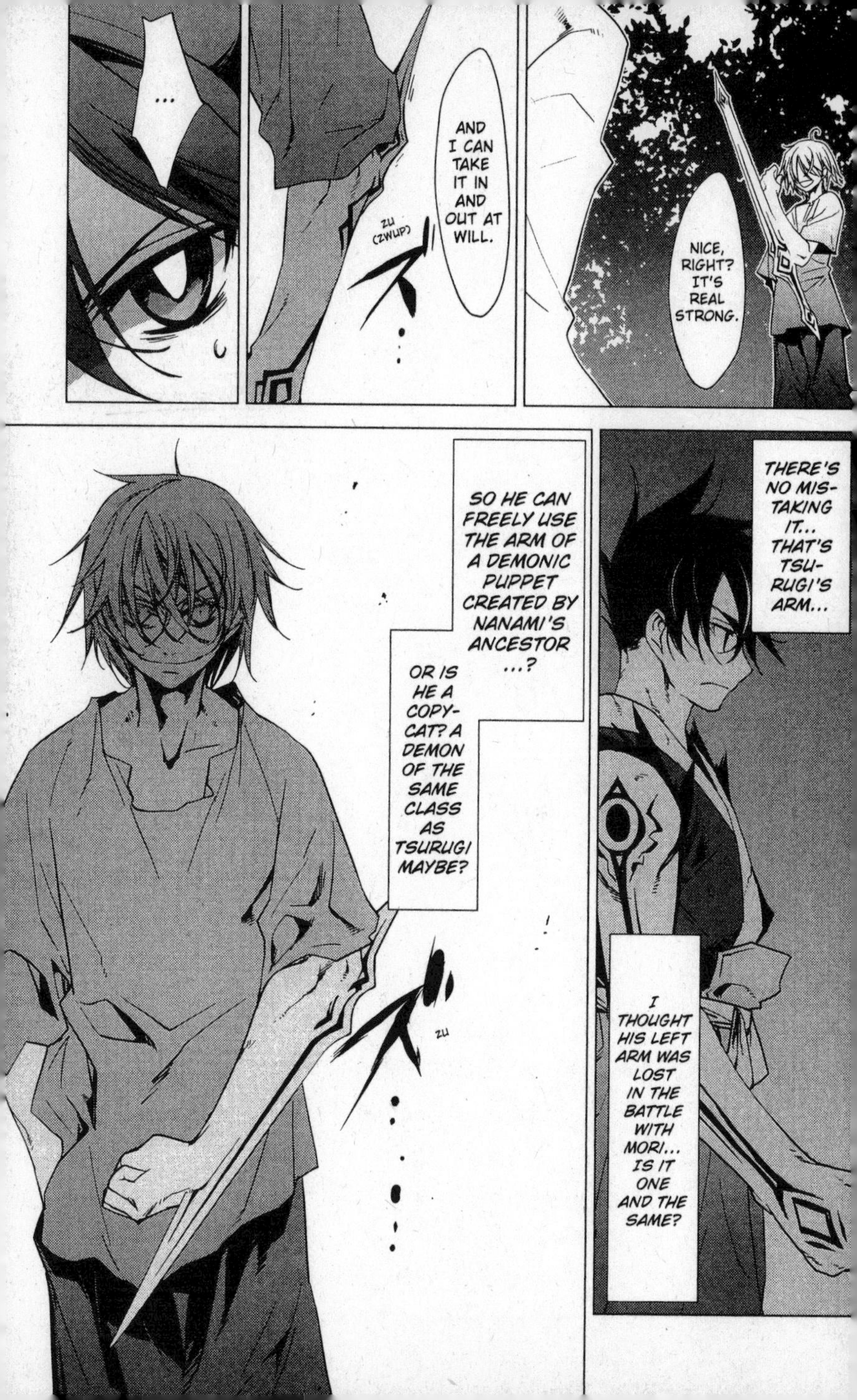
NICE, RIGHT? IT'S REAL STRONG.
AND I CAN TAKE IT IN AND OUT AT WILL.
ZU (ZWUP)
...
THERE'S NO MISTAKING IT... THAT'S TSURUGI'S ARM...
I THOUGHT HIS LEFT ARM WAS LOST IN THE BATTLE WITH MORI... IS IT ONE AND THE SAME?
SO HE CAN FREELY USE THE ARM OF A DEMONIC PUPPET CREATED BY NANAMI'S ANCESTOR ...?
OR IS HE A COPYCAT? A DEMON OF THE SAME CLASS AS TSURUGI MAYBE?
ZU

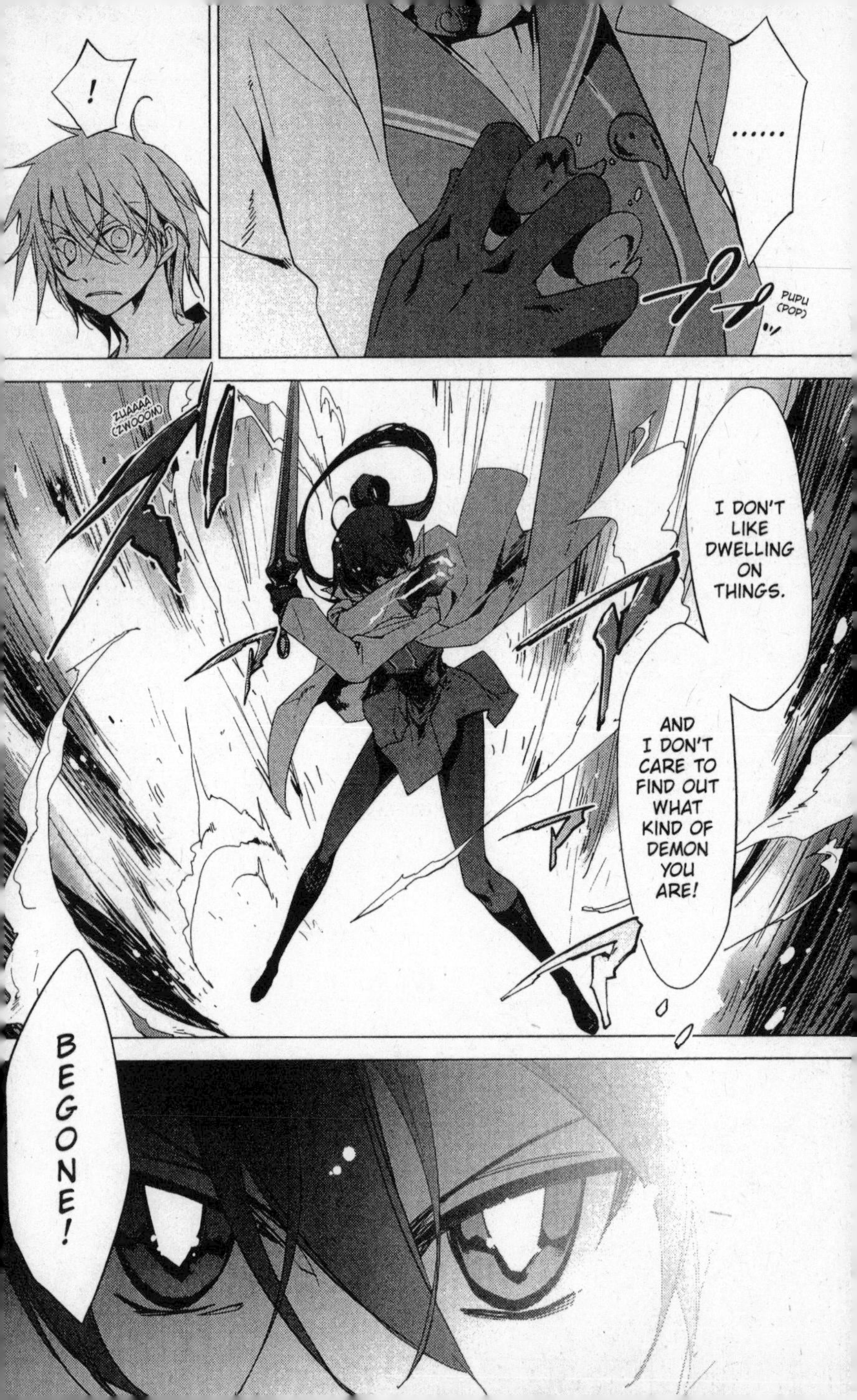
……
PUPU (POP)
!
ZUAAAA (ZWOOOM)
I DON'T LIKE DWELLING ON THINGS.
AND I DON'T CARE TO FIND OUT WHAT KIND OF DEMON YOU ARE!
BEGONE!

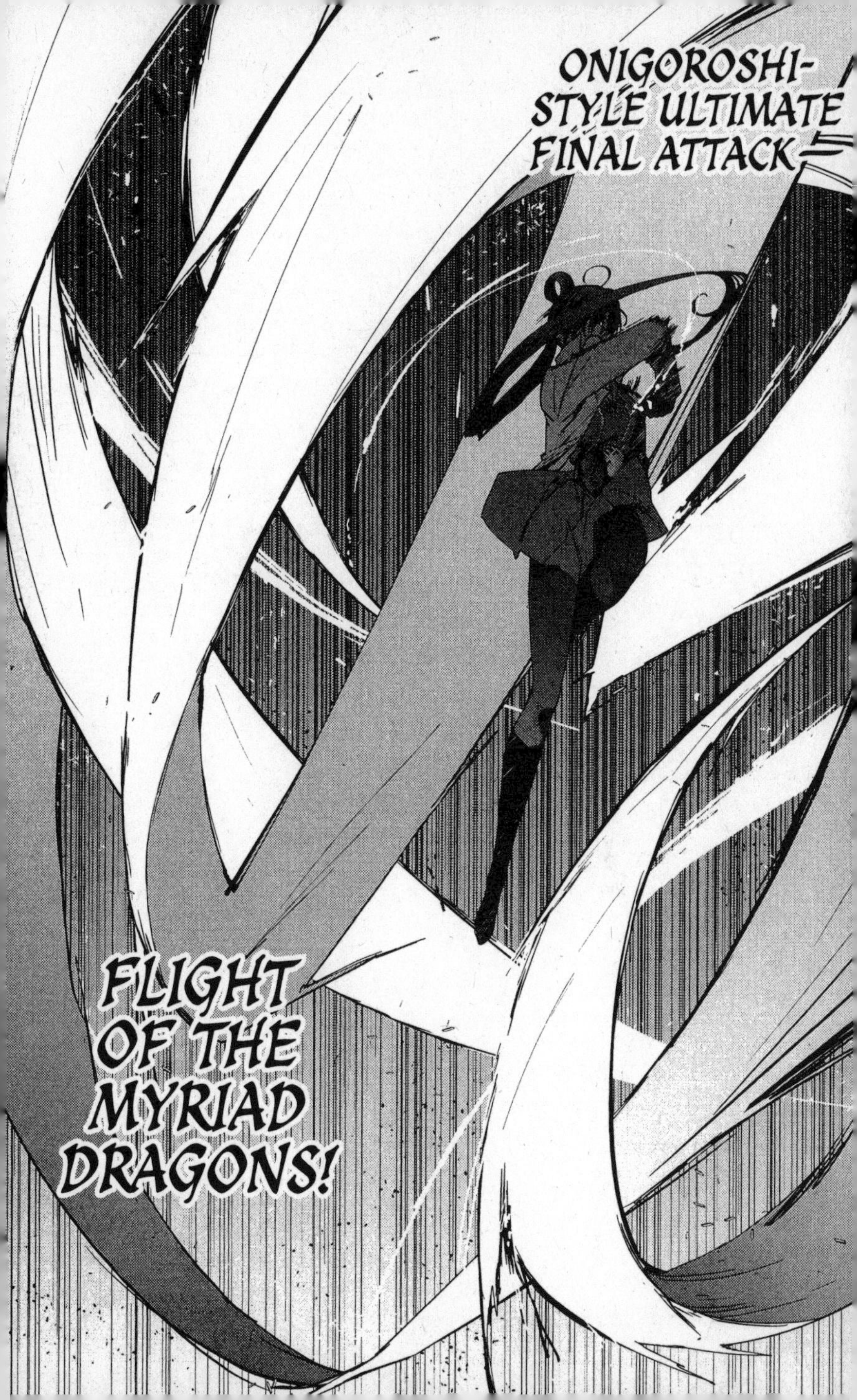
ONIGOROSHI-STYLE ULTIMATE FINAL ATTACK—
FLIGHT OF THE MYRIAD DRAGONS!

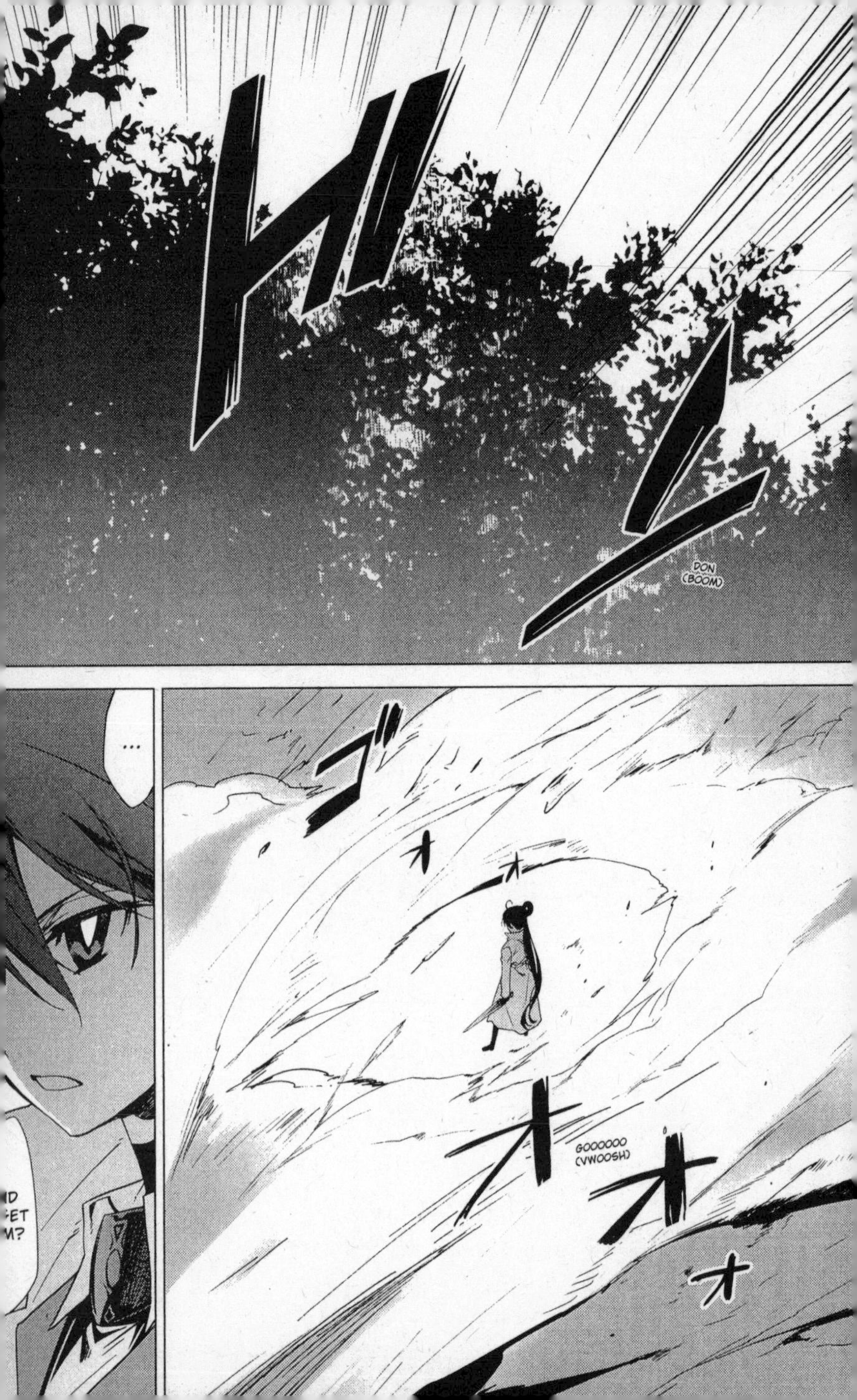
DON
(BOOM)
GOOOOOO
(VWOOSH)
...
ID
FET
M?

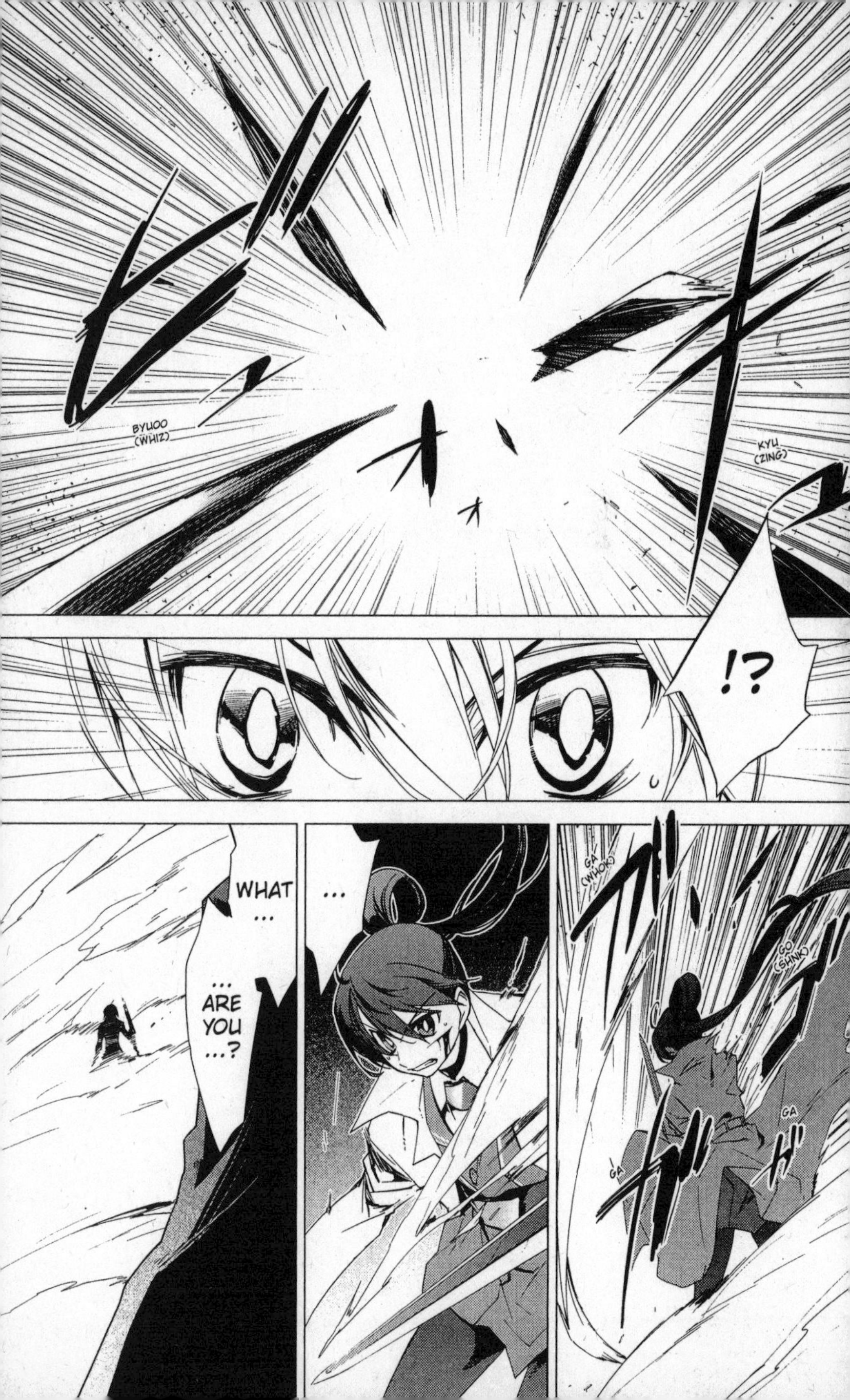
KYU (ZING)
BYUOO (WHIZ)
!?
GA (WHOK)
GO (SHNK)
GA
GA
...
WHAT ...
... ARE YOU ...?

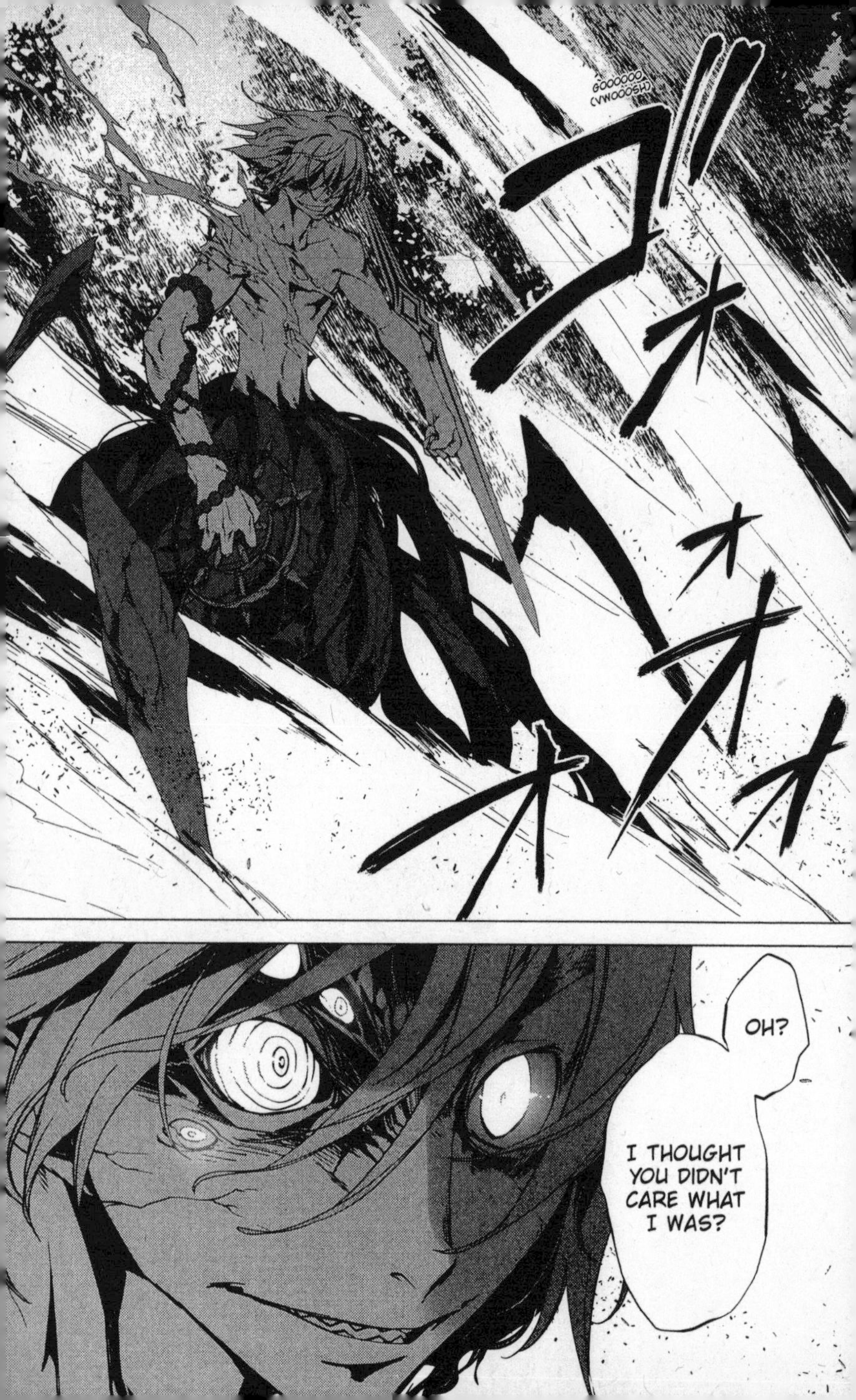
GOOOOOO
(VWOOOSH)
OH?
I THOUGHT YOU DIDN'T CARE WHAT I WAS?

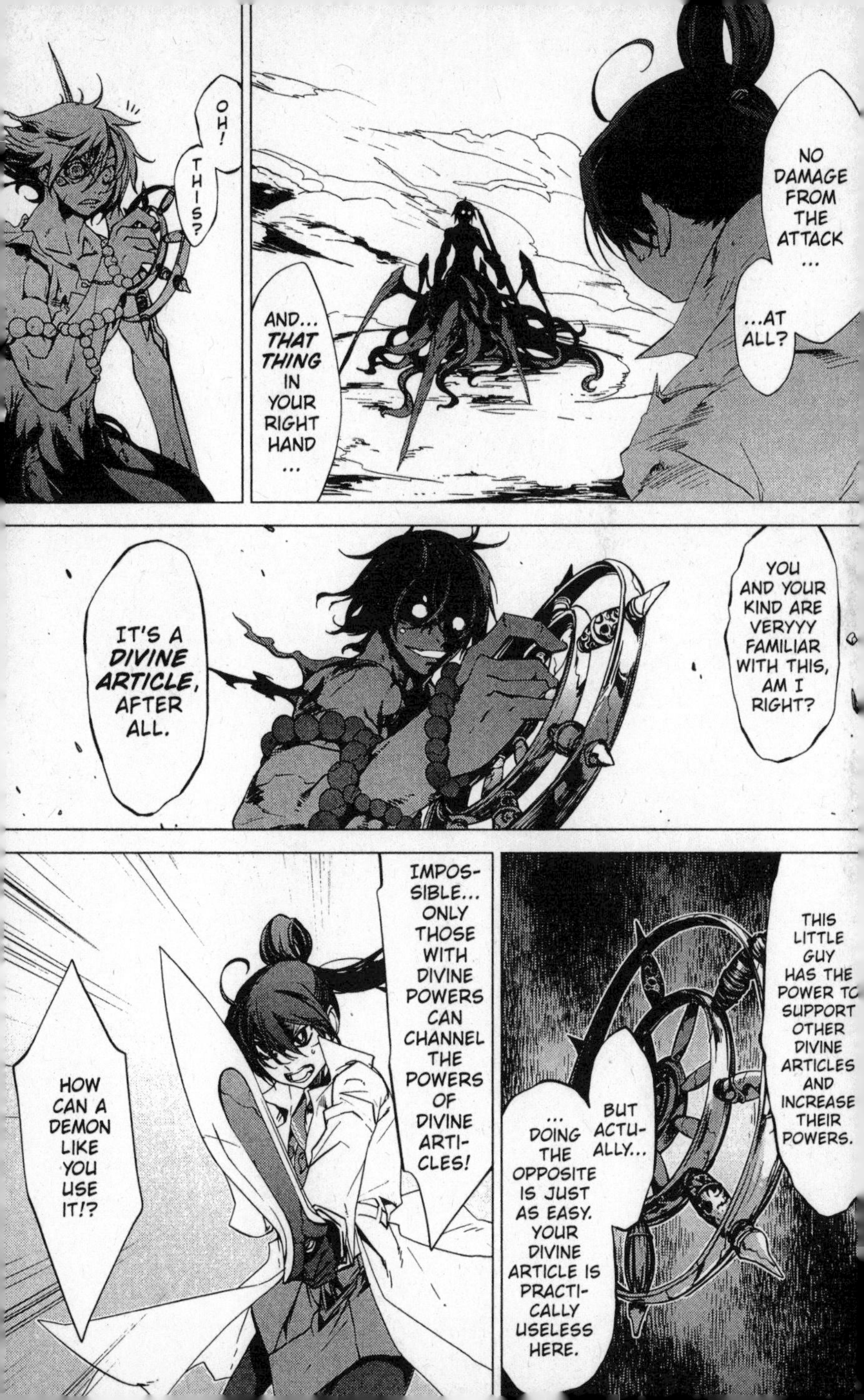
NO DAMAGE FROM THE ATTACK ...
...AT ALL?
AND... THAT THING IN YOUR RIGHT HAND ...
OH! THIS?
YOU AND YOUR KIND ARE VERYYY FAMILIAR WITH THIS, AM I RIGHT?
IT'S A DIVINE ARTICLE, AFTER ALL.
THIS LITTLE GUY HAS THE POWER TO SUPPORT OTHER DIVINE ARTICLES AND INCREASE THEIR POWERS.
BUT ACTU-ALLY...
... DOING THE OPPOSITE IS JUST AS EASY. YOUR DIVINE ARTICLE IS PRACTI-CALLY USELESS HERE.
IMPOS-SIBLE... ONLY THOSE WITH DIVINE POWERS CAN CHANNEL THE POWERS OF DIVINE ARTI-CLES!
HOW CAN A DEMON LIKE YOU USE IT!?

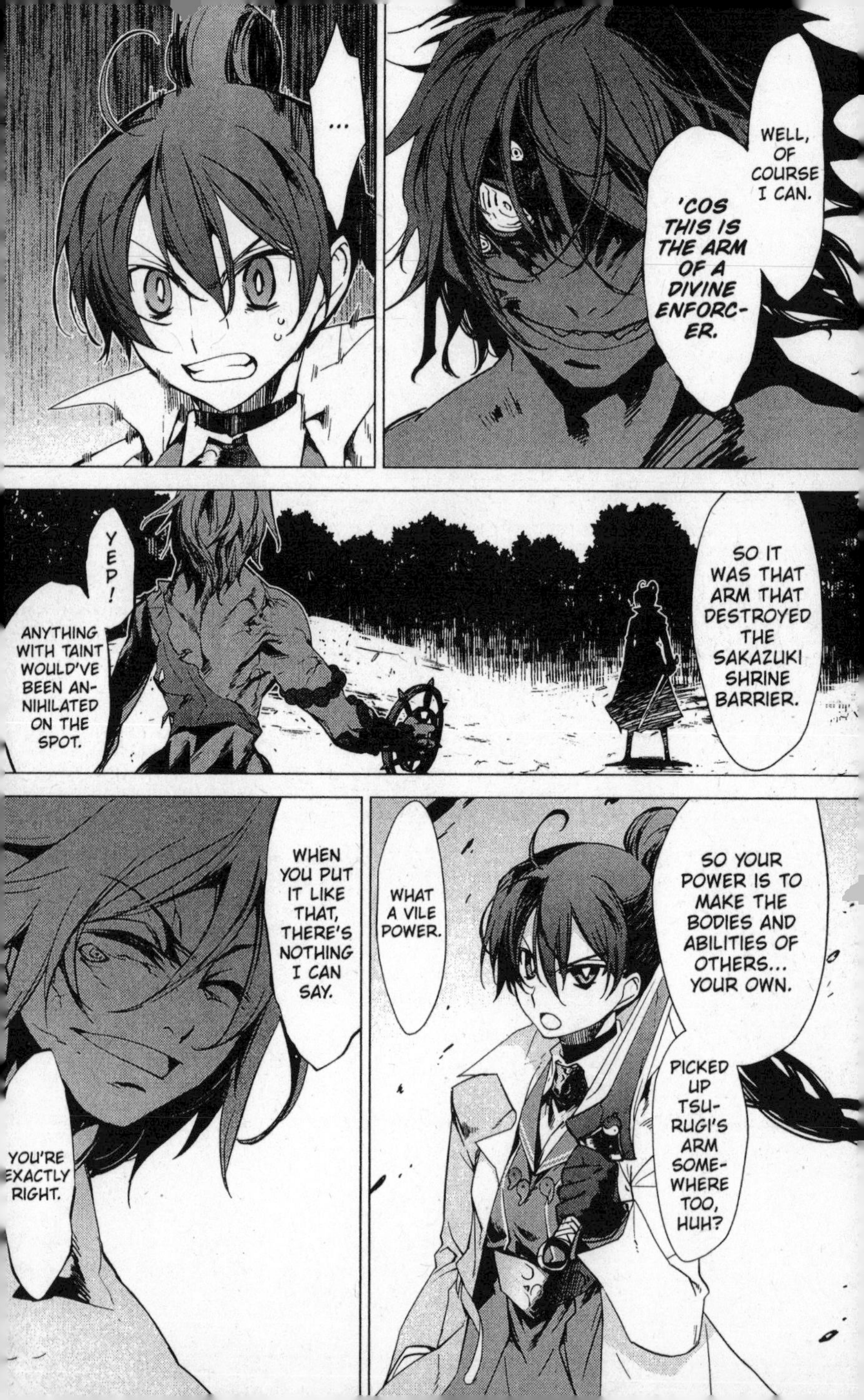
WELL, OF COURSE I CAN.
'COS THIS IS THE ARM OF A DIVINE ENFORCER.
...
SO IT WAS THAT ARM THAT DESTROYED THE SAKAZUKI SHRINE BARRIER.
YEP!
ANYTHING WITH TAINT WOULD'VE BEEN ANNIHILATED ON THE SPOT.
SO YOUR POWER IS TO MAKE THE BODIES AND ABILITIES OF OTHERS... YOUR OWN.
PICKED UP TSURUGI'S ARM SOMEWHERE TOO, HUH?
WHAT A VILE POWER.
WHEN YOU PUT IT LIKE THAT, THERE'S NOTHING I CAN SAY.
YOU'RE EXACTLY RIGHT.

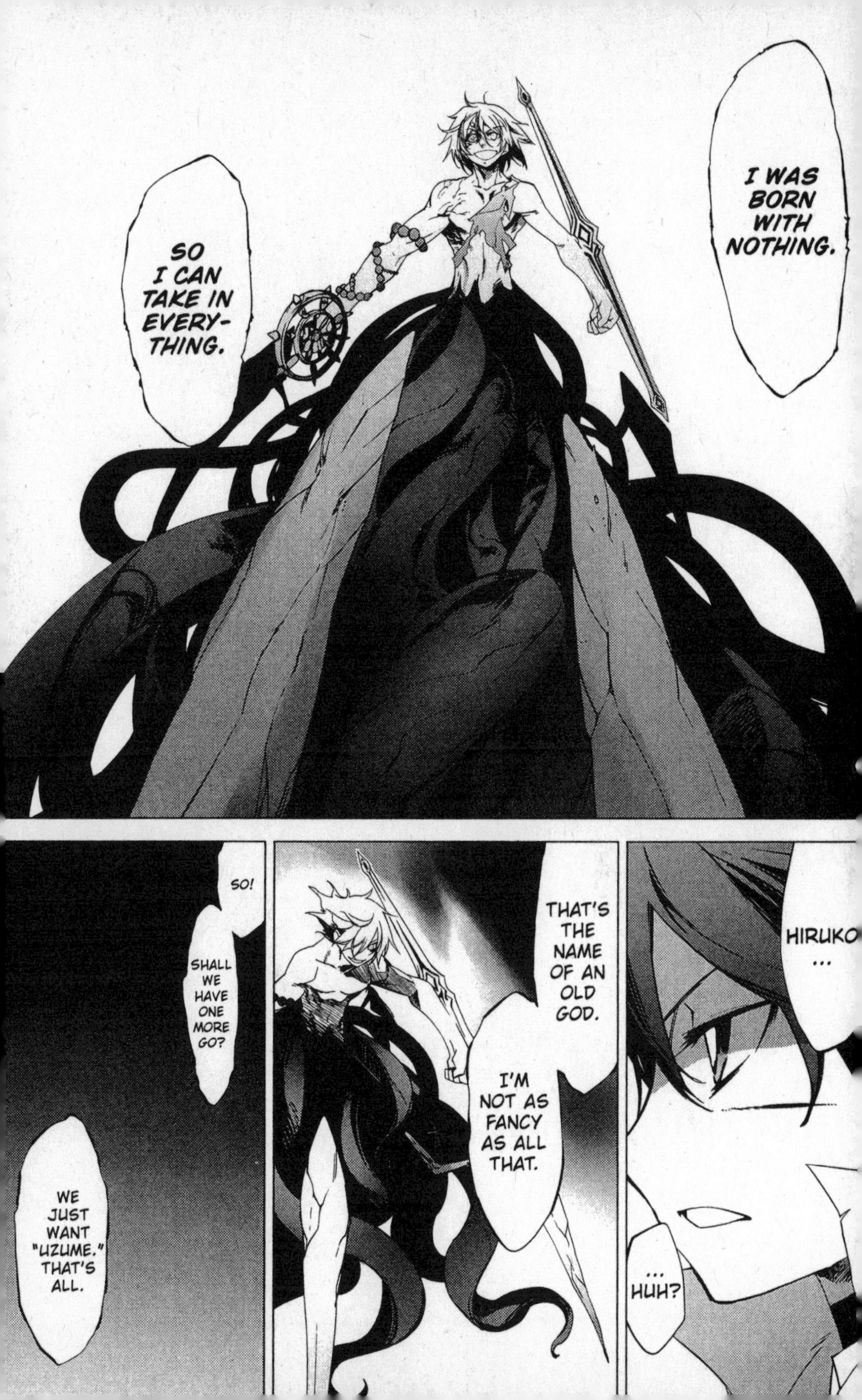
I WAS BORN WITH NOTHING.
SO I CAN TAKE IN EVERY-THING.
HIRUKO...
...HUH?
THAT'S THE NAME OF AN OLD GOD.
I'M NOT AS FANCY AS ALL THAT.
SO!
SHALL WE HAVE ONE MORE GO?
WE JUST WANT "UZUME." THAT'S ALL.

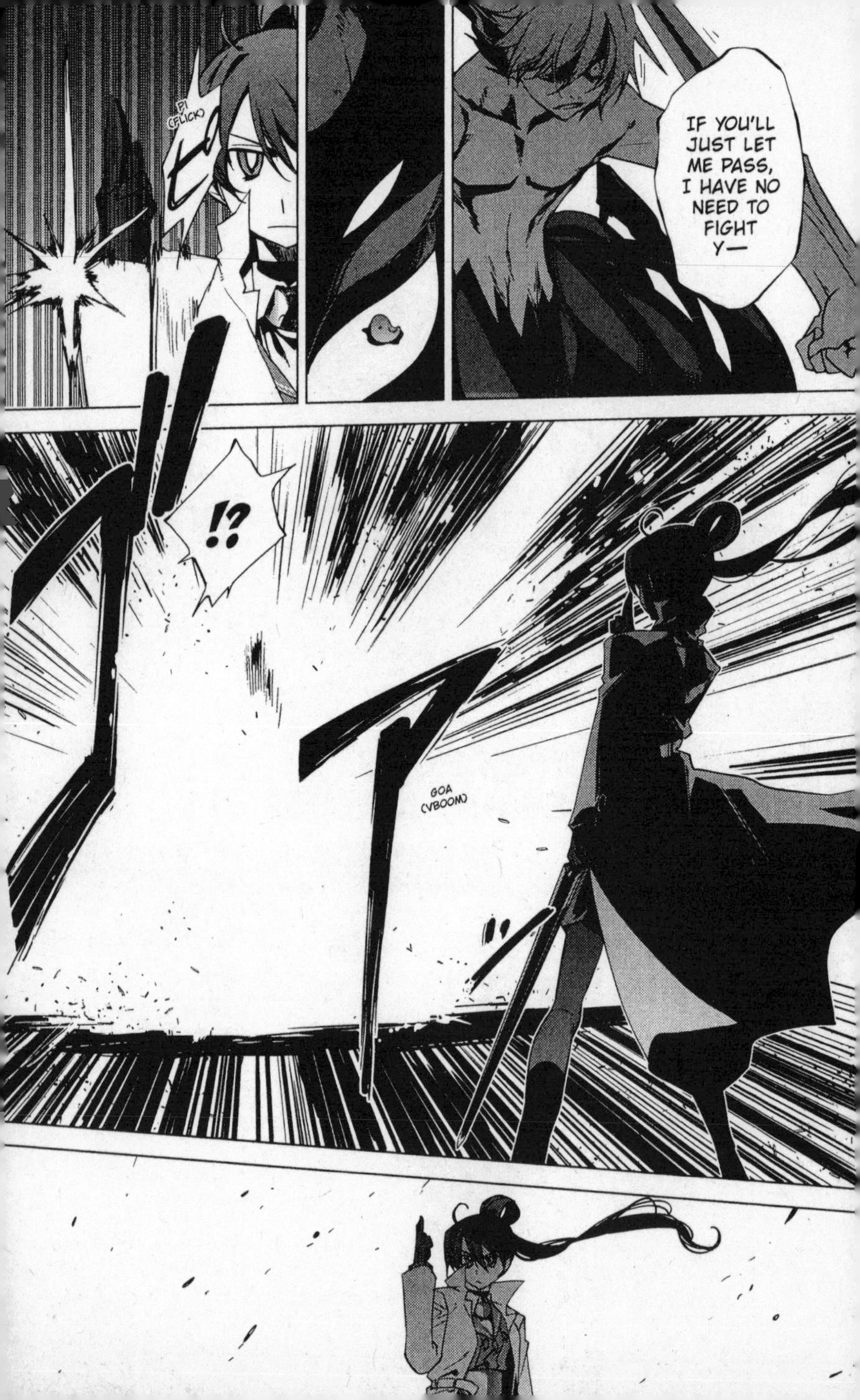
IF YOU'LL JUST LET ME PASS, I HAVE NO NEED TO FIGHT Y—
PI (FLICK)
!?
GOA (VBOOM)

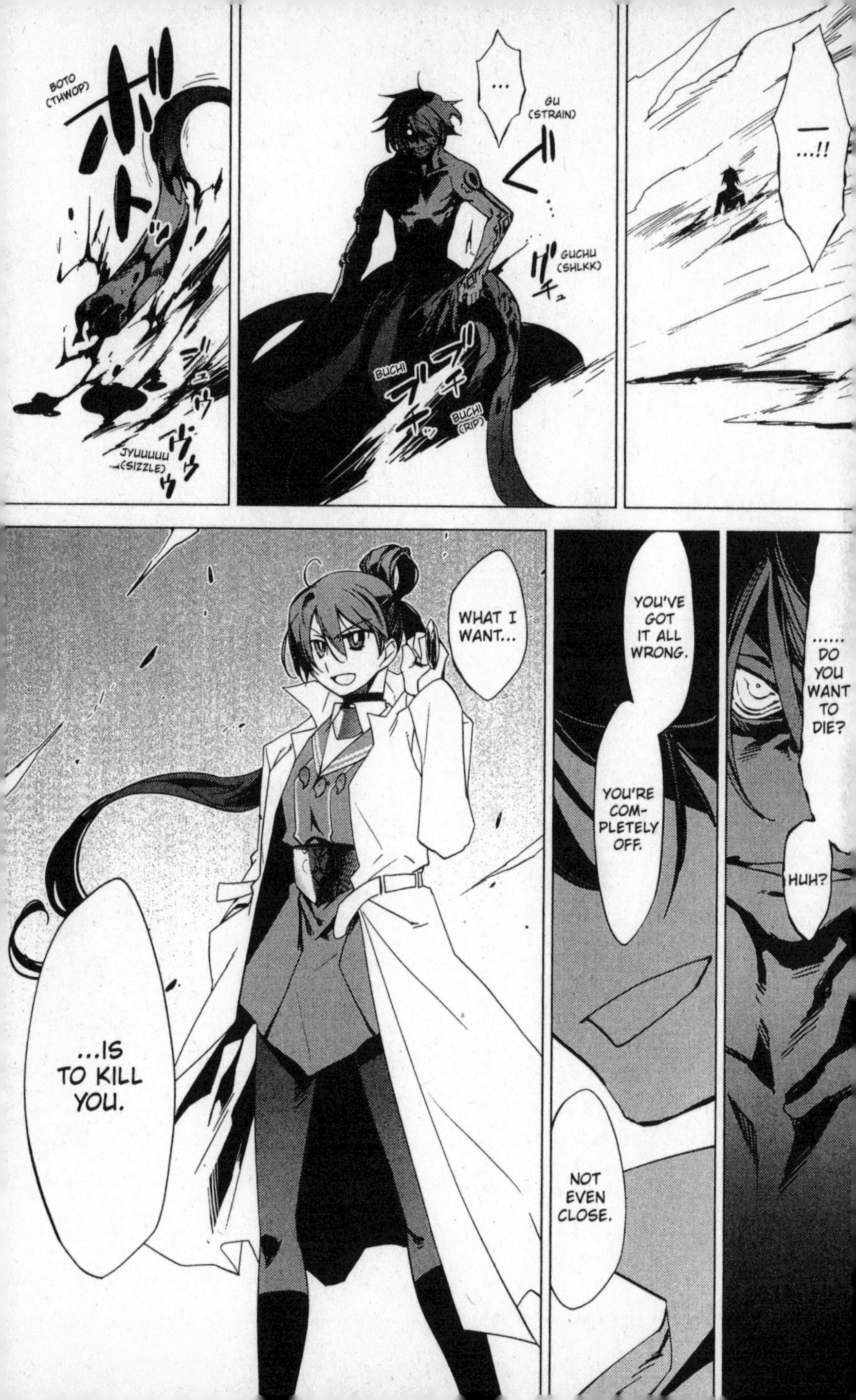
—
...!!
...
GU (STRAIN)
GUCHU (SHLKK)
BUCHI
BUCHI (RIP)
BOTO (THWOP)
JYUUUUUU (SIZZLE)
...... DO YOU WANT TO DIE?
HUH?
YOU'VE GOT IT ALL WRONG.
YOU'RE COMPLETELY OFF.
NOT EVEN CLOSE.
WHAT I WANT...
...IS TO KILL YOU.

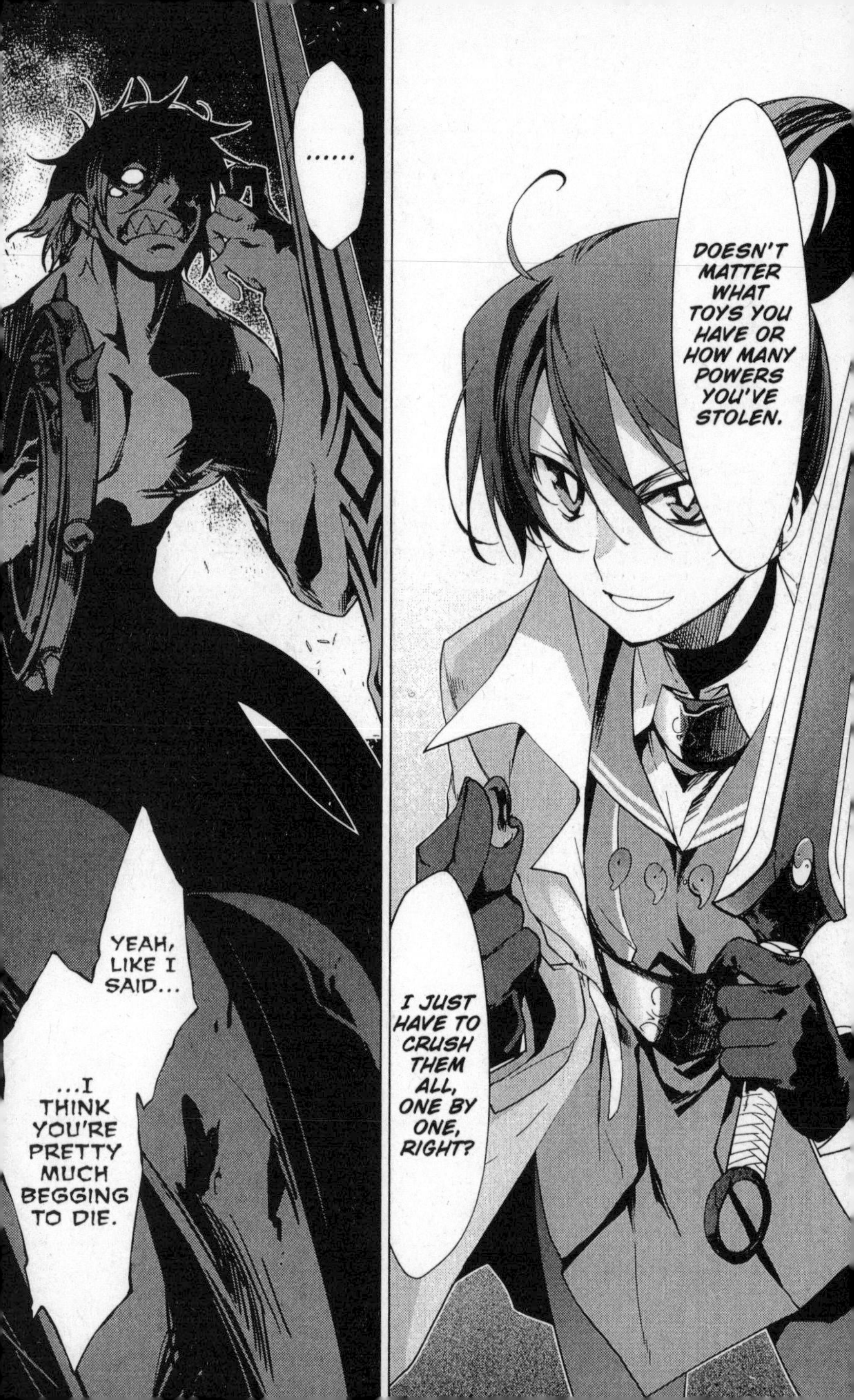
DOESN'T MATTER WHAT TOYS YOU HAVE OR HOW MANY POWERS YOU'VE STOLEN.
I JUST HAVE TO CRUSH THEM ALL, ONE BY ONE, RIGHT?
......
YEAH, LIKE I SAID...
...I THINK YOU'RE PRETTY MUCH BEGGING TO DIE.

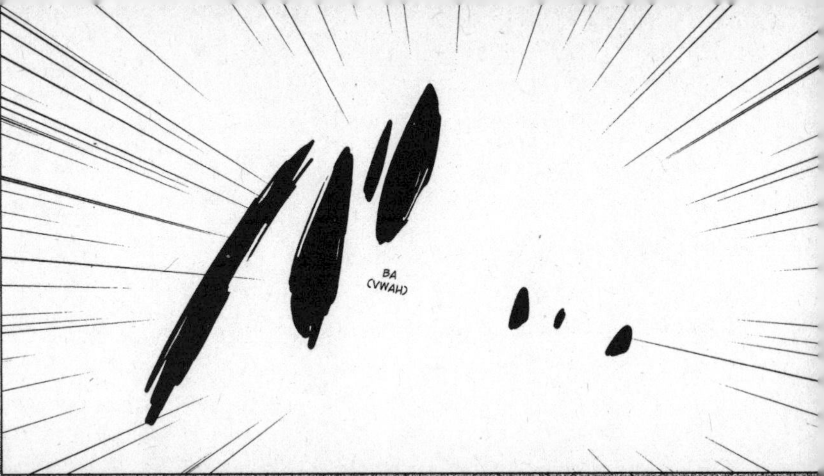
BA
(VWAH)

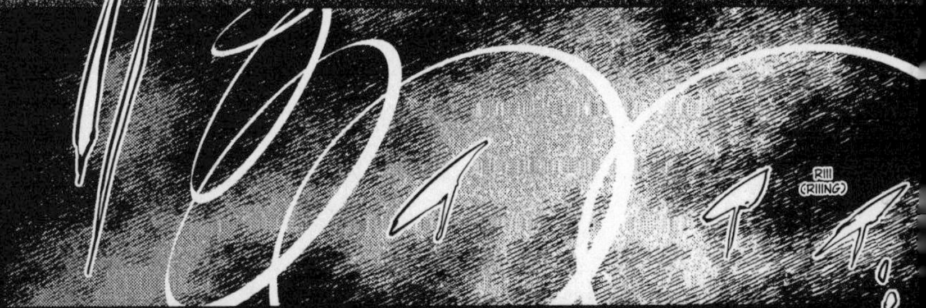
RIII
(RIIING)

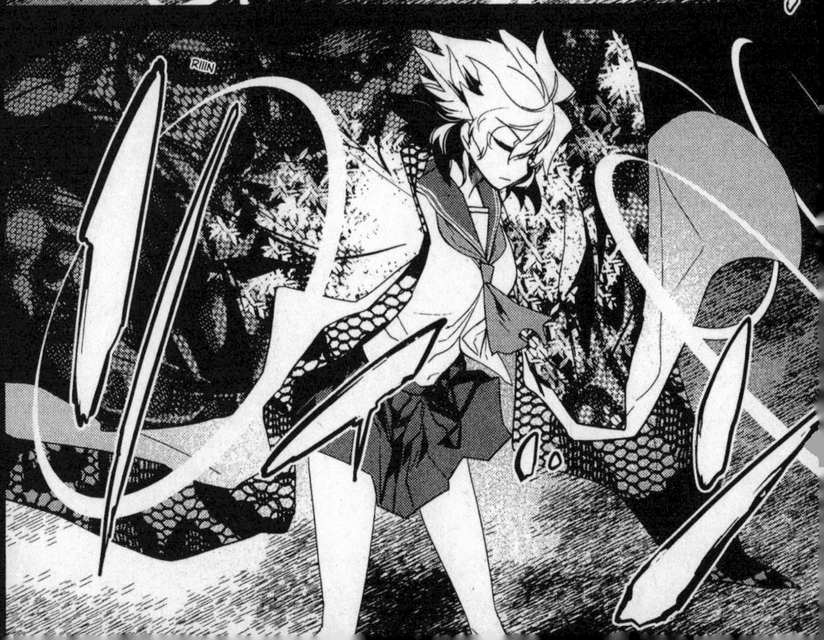
RIIIN

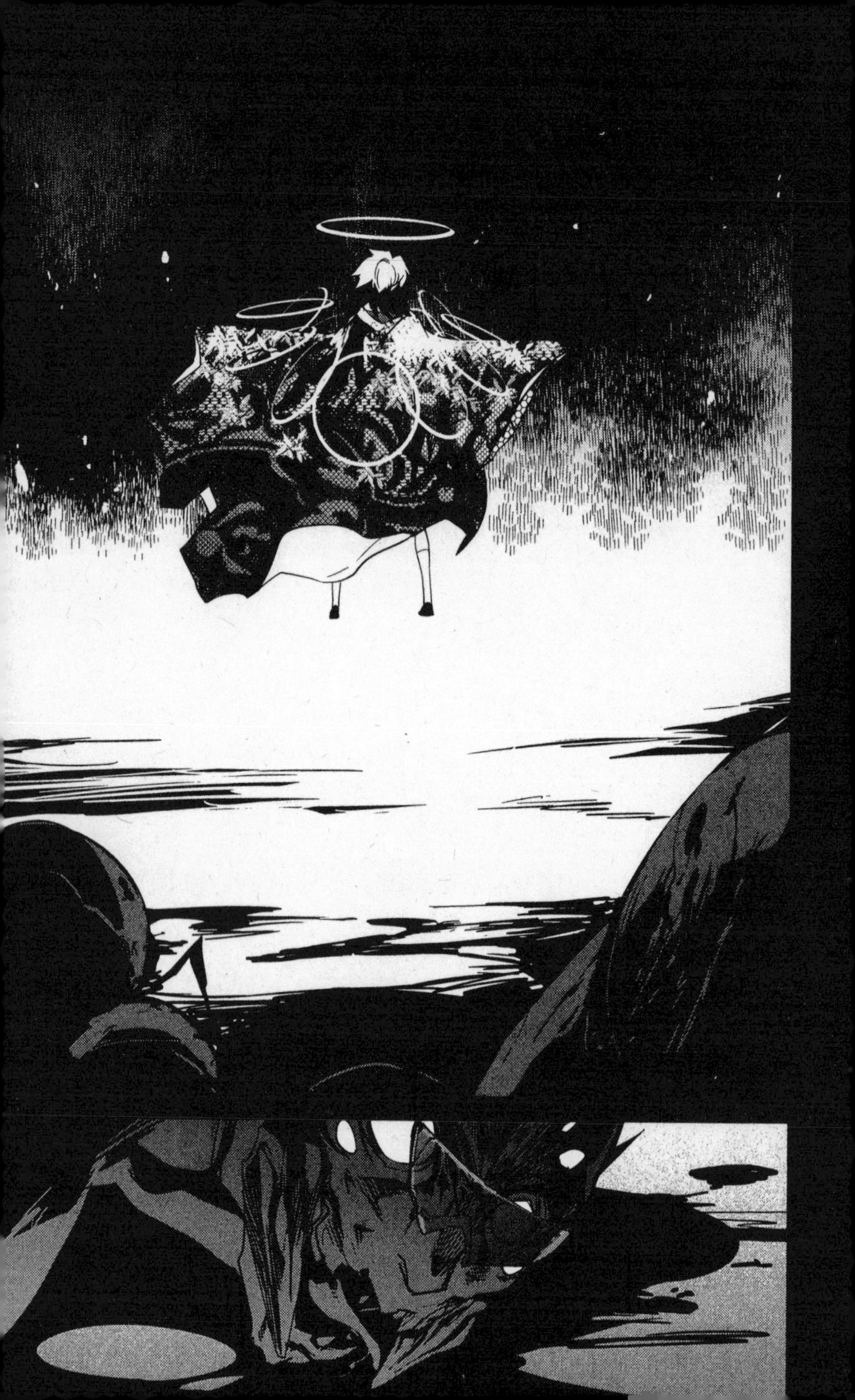

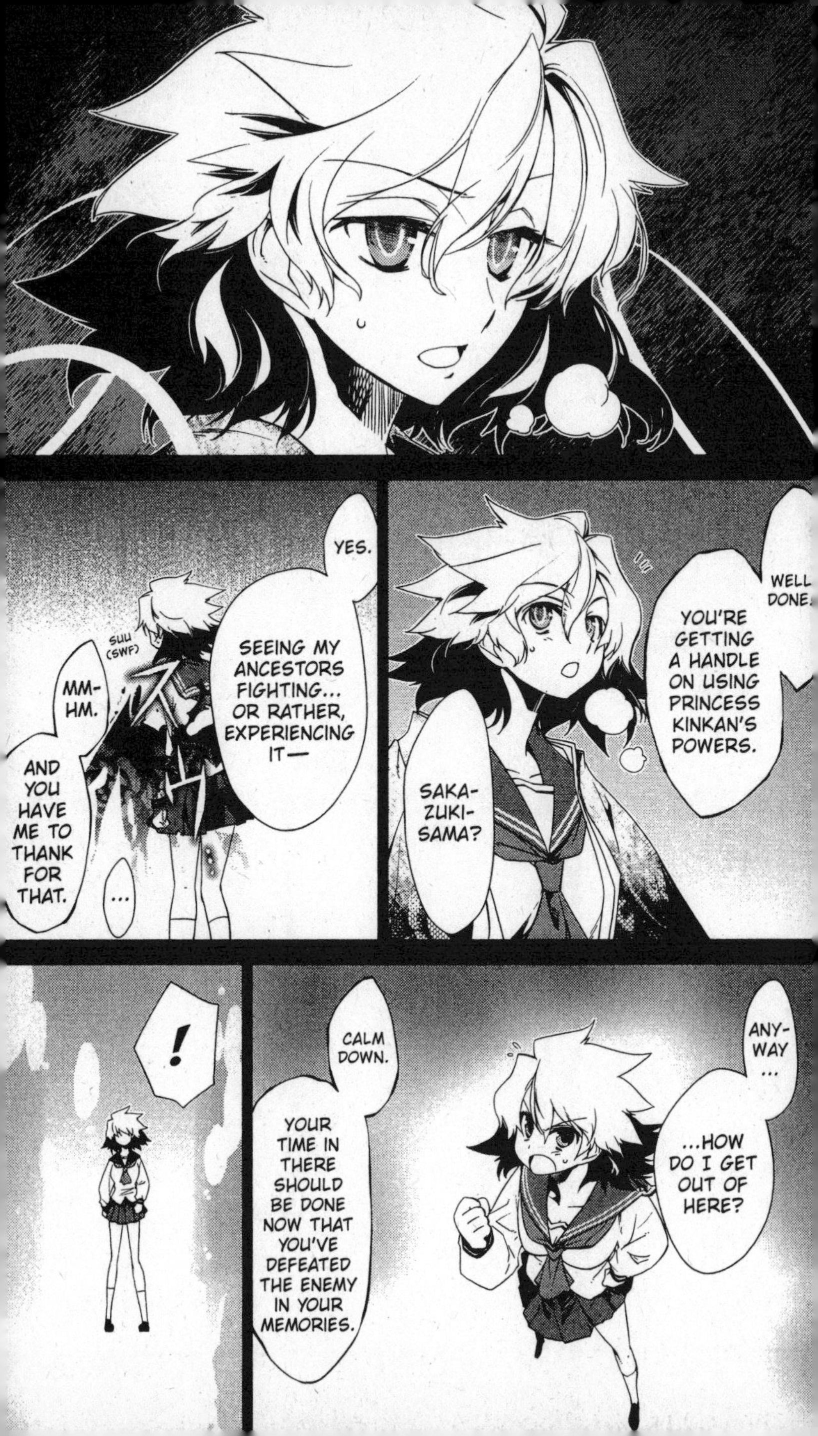
WELL DONE.
YOU'RE GETTING A HANDLE ON USING PRINCESS KINKAN'S POWERS.
SAKA-ZUKI-SAMA?
YES.
SEEING MY ANCESTORS FIGHTING... OR RATHER, EXPERIENCING IT—
SUU (SWF)
MM-HM.
AND YOU HAVE ME TO THANK FOR THAT.
...
ANY-WAY...
...HOW DO I GET OUT OF HERE?
CALM DOWN.
YOUR TIME IN THERE SHOULD BE DONE NOW THAT YOU'VE DEFEATED THE ENEMY IN YOUR MEMORIES.
!

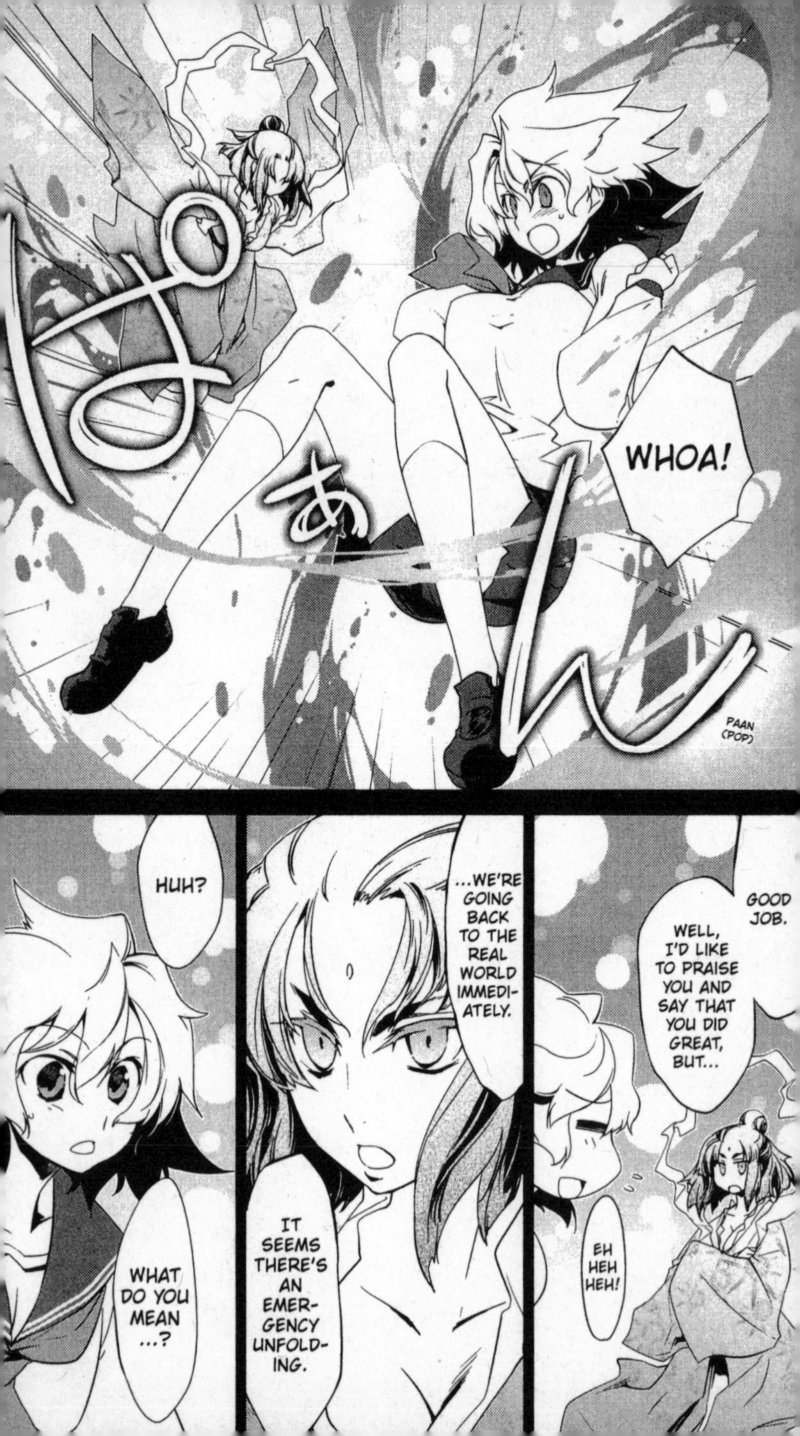
ぱあん
WHOA!
PAAN (POP)
GOOD JOB.
WELL, I'D LIKE TO PRAISE YOU AND SAY THAT YOU DID GREAT, BUT...
EH HEH HEH!
...WE'RE GOING BACK TO THE REAL WORLD IMMEDIATELY.
IT SEEMS THERE'S AN EMERGENCY UNFOLDING.
HUH?
WHAT DO YOU MEAN ...?

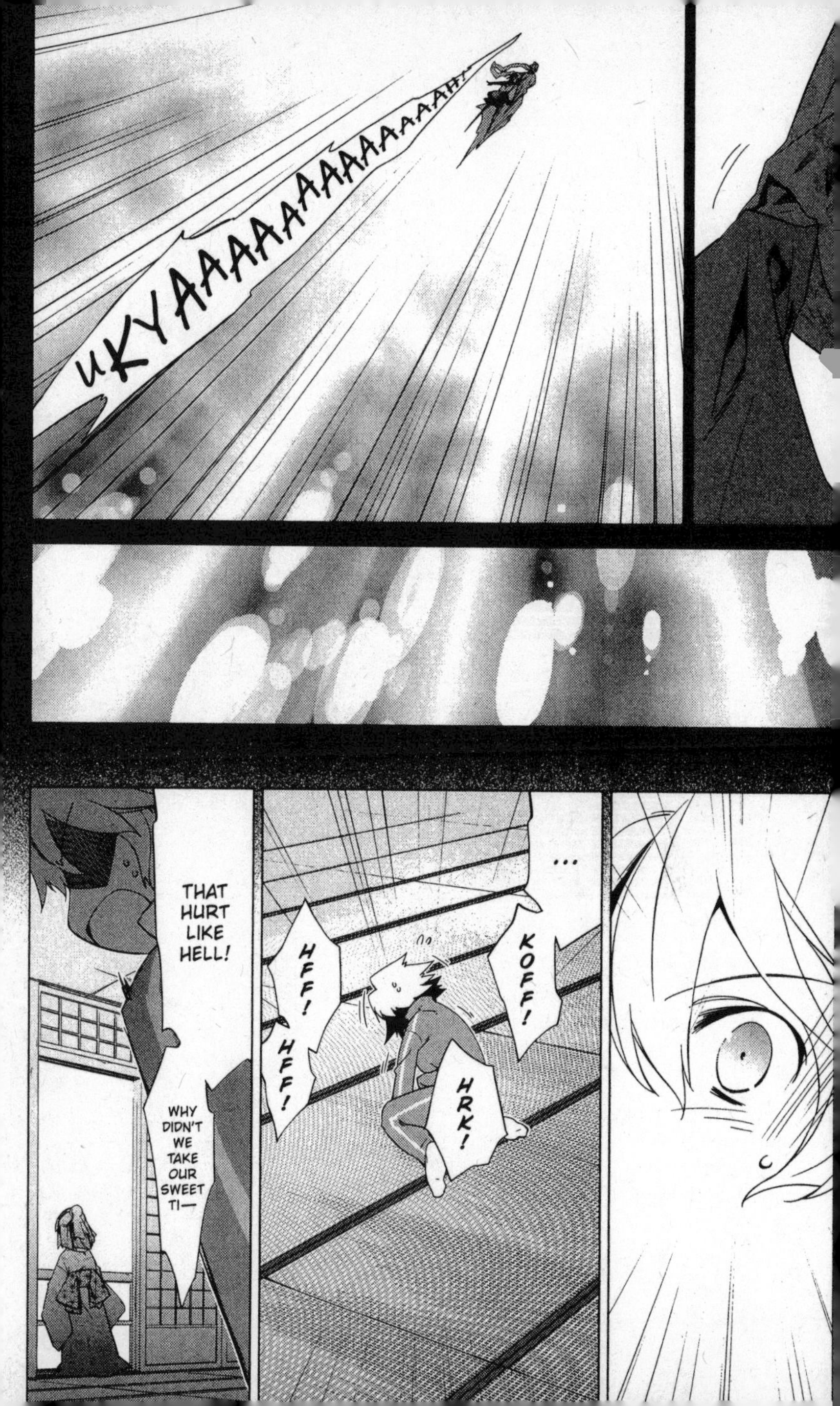
UKYAAAAAAAAAAAAAAAAH!!
...
KOFF!
HRK!
HFF!
HFF!
THAT HURT LIKE HELL!
WHY DIDN'T WE TAKE OUR SWEET TI—

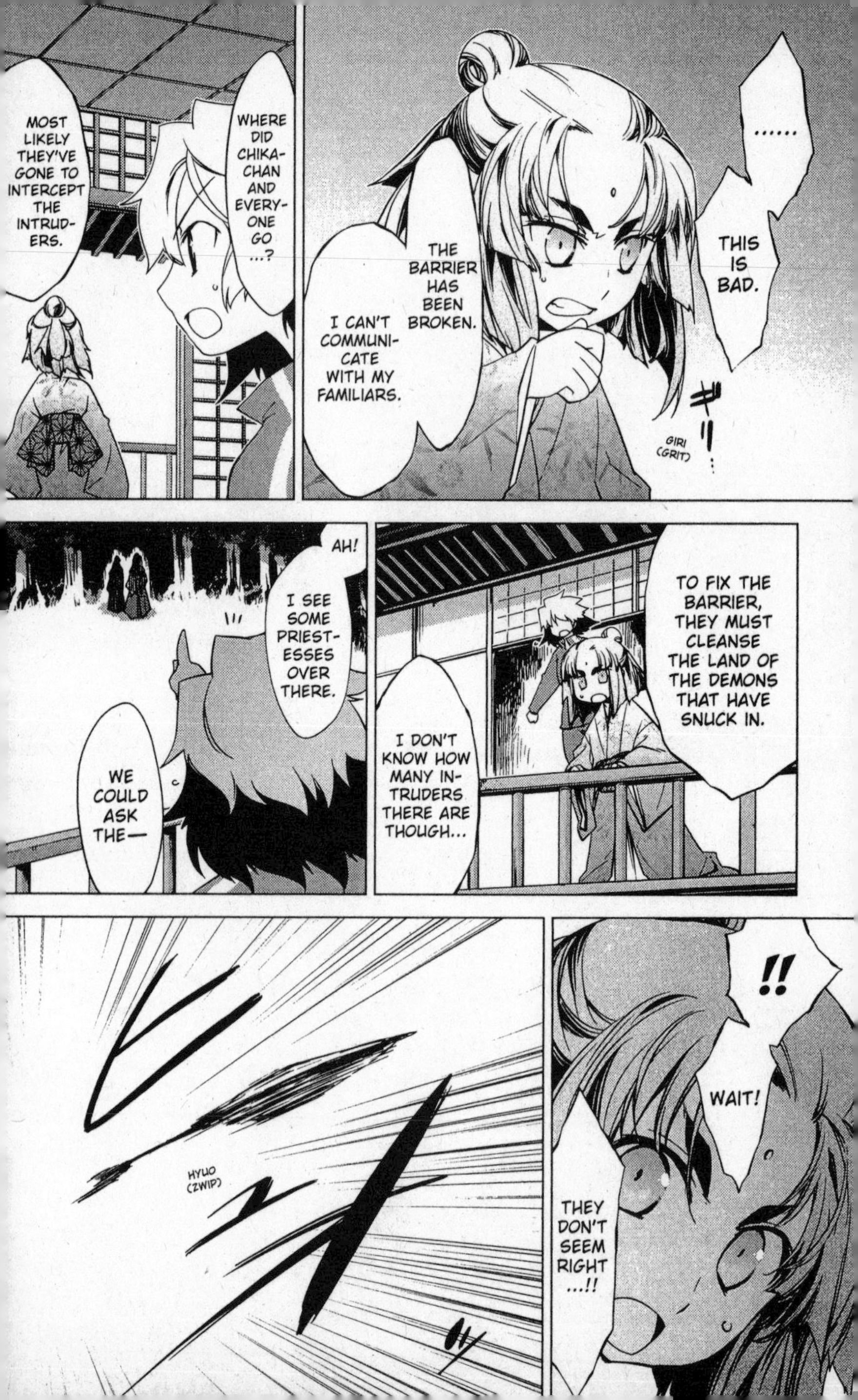
......
THIS IS BAD.
GIRI (GRIT)
THE BARRIER HAS BEEN BROKEN.
I CAN'T COMMUNICATE WITH MY FAMILIARS.
WHERE DID CHIKA-CHAN AND EVERYONE GO ...?
MOST LIKELY THEY'VE GONE TO INTERCEPT THE INTRUDERS.
TO FIX THE BARRIER, THEY MUST CLEANSE THE LAND OF THE DEMONS THAT HAVE SNUCK IN.
I DON'T KNOW HOW MANY INTRUDERS THERE ARE THOUGH...
AH!
I SEE SOME PRIESTESSES OVER THERE.
WE COULD ASK THE—
!!
WAIT!
THEY DON'T SEEM RIGHT ...!!
HYUO (ZWIP)

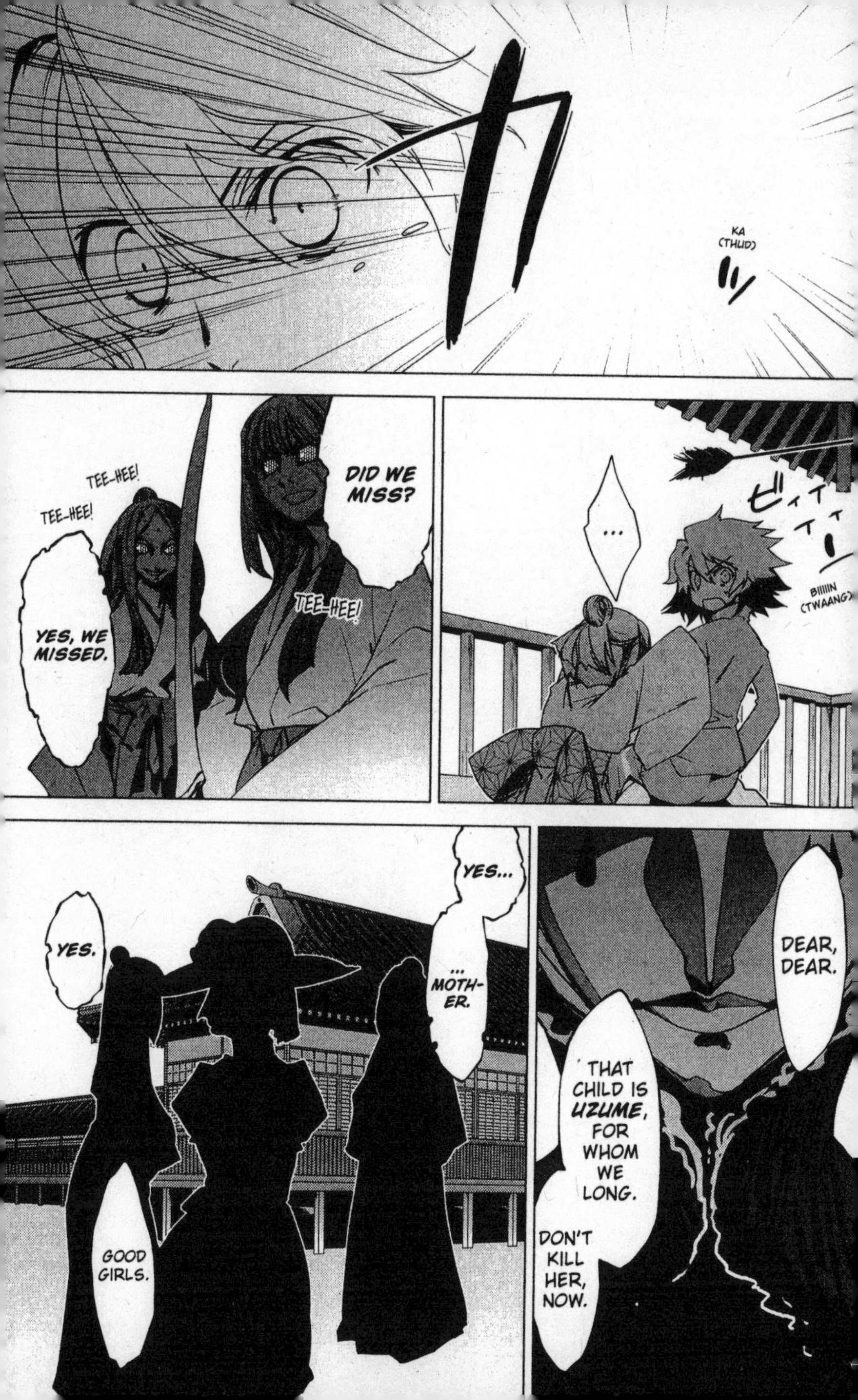
KA (THUD)
...
BIIIIIN (TWAANG)
DID WE MISS?
TEE-HEE!
TEE-HEE!
TEE-HEE!
YES, WE MISSED.
DEAR, DEAR.
THAT CHILD IS UZUME, FOR WHOM WE LONG.
DON'T KILL HER, NOW.
YES...
...MOTHER.
YES.
GOOD GIRLS.

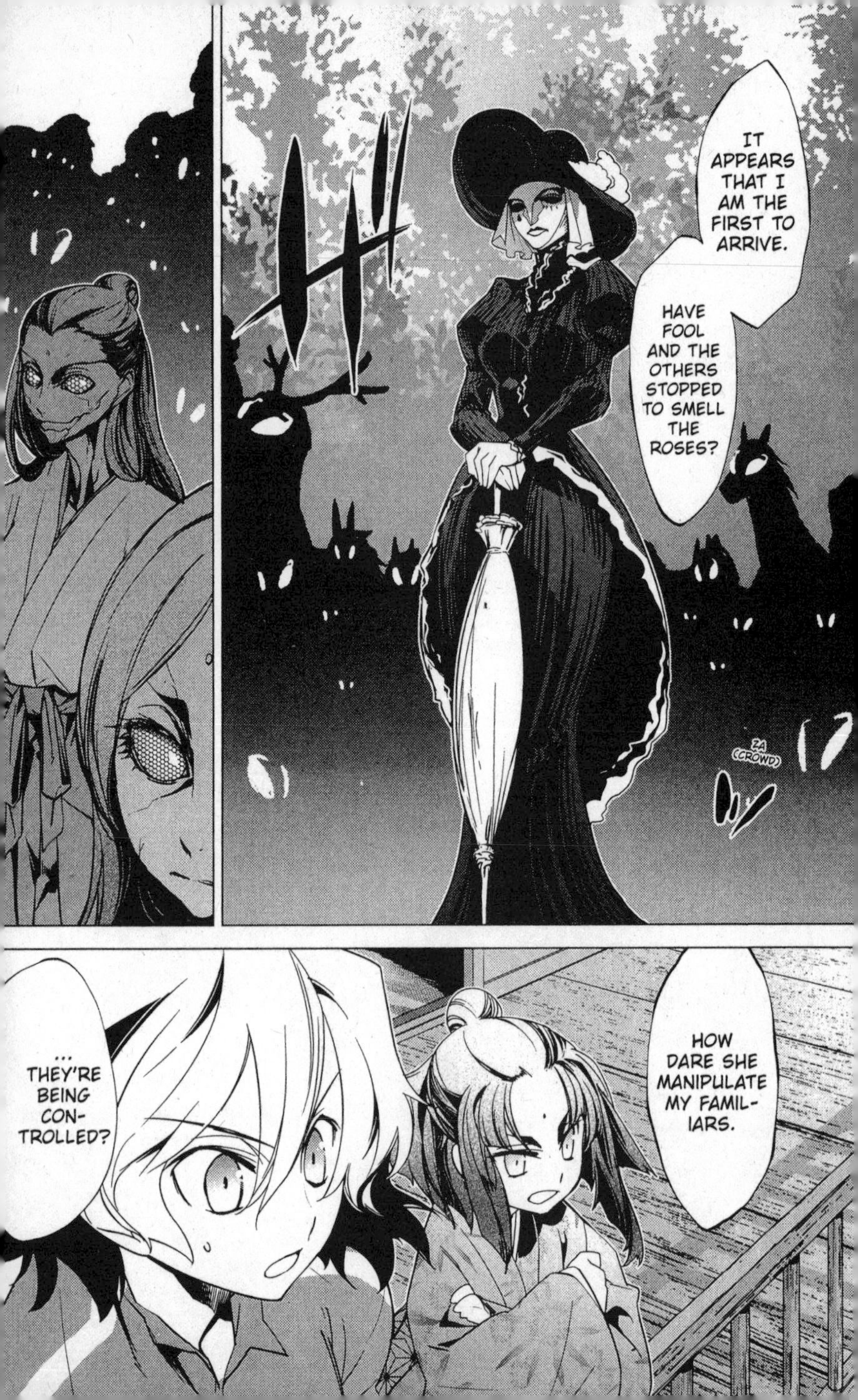
IT APPEARS THAT I AM THE FIRST TO ARRIVE.
HAVE FOOL AND THE OTHERS STOPPED TO SMELL THE ROSES?
ZA (CROWD)
HOW DARE SHE MANIPULATE MY FAMIL-IARS.
... THEY'RE BEING CON-TROLLED?

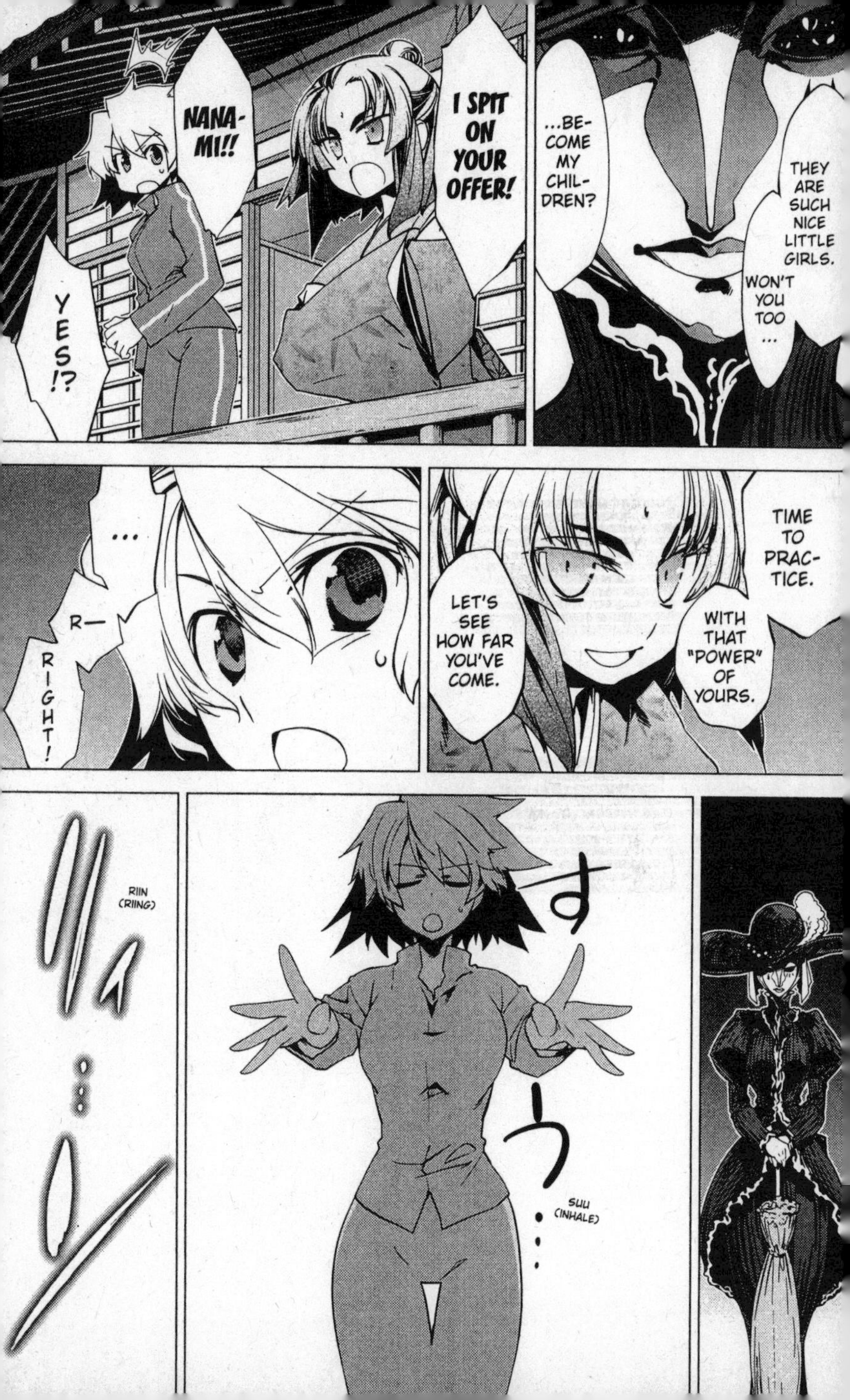
THEY ARE SUCH NICE LITTLE GIRLS.
WON'T YOU TOO ...
...BE-COME MY CHIL-DREN?
I SPIT ON YOUR OFFER!
NANA-MI!!
YES!?
TIME TO PRAC-TICE.
WITH THAT "POWER" OF YOURS.
LET'S SEE HOW FAR YOU'VE COME.
...
R— RIGHT!
すう…
SUU (INHALE)
リィ…ン
RIIN (RIING)

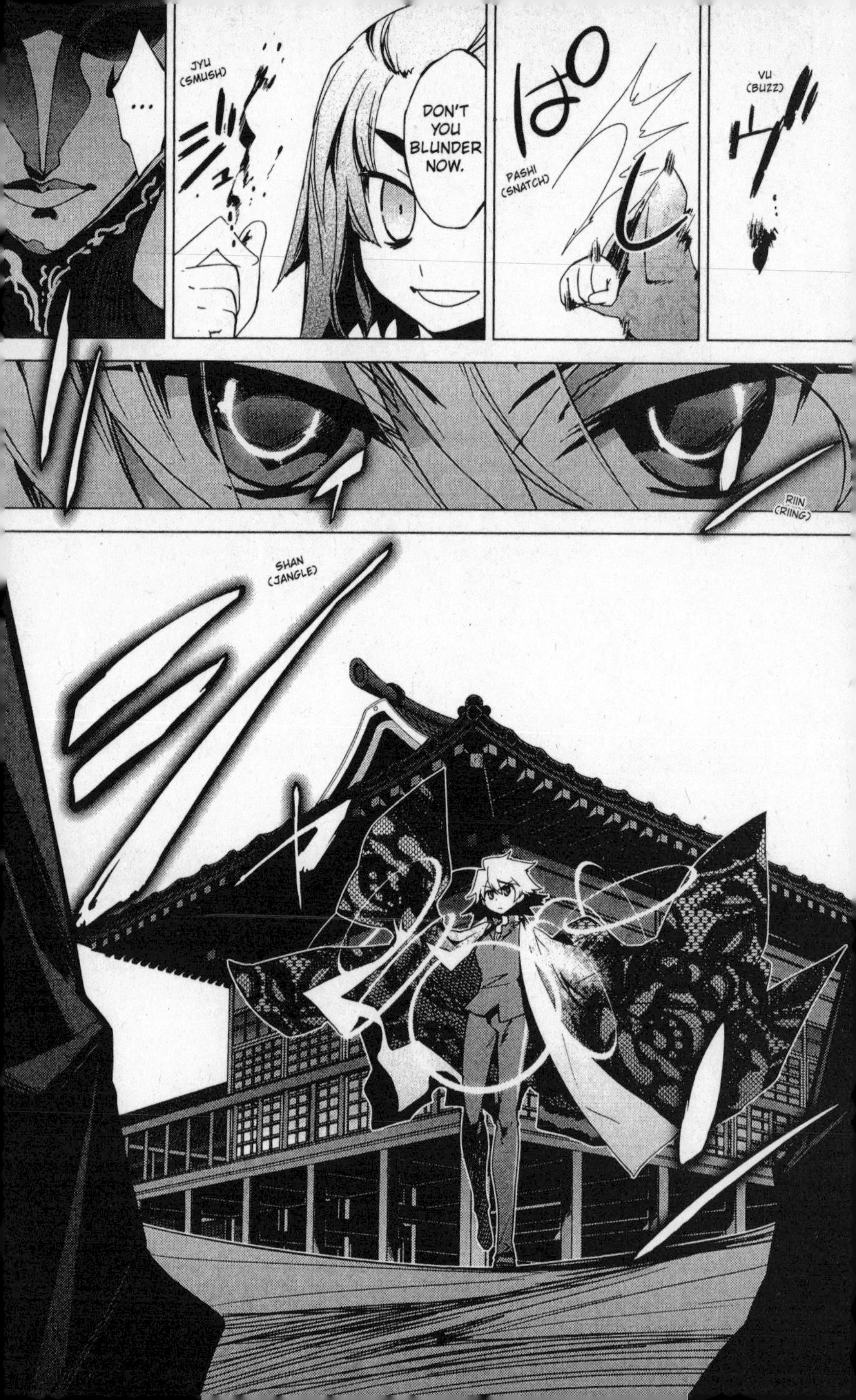
VU (BUZZ)
PASHI (SNATCH)
DON'T YOU BLUNDER NOW.
JYU (SMUSH)
...
RIIN (RIING)
SHAN (JANGLE)

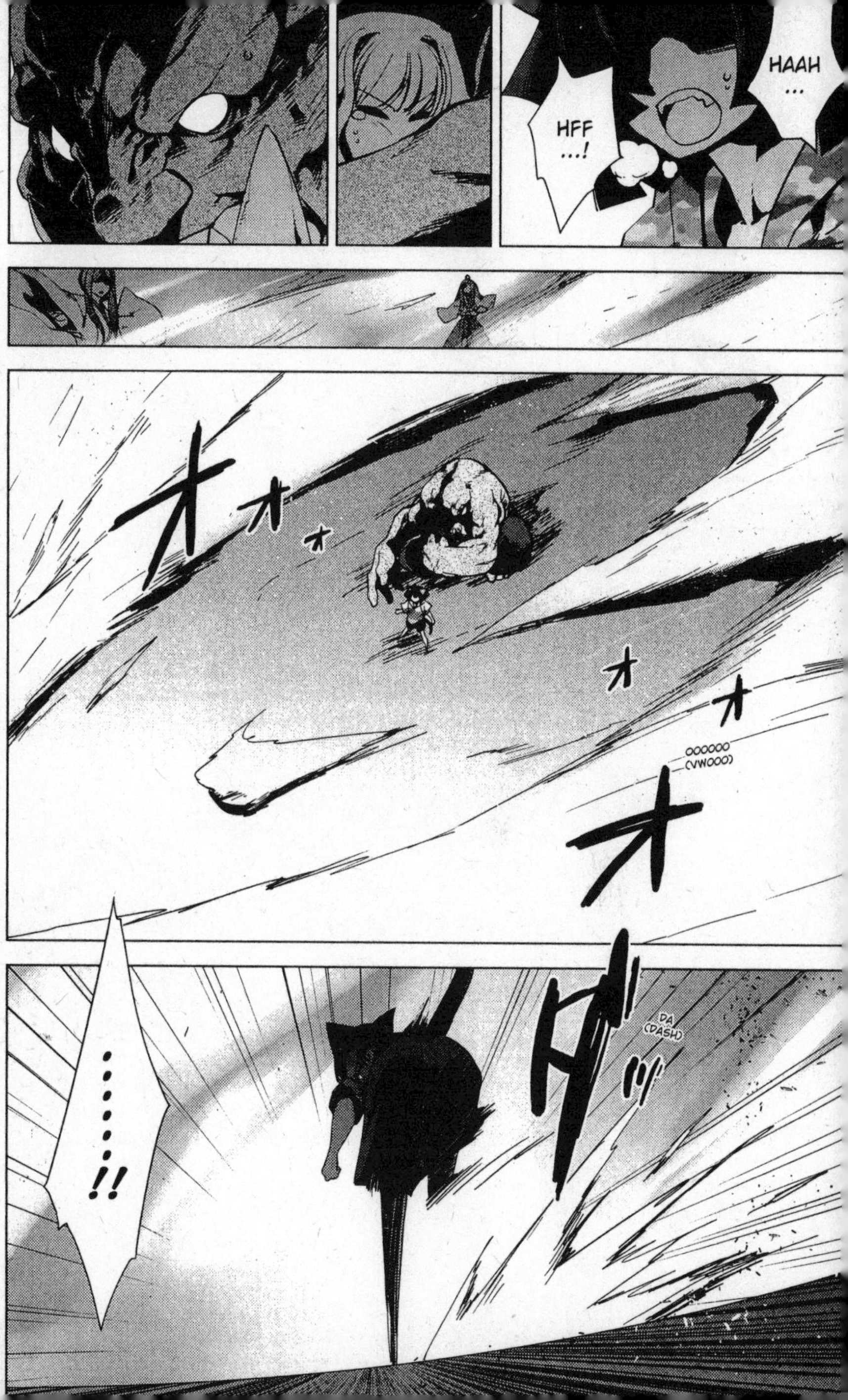
HAAH ...
HFF ...!
オオオオオオ
OOOOOO (VWOOO)
ダッ
DA (DASH)
......!!

ーザー
(VWIP)

OOOO
(FWOOH)

オ
オ
オ
オ

ZUOOO
(VWOOSH)

!?

OH PLEASE ...

THIS STUPID FOG...

I'LL CUT RIGHT THROUGH IT, AND—

...

......

ガ
く
GAKU
(SLUMP)

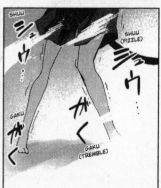
SHUU
(FIZZLE)

シュ
ウ
...

SHUU
(FIZZLE)

シュ
ウ
...

GAKU

ガ
く

ガ
く
GAKU
(TREMBLE)

ACT TWENTY-FIVE.

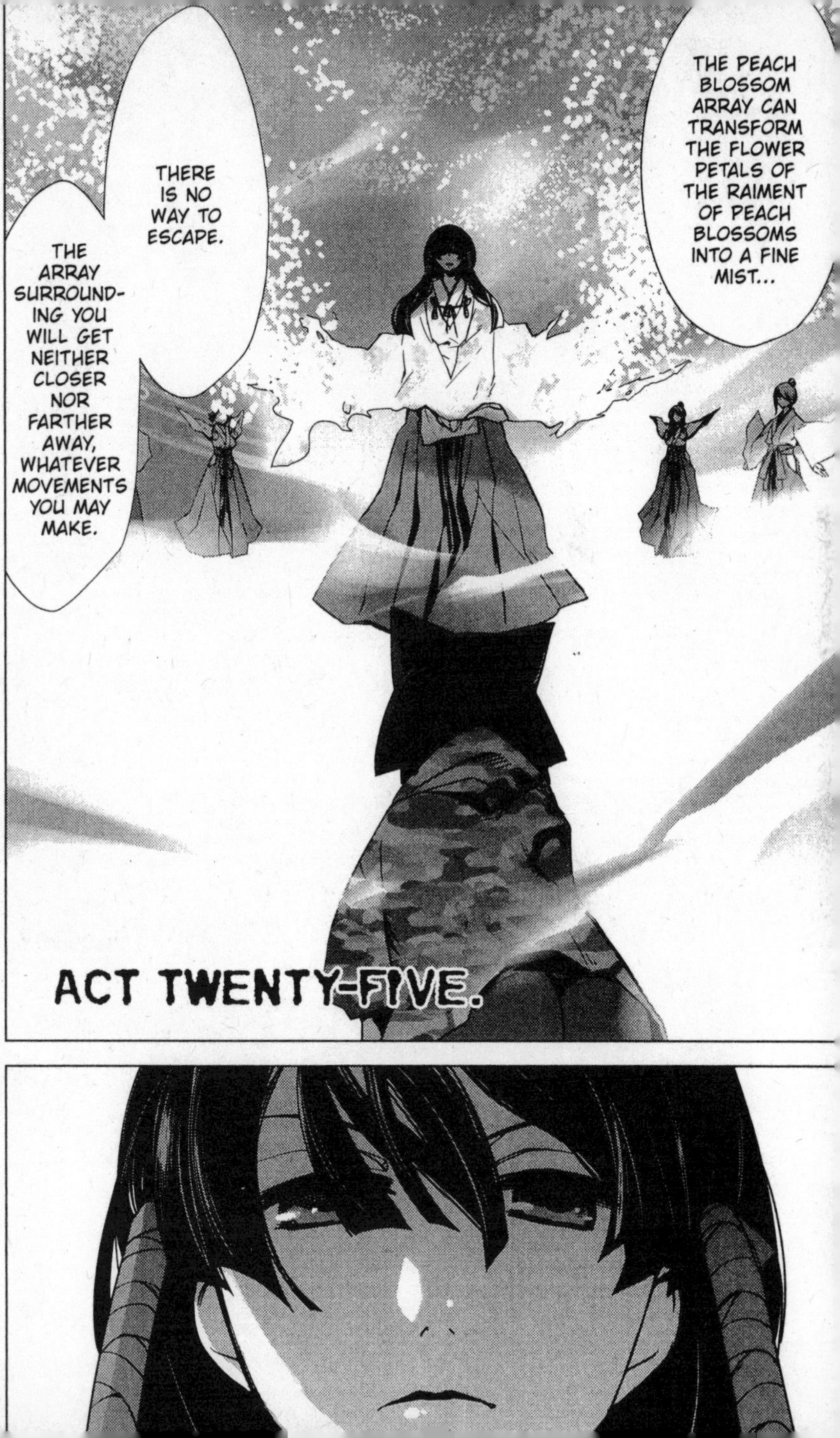
THE PEACH BLOSSOM ARRAY CAN TRANSFORM THE FLOWER PETALS OF THE RAIMENT OF PEACH BLOSSOMS INTO A FINE MIST...
THERE IS NO WAY TO ESCAPE.
THE ARRAY SURROUND-ING YOU WILL GET NEITHER CLOSER NOR FARTHER AWAY, WHATEVER MOVEMENTS YOU MAY MAKE.

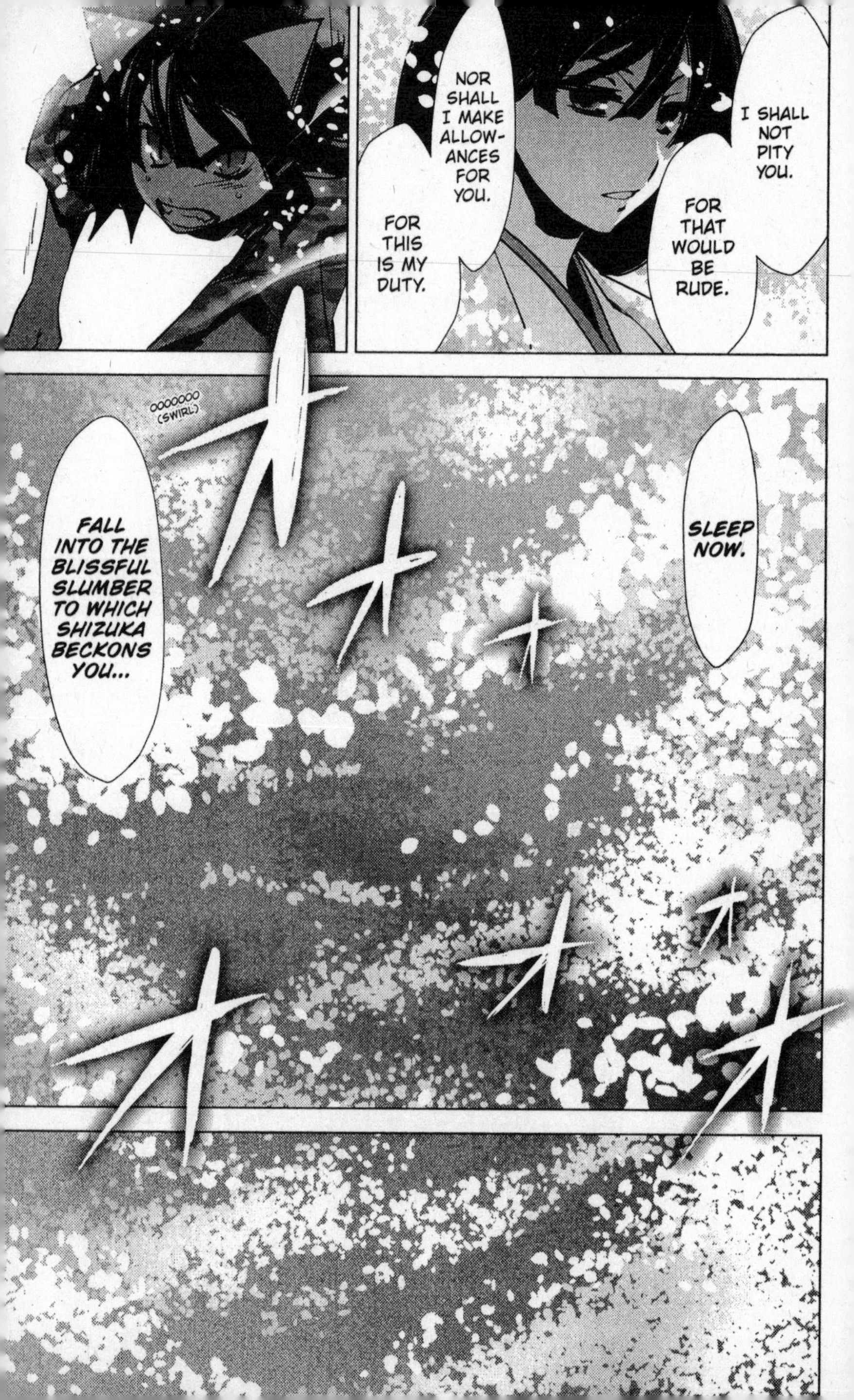
I SHALL NOT PITY YOU.
FOR THAT WOULD BE RUDE.
NOR SHALL I MAKE ALLOW-ANCES FOR YOU.
FOR THIS IS MY DUTY.
SLEEP NOW.
OOOOOOO (SWIRL)
FALL INTO THE BLISSFUL SLUMBER TO WHICH SHIZUKA BECKONS YOU...

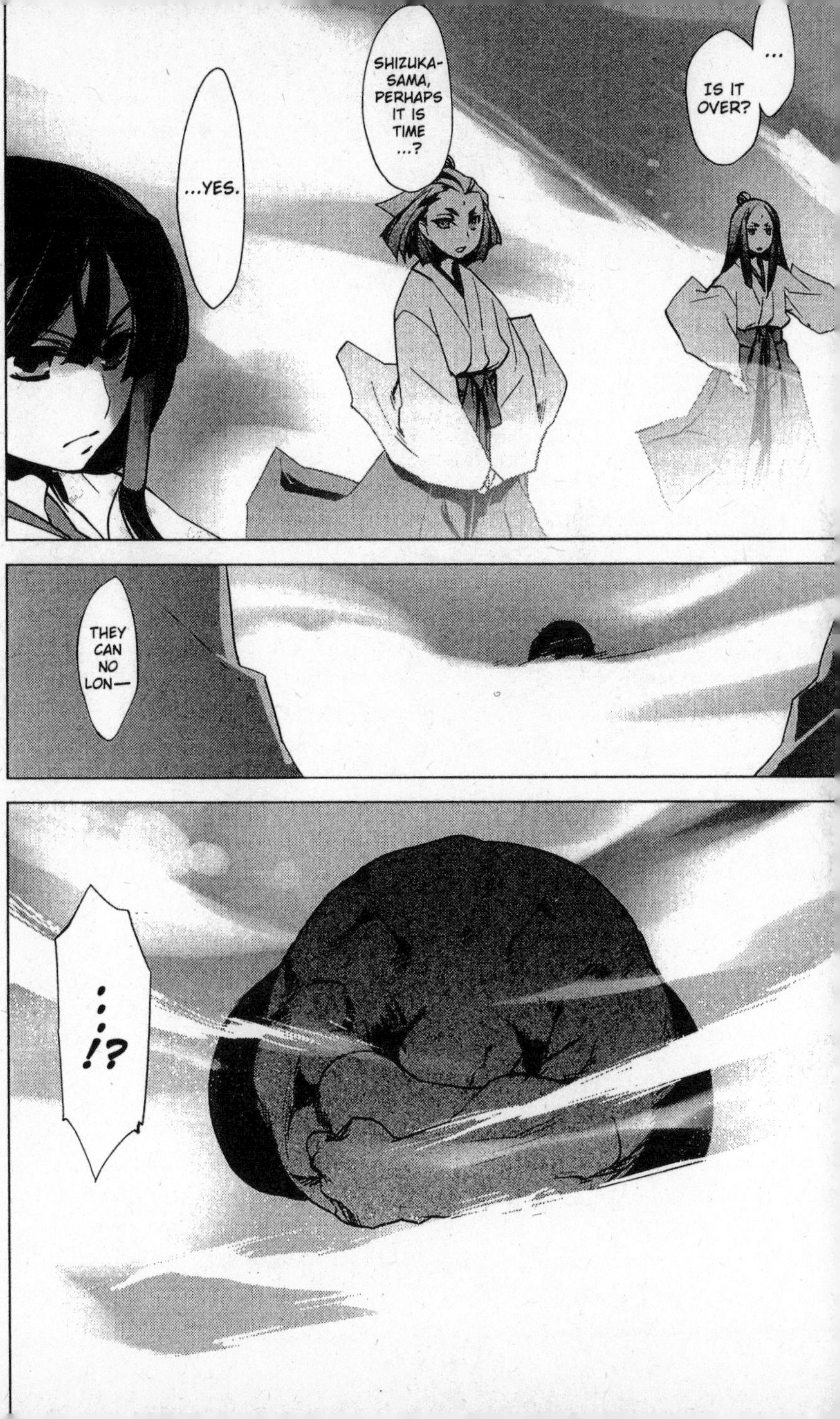

... IS IT OVER?
SHIZUKA-SAMA, PERHAPS IT IS TIME ...?
...YES.
THEY CAN NO LON—
...!?

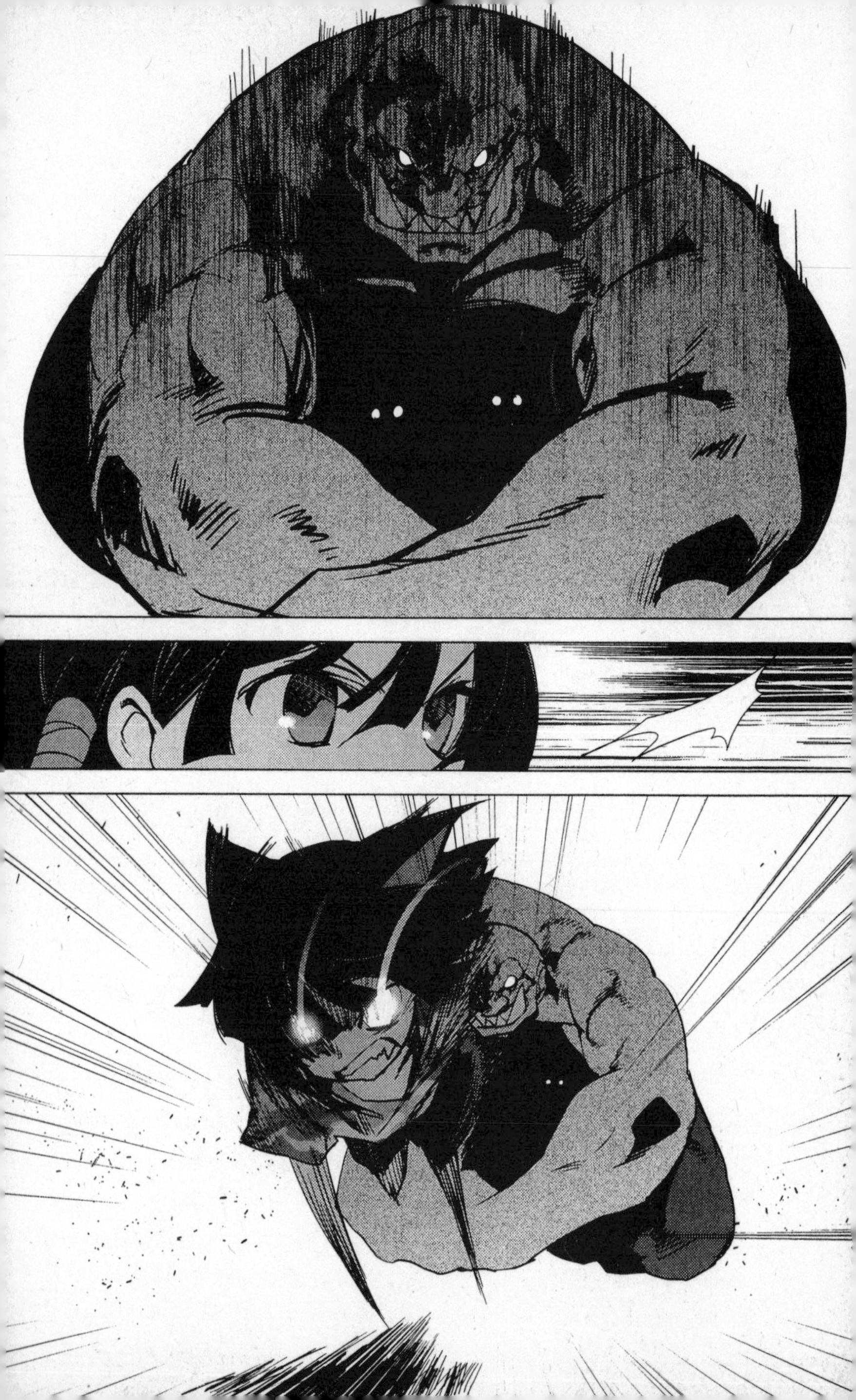

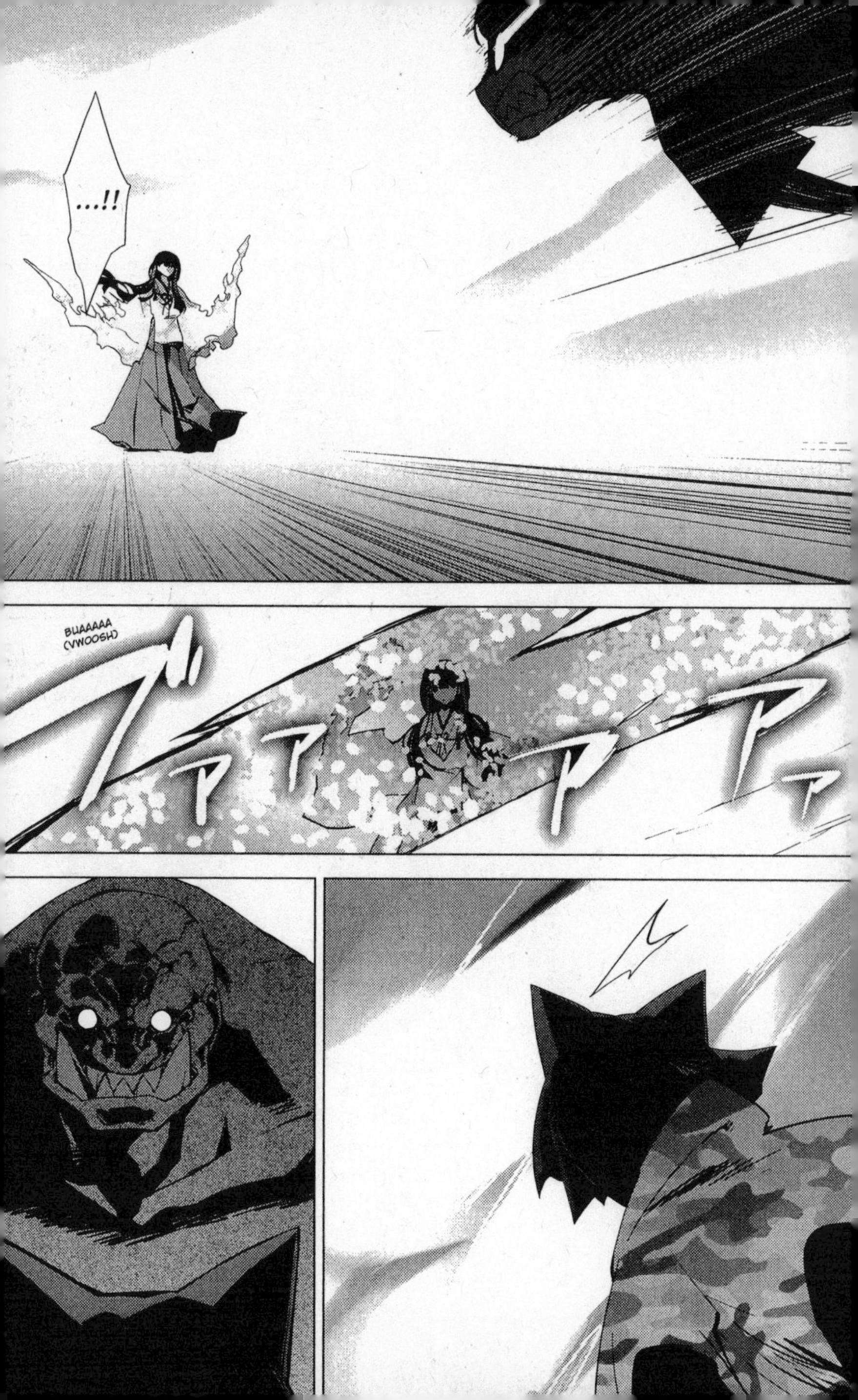
...!!
BUAAAAA (VWOOSH)
ブァァァァァ

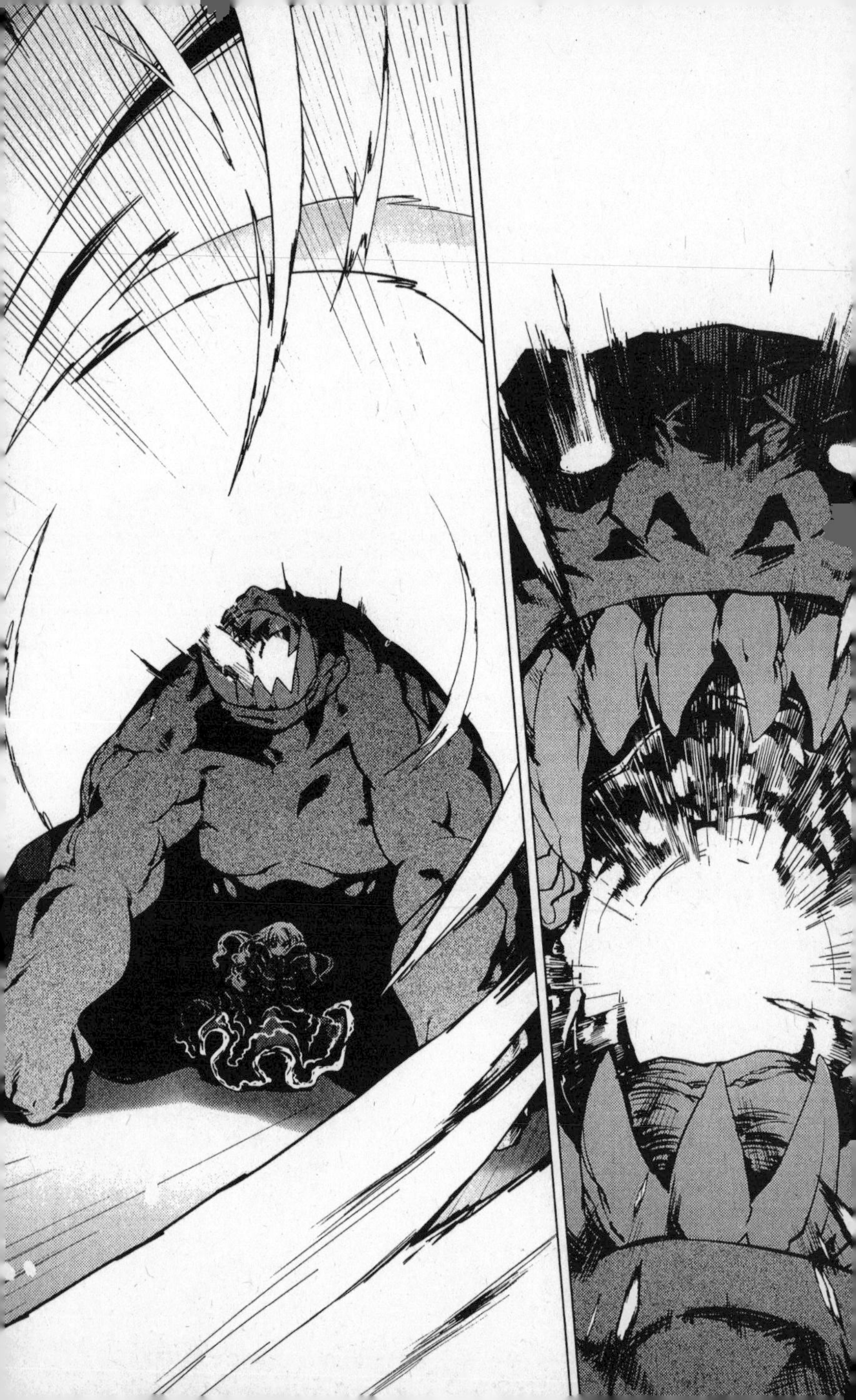

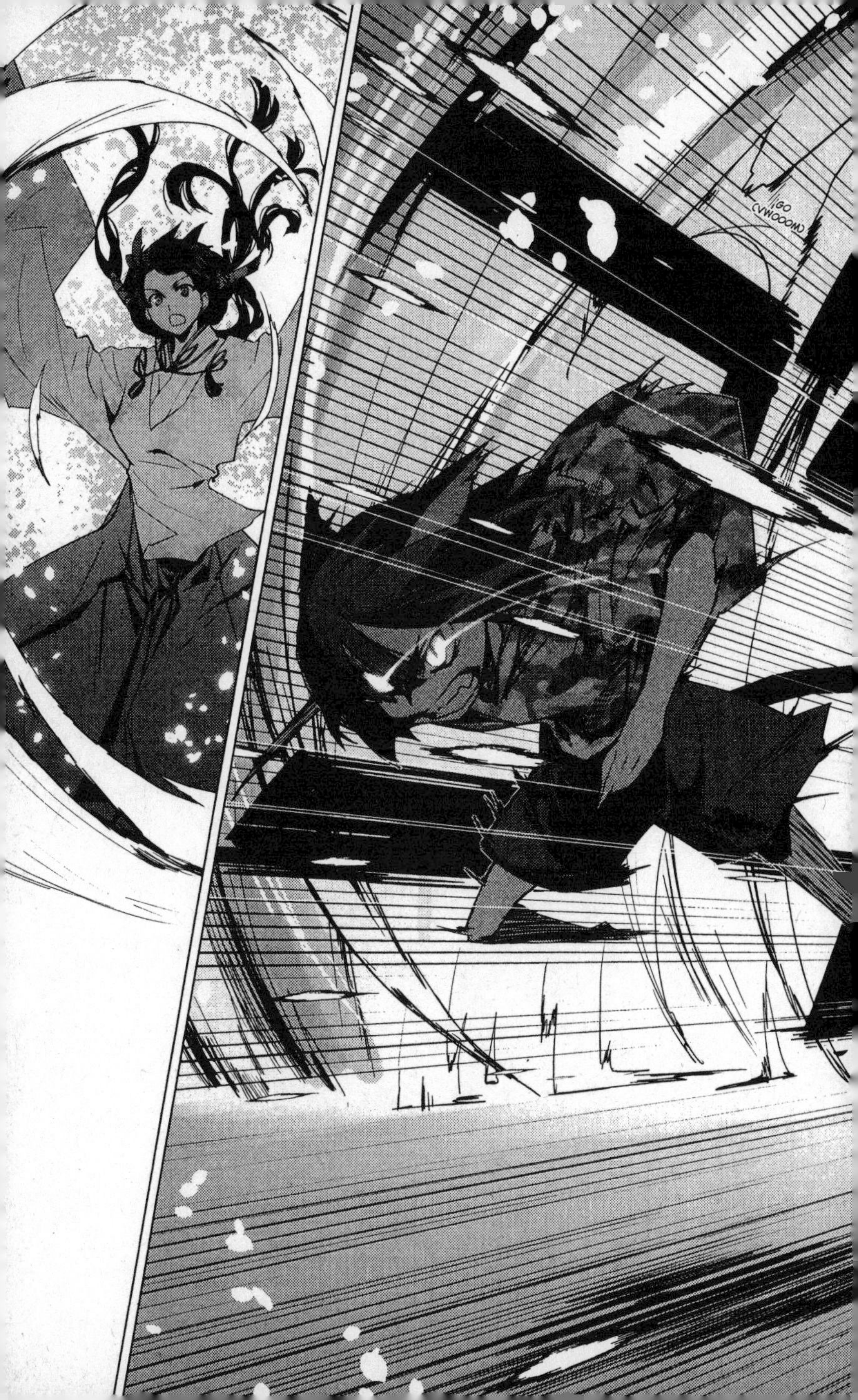
GO
(VWOOOM)

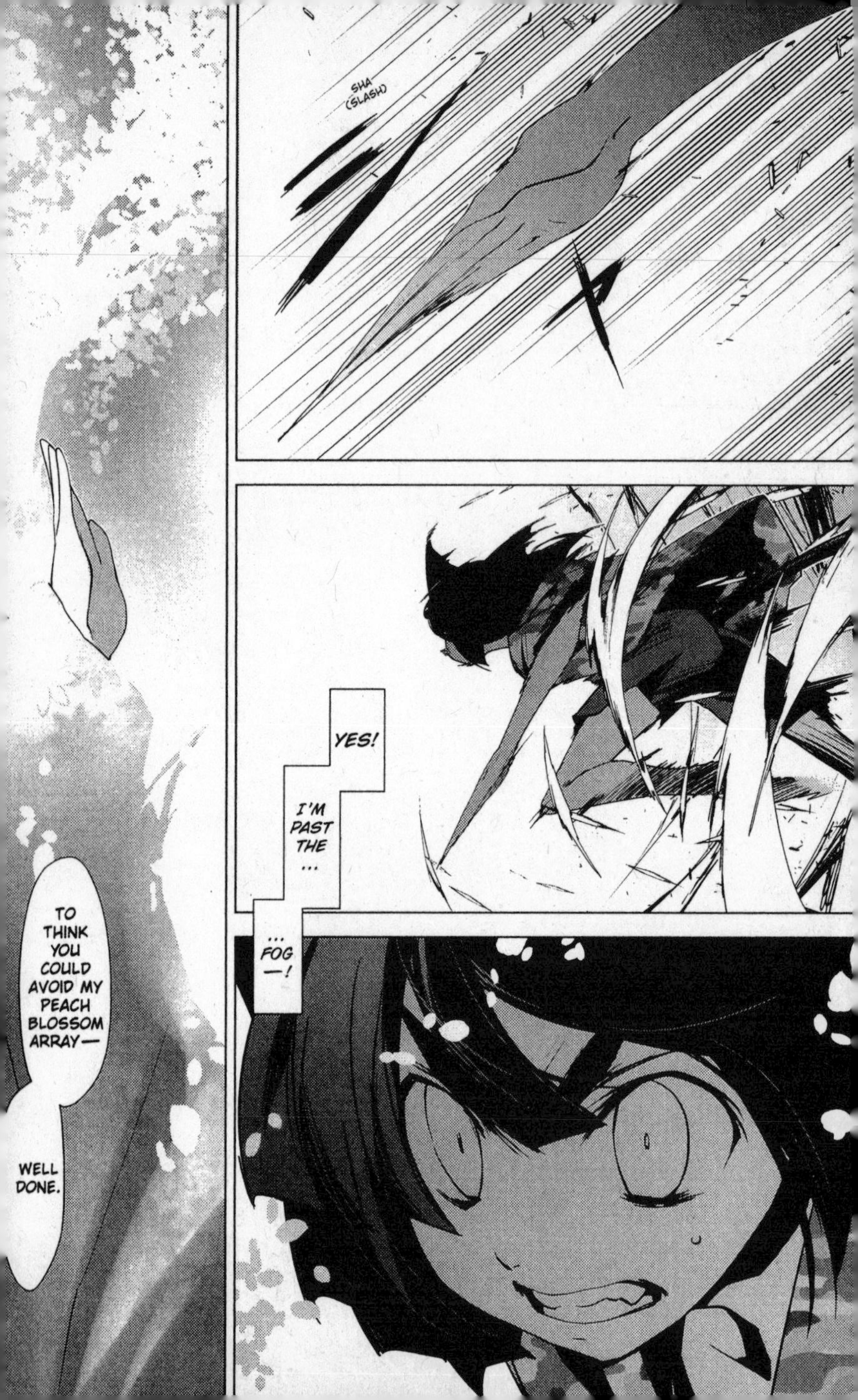
SHA (SLASH)
YES!
I'M PAST THE ...
... FOG—!
TO THINK YOU COULD AVOID MY PEACH BLOSSOM ARRAY—
WELL DONE.

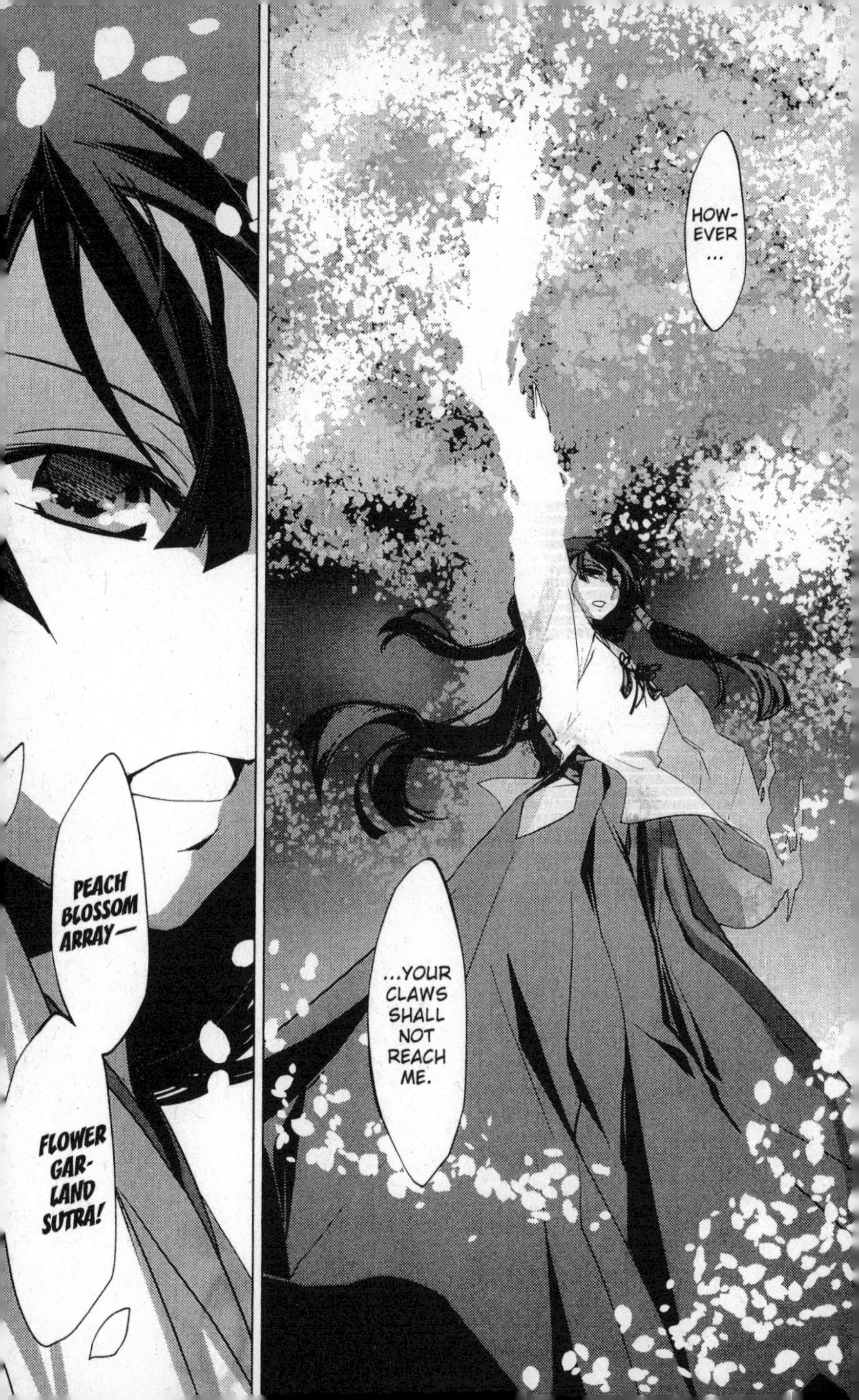
HOW-EVER ...
...YOUR CLAWS SHALL NOT REACH ME.
PEACH BLOSSOM ARRAY—
FLOWER GAR-LAND SUTRA!

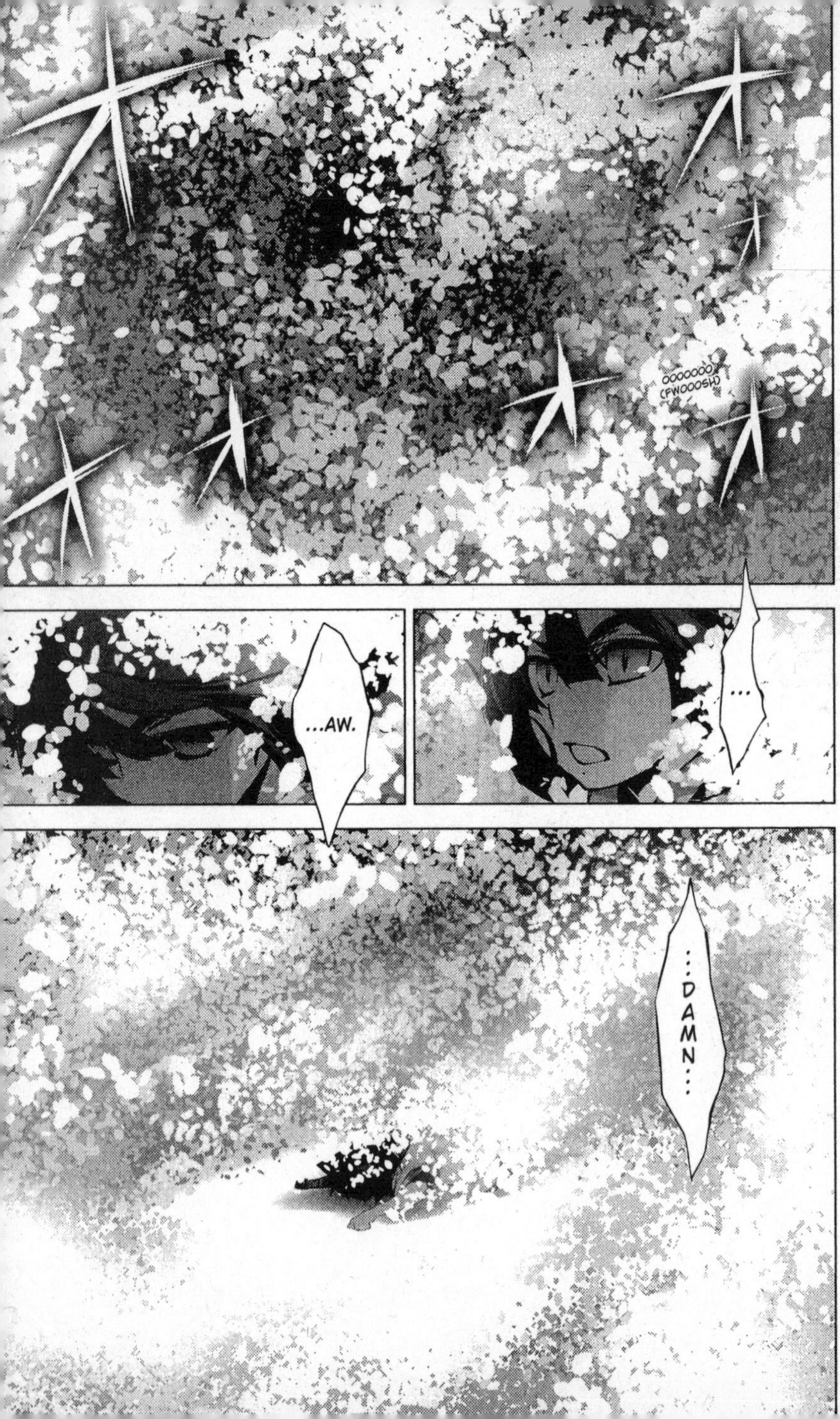
OOOOOOO
(FWOOOSH)
...
...AW.
...DAMN...

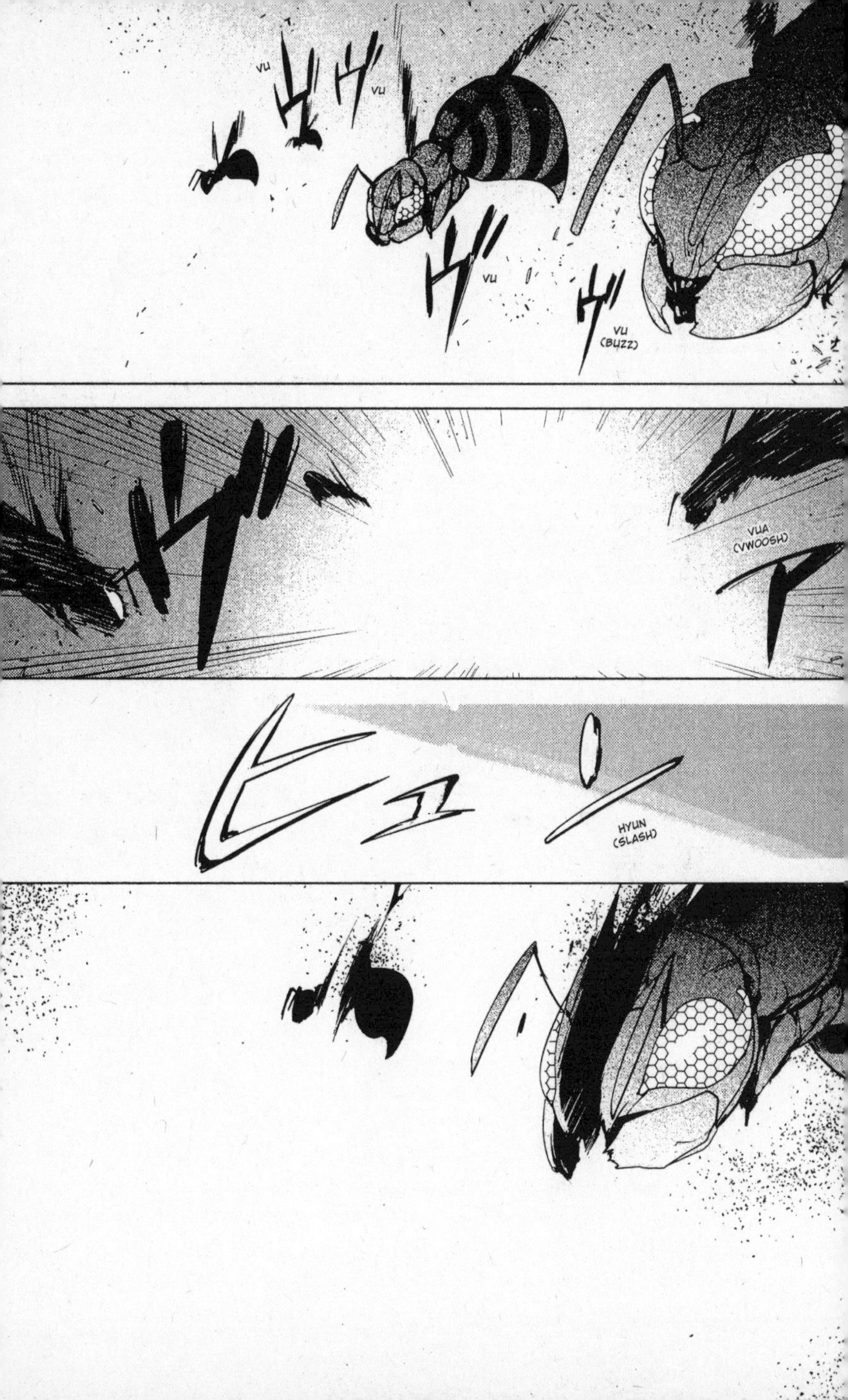
VU
VU
VU
VU
(BUZZ)
VUA
(VWOOSH)
HYUN
(SLASH)

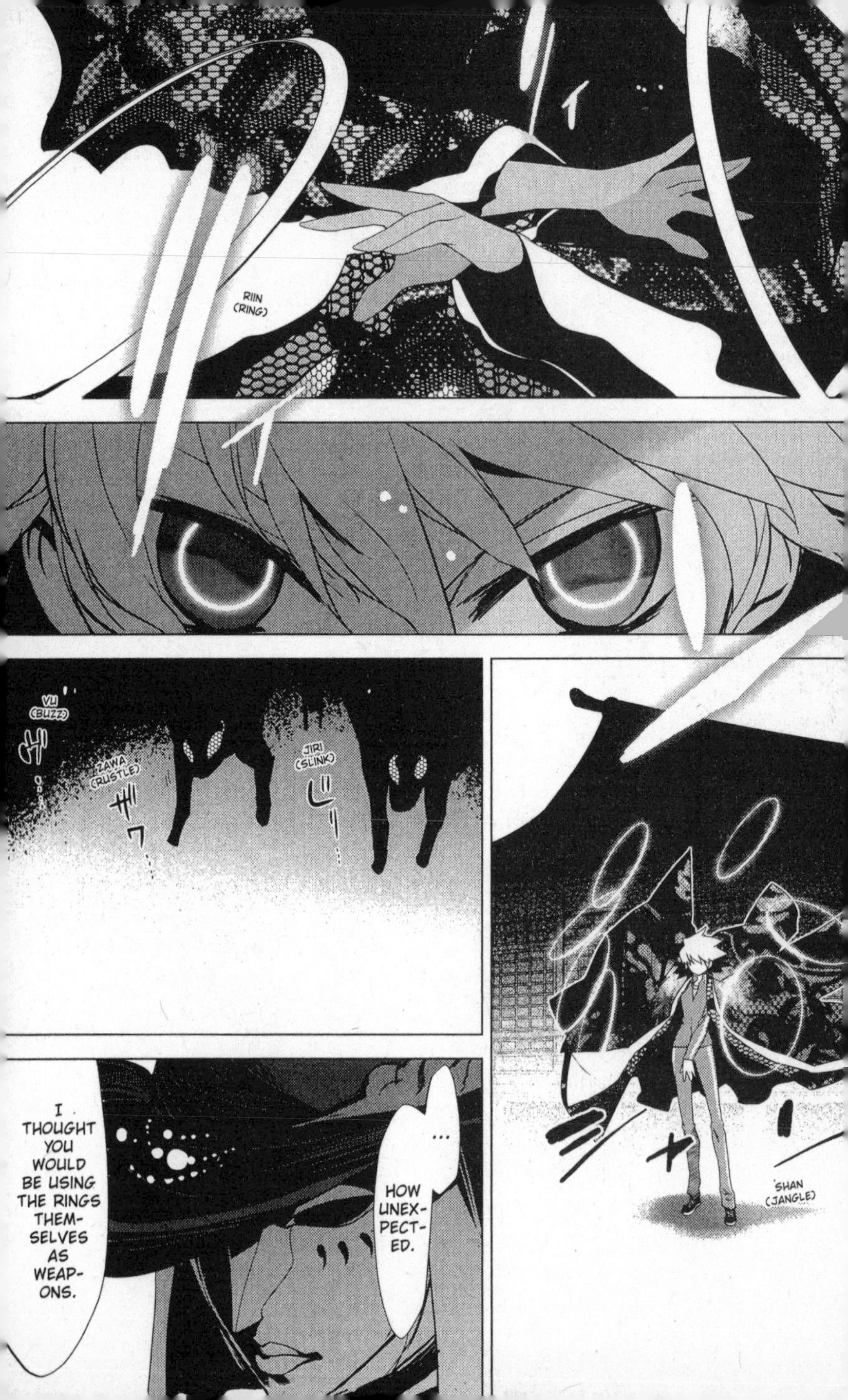
RIIN (RING)
SHAN (JANGLE)
JIRI (SLINK)
ZAWA (RUSTLE)
VU (BUZZ)
... HOW UNEXPECTED.
I THOUGHT YOU WOULD BE USING THE RINGS THEMSELVES AS WEAPONS.

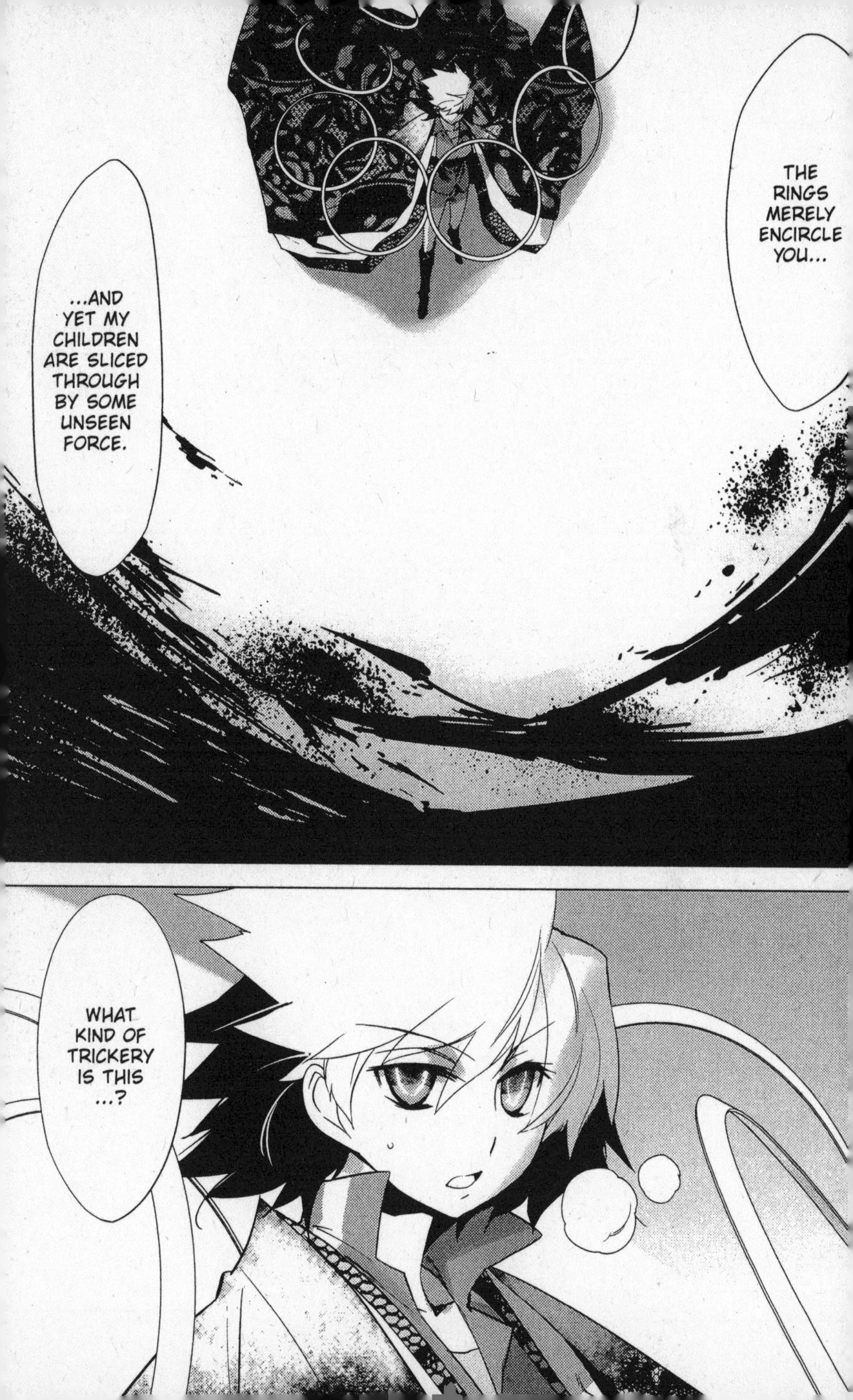
THE RINGS MERELY ENCIRCLE YOU...
...AND YET MY CHILDREN ARE SLICED THROUGH BY SOME UNSEEN FORCE.
WHAT KIND OF TRICKERY IS THIS ...?

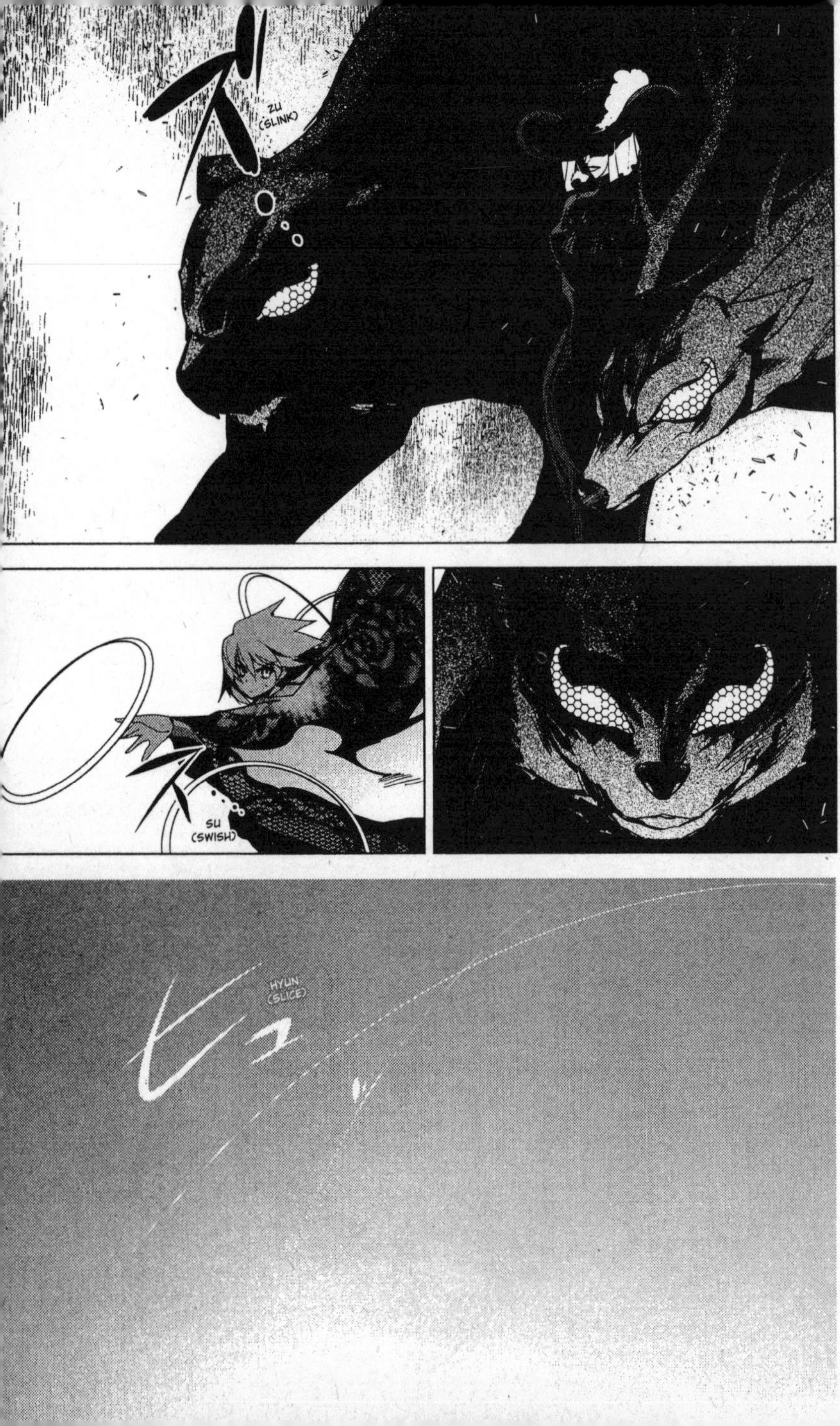
ZU
(SLINK)
SU
(SWISH)
HYUN
(SLICE)

GYAGG
(VWEEN)

GIN
(ZING)

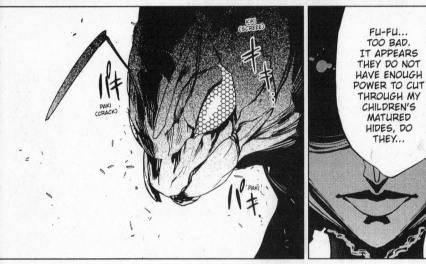

KIKI
(SCREE)

PAKI
(CRACK)

PAKI

FU-FU...
TOO BAD.
IT APPEARS
THEY DO NOT
HAVE ENOUGH
POWER TO CUT
THROUGH MY
CHILDREN'S
MATURED
HIDES, DO
THEY...

...THOSE
THREADS
OF
YOURS?

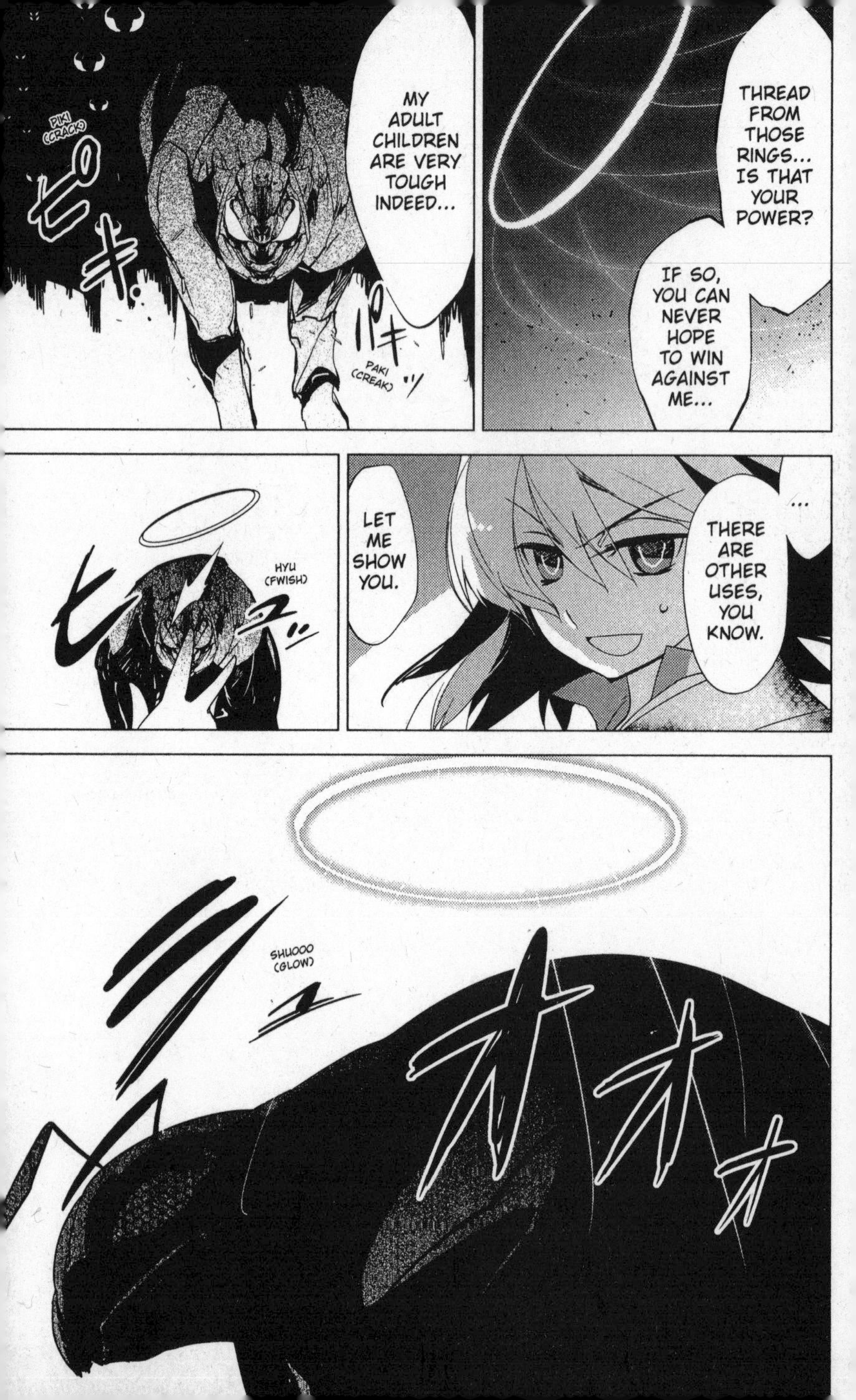
THREAD FROM THOSE RINGS... IS THAT YOUR POWER?
IF SO, YOU CAN NEVER HOPE TO WIN AGAINST ME...
MY ADULT CHILDREN ARE VERY TOUGH INDEED...
PIKI (CRACK)
PAKI (CREAK)
...
THERE ARE OTHER USES, YOU KNOW.
LET ME SHOW YOU.
HYU (FWISH)
SHUOOO (GLOW)

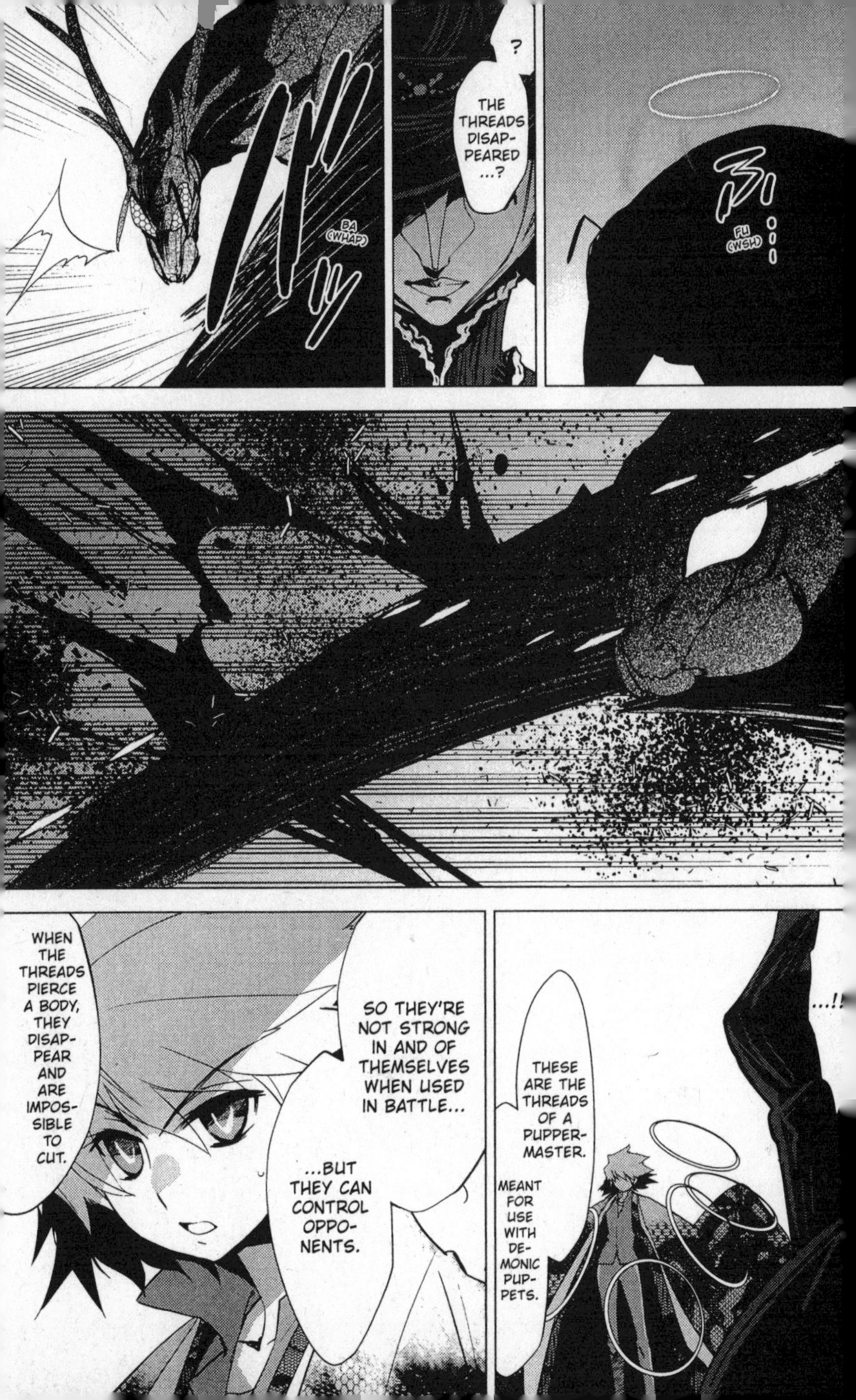
FU (WSH)
?
THE THREADS DISAPPEARED...?
BA (WHAP)
...!!
THESE ARE THE THREADS OF A PUPPER-MASTER.
MEANT FOR USE WITH DEMONIC PUPPETS.
WHEN THE THREADS PIERCE A BODY, THEY DISAPPEAR AND ARE IMPOSSIBLE TO CUT.
SO THEY'RE NOT STRONG IN AND OF THEMSELVES WHEN USED IN BATTLE...
...BUT THEY CAN CONTROL OPPONENTS.

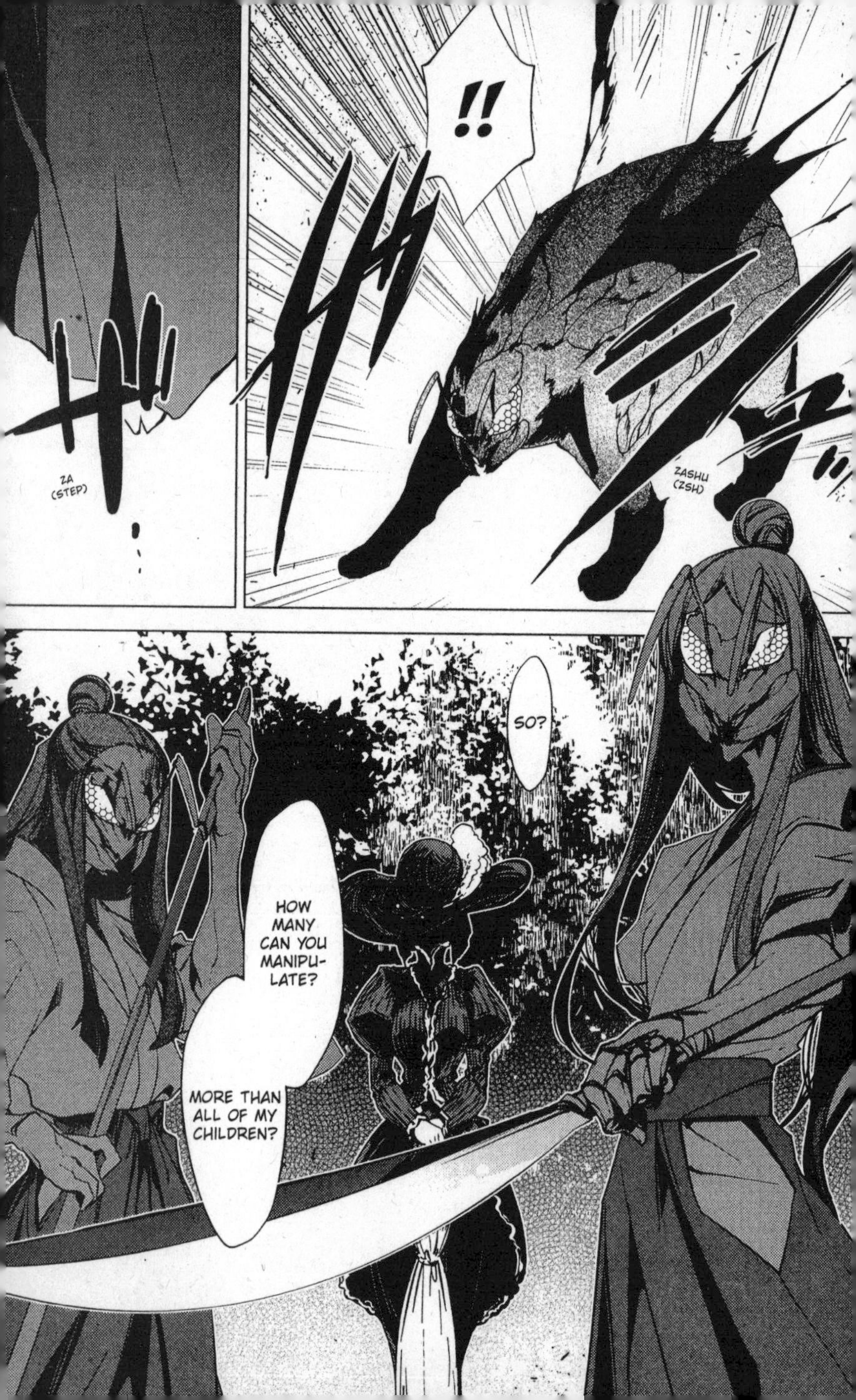
!!
ZASHU (ZSH)
ZA (STEP)
SO?
HOW MANY CAN YOU MANIPULATE?
MORE THAN ALL OF MY CHILDREN?

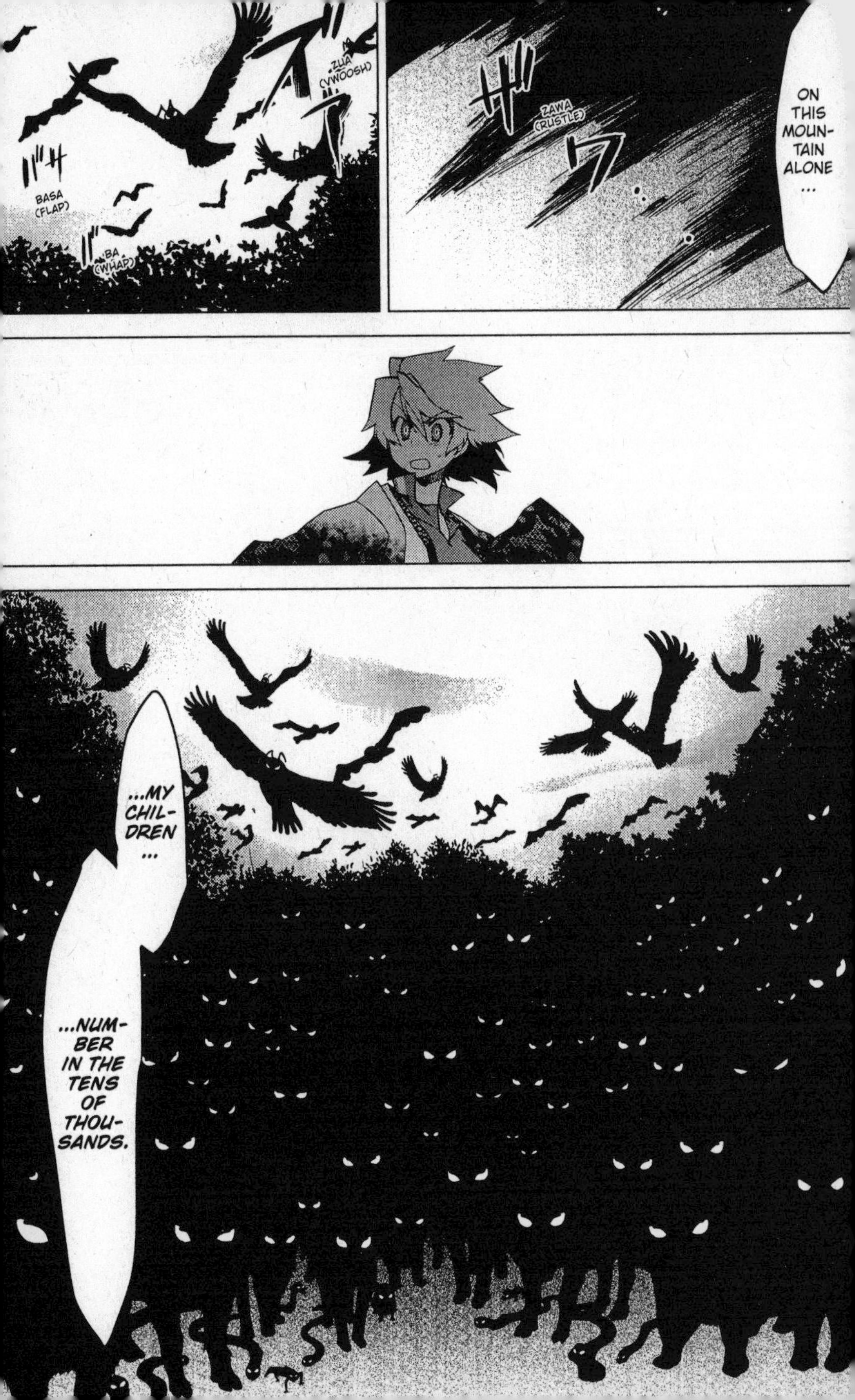
ON THIS MOUNTAIN ALONE...
ZAWA (RUSTLE)
ZUA (VWOOSH)
BASA (FLAP)
BA (WHAP)
...MY CHILDREN...
...NUMBER IN THE TENS OF THOUSANDS.

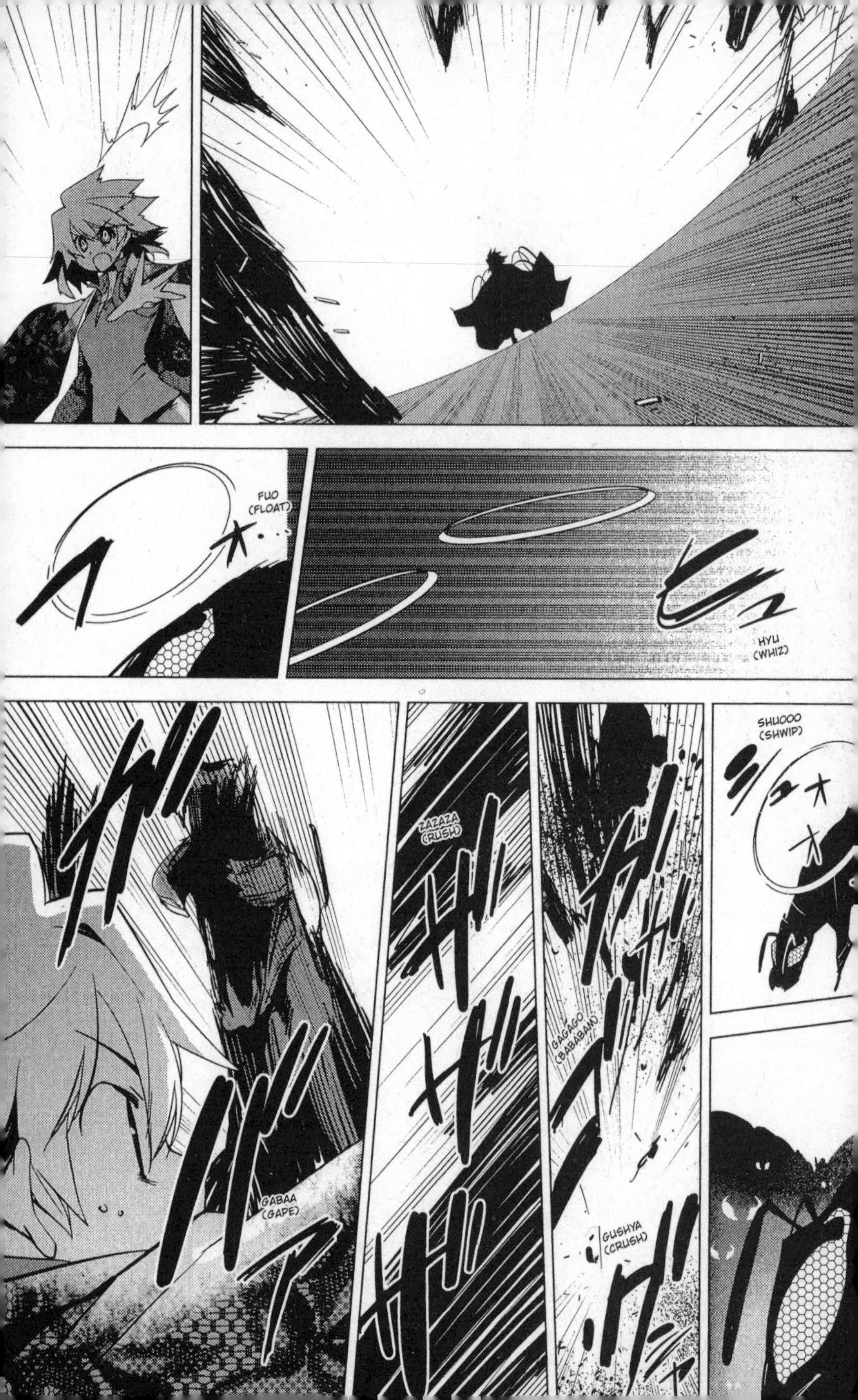
HYU
(WHIZ)
FUO
(FLOAT)
SHUOOO
(SHWIP)
GAGAGO
(BABABAM)
GUSHYA
(CRUSH)
ZAZAZA
(RUSH)
GABAA
(GAPE)

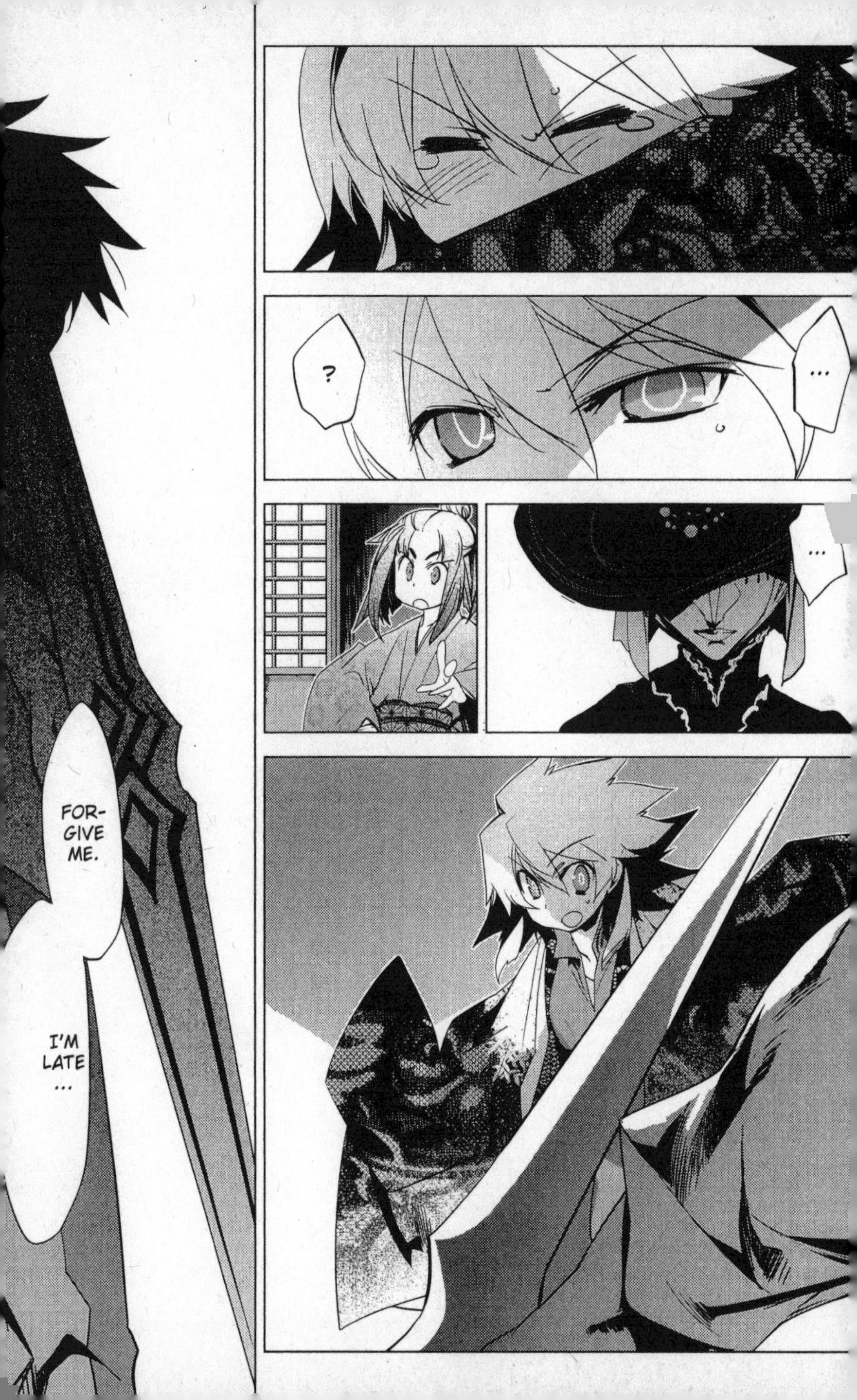
...
?
...
FOR-GIVE ME.
I'M LATE ...

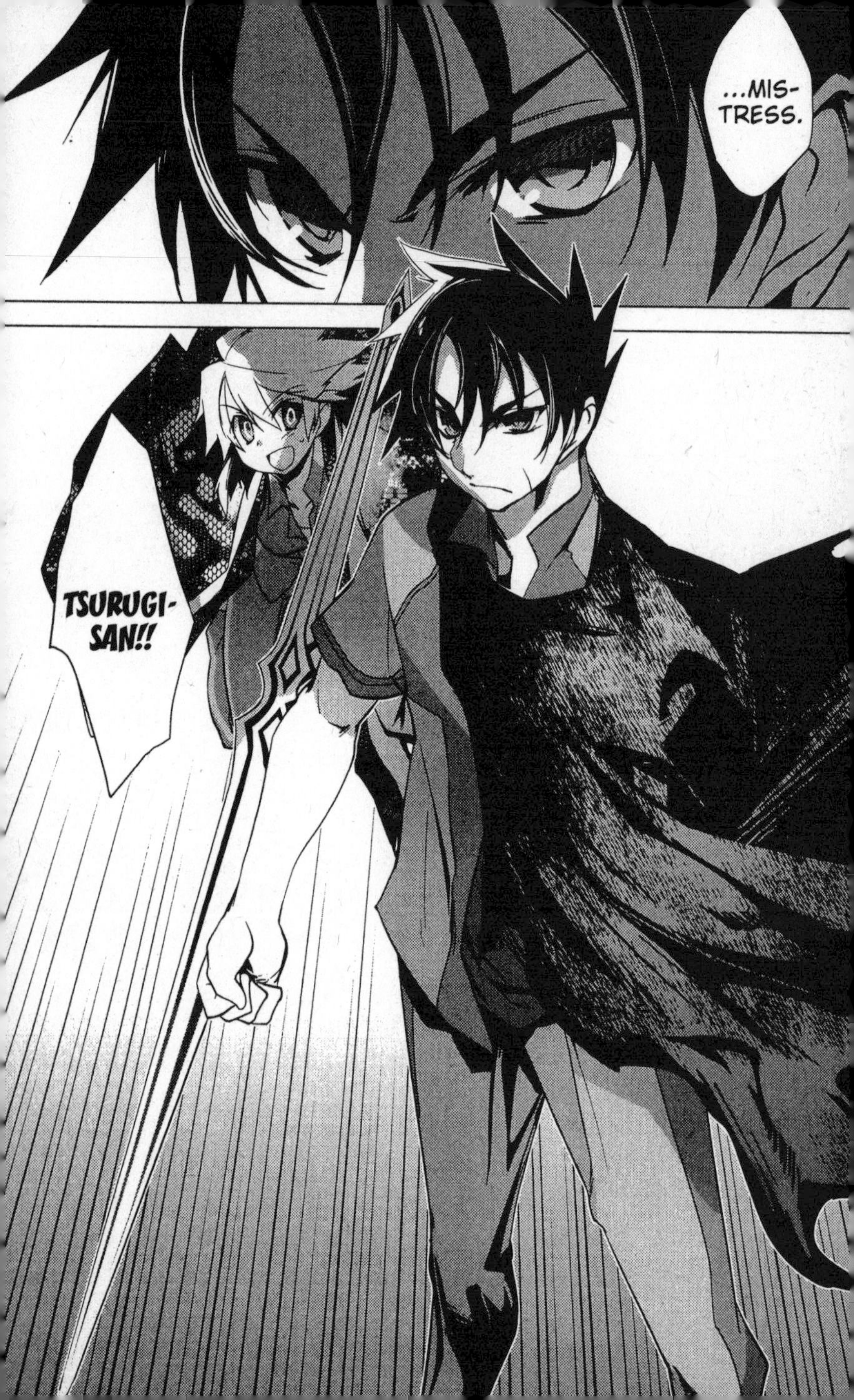
...MIS-
TRESS.
TSURUGI-
SAN!!

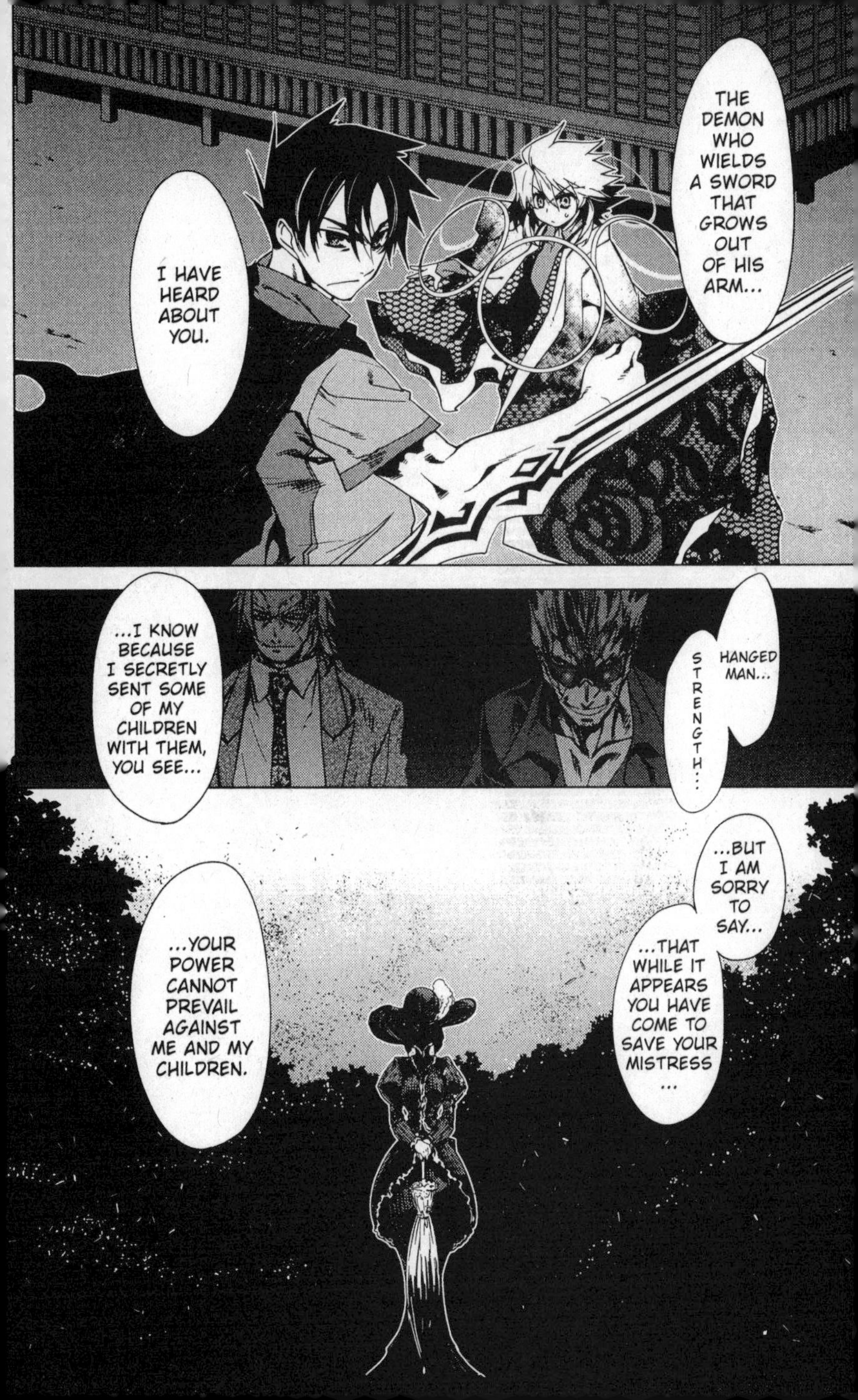
THE DEMON WHO WIELDS A SWORD THAT GROWS OUT OF HIS ARM...
I HAVE HEARD ABOUT YOU.
HANGED MAN...
STRENGTH...
...I KNOW BECAUSE I SECRETLY SENT SOME OF MY CHILDREN WITH THEM, YOU SEE...
...BUT I AM SORRY TO SAY...
...THAT WHILE IT APPEARS YOU HAVE COME TO SAVE YOUR MISTRESS...
...YOUR POWER CANNOT PREVAIL AGAINST ME AND MY CHILDREN.

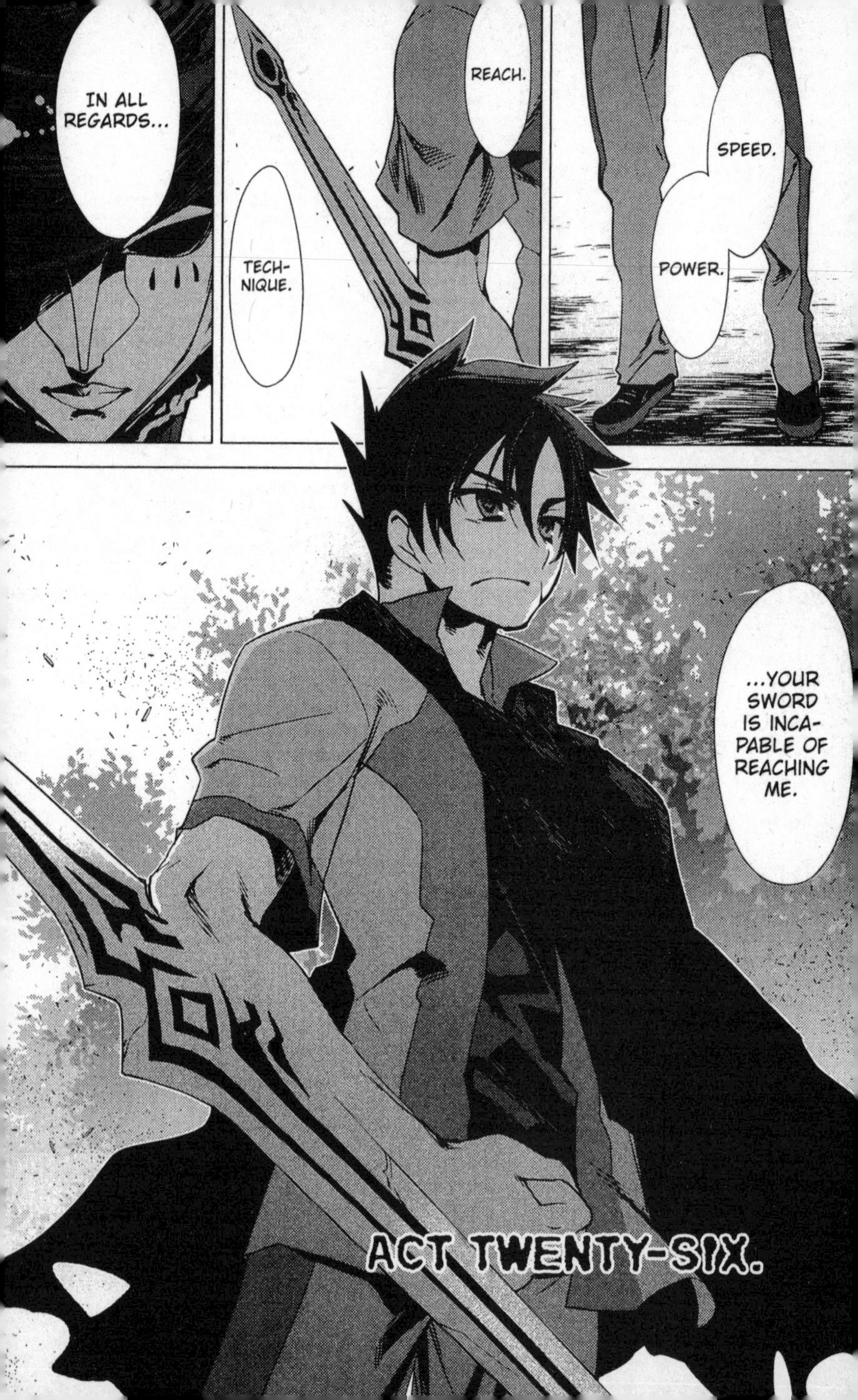
SPEED.
POWER.
REACH.
TECH-NIQUE.
IN ALL REGARDS...
...YOUR SWORD IS INCA-PABLE OF REACHING ME.
ACT TWENTY-SIX.

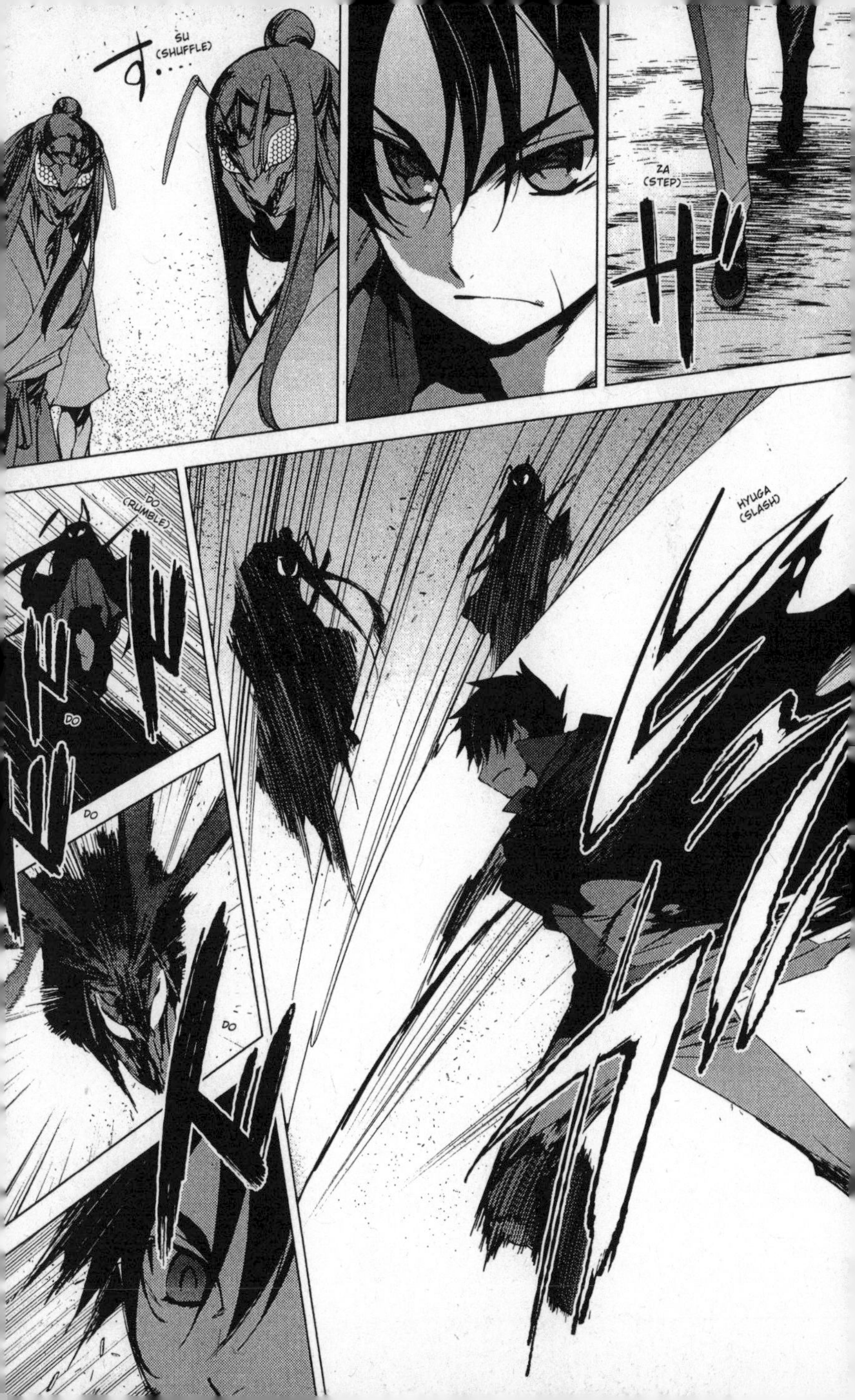
ZA
(STEP)
SU
(SHUFFLE)
す....
HYUGA
(SLASH)
DO
(RUMBLE)
DO
DO
DO

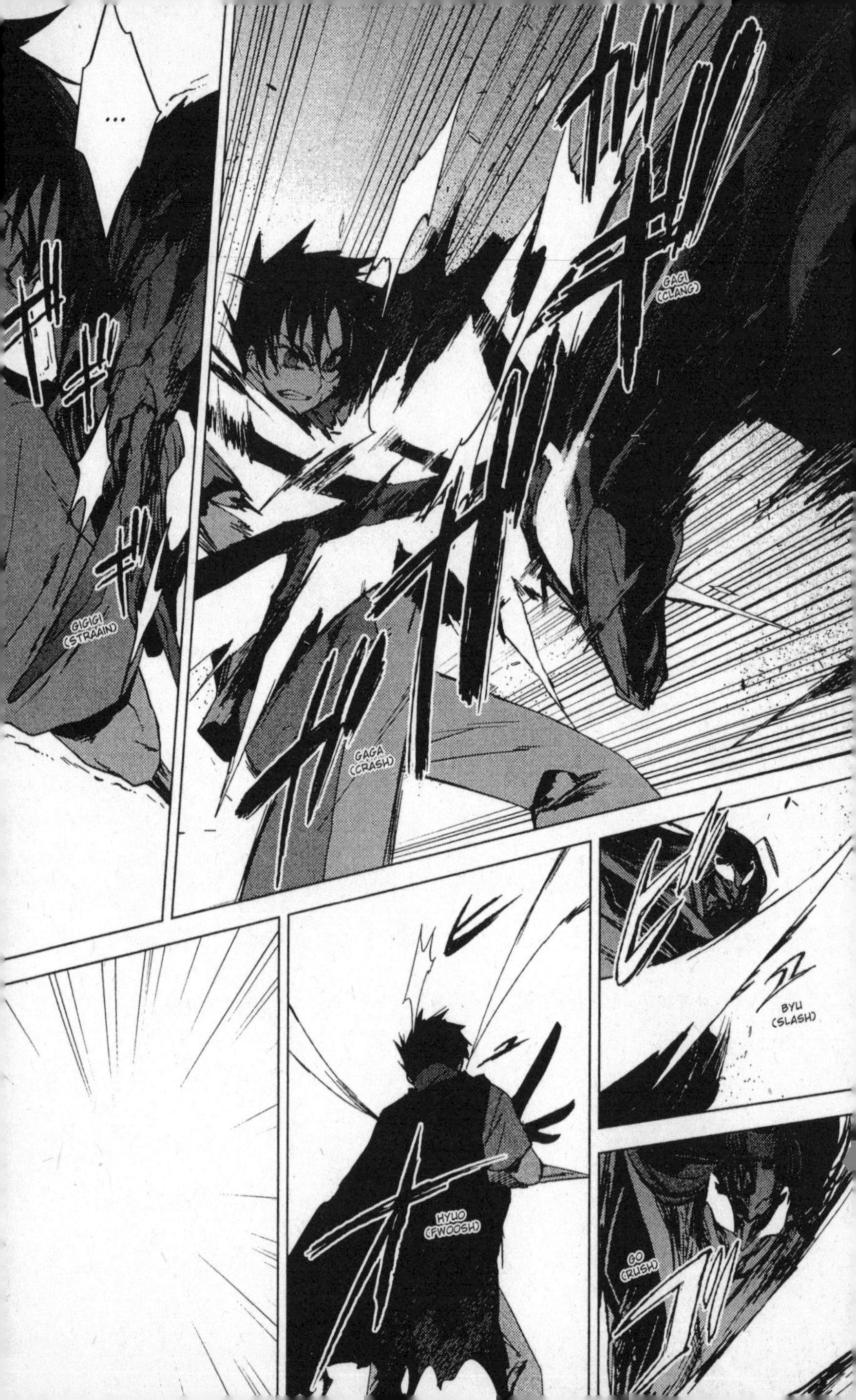
GAGI (CLANG)
GAGA (CRASH)
...
GIGIGI (STRAAIN)
BYU (SLASH)
GO (RUSH)
HYUO (FWOOSH)

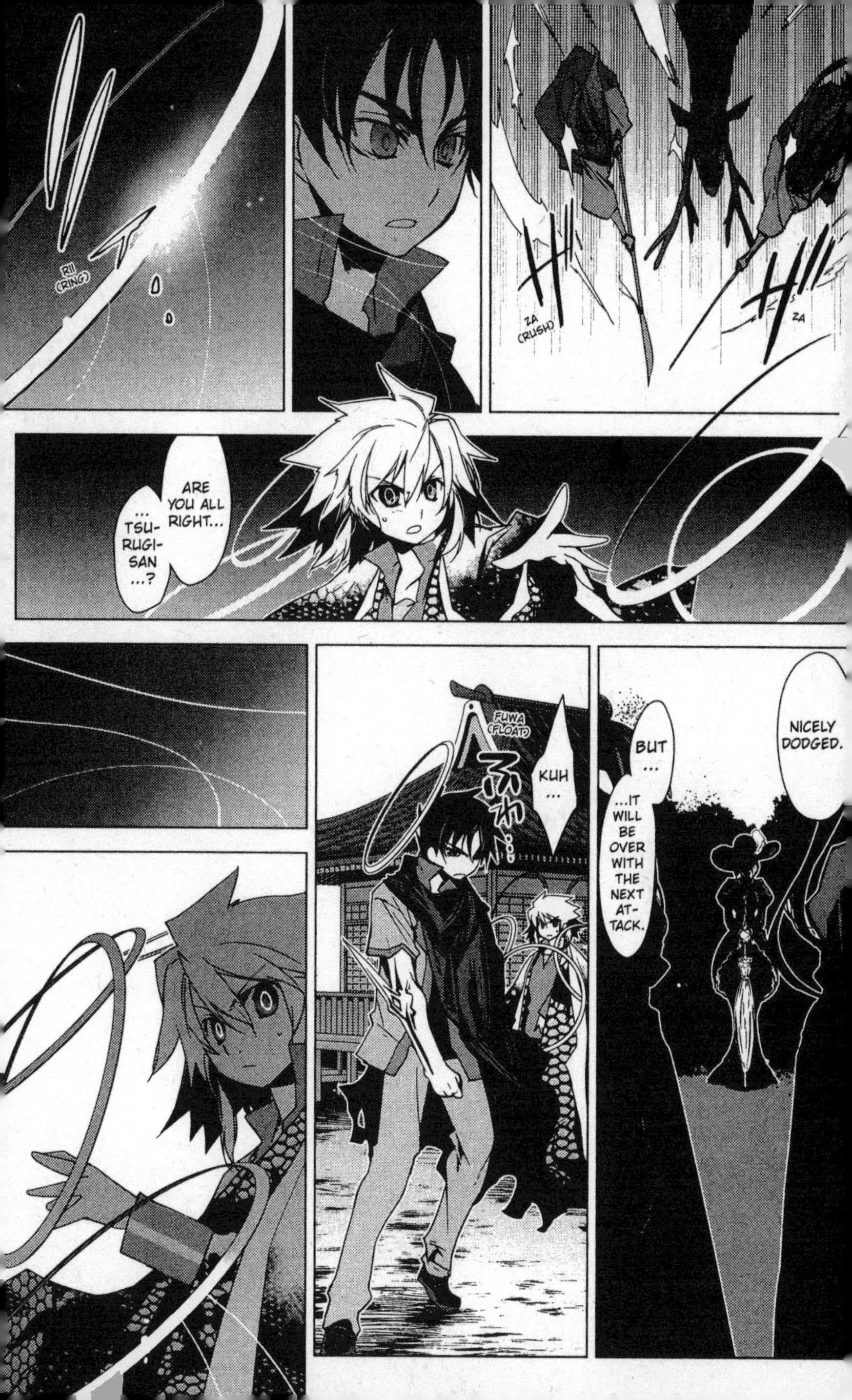

ZA (RUSH)
ZA
RII (RING)
ARE YOU ALL RIGHT...
...TSURUGI-SAN...?
NICELY DODGED.
BUT...
...IT WILL BE OVER WITH THE NEXT AT-TACK.
KUH...
FUWA (FLOAT)
ふわ…

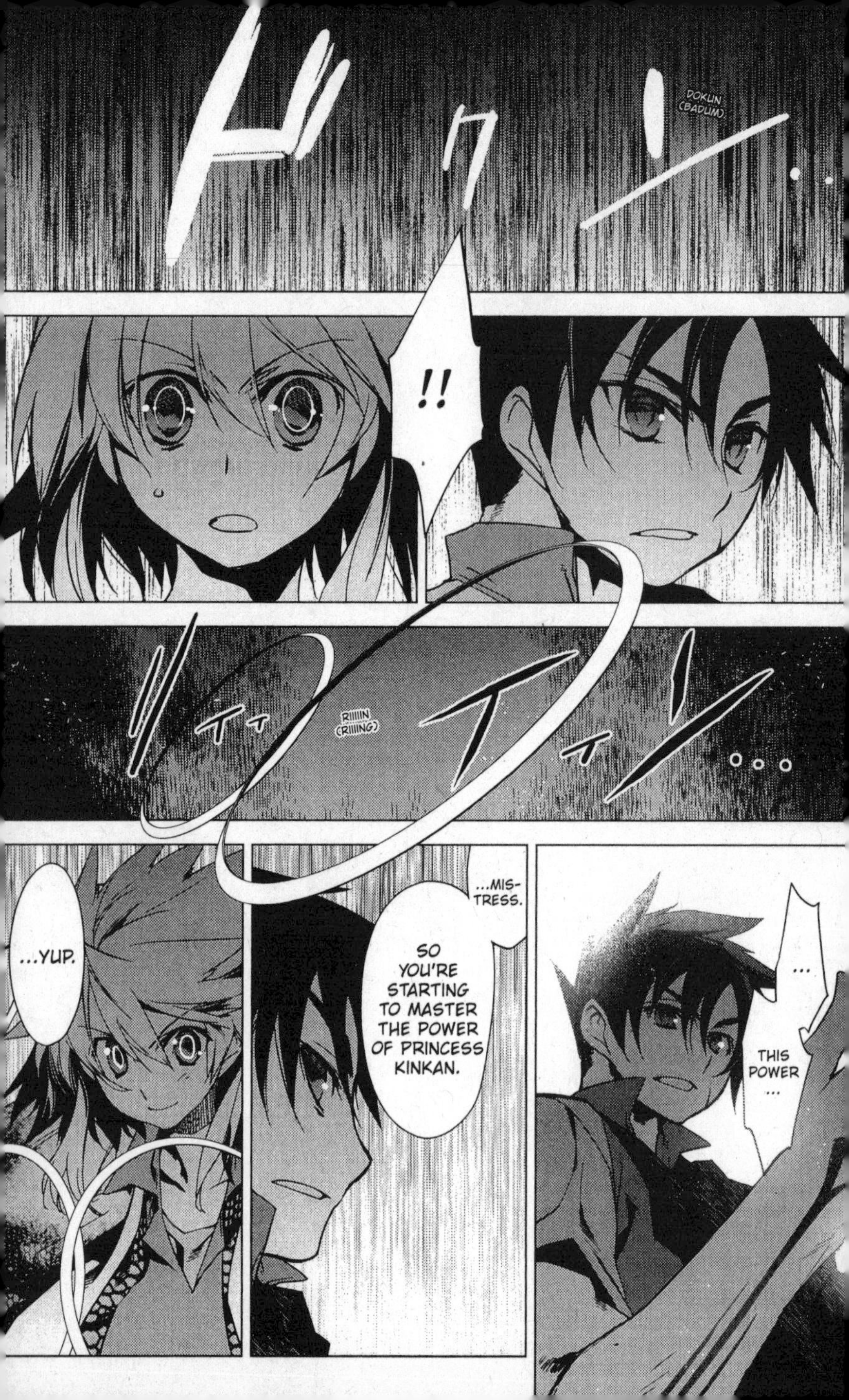
DOKUN (BADUM)
!!
RIIIIN (RIIIING)
...
THIS POWER ...
...MIS-TRESS.
SO YOU'RE STARTING TO MASTER THE POWER OF PRINCESS KINKAN.
...YUP.

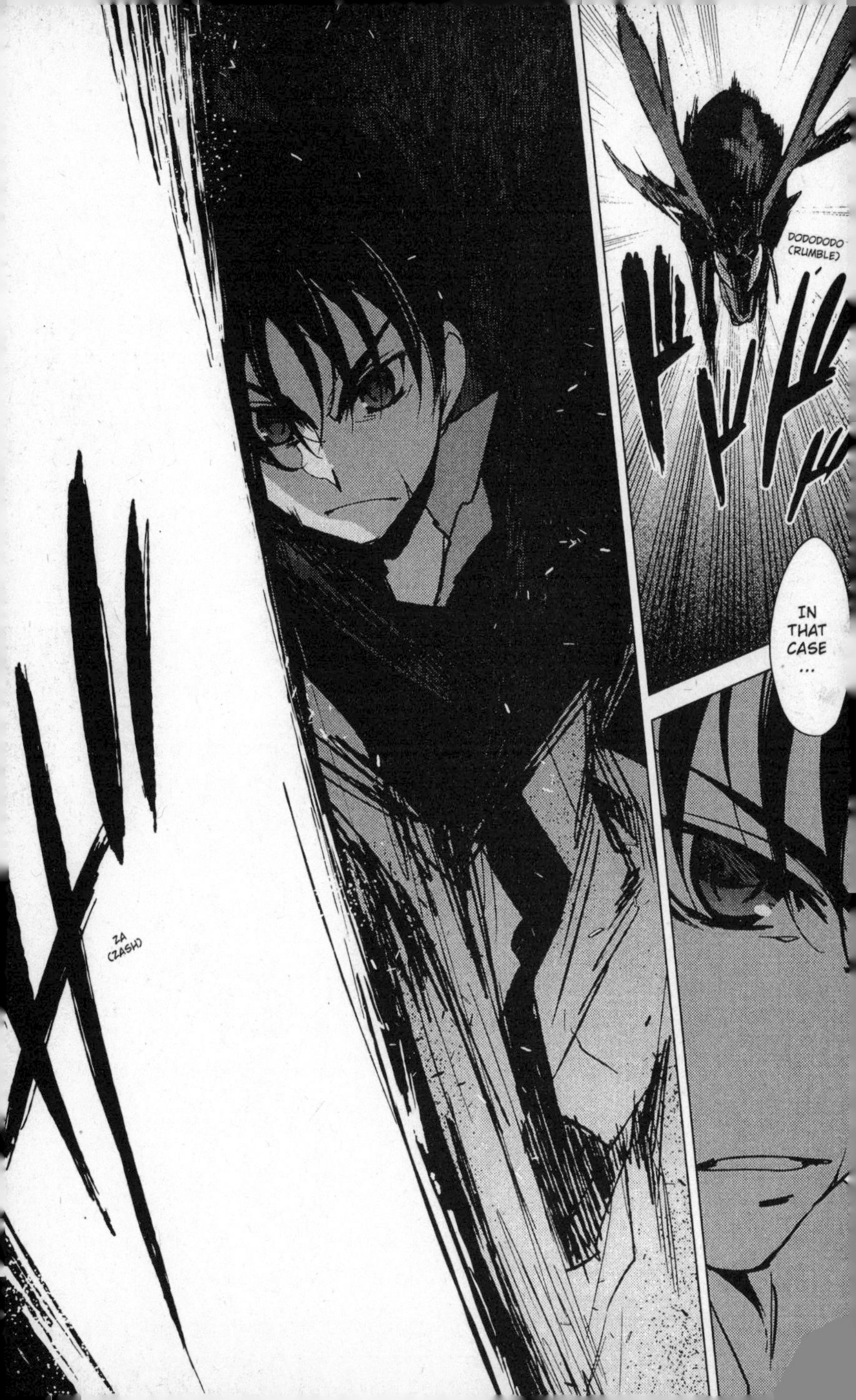
DODODODO (RUMBLE)
IN THAT CASE ...
ZA (ZASH)

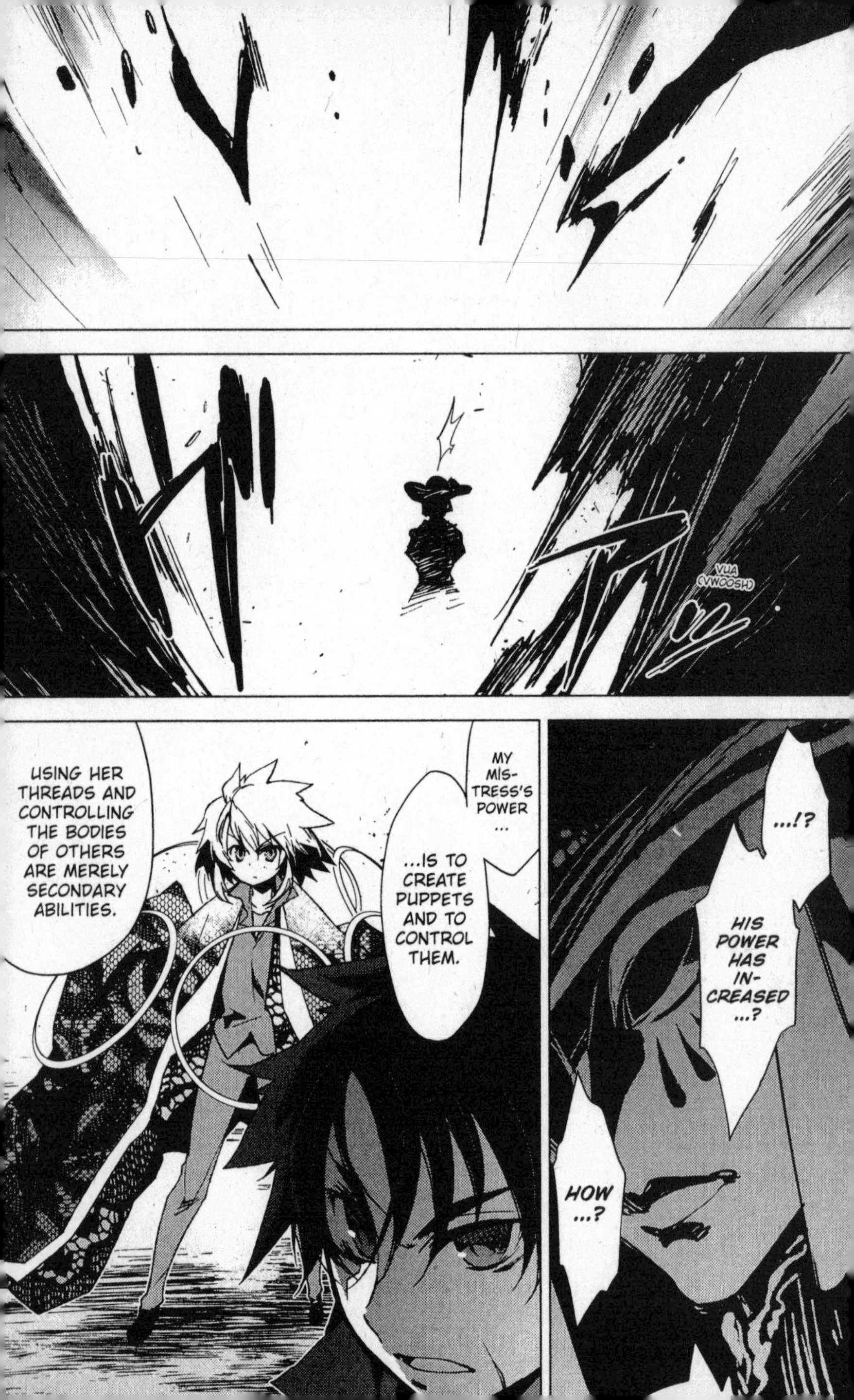
VUA (VWOOSH)
...!?
HIS POWER HAS IN-CREASED ...?
HOW ...?
MY MIS-TRESS'S POWER ...
...IS TO CREATE PUPPETS AND TO CONTROL THEM.
USING HER THREADS AND CONTROLLING THE BODIES OF OTHERS ARE MERELY SECONDARY ABILITIES.

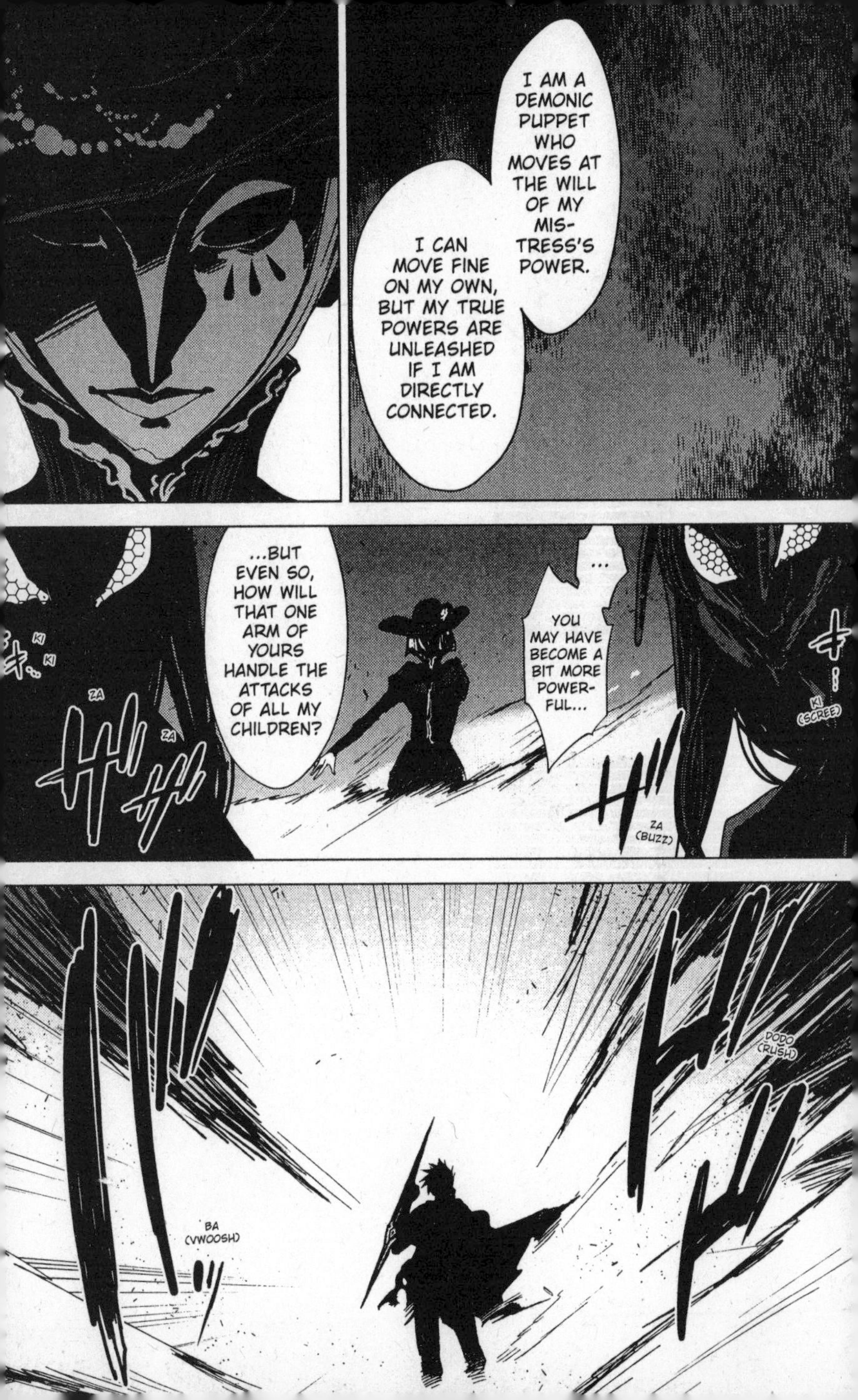
I AM A DEMONIC PUPPET WHO MOVES AT THE WILL OF MY MIS-TRESS'S POWER.
I CAN MOVE FINE ON MY OWN, BUT MY TRUE POWERS ARE UNLEASHED IF I AM DIRECTLY CONNECTED.
KI (SCREE)
...
YOU MAY HAVE BECOME A BIT MORE POWER-FUL...
ZA (BUZZ)
...BUT EVEN SO, HOW WILL THAT ONE ARM OF YOURS HANDLE THE ATTACKS OF ALL MY CHILDREN?
ZA
ZA
KI
KI
DODO (RUSH)
BA (VWOOSH)

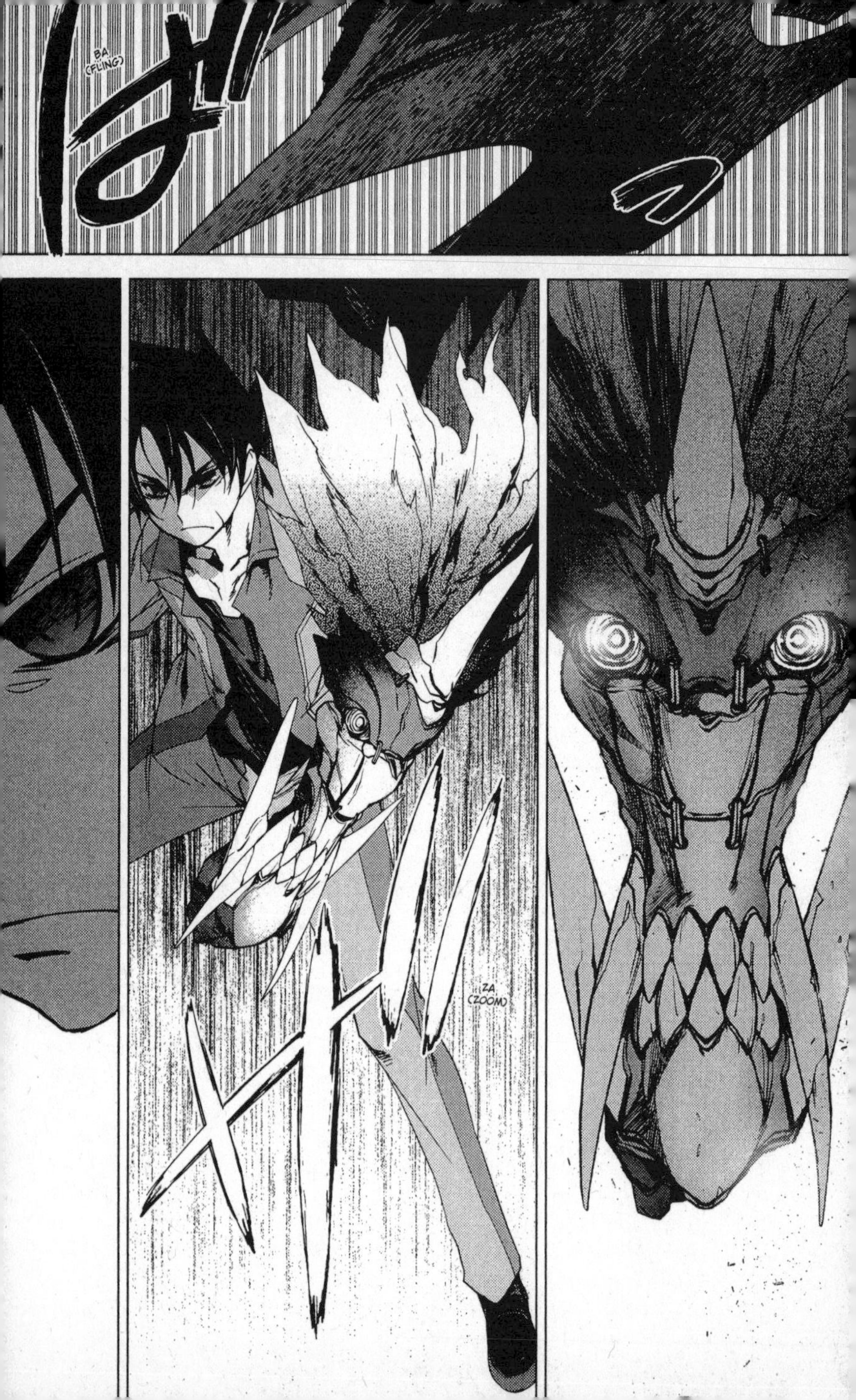
BA (FLING)
ZA (ZOOM)

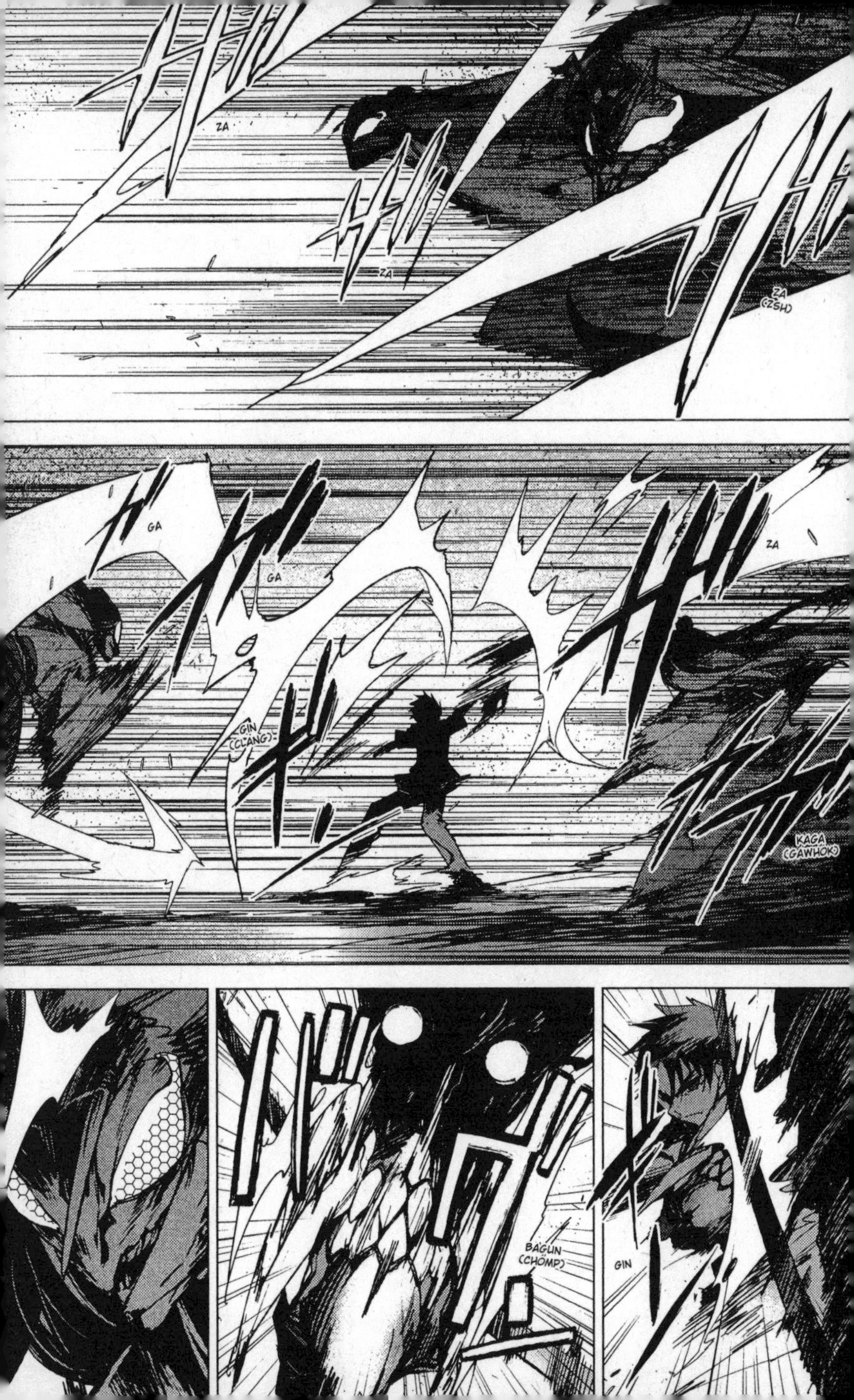
ZA
(ZSH)
ZA
ZA
ZA
KAGA
(GAWHOK)
GA
GA
GIN
(CLANG)
GIN
BAGUN
(CHOMP)

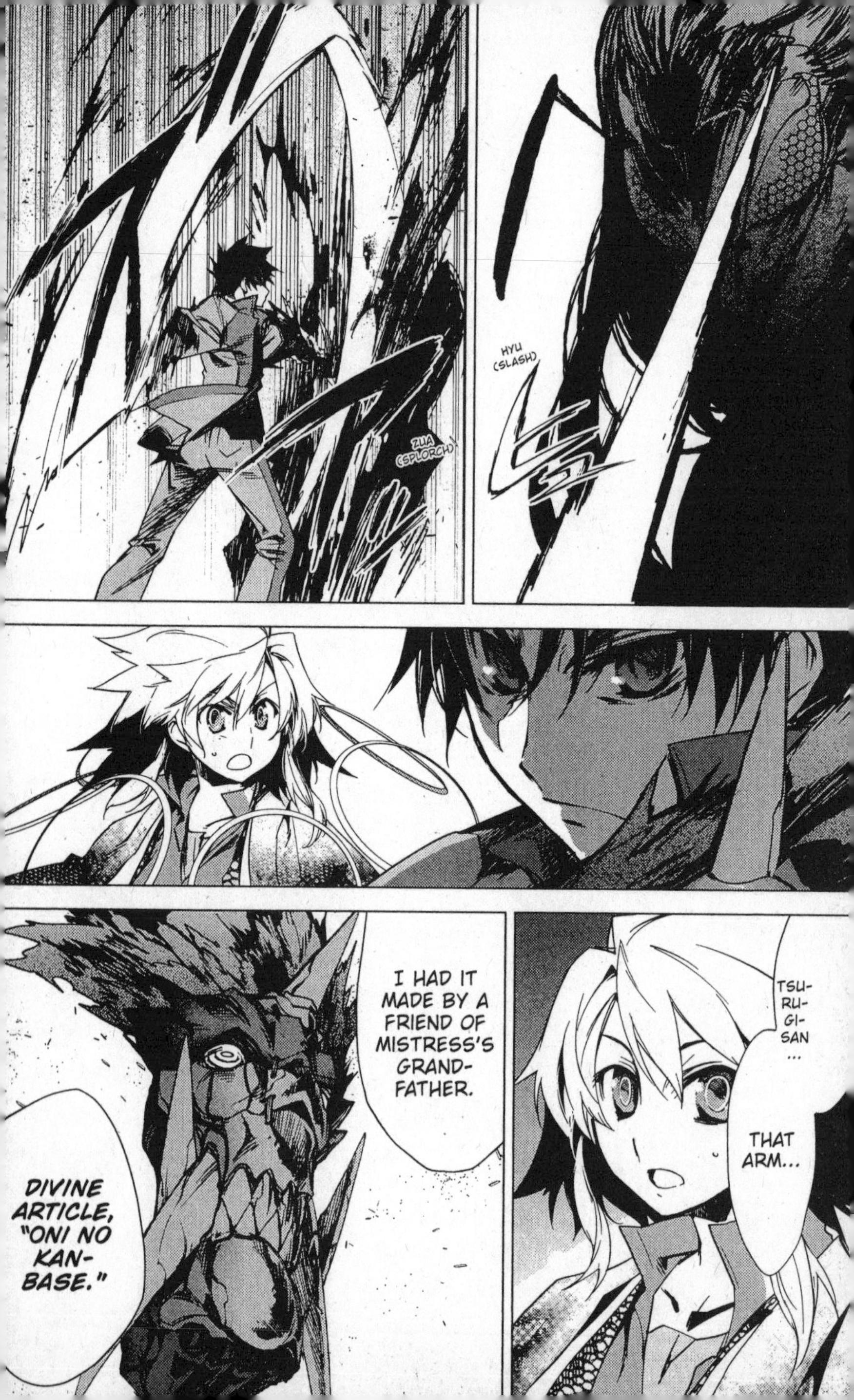
HYU (SLASH)
ZUA (SPLORCH)
TSU-RU-GI-SAN...
THAT ARM...
I HAD IT MADE BY A FRIEND OF MISTRESS'S GRAND-FATHER.
DIVINE ARTICLE, "ONI NO KAN-BASE."

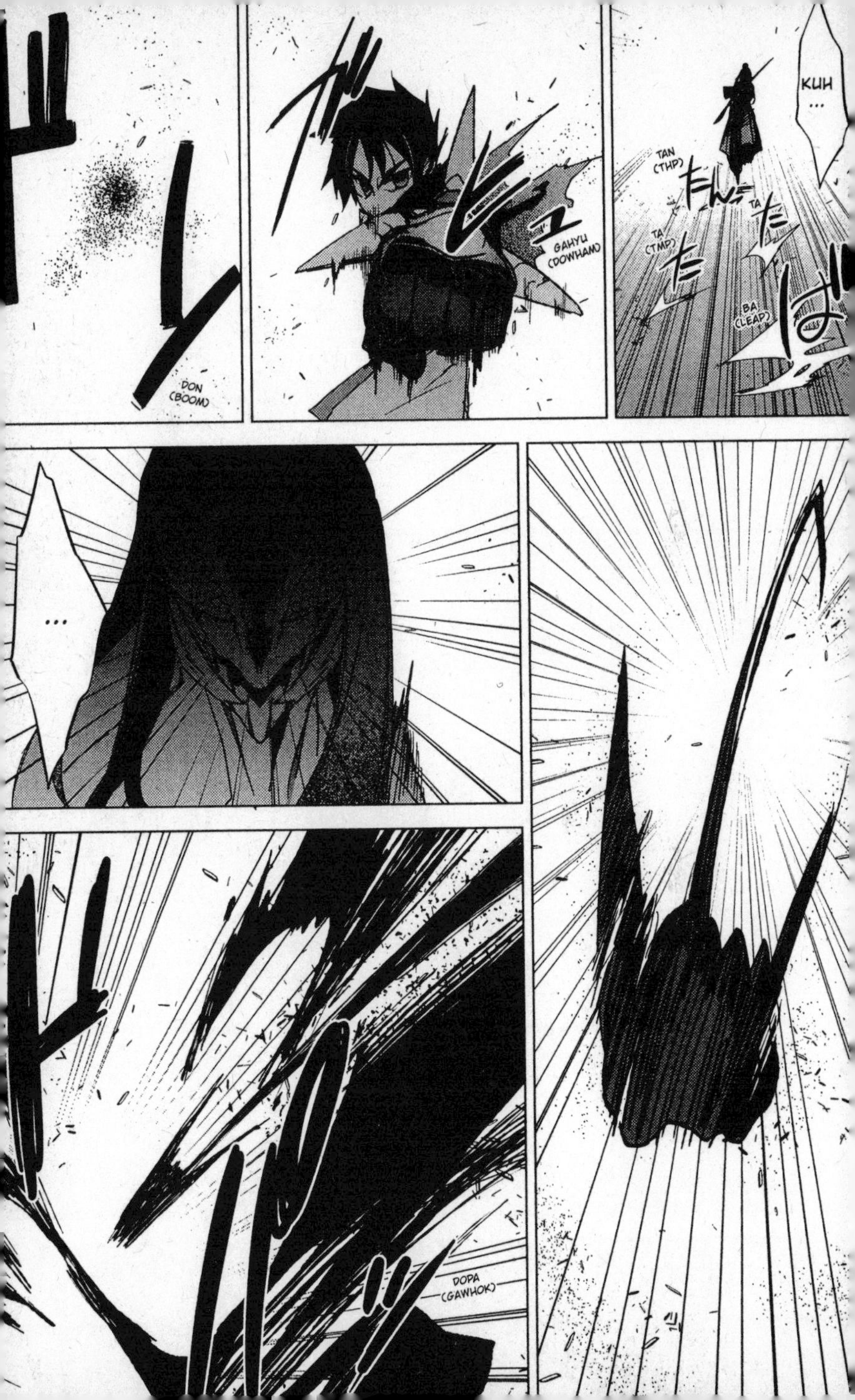
KUH ...
TAN (THP)
TA (TMP)
TA
BA (LEAP)
GAHYU (DOWHAM)
DON (BOOM)
...
DOPA (GAWHOK)

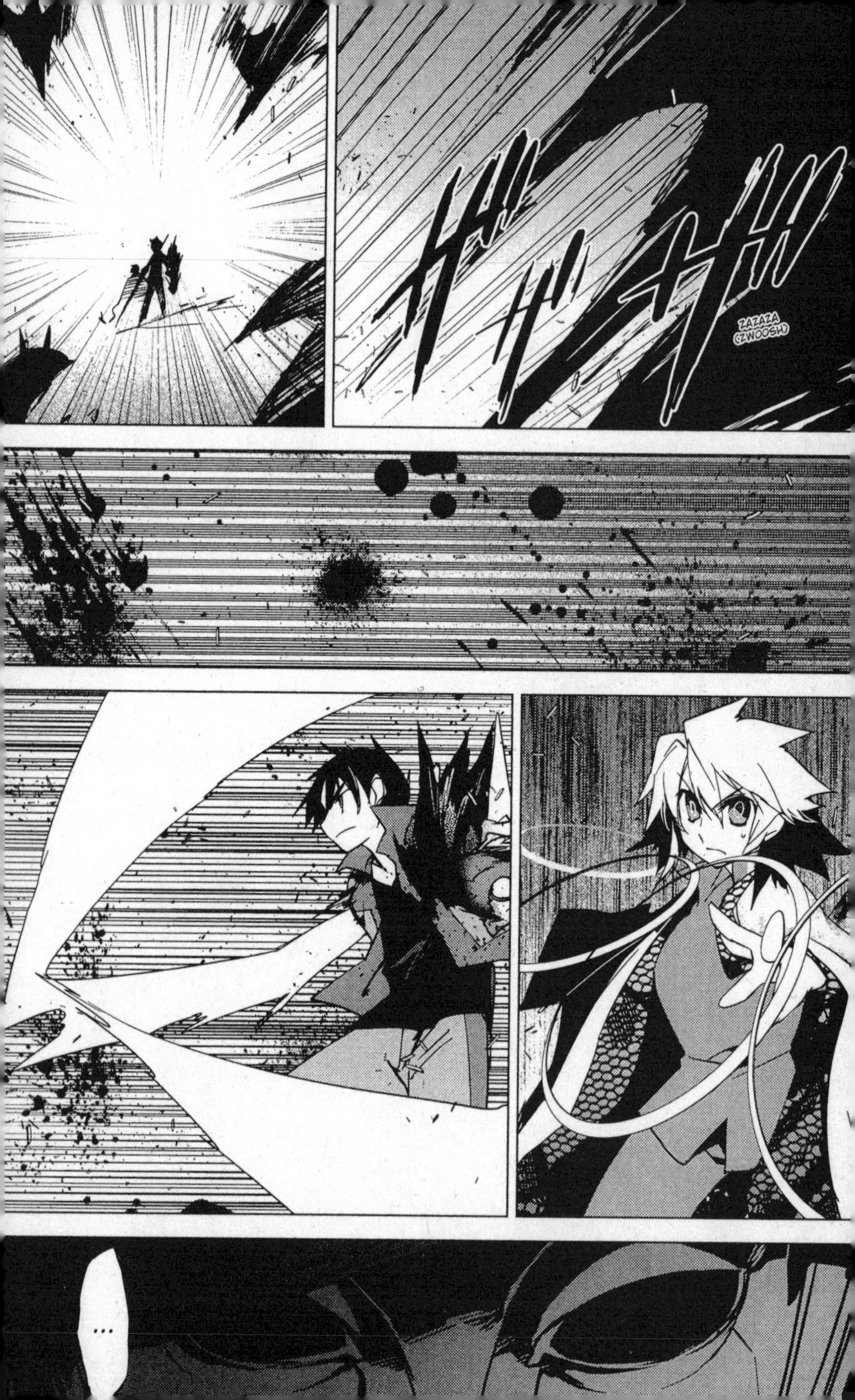
ZAZAZA (ZWOOSH)
...

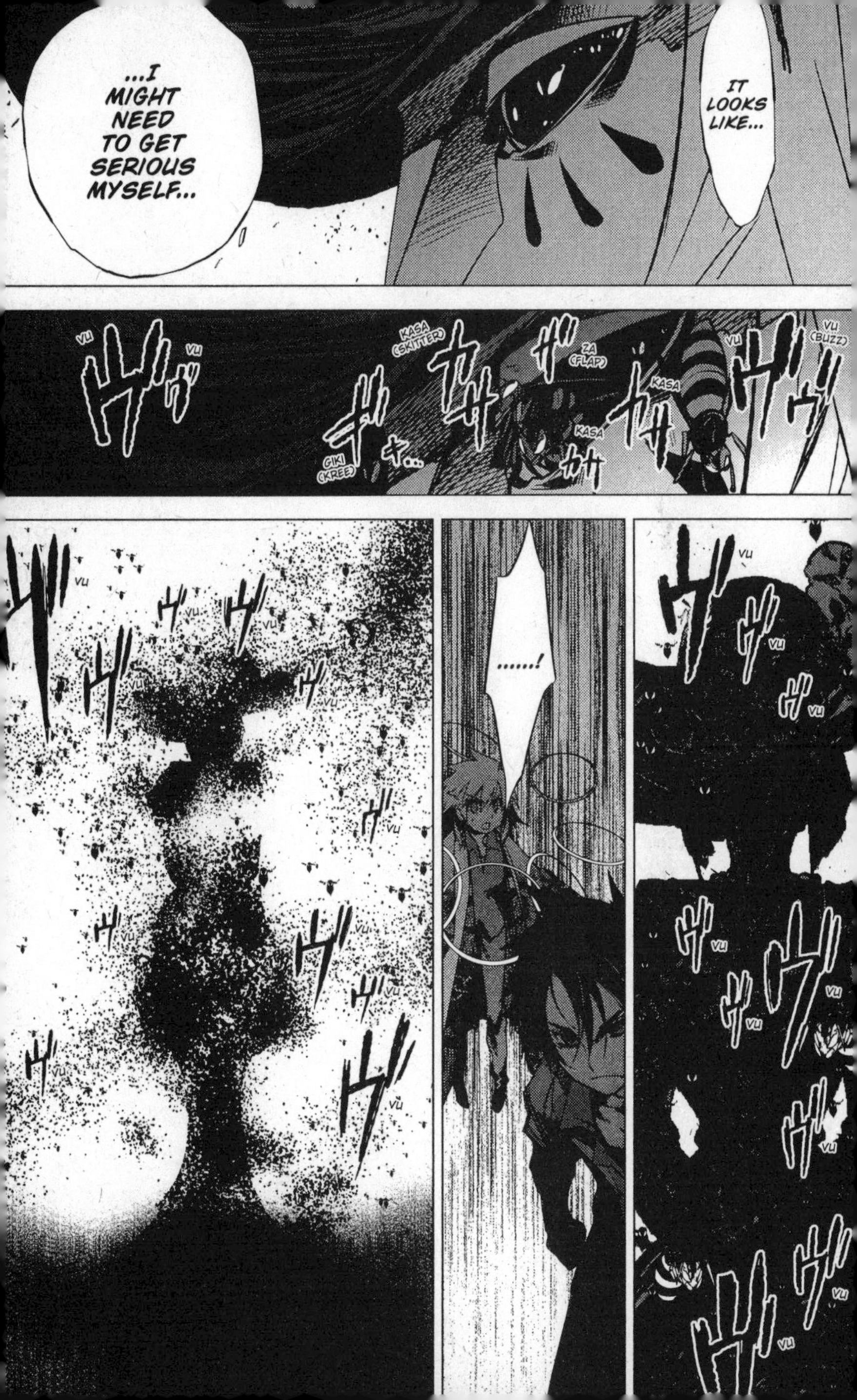
IT LOOKS LIKE...
...I MIGHT NEED TO GET SERIOUS MYSELF...
VU (BUZZ)
VU
KASA
KASA
ZA (FLAP)
KASA (SKITTER)
GIKI (KREE)
VU
VU
VU
VU
VU
VU
VU
VU
VU
VU
VU
......!
VU
VU
VU
VU
VU
VU
VU
VU
VU
VU
VU

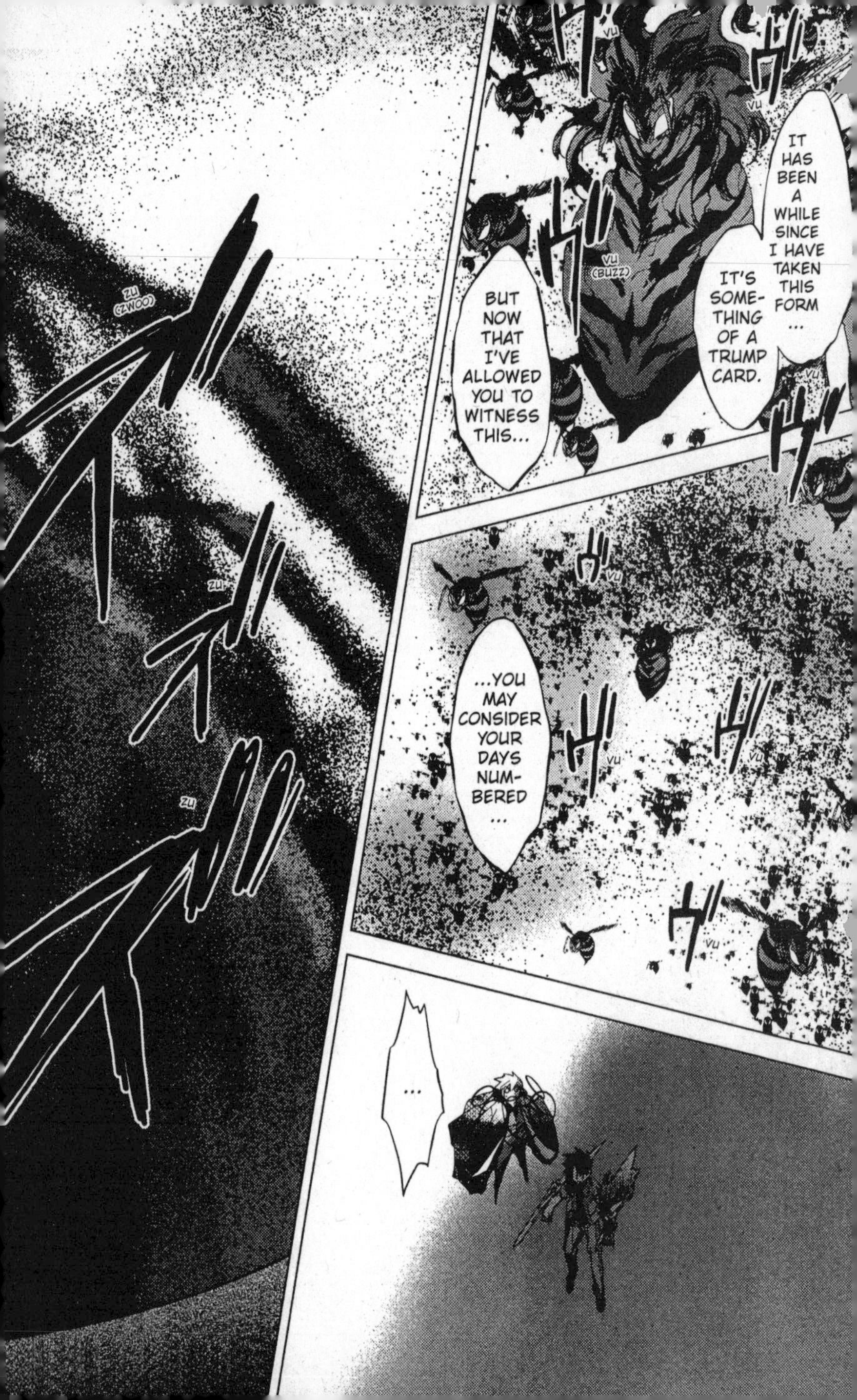
VU
VU (BUZZ)
IT HAS BEEN A WHILE SINCE I HAVE TAKEN THIS FORM...
IT'S SOMETHING OF A TRUMP CARD.
BUT NOW THAT I'VE ALLOWED YOU TO WITNESS THIS...
VU
...YOU MAY CONSIDER YOUR DAYS NUMBERED...
VU
...
ZU (ZWOO)
ZU
ZU

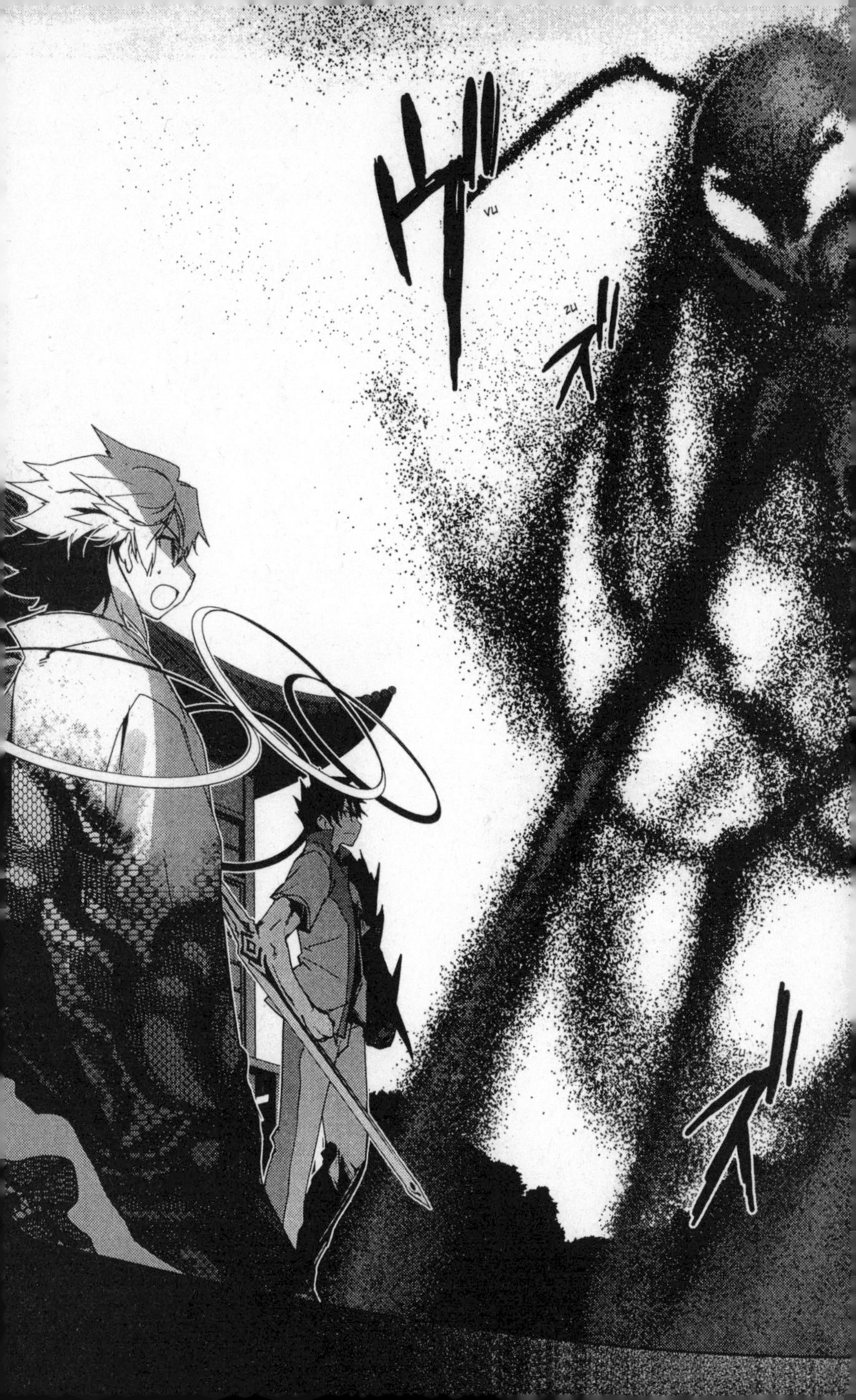
vu
zu
zu

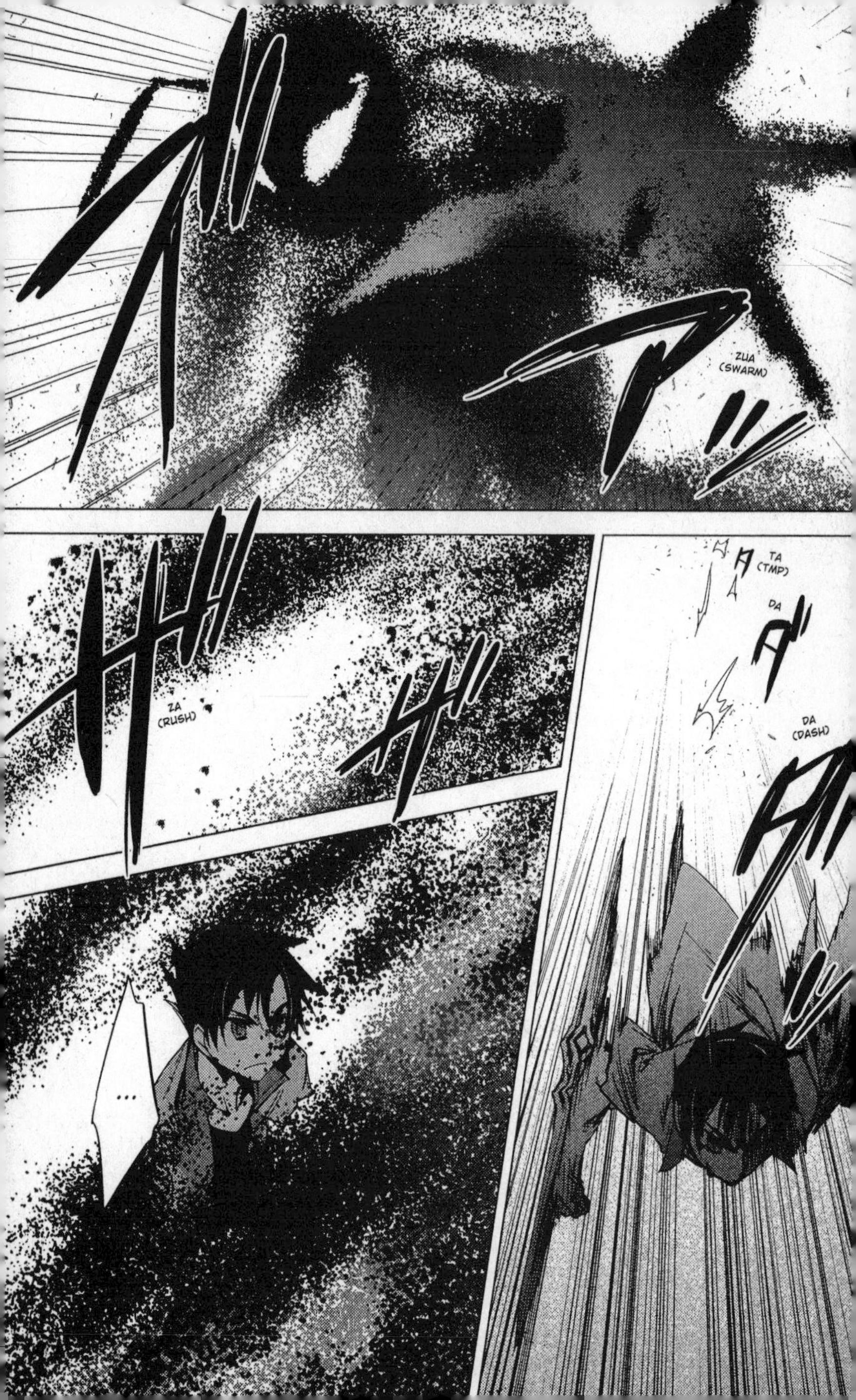
ZUA (SWARM)
TA (TMP)
DA
DA (DASH)
ZA (RUSH)
ZA
...

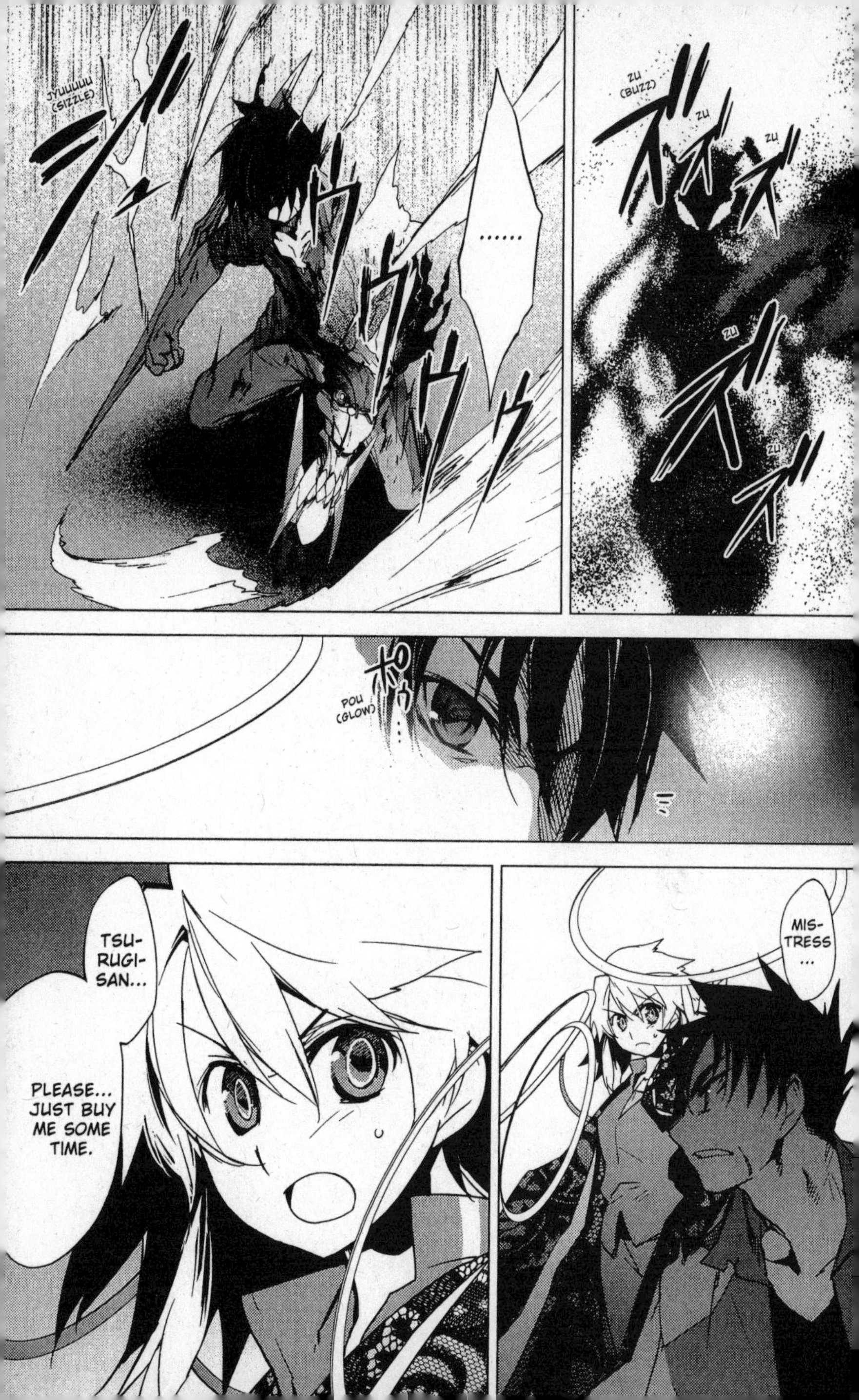
ZU (BUZZ)
ZU
ZU
ZU
ZU
JYUUUUU (SIZZLE)
......
POU (GLOW)
MIS-TRESS...
TSURUGI-SAN...
PLEASE... JUST BUY ME SOME TIME.

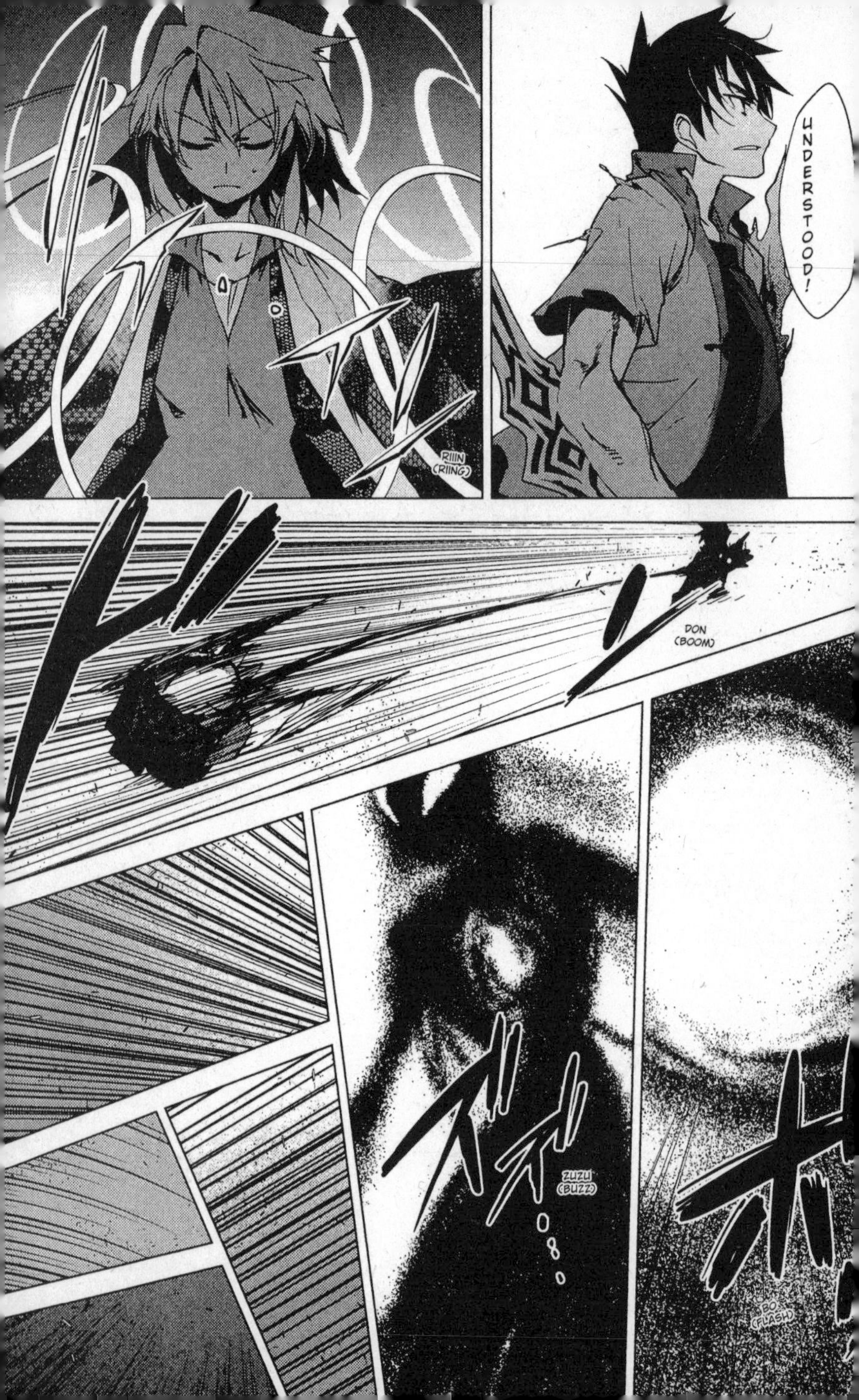
UNDERSTOOD!
RIIN (RIING)
DON (BOOM)
BO (FLASH)
ZUZU (BUZZ)

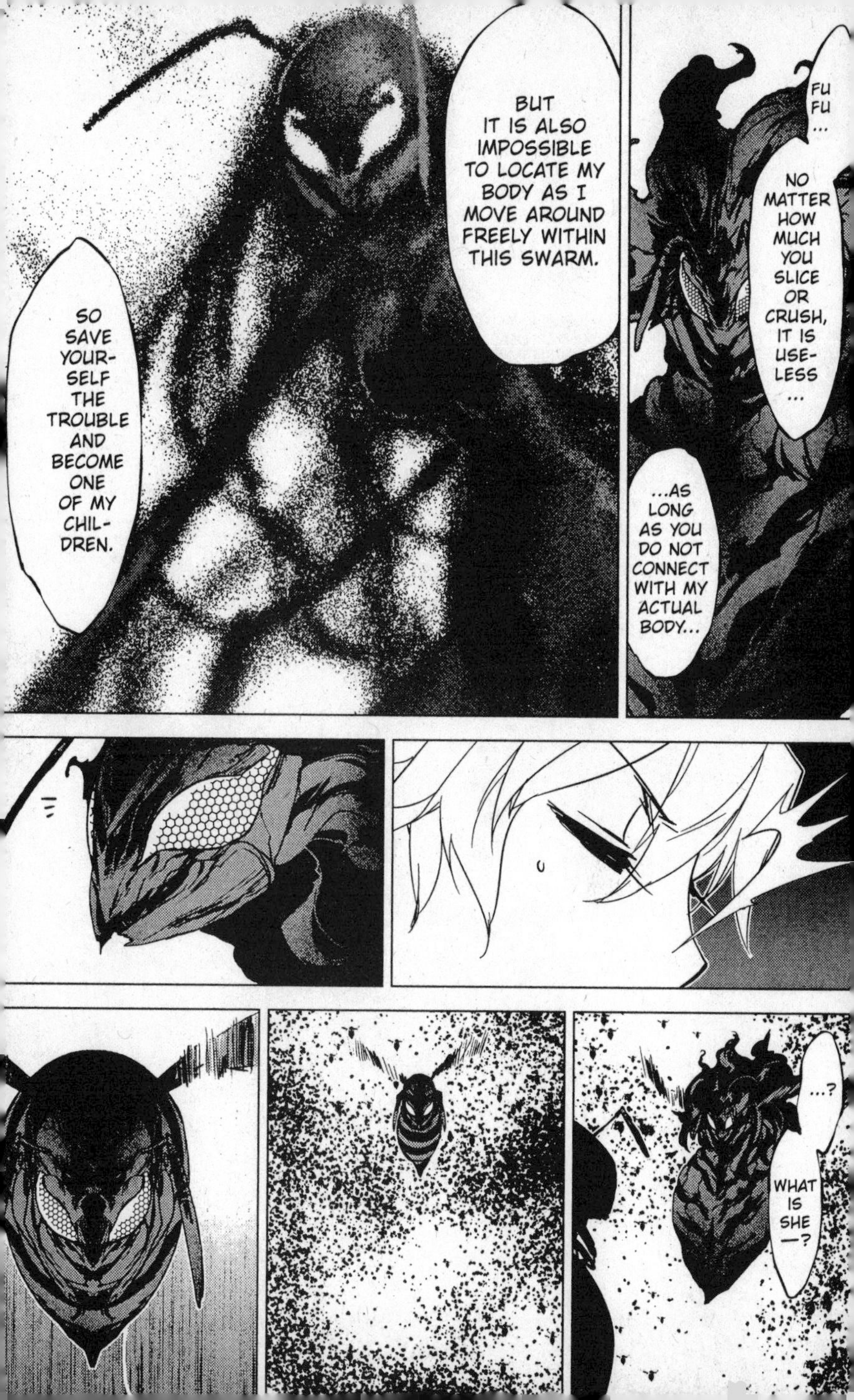
FU FU ...
NO MATTER HOW MUCH YOU SLICE OR CRUSH, IT IS USELESS ...
...AS LONG AS YOU DO NOT CONNECT WITH MY ACTUAL BODY...
BUT IT IS ALSO IMPOSSIBLE TO LOCATE MY BODY AS I MOVE AROUND FREELY WITHIN THIS SWARM.
SO SAVE YOURSELF THE TROUBLE AND BECOME ONE OF MY CHILDREN.
...?
WHAT IS SHE—?

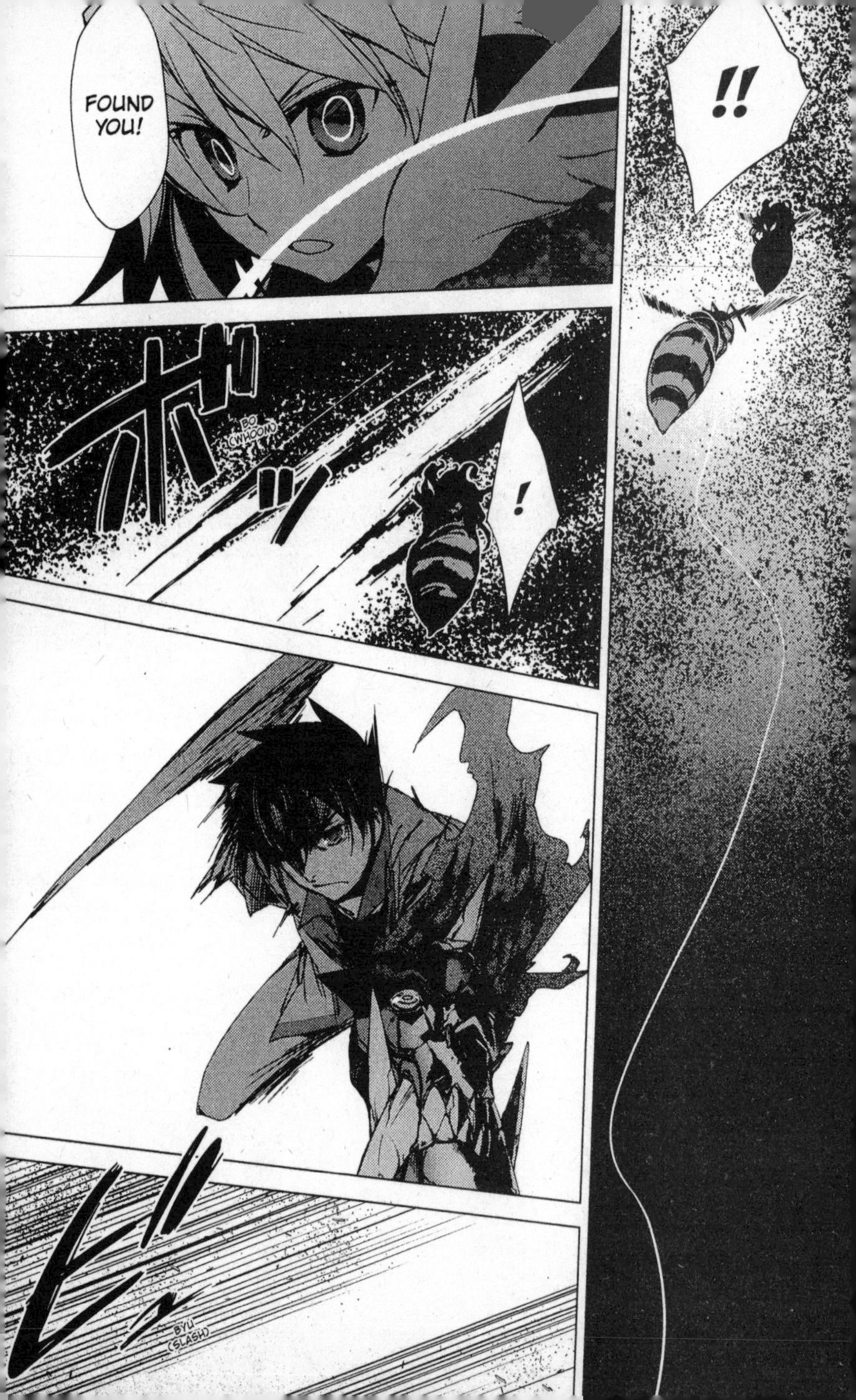
!!
FOUND YOU!
BO (WHOOM)
!
BYU (SLASH)

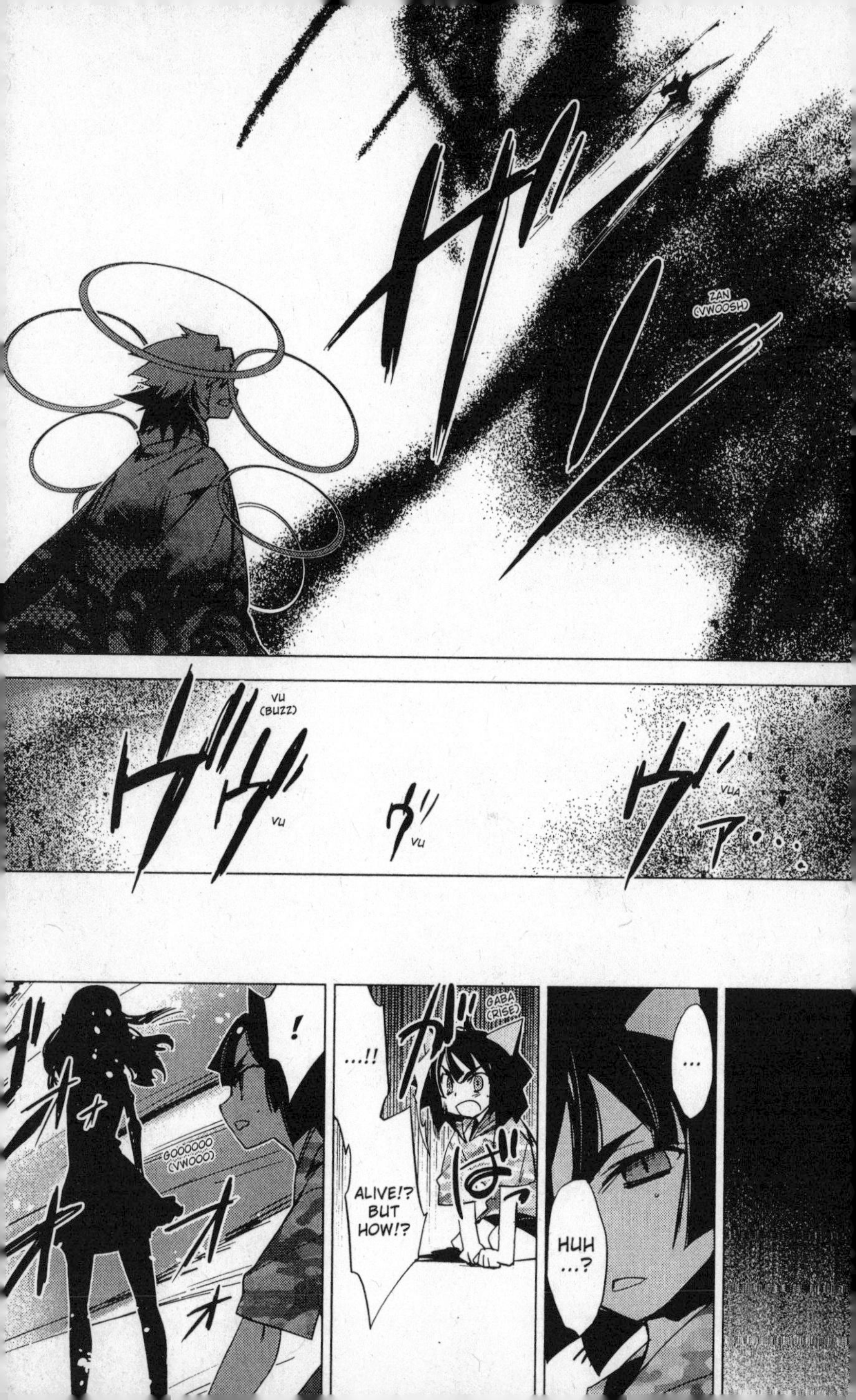
ZAN
(VWOOSH)
VUA
VU
VU
(BUZZ)
VU
...
HUH
...?
GABA
(RISE)
...!!
ALIVE!? BUT HOW!?
!
GOOOOOO
(VWOOO)

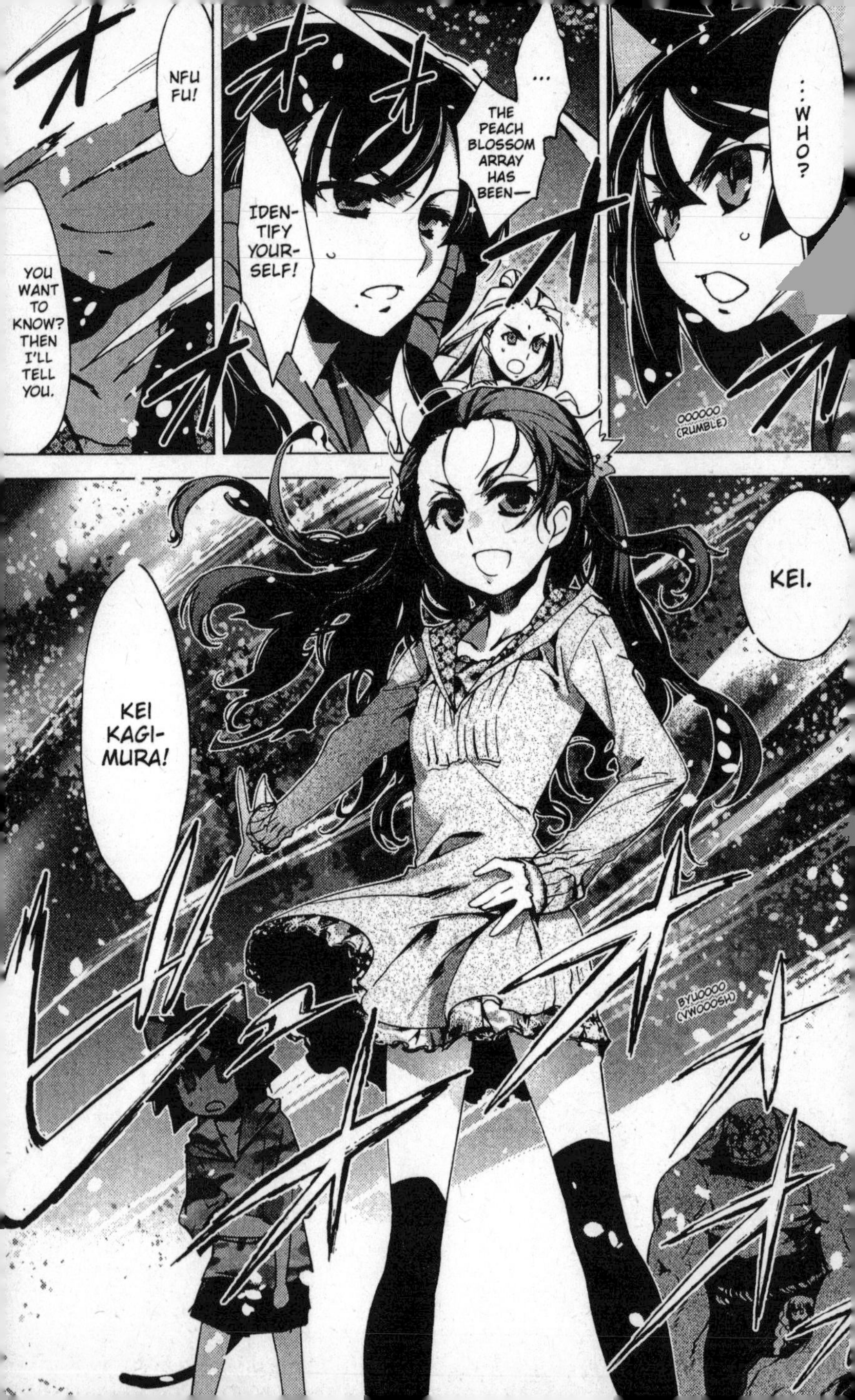
...WHO?
OOOOOO (RUMBLE)
...
THE PEACH BLOSSOM ARRAY HAS BEEN—
IDEN-TIFY YOUR-SELF!
NFU FU!
YOU WANT TO KNOW? THEN I'LL TELL YOU.
KEI.
KEI KAGI-MURA!
BYUOOOO (VWOOOSH)

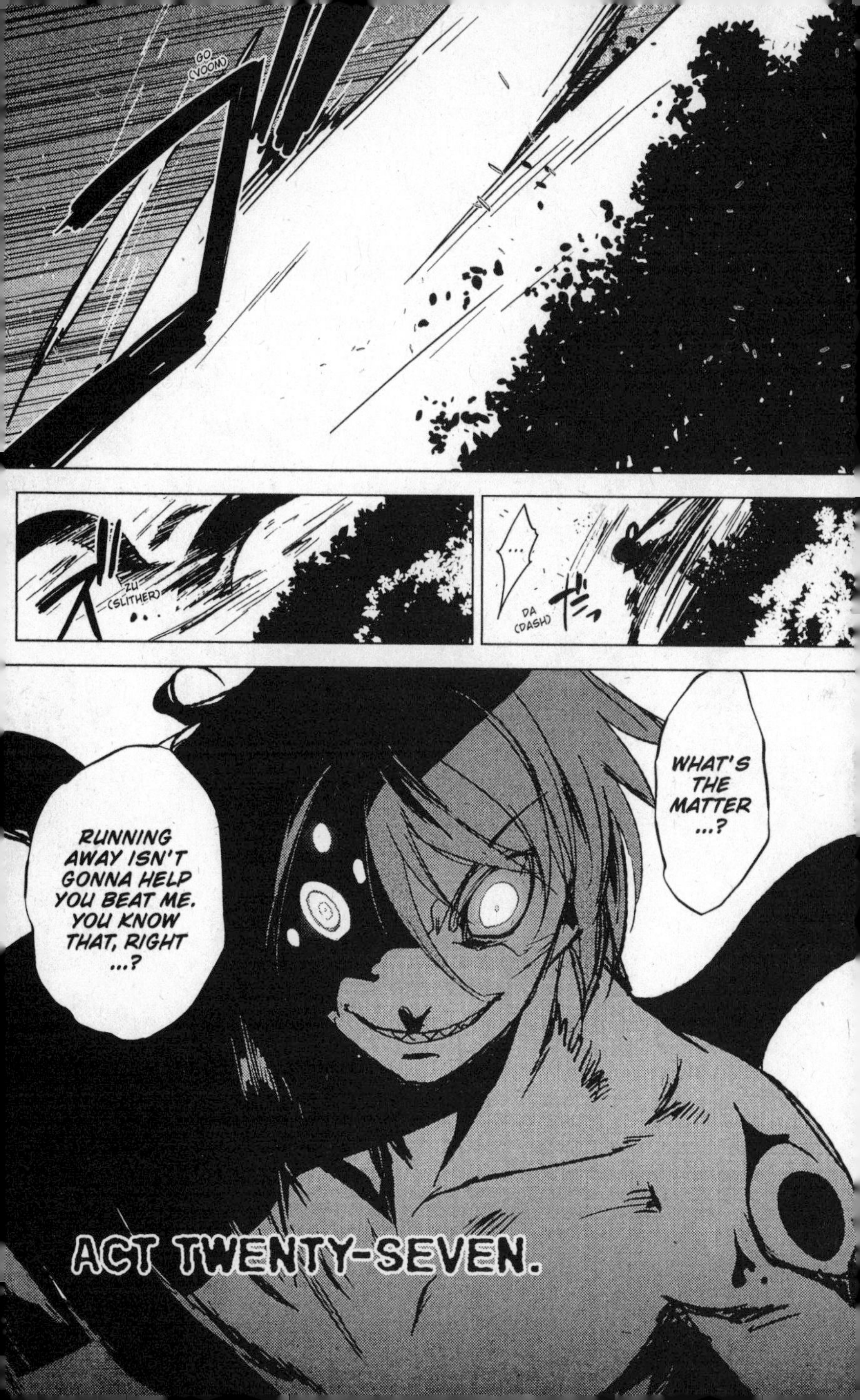
GO (VOOM)
...
DA (DASH)
ZU (SLITHER)
...
WHAT'S THE MATTER ...?
RUNNING AWAY ISN'T GONNA HELP YOU BEAT ME. YOU KNOW THAT, RIGHT ...?
ACT TWENTY-SEVEN.

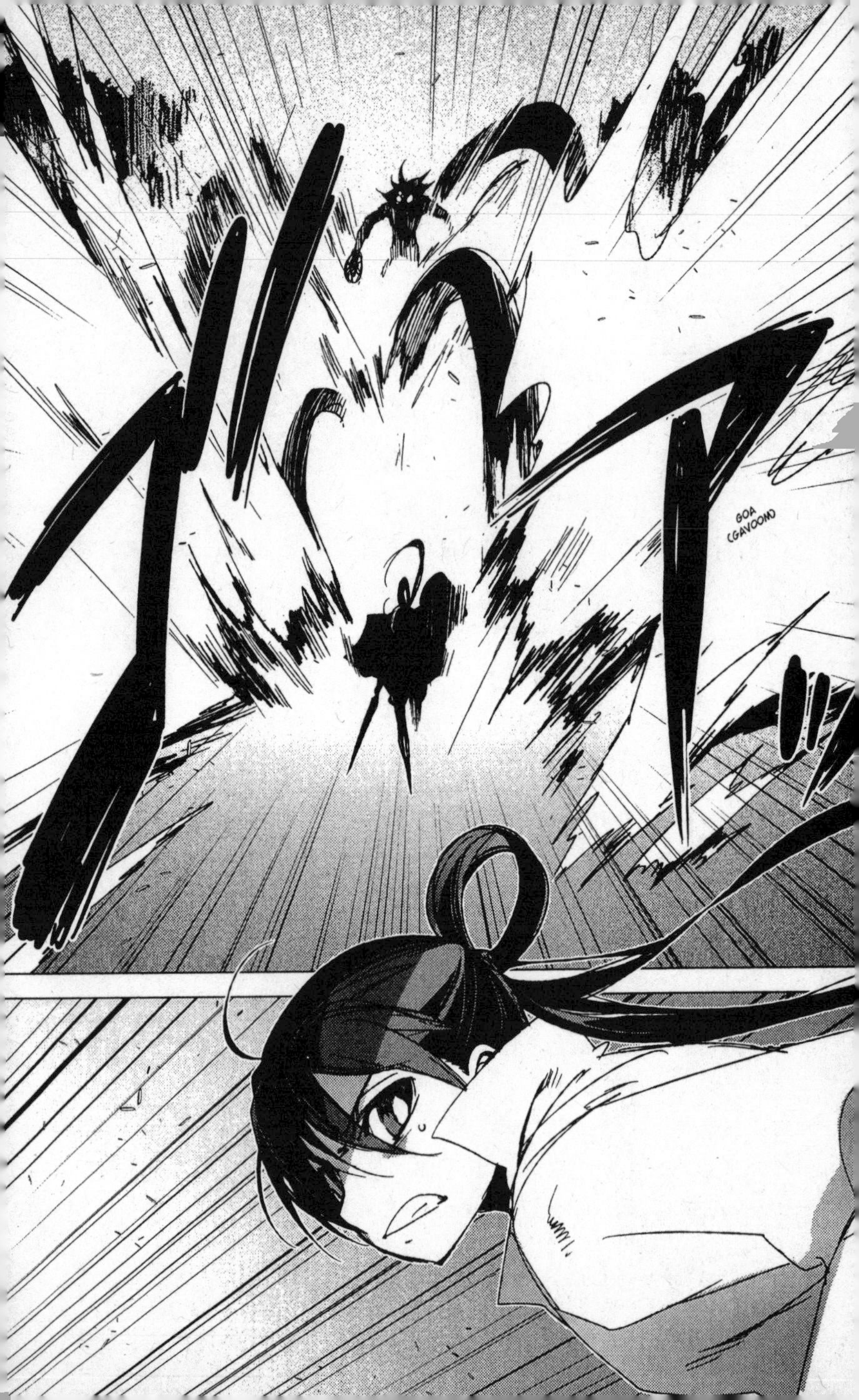
GOA
(GAVOOM)

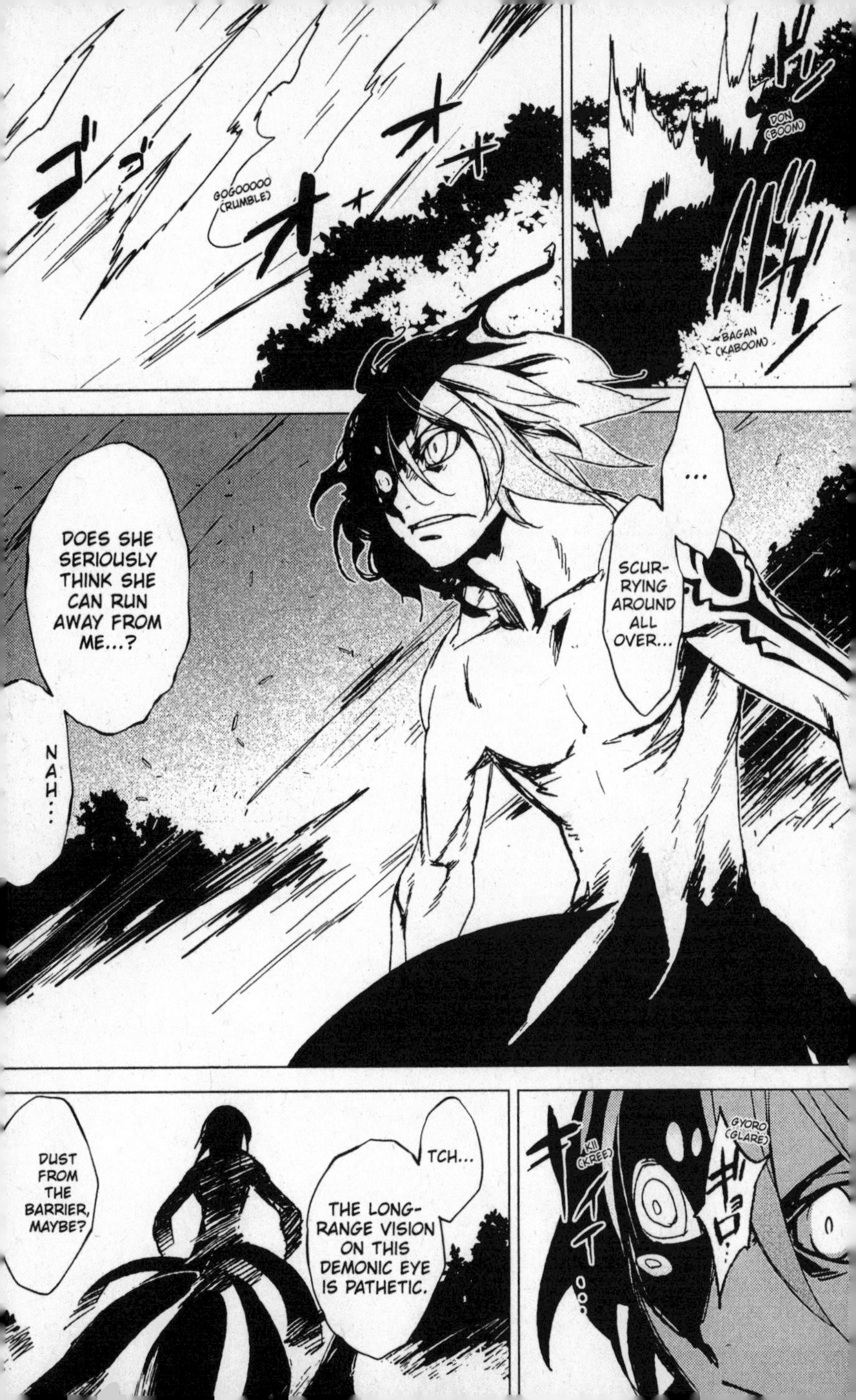
DON (BOOM)
BAGAN (KABOOM)
GOGOOOOO (RUMBLE)
...
SCUR-RYING AROUND ALL OVER...
DOES SHE SERIOUSLY THINK SHE CAN RUN AWAY FROM ME...?
NAH...
GYORO (GLARE)
KII (KREE)
TCH...
THE LONG-RANGE VISION ON THIS DEMONIC EYE IS PATHETIC.
DUST FROM THE BARRIER, MAYBE?

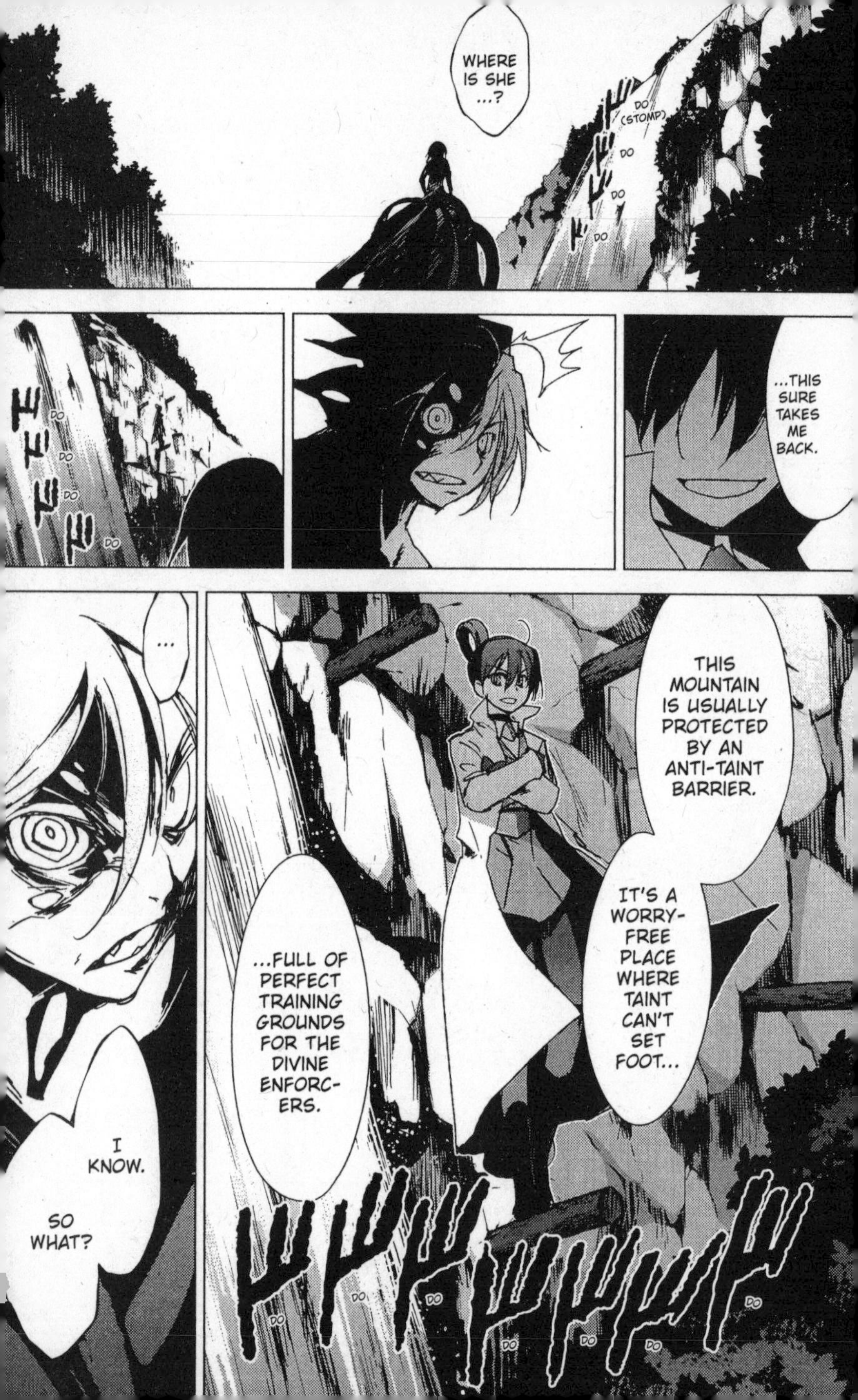
WHERE IS SHE ...?
DO (STOMP)
DO
DO
DO
...THIS SURE TAKES ME BACK.
DO
DO
DO
DO
THIS MOUNTAIN IS USUALLY PROTECTED BY AN ANTI-TAINT BARRIER.
IT'S A WORRY-FREE PLACE WHERE TAINT CAN'T SET FOOT...
...FULL OF PERFECT TRAINING GROUNDS FOR THE DIVINE ENFORCERS.
DO DO DO DO DO DO DO
...
I KNOW.
SO WHAT?

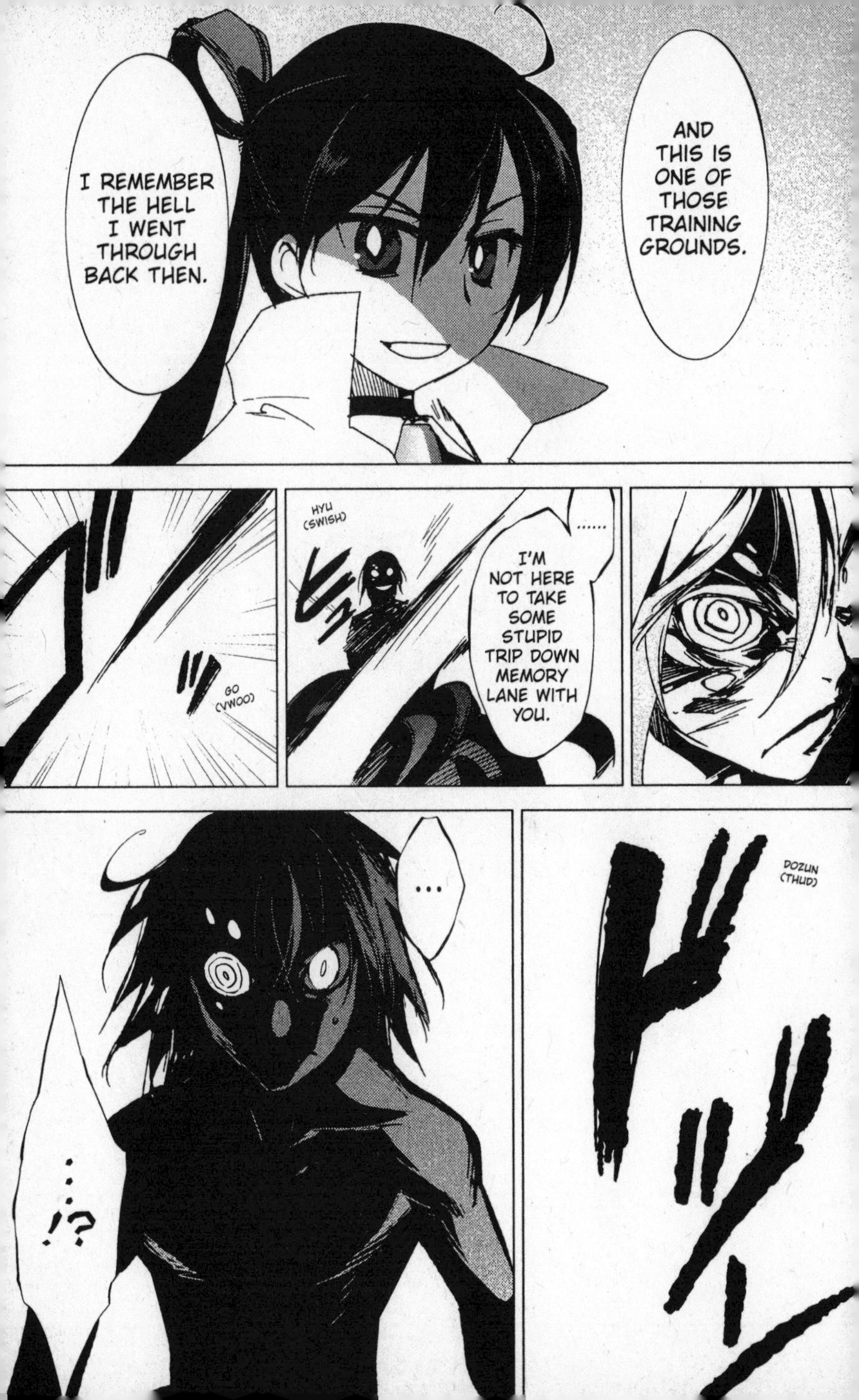
AND THIS IS ONE OF THOSE TRAINING GROUNDS.
I REMEMBER THE HELL I WENT THROUGH BACK THEN.
......
I'M NOT HERE TO TAKE SOME STUPID TRIP DOWN MEMORY LANE WITH YOU.
HYU (SWISH)
GO (VWOO)
DOZUN (THUD)
...
...!?

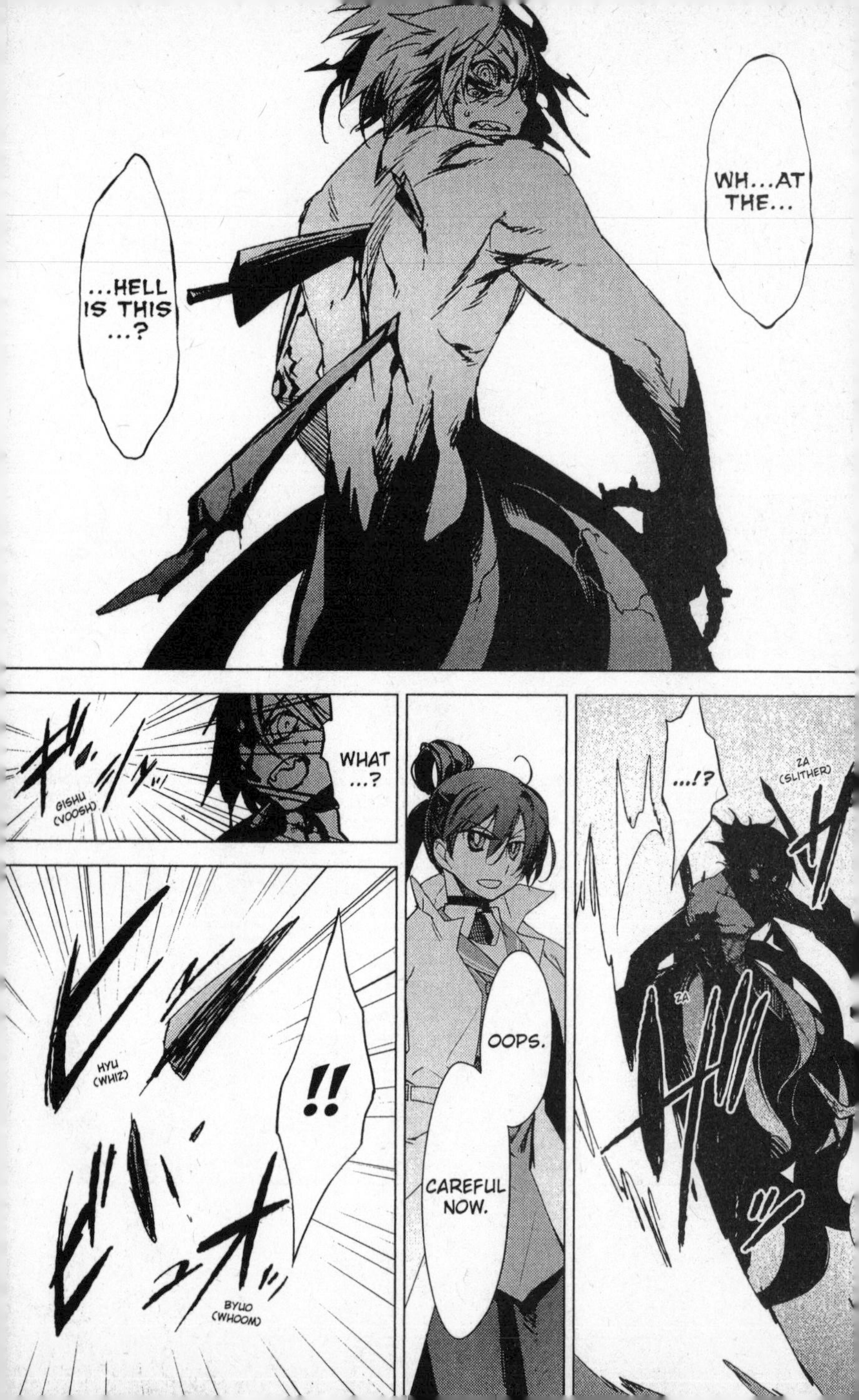
WH...AT THE...
...HELL IS THIS ...?
...!?
ZA (SLITHER)
ZA
OOPS.
CAREFUL NOW.
GISHU (VOOSH)
WHAT ...?
HYU (WHIZ)
!!
BYUO (WHOOM)

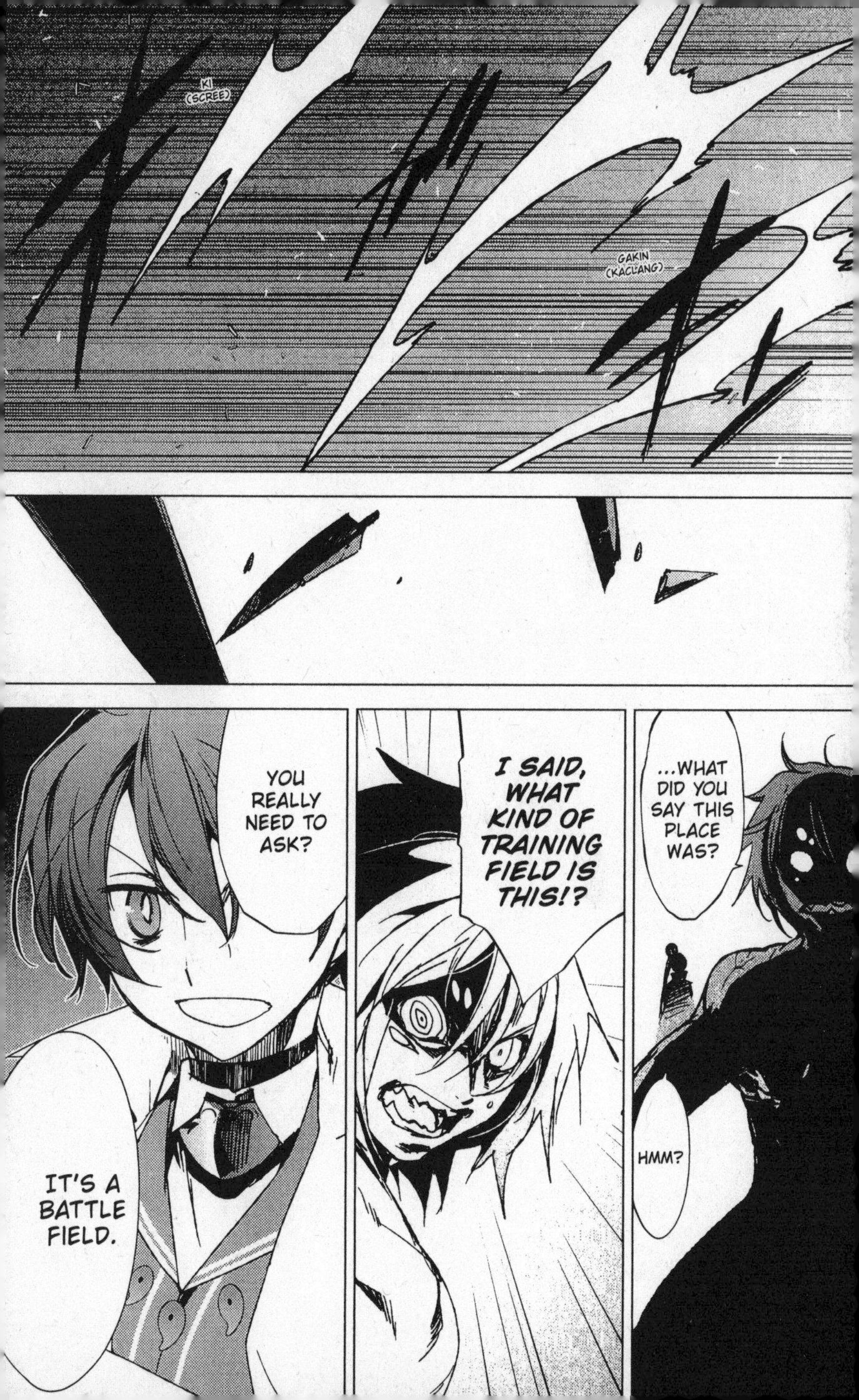
KI
(SCREE)
GAKIN
(KACLANG)
...WHAT DID YOU SAY THIS PLACE WAS?
HMM?
I SAID, WHAT KIND OF TRAINING FIELD IS THIS!?
YOU REALLY NEED TO ASK?
IT'S A BATTLE FIELD.

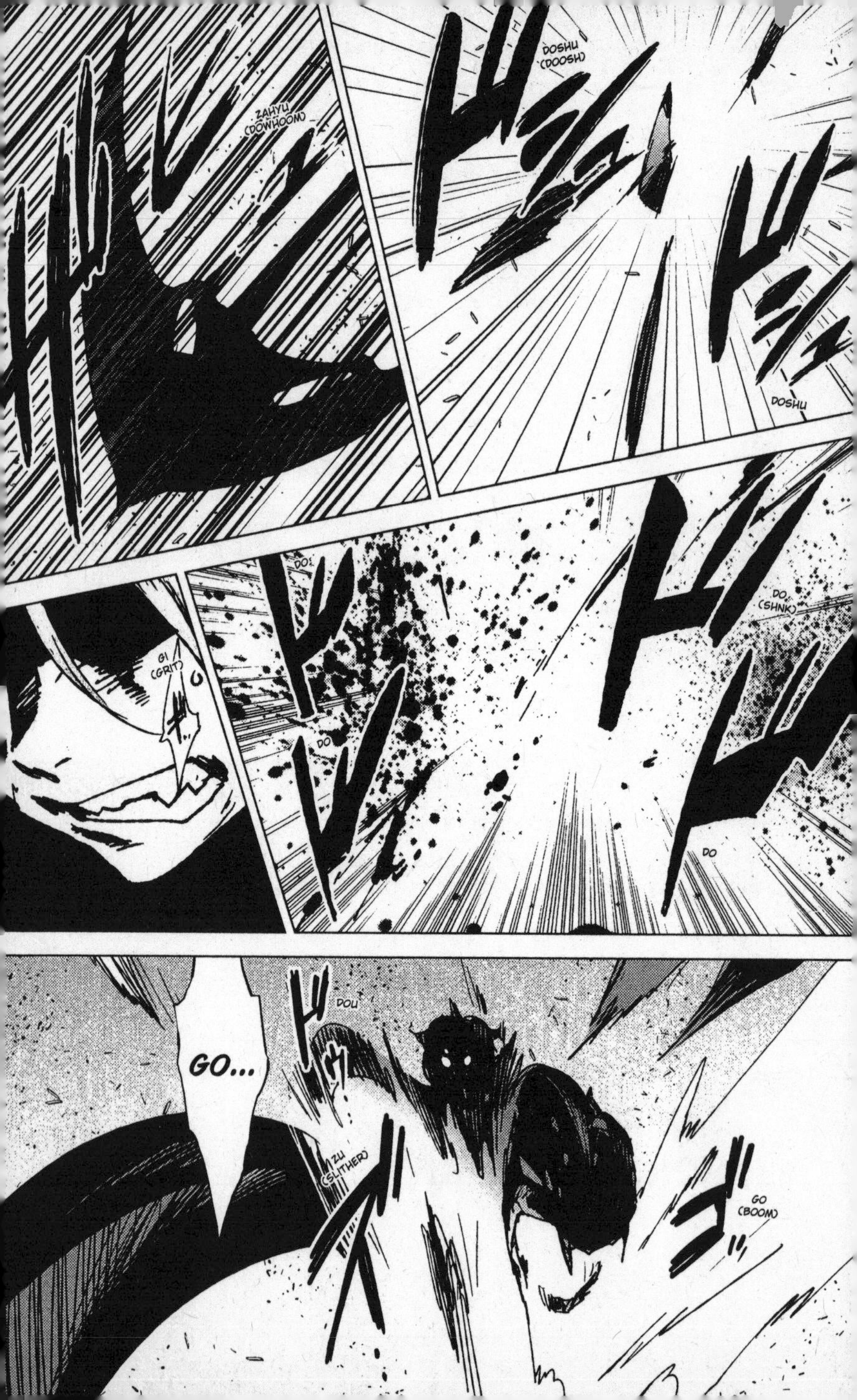
DOSHU (DOOSH)
DOSHU
ZAHYU (DOWHOOM)
DO (SHNK)
DO:
DO
DO
GI (GRIT)
DOU
GO...
GO (BOOM)
ZU (SLITHER)

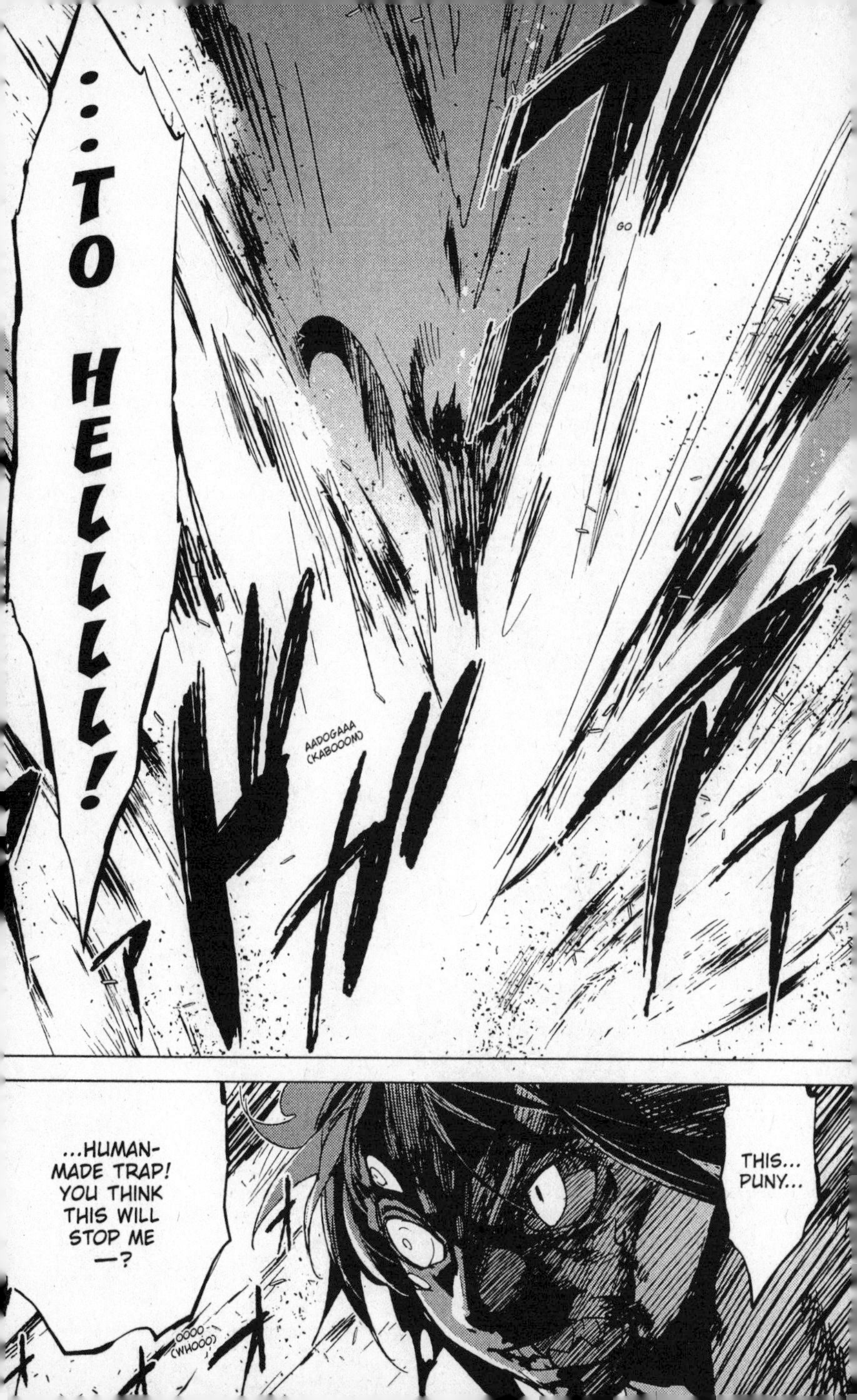
GO
AADOGAAA (KABOOOM)
...TO HELLLL!
THIS... PUNY...
...HUMAN-MADE TRAP! YOU THINK THIS WILL STOP ME—?
OOOO (WHOOO)

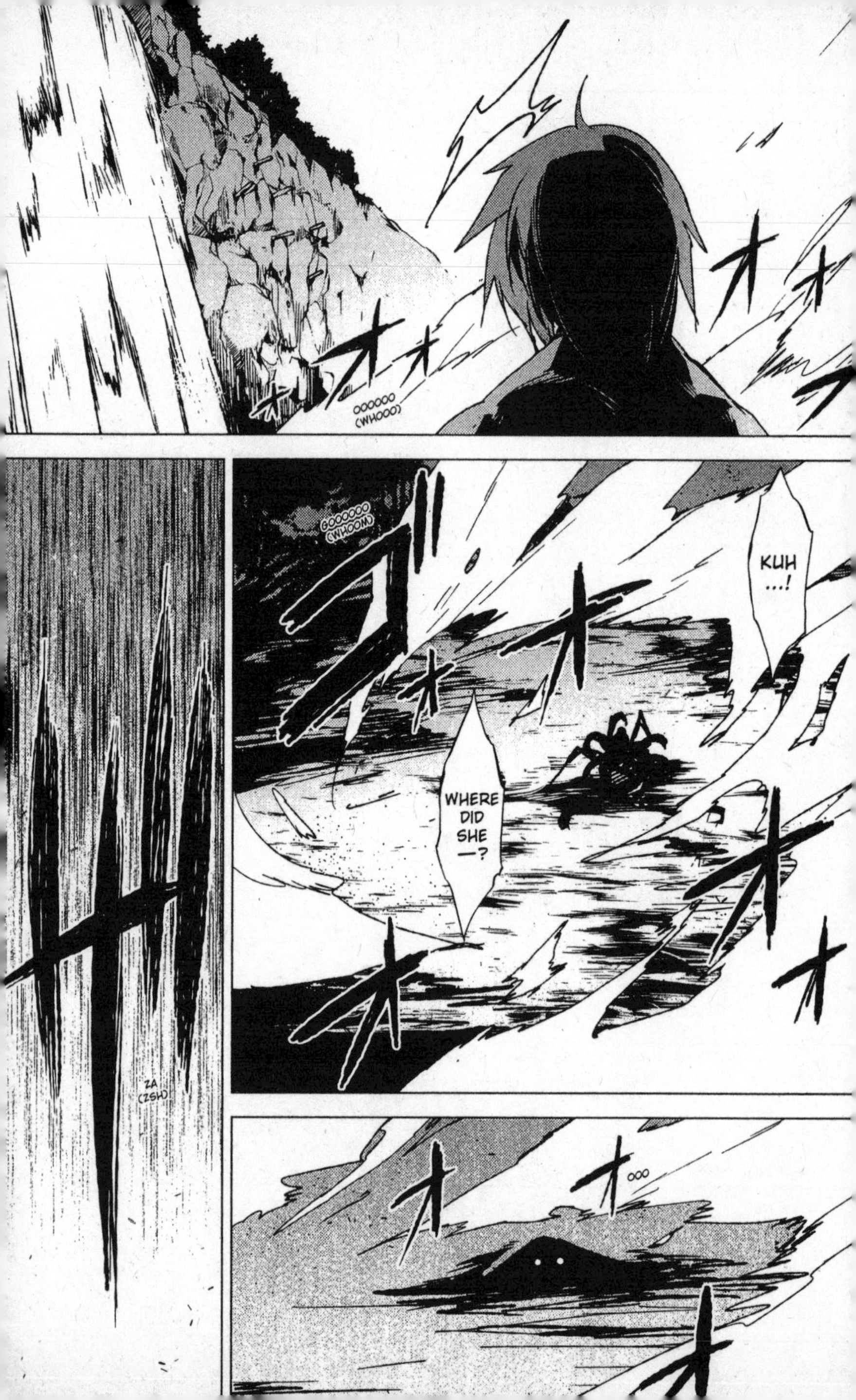
OOOOOO (WHOOO)
KUH ...!
GOOOOOO (WHOOM)
WHERE DID SHE—?
OOO
ZA (ZSH)

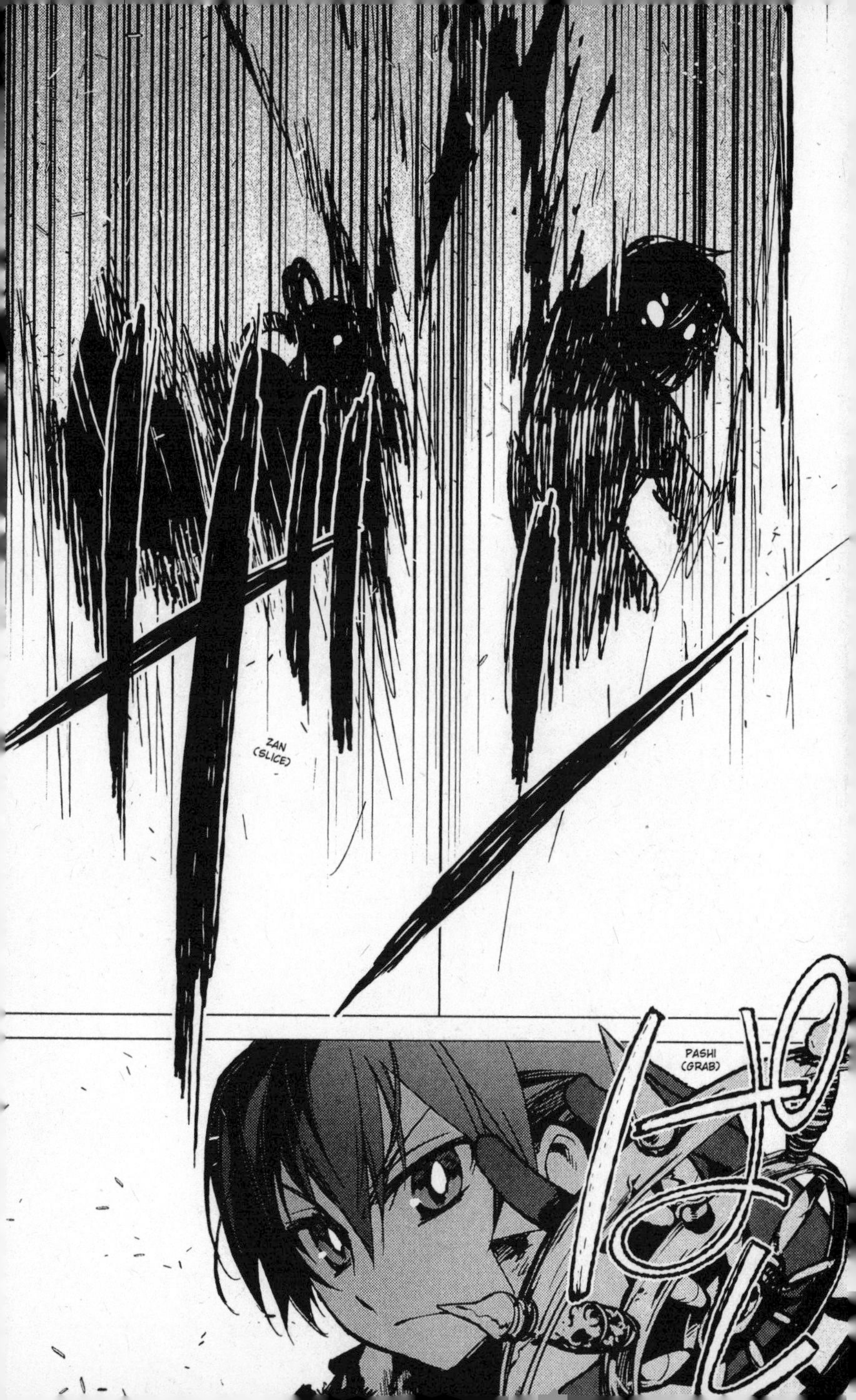
ZAN (SLICE)
PASHI (GRAB)

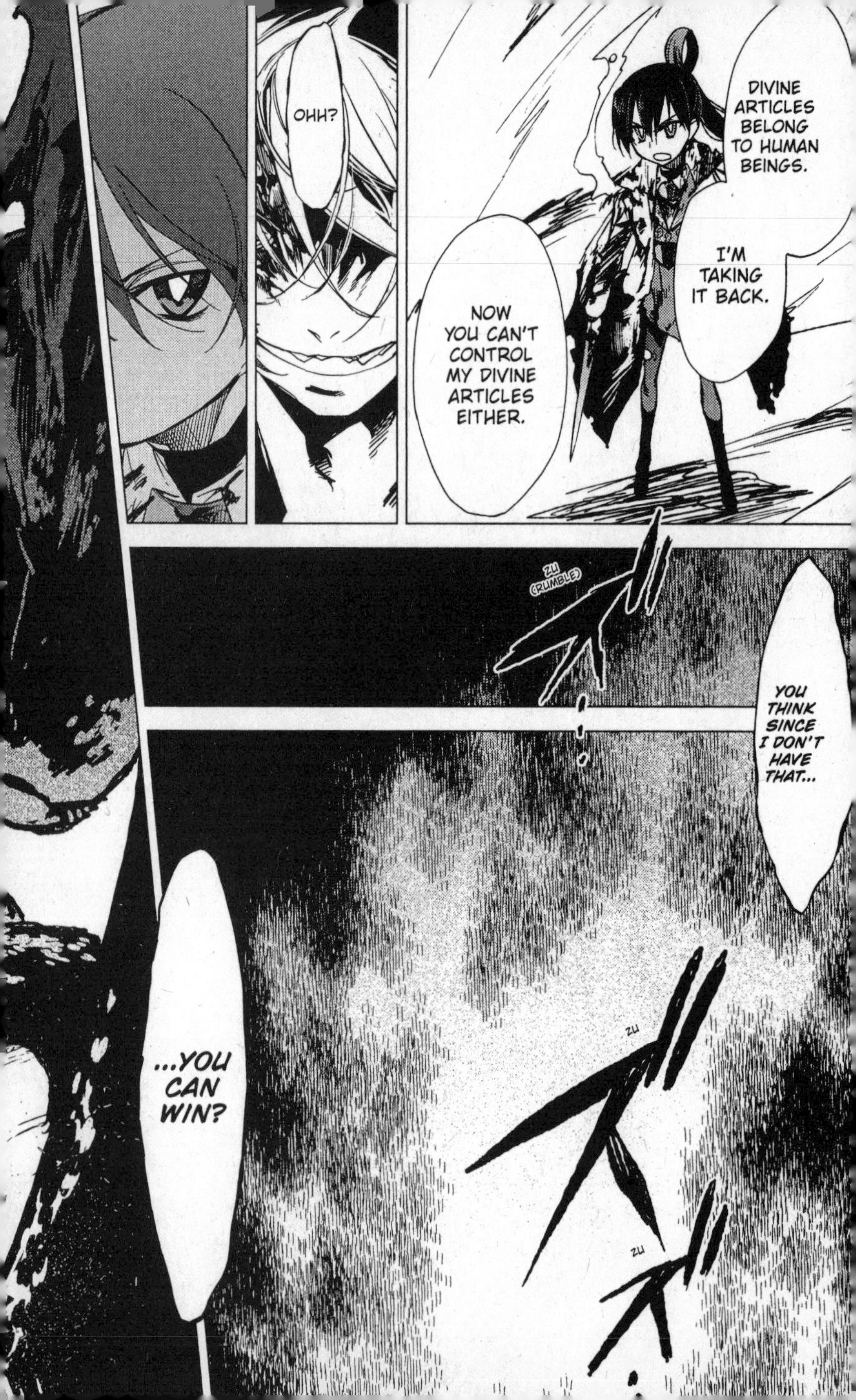
DIVINE ARTICLES BELONG TO HUMAN BEINGS.
I'M TAKING IT BACK.
NOW YOU CAN'T CONTROL MY DIVINE ARTICLES EITHER.
OHH?
ZU (RUMBLE)
YOU THINK SINCE I DON'T HAVE THAT...
ZU
ZU
...YOU CAN WIN?

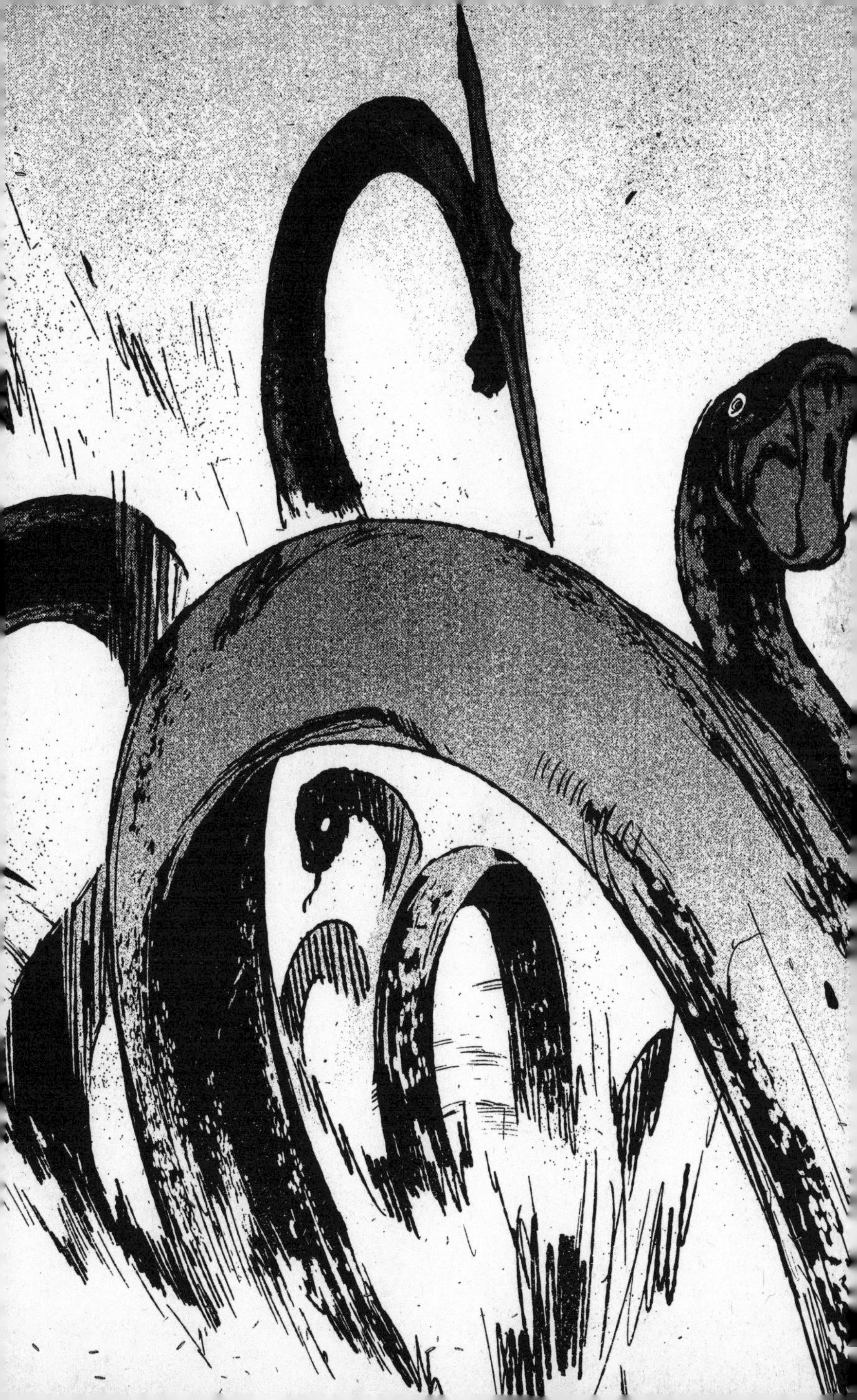

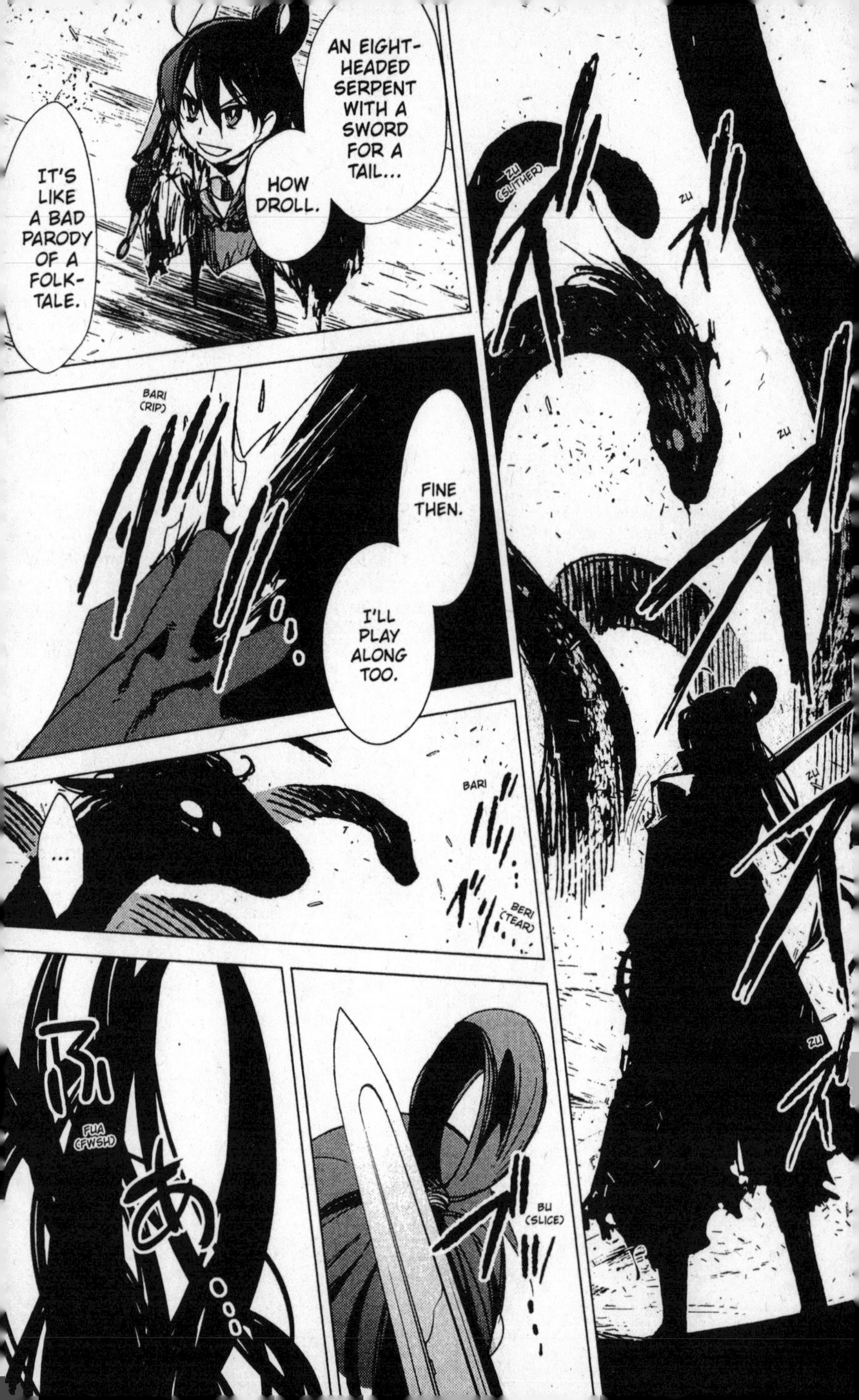
ZU (SLITHER)
ZU
ZU
ZU
ZU
AN EIGHT-HEADED SERPENT WITH A SWORD FOR A TAIL...
HOW DROLL.
IT'S LIKE A BAD PARODY OF A FOLK-TALE.
FINE THEN.
I'LL PLAY ALONG TOO.
BARI (RIP)
BARI
BERI (TEAR)
...
BU (SLICE)
FUA (FWSH)

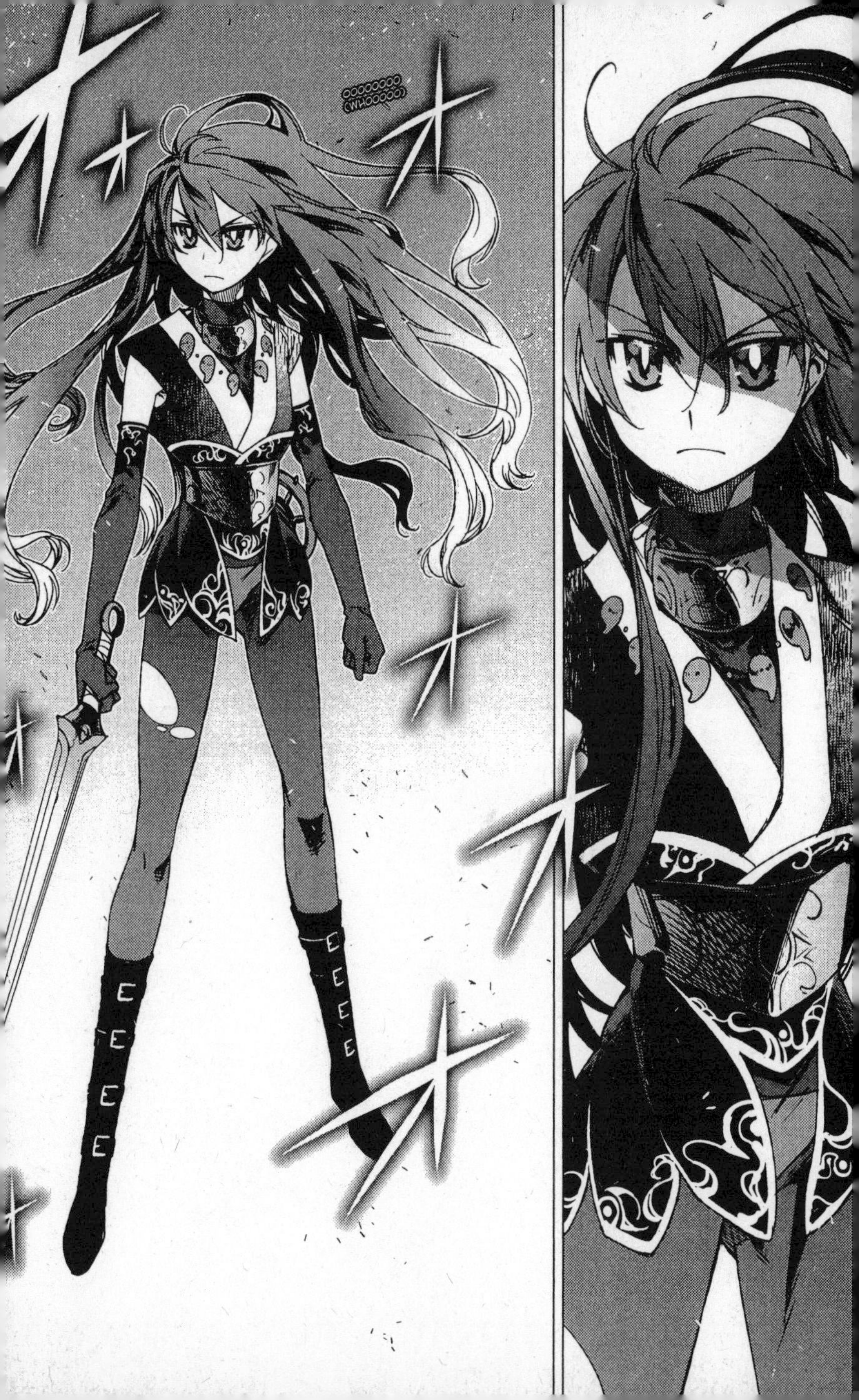
OOOOOOOO
(WHOOOOOO)

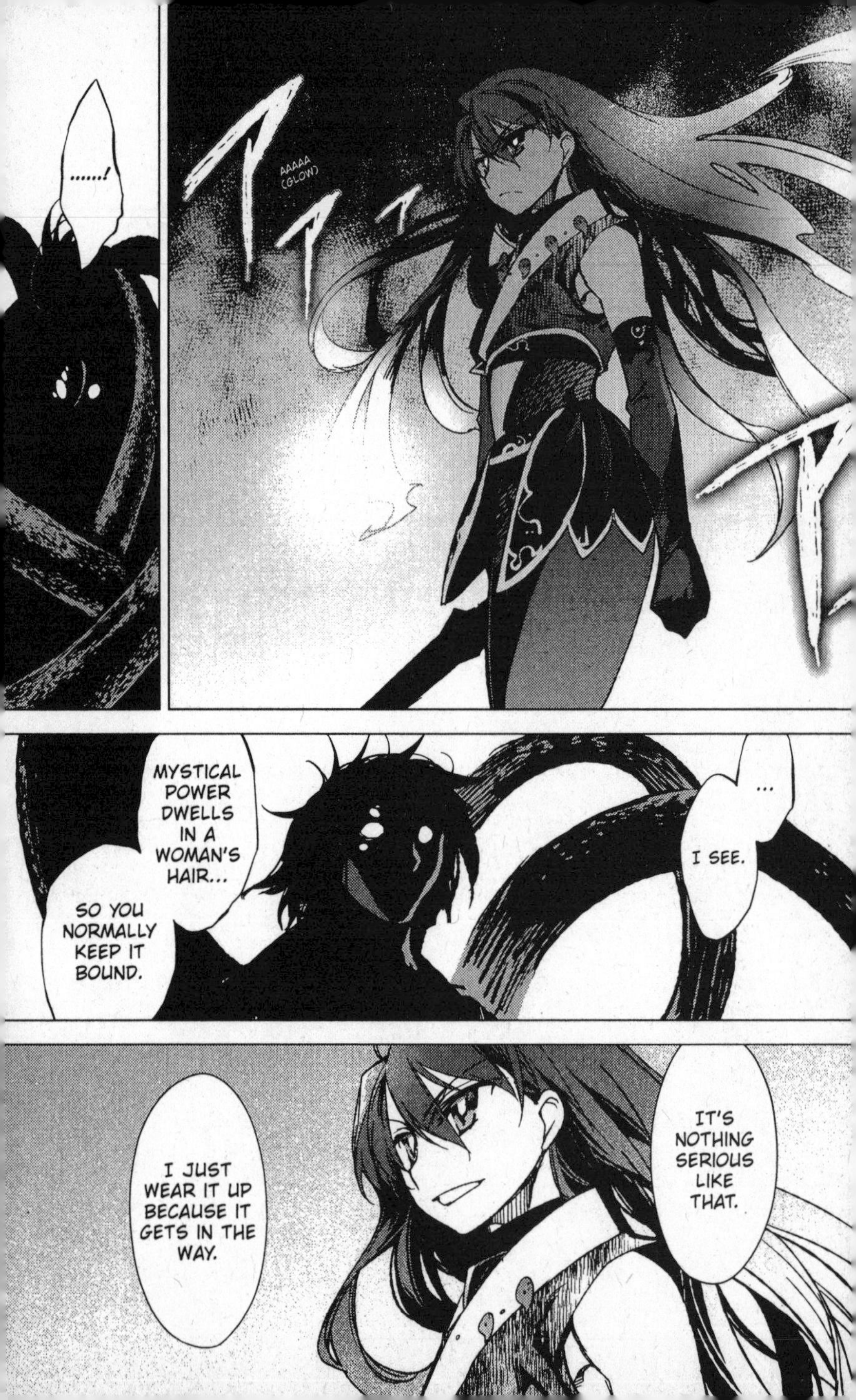
AAAAA (GLOW)
......!
...
I SEE.
MYSTICAL POWER DWELLS IN A WOMAN'S HAIR...
SO YOU NORMALLY KEEP IT BOUND.
IT'S NOTHING SERIOUS LIKE THAT.
I JUST WEAR IT UP BECAUSE IT GETS IN THE WAY.

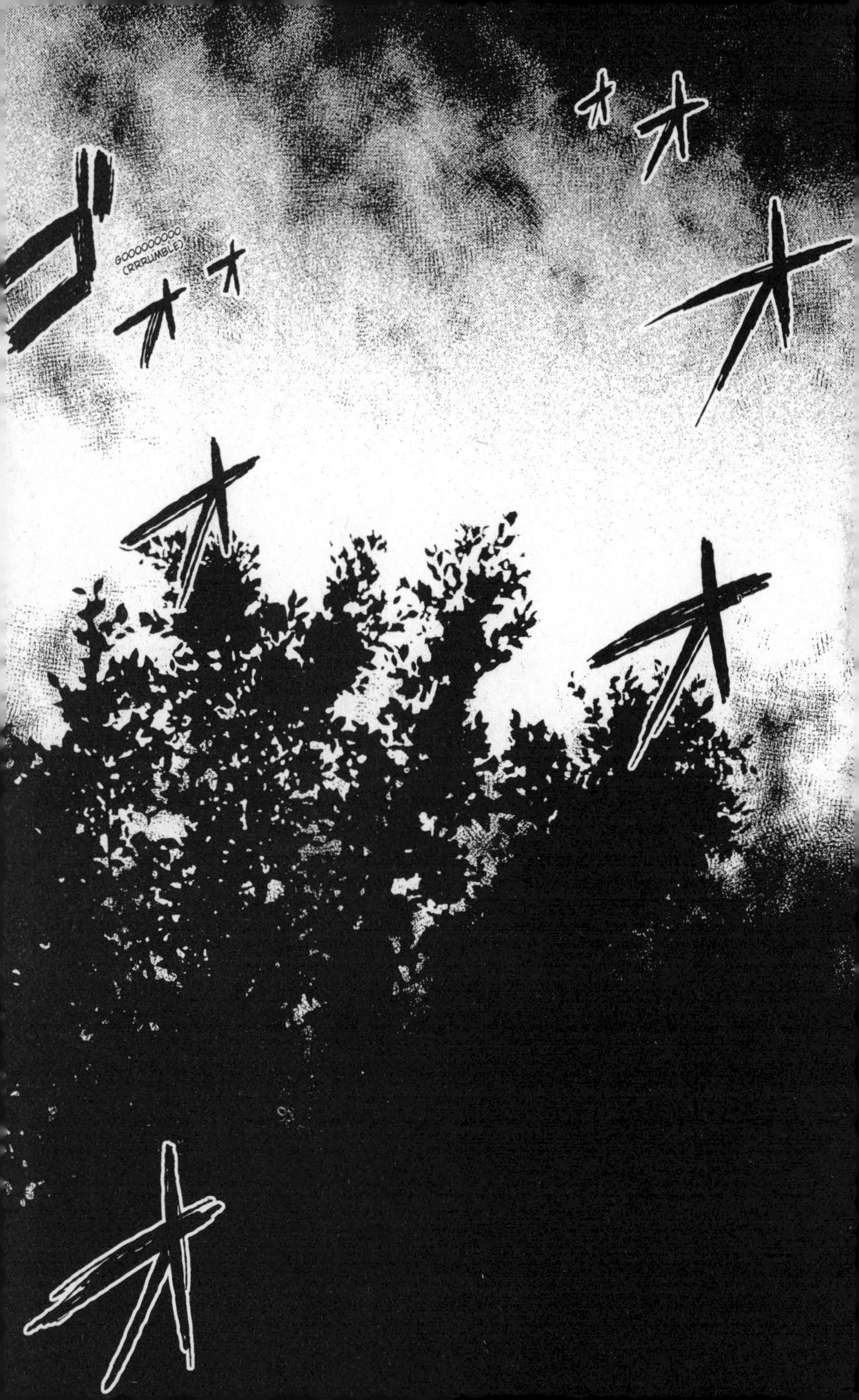
ゴオオオオオオオオオ
GOOOOOOOOO
(RRRUMBLE)

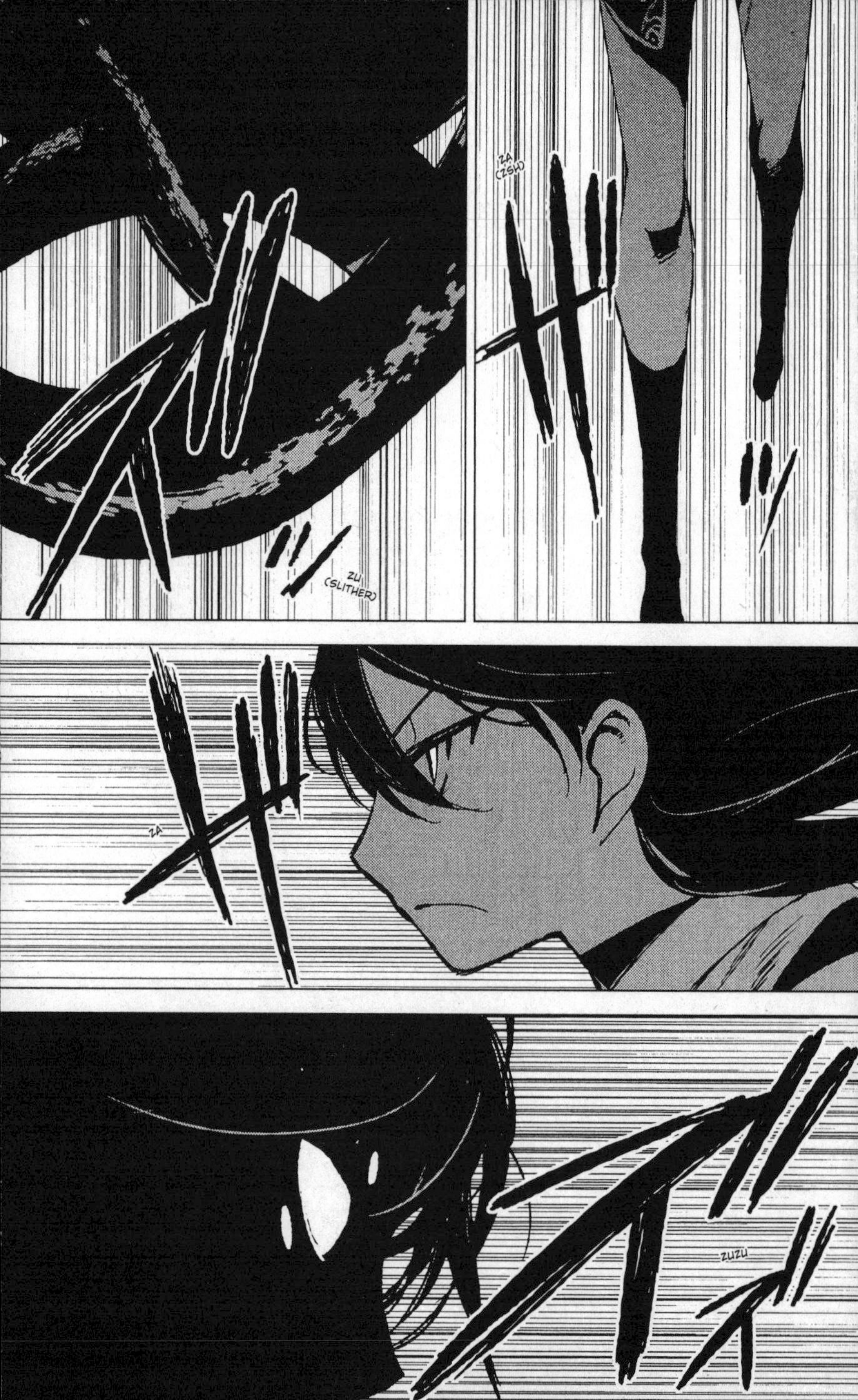
ZA
(ZSH)
ZU
(SLITHER)
ZA
ZUZU

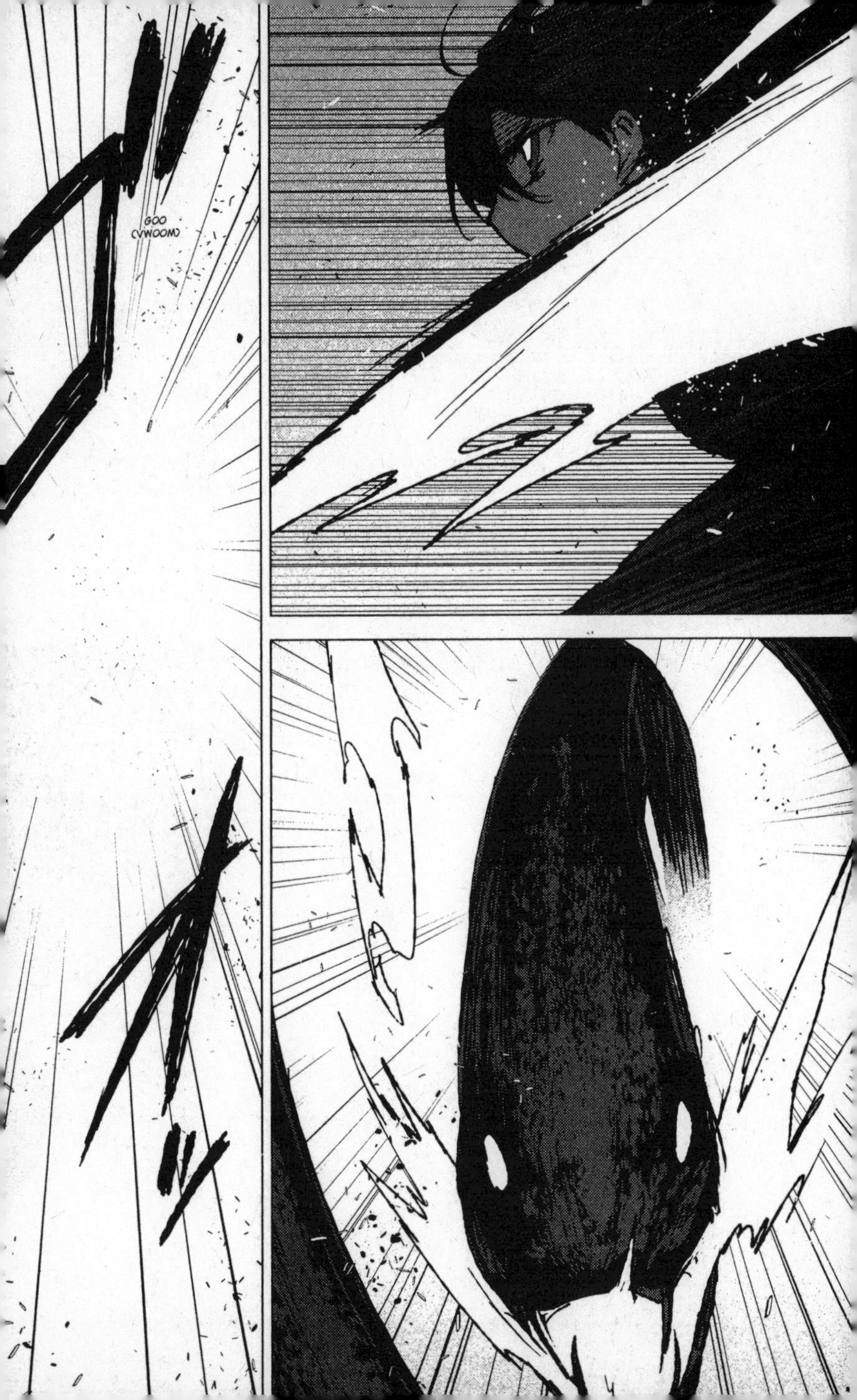
GOO
(VWOOM)

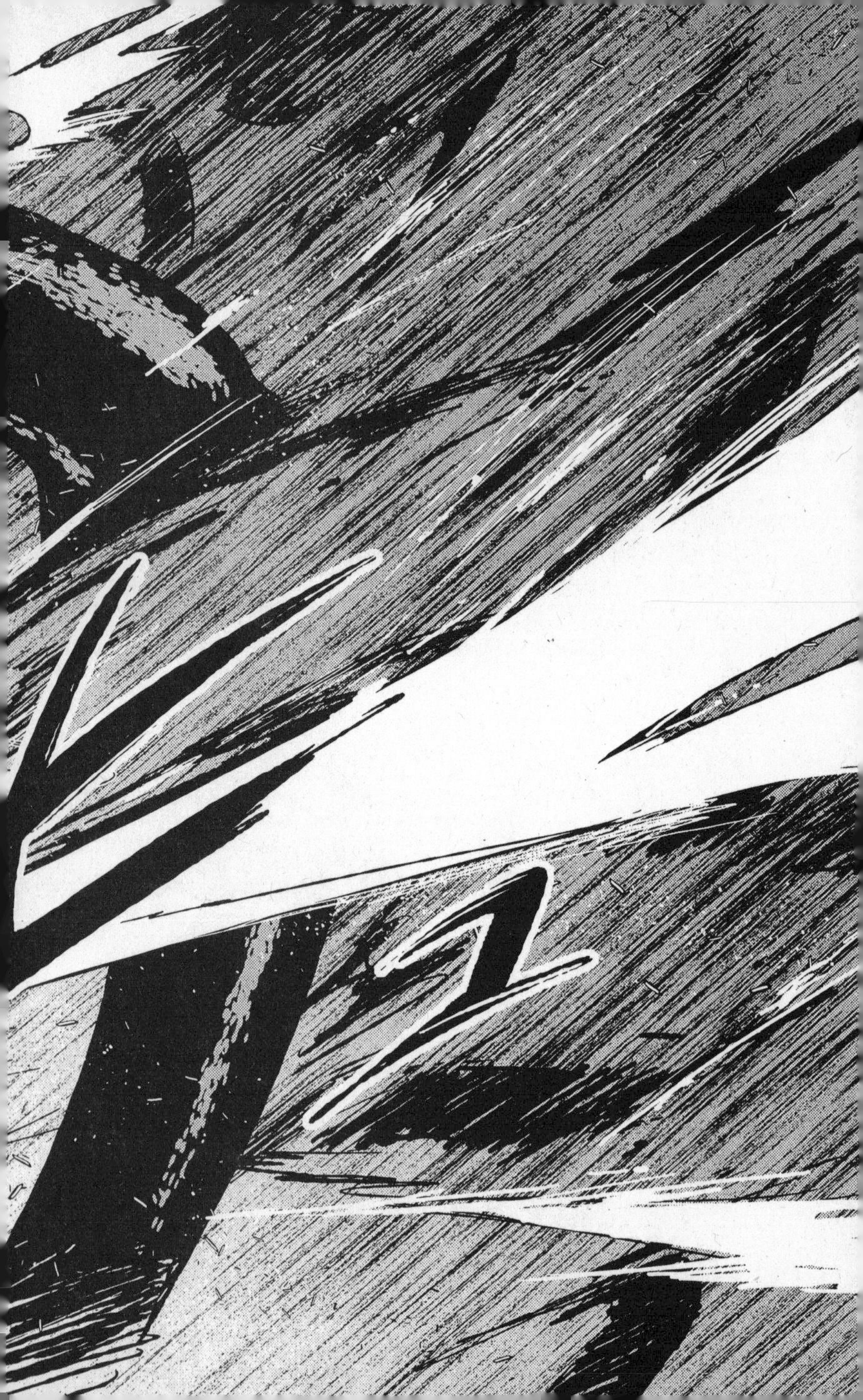

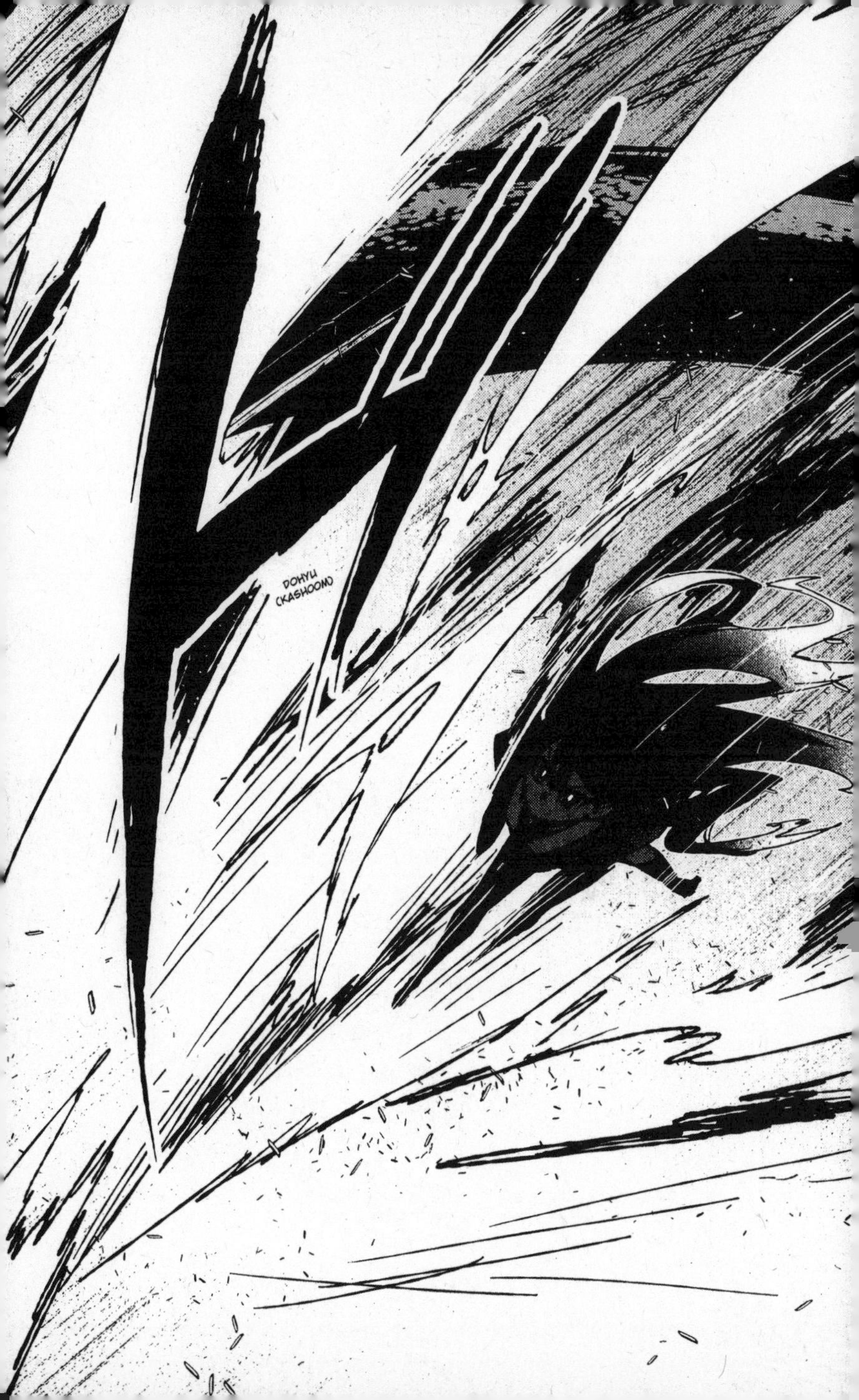
DOHYU
(KASHOOM)

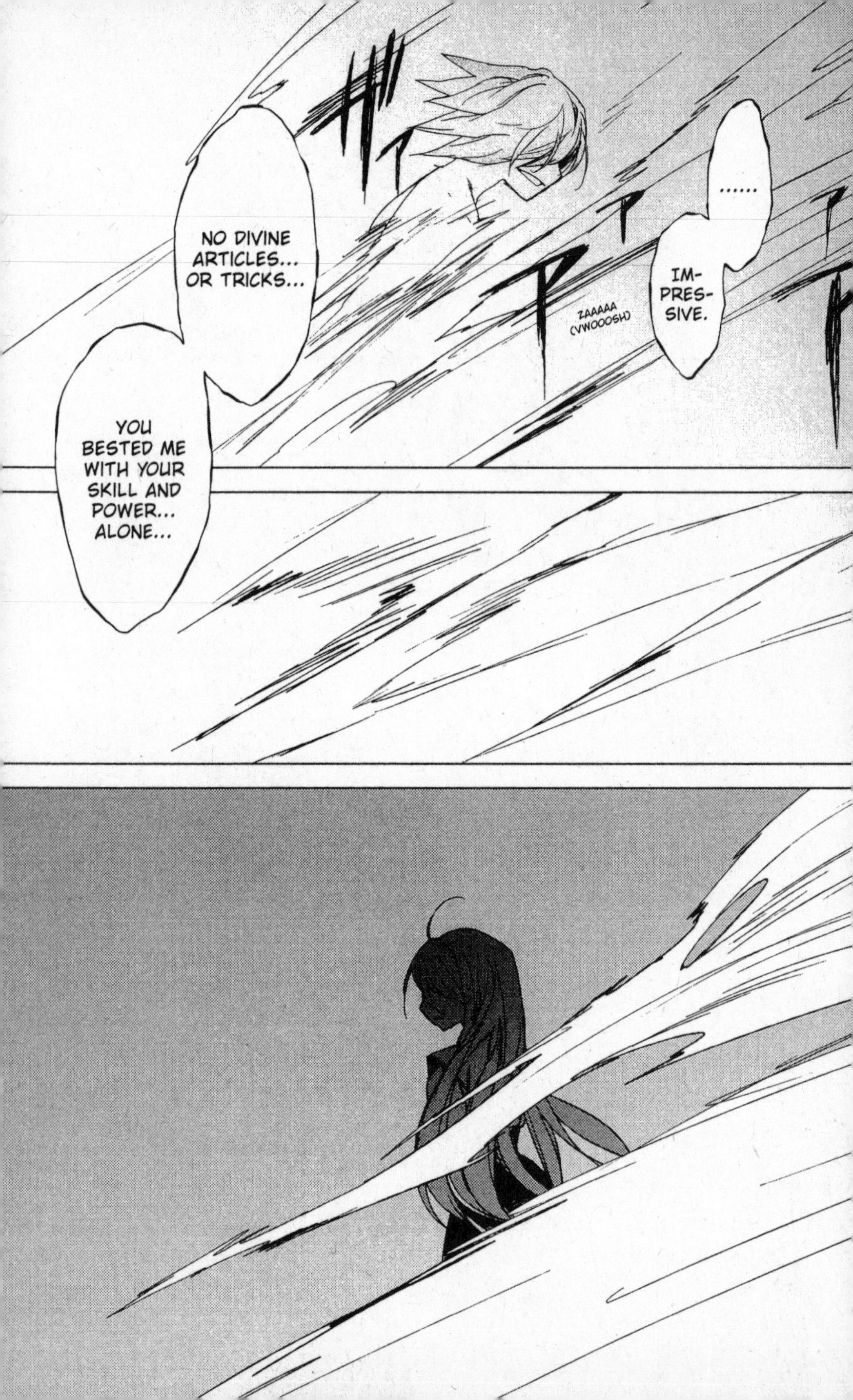
......
IM-PRES-SIVE.
ZAAAAA (VWOOOSH)
NO DIVINE ARTICLES... OR TRICKS...
YOU BESTED ME WITH YOUR SKILL AND POWER... ALONE...

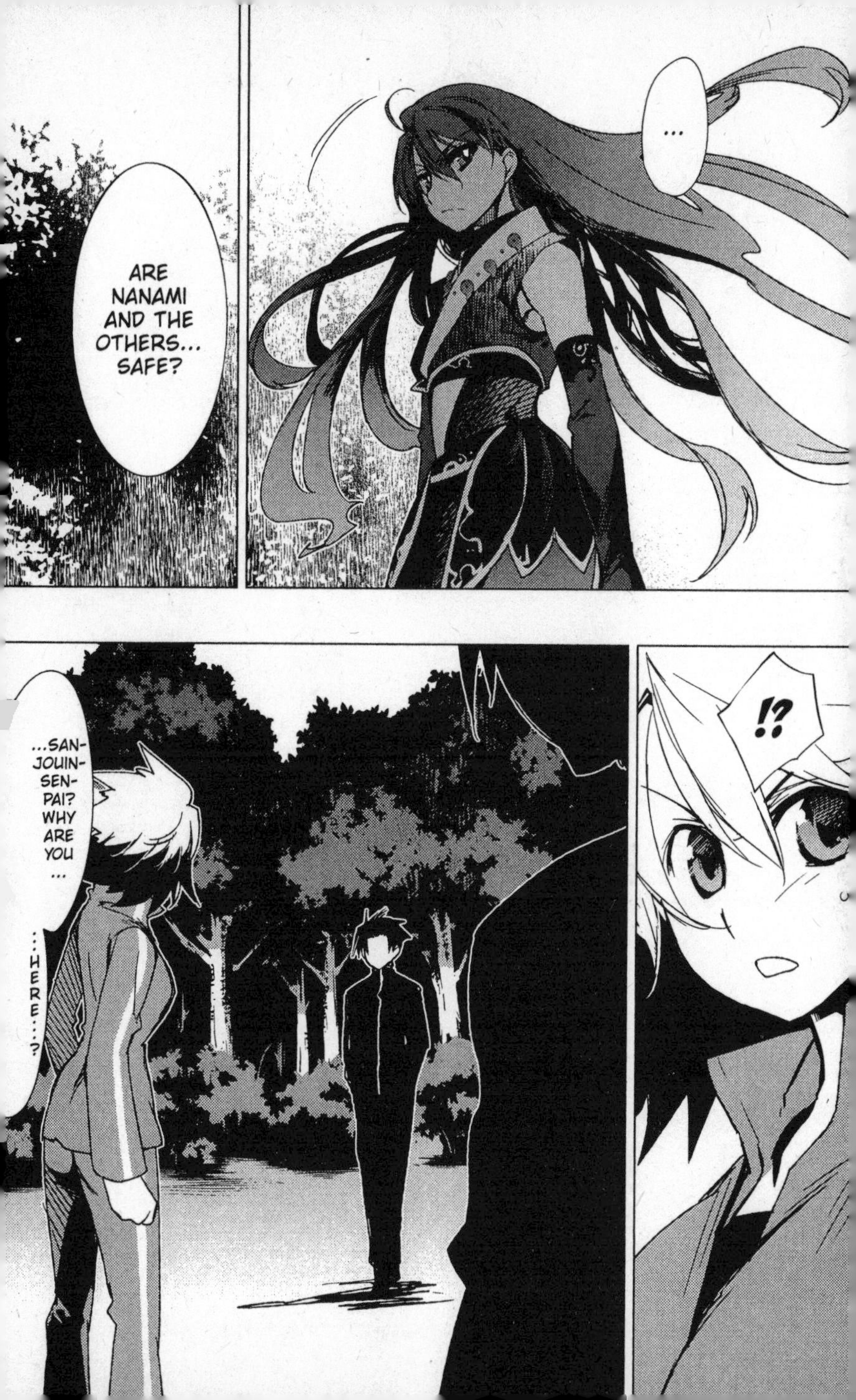
...
ARE NANAMI AND THE OTHERS... SAFE?
!?
...SANJOUIN-SENPAI? WHY ARE YOU ...
...HERE...?

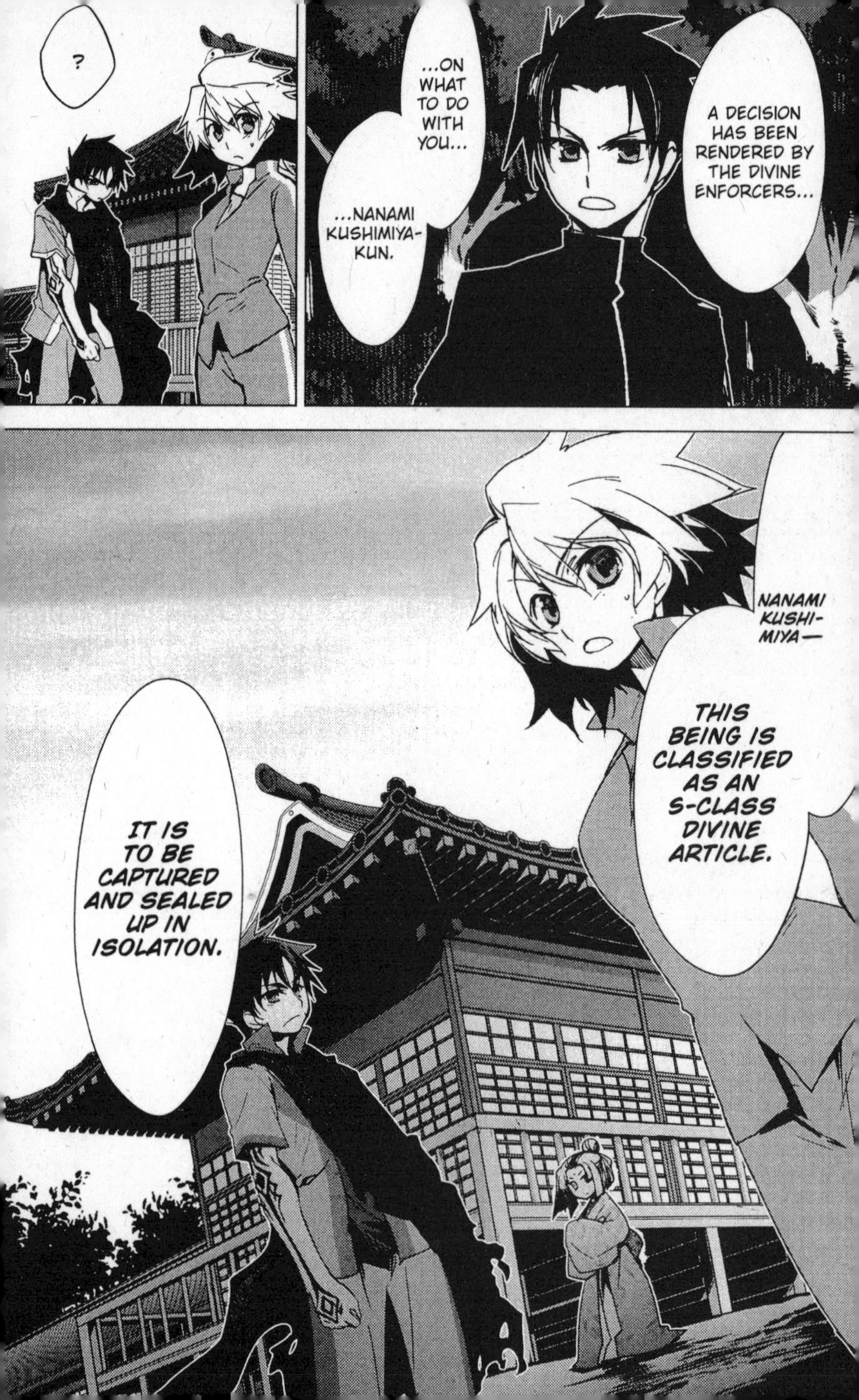
A DECISION HAS BEEN RENDERED BY THE DIVINE ENFORCERS...
...ON WHAT TO DO WITH YOU...
...NANAMI KUSHIMIYA-KUN.
?
NANAMI KUSHIMIYA—
THIS BEING IS CLASSIFIED AS AN S-CLASS DIVINE ARTICLE.
IT IS TO BE CAPTURED AND SEALED UP IN ISOLATION.

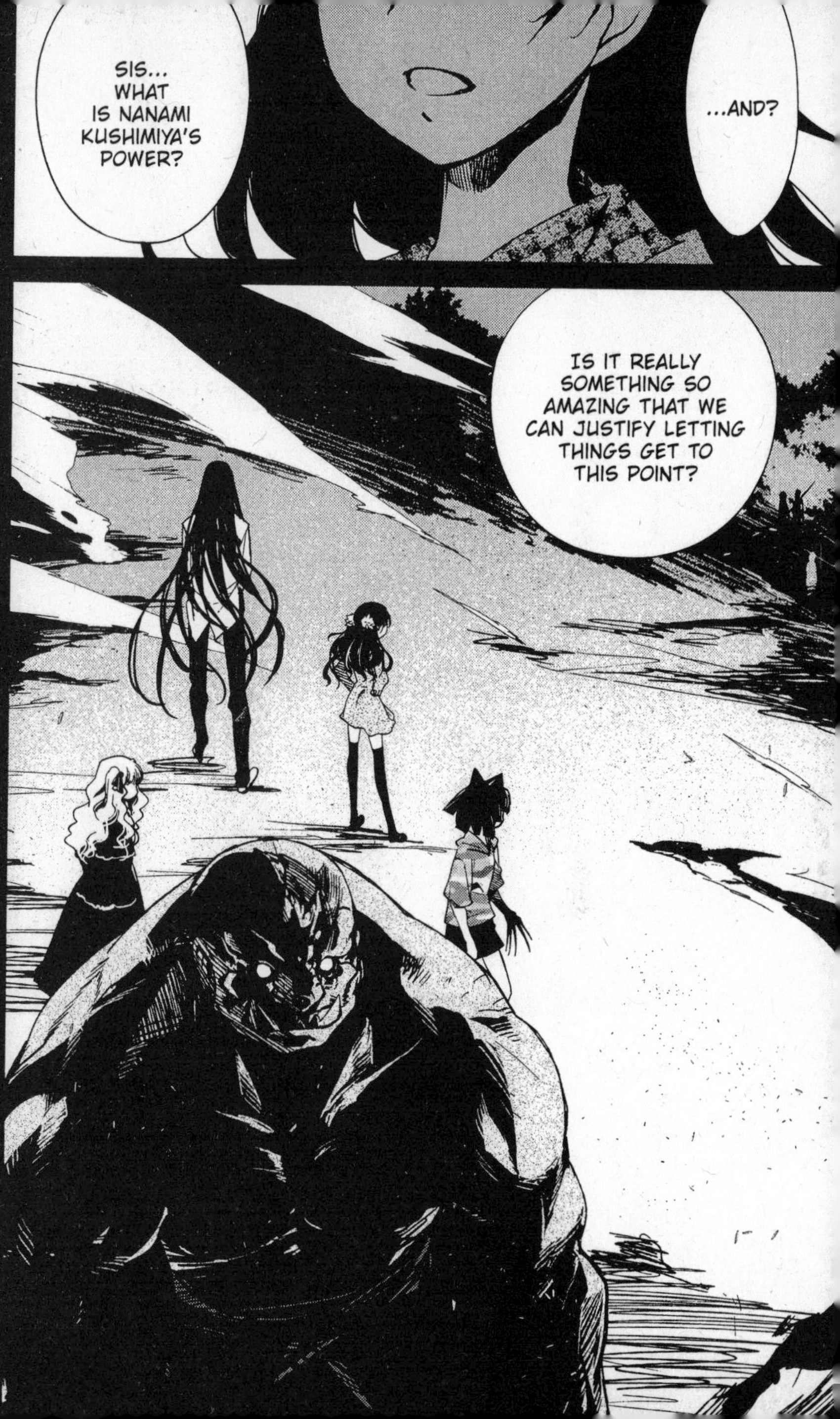
...AND?
SIS... WHAT IS NANAMI KUSHIMIYA'S POWER?
IS IT REALLY SOMETHING SO AMAZING THAT WE CAN JUSTIFY LETTING THINGS GET TO THIS POINT?

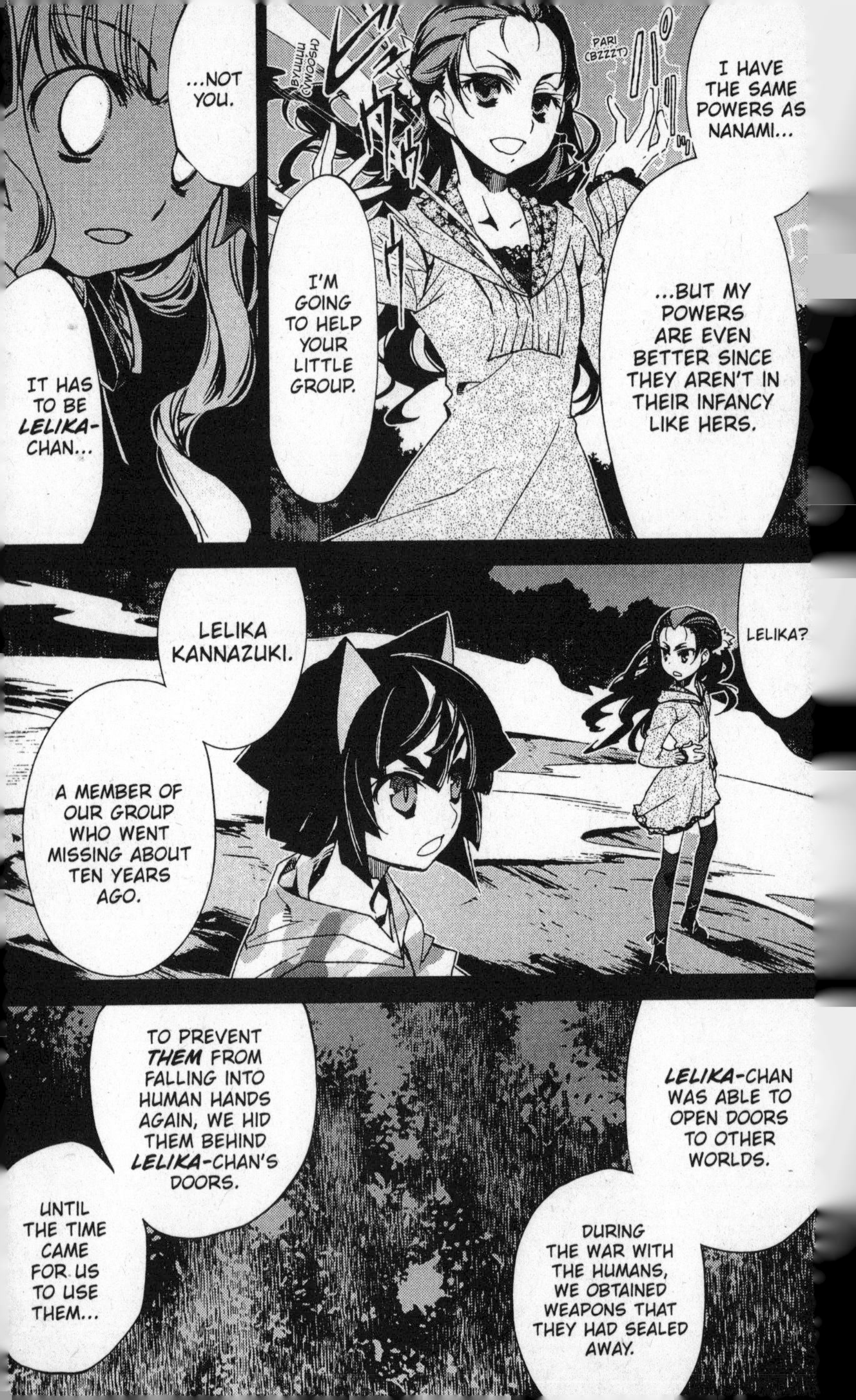
I HAVE THE SAME POWERS AS NANAMI...
PARI (BZZZT)
...BUT MY POWERS ARE EVEN BETTER SINCE THEY AREN'T IN THEIR INFANCY LIKE HERS.
BYUHHH (VWOOSH)
I'M GOING TO HELP YOUR LITTLE GROUP.
...NOT YOU.
IT HAS TO BE *LELIKA*-CHAN...
LELIKA?
LELIKA KANNAZUKI.
A MEMBER OF OUR GROUP WHO WENT MISSING ABOUT TEN YEARS AGO.
LELIKA-CHAN WAS ABLE TO OPEN DOORS TO OTHER WORLDS.
DURING THE WAR WITH THE HUMANS, WE OBTAINED WEAPONS THAT THEY HAD SEALED AWAY.
TO PREVENT *THEM* FROM FALLING INTO HUMAN HANDS AGAIN, WE HID THEM BEHIND *LELIKA*-CHAN'S DOORS.
UNTIL THE TIME CAME FOR US TO USE THEM...

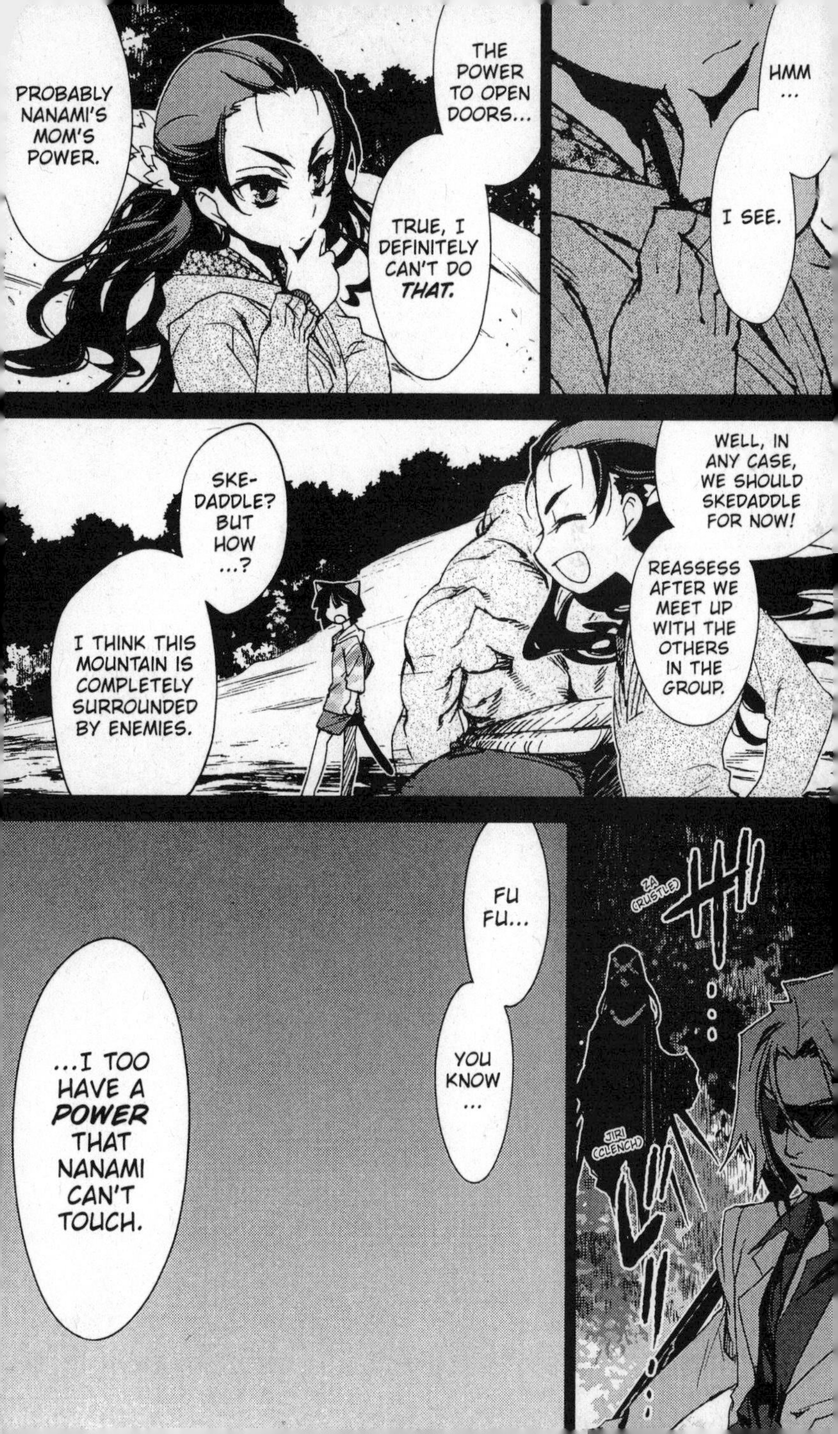
HMM ...
I SEE.
THE POWER TO OPEN DOORS...
PROBABLY NANAMI'S MOM'S POWER.
TRUE, I DEFINITELY CAN'T DO *THAT.*
WELL, IN ANY CASE, WE SHOULD SKEDADDLE FOR NOW!
REASSESS AFTER WE MEET UP WITH THE OTHERS IN THE GROUP.
SKE-DADDLE? BUT HOW ...?
I THINK THIS MOUNTAIN IS COMPLETELY SURROUNDED BY ENEMIES.
ZA (RUSTLE)
JIRI (CLENCH)
FU FU...
YOU KNOW ...
...I TOO HAVE A *POWER* THAT NANAMI CAN'T TOUCH.

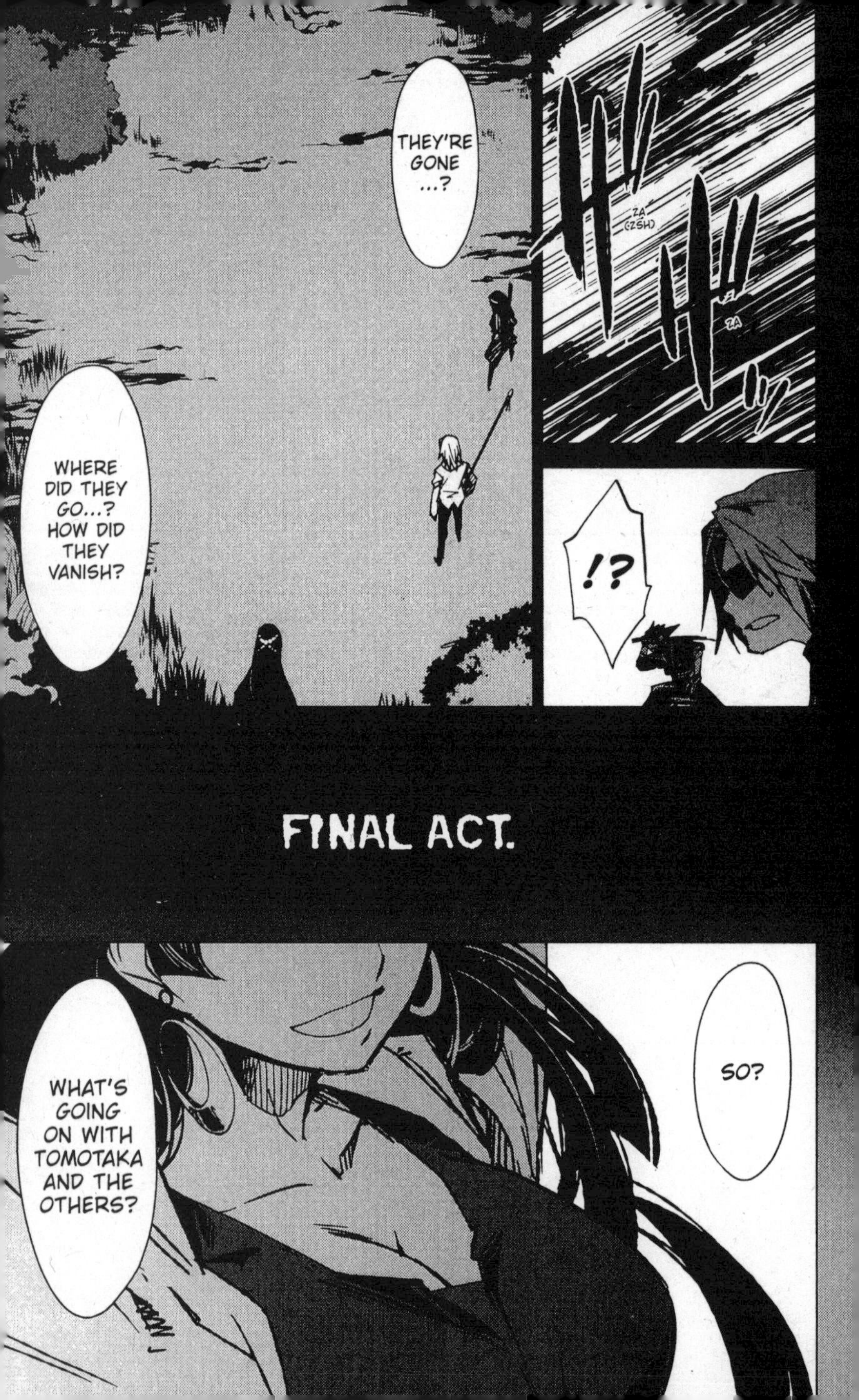
ZA (ZSH)
ZA
!?
THEY'RE GONE ...?
WHERE DID THEY GO...? HOW DID THEY VANISH?
FINAL ACT.
SO?
WHAT'S GOING ON WITH TOMOTAKA AND THE OTHERS?

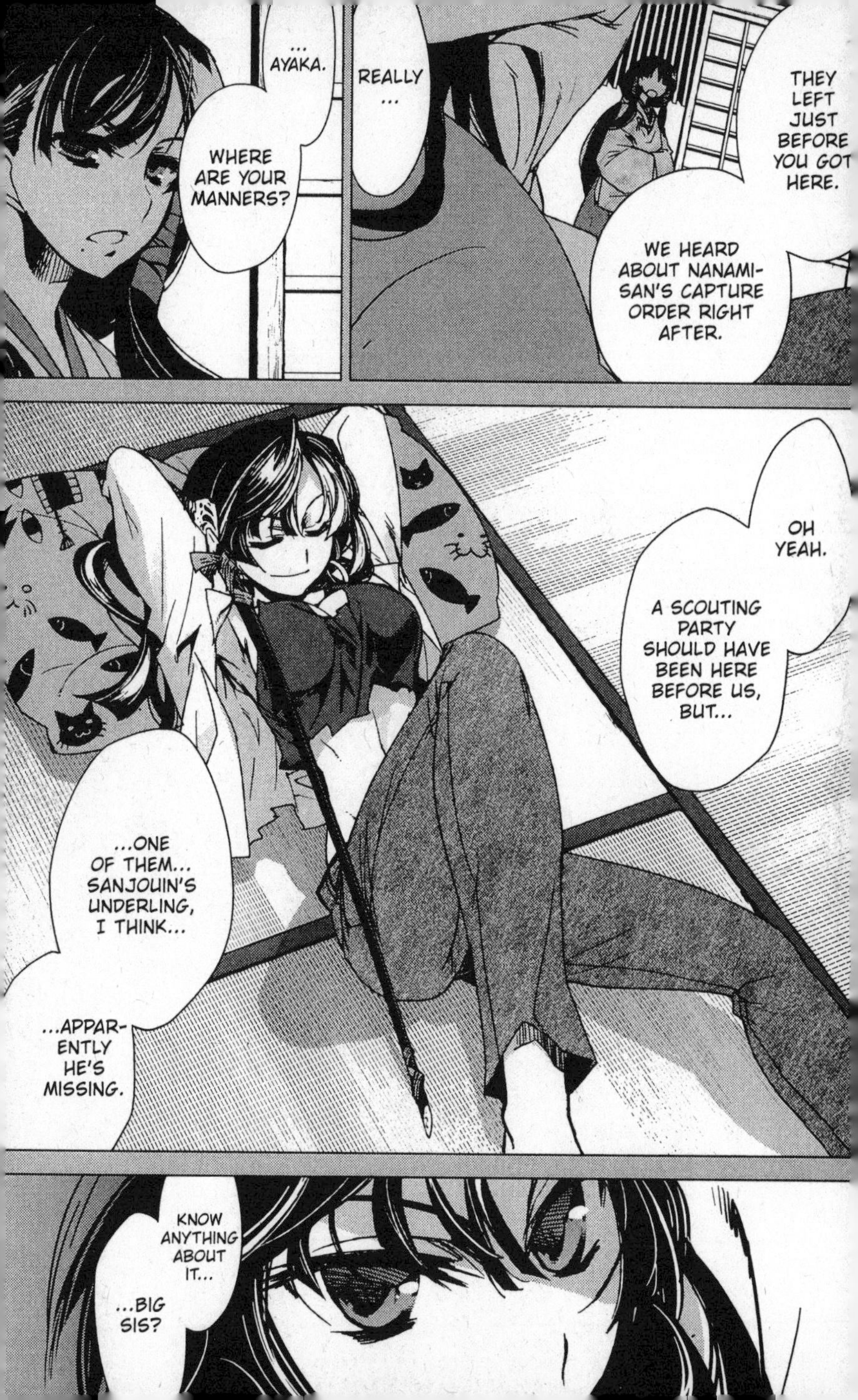
THEY LEFT JUST BEFORE YOU GOT HERE.
WE HEARD ABOUT NANAMI-SAN'S CAPTURE ORDER RIGHT AFTER.
REALLY...
...AYAKA.
WHERE ARE YOUR MANNERS?
OH YEAH.
A SCOUTING PARTY SHOULD HAVE BEEN HERE BEFORE US, BUT...
...ONE OF THEM... SANJOUIN'S UNDERLING, I THINK...
...APPAR-ENTLY HE'S MISSING.
KNOW ANYTHING ABOUT IT...
...BIG SIS?

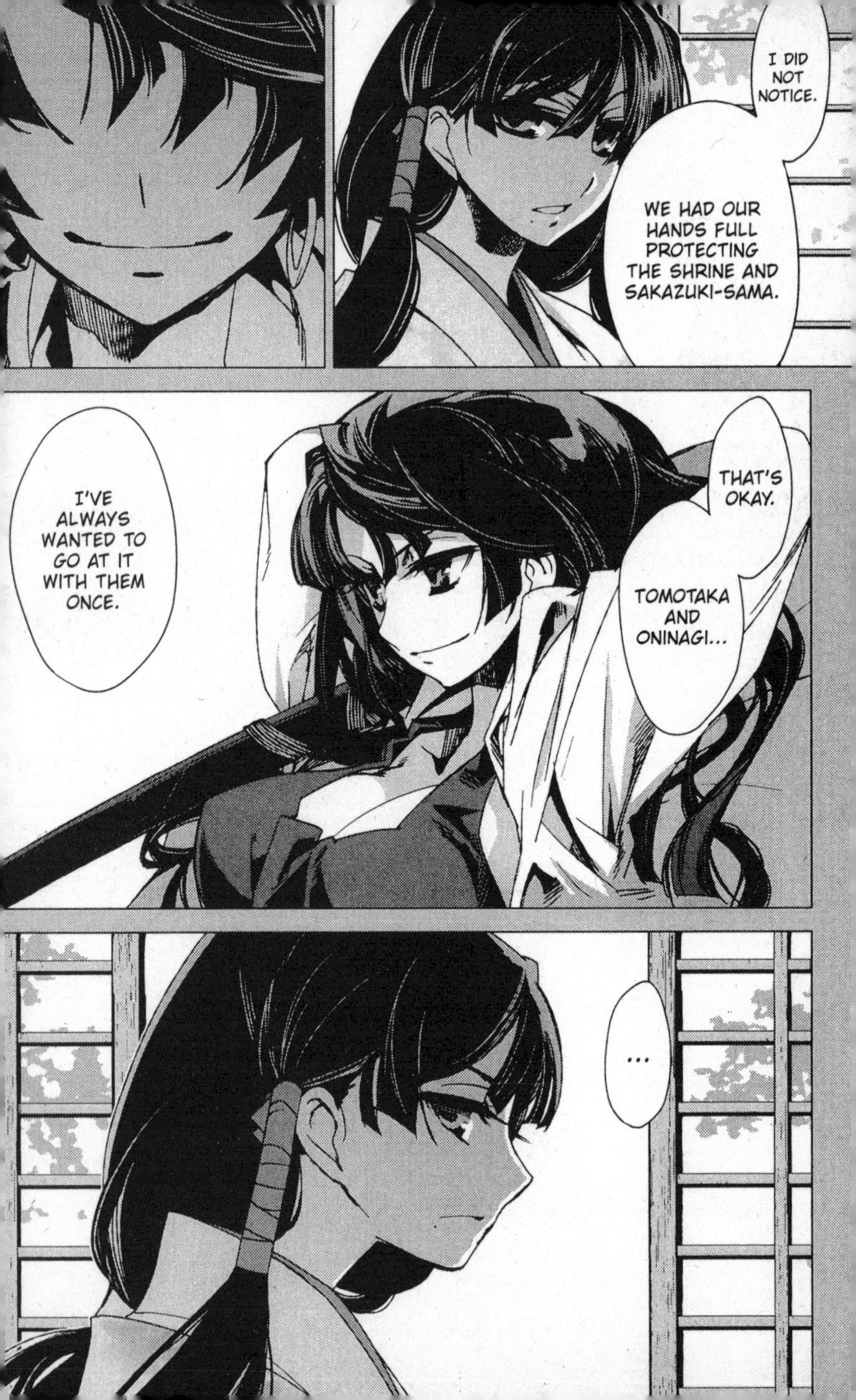
I DID NOT NOTICE.
WE HAD OUR HANDS FULL PROTECTING THE SHRINE AND SAKAZUKI-SAMA.
THAT'S OKAY.
TOMOTAKA AND ONINAGI...
I'VE ALWAYS WANTED TO GO AT IT WITH THEM ONCE.
...

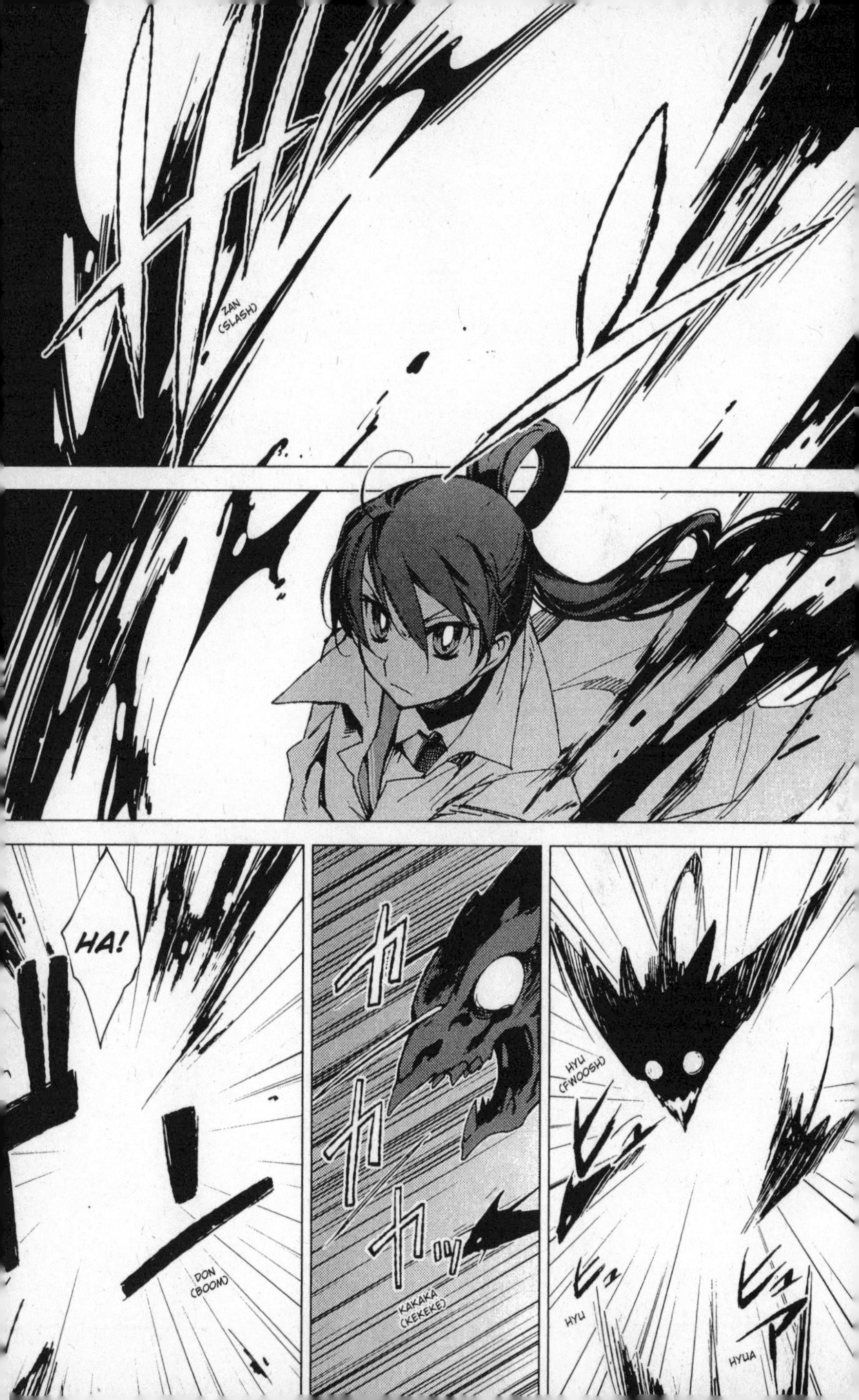
ZAN (SLASH)
HYU (FWOOSH)
HYU
HYUA
KAKAKA (KEKEKE)
HA!
DON (BOOM)

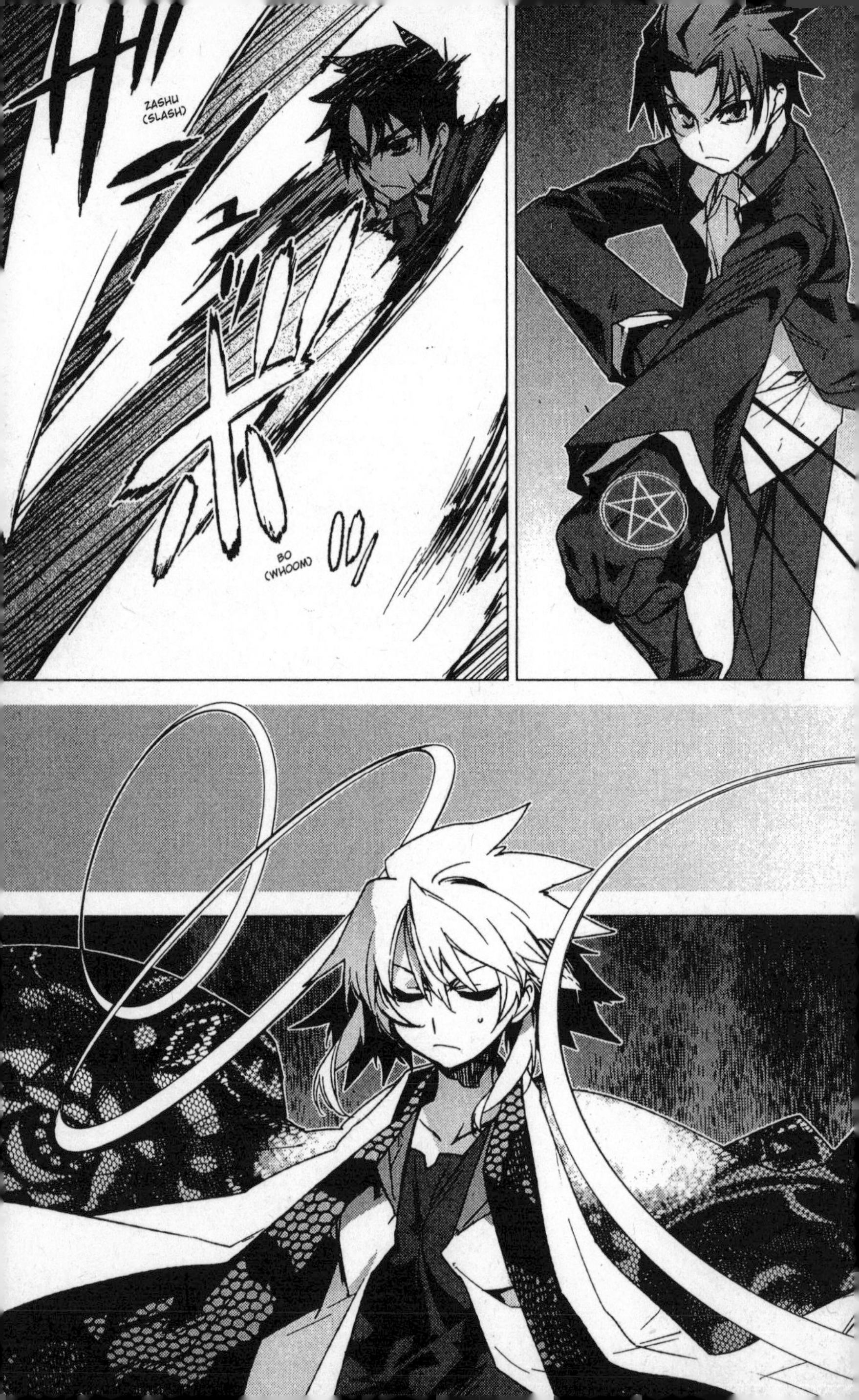
ZASHU (SLASH)
BO (WHOOM)

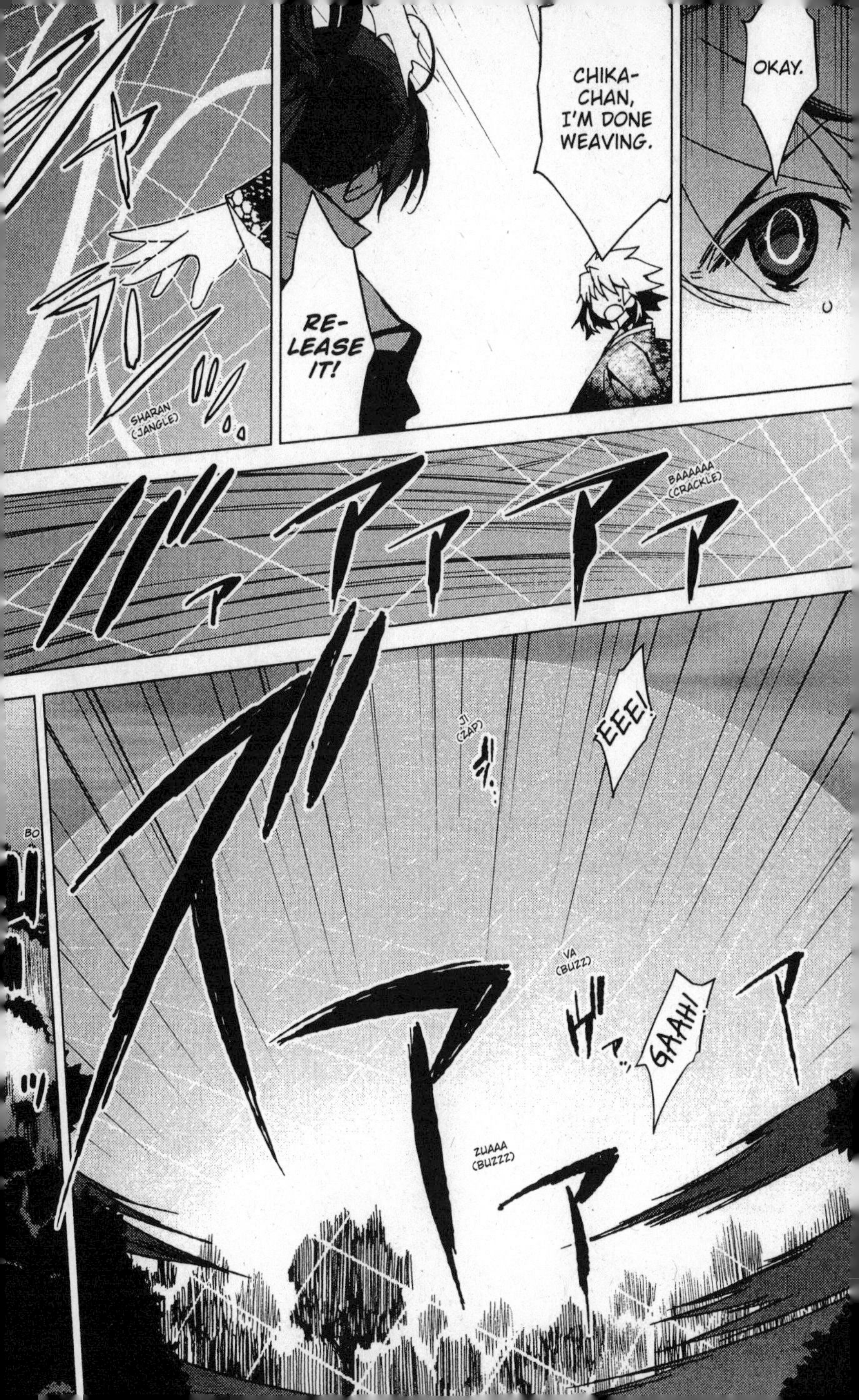
OKAY.
CHIKA-CHAN, I'M DONE WEAVING.
RE-LEASE IT!
SHARAN (JANGLE)
BAAAAAA (CRACKLE)
EEE!
JI (ZAP)
BO
VA (BUZZ)
GAAH!
ZUAAA (BUZZZ)

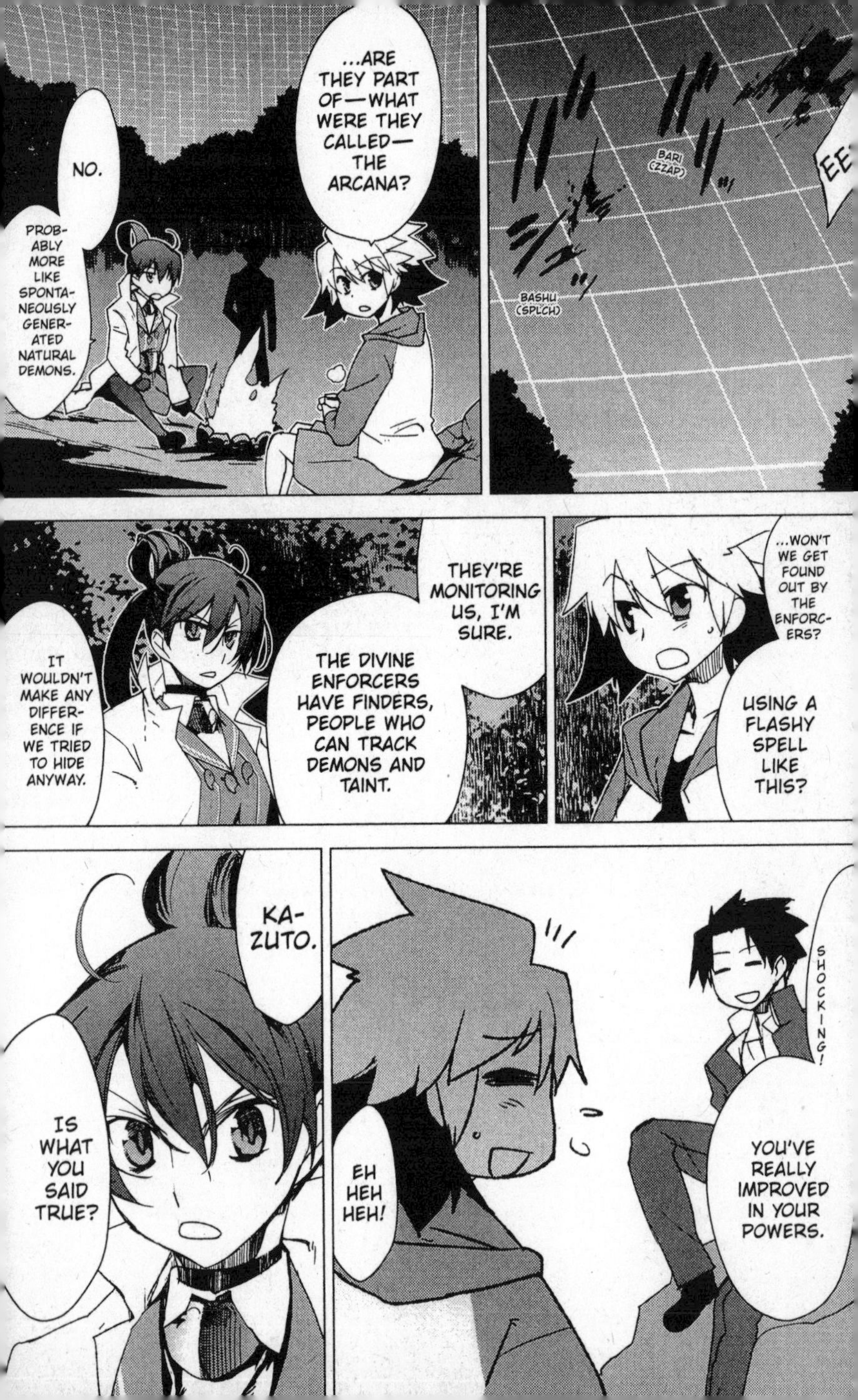
BARI (ZZAP)
BASHU (SPLCH)
...ARE THEY PART OF—WHAT WERE THEY CALLED—THE ARCANA?
NO.
PROBABLY MORE LIKE SPONTANEOUSLY GENERATED NATURAL DEMONS.
...WON'T WE GET FOUND OUT BY THE ENFORCERS?
USING A FLASHY SPELL LIKE THIS?
THEY'RE MONITORING US, I'M SURE.
THE DIVINE ENFORCERS HAVE FINDERS, PEOPLE WHO CAN TRACK DEMONS AND TAINT.
IT WOULDN'T MAKE ANY DIFFERENCE IF WE TRIED TO HIDE ANYWAY.
SHOCKING!
YOU'VE REALLY IMPROVED IN YOUR POWERS.
EH HEH HEH!
KAZUTO.
IS WHAT YOU SAID TRUE?

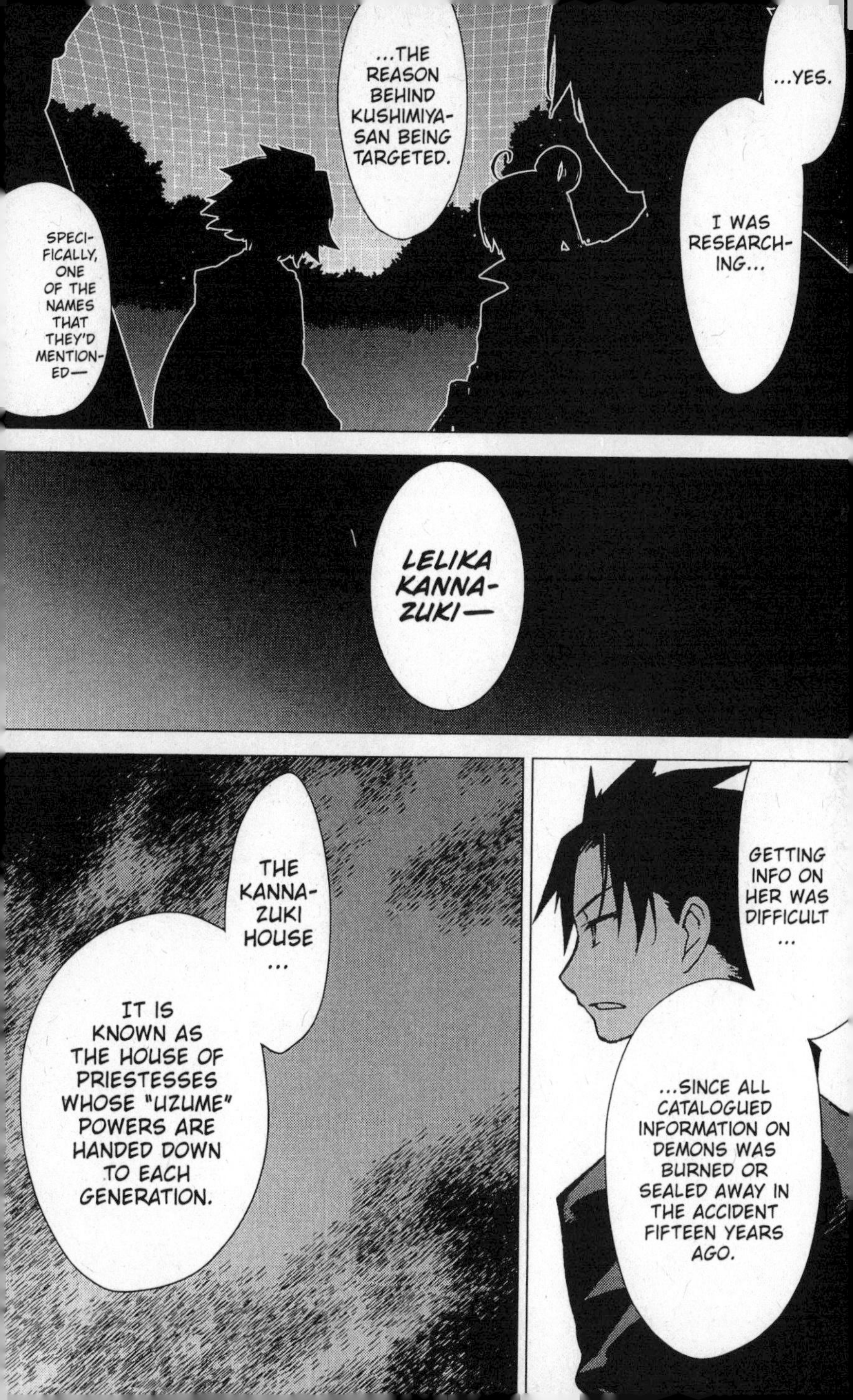
...YES.
I WAS RESEARCHING...
...THE REASON BEHIND KUSHIMIYA-SAN BEING TARGETED.
SPECIFICALLY, ONE OF THE NAMES THAT THEY'D MENTIONED—
LELIKA KANNAZUKI—
GETTING INFO ON HER WAS DIFFICULT...
...SINCE ALL CATALOGUED INFORMATION ON DEMONS WAS BURNED OR SEALED AWAY IN THE ACCIDENT FIFTEEN YEARS AGO.
THE KANNAZUKI HOUSE...
IT IS KNOWN AS THE HOUSE OF PRIESTESSES WHOSE "UZUME" POWERS ARE HANDED DOWN TO EACH GENERATION.

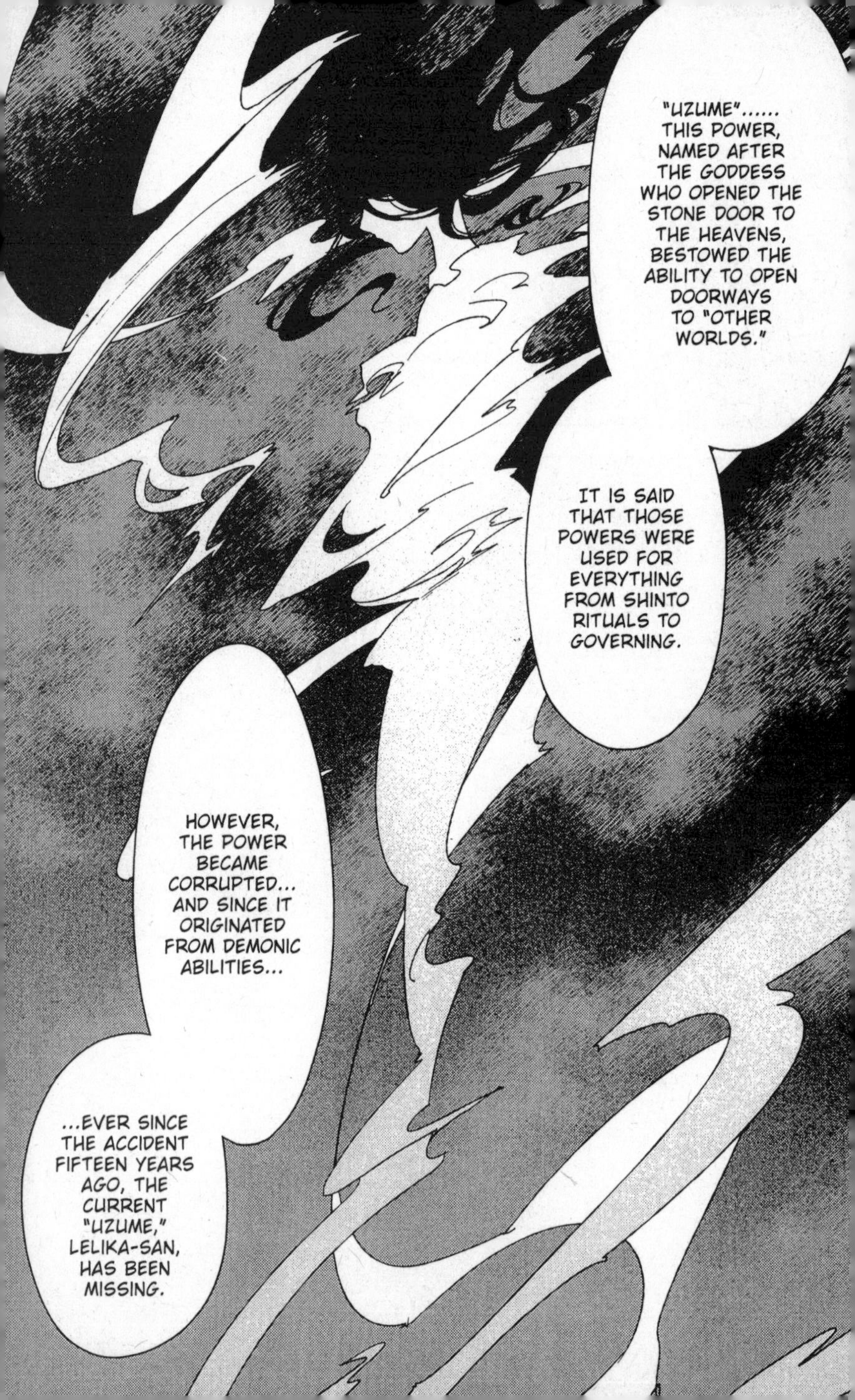
"UZUME"...... THIS POWER, NAMED AFTER THE GODDESS WHO OPENED THE STONE DOOR TO THE HEAVENS, BESTOWED THE ABILITY TO OPEN DOORWAYS TO "OTHER WORLDS."
IT IS SAID THAT THOSE POWERS WERE USED FOR EVERYTHING FROM SHINTO RITUALS TO GOVERNING.
HOWEVER, THE POWER BECAME CORRUPTED... AND SINCE IT ORIGINATED FROM DEMONIC ABILITIES...
...EVER SINCE THE ACCIDENT FIFTEEN YEARS AGO, THE CURRENT "UZUME," LELIKA-SAN, HAS BEEN MISSING.

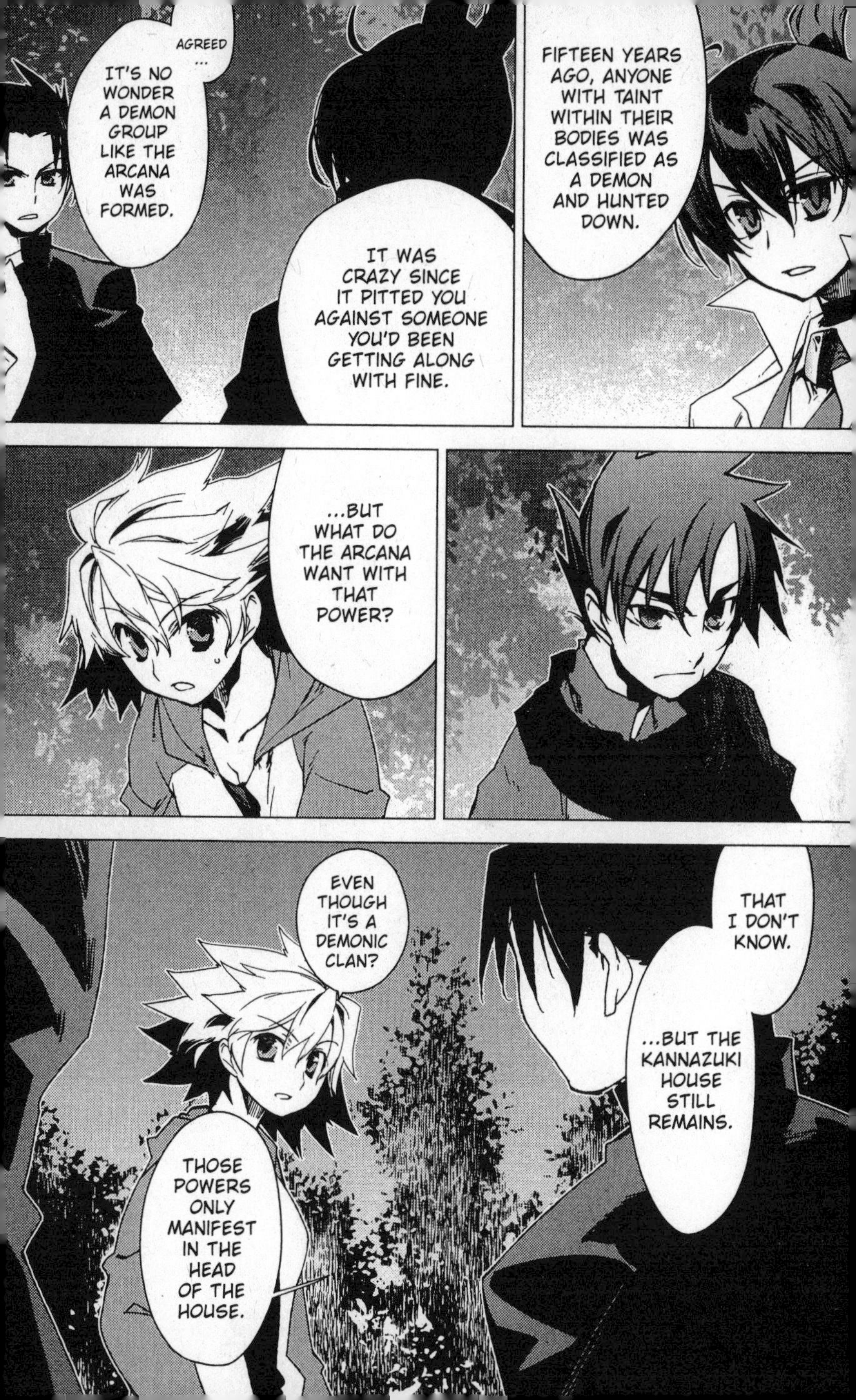
FIFTEEN YEARS AGO, ANYONE WITH TAINT WITHIN THEIR BODIES WAS CLASSIFIED AS A DEMON AND HUNTED DOWN.
IT WAS CRAZY SINCE IT PITTED YOU AGAINST SOMEONE YOU'D BEEN GETTING ALONG WITH FINE.
AGREED ...
IT'S NO WONDER A DEMON GROUP LIKE THE ARCANA WAS FORMED.
...BUT WHAT DO THE ARCANA WANT WITH THAT POWER?
THAT I DON'T KNOW.
...BUT THE KANNAZUKI HOUSE STILL REMAINS.
EVEN THOUGH IT'S A DEMONIC CLAN?
THOSE POWERS ONLY MANIFEST IN THE HEAD OF THE HOUSE.

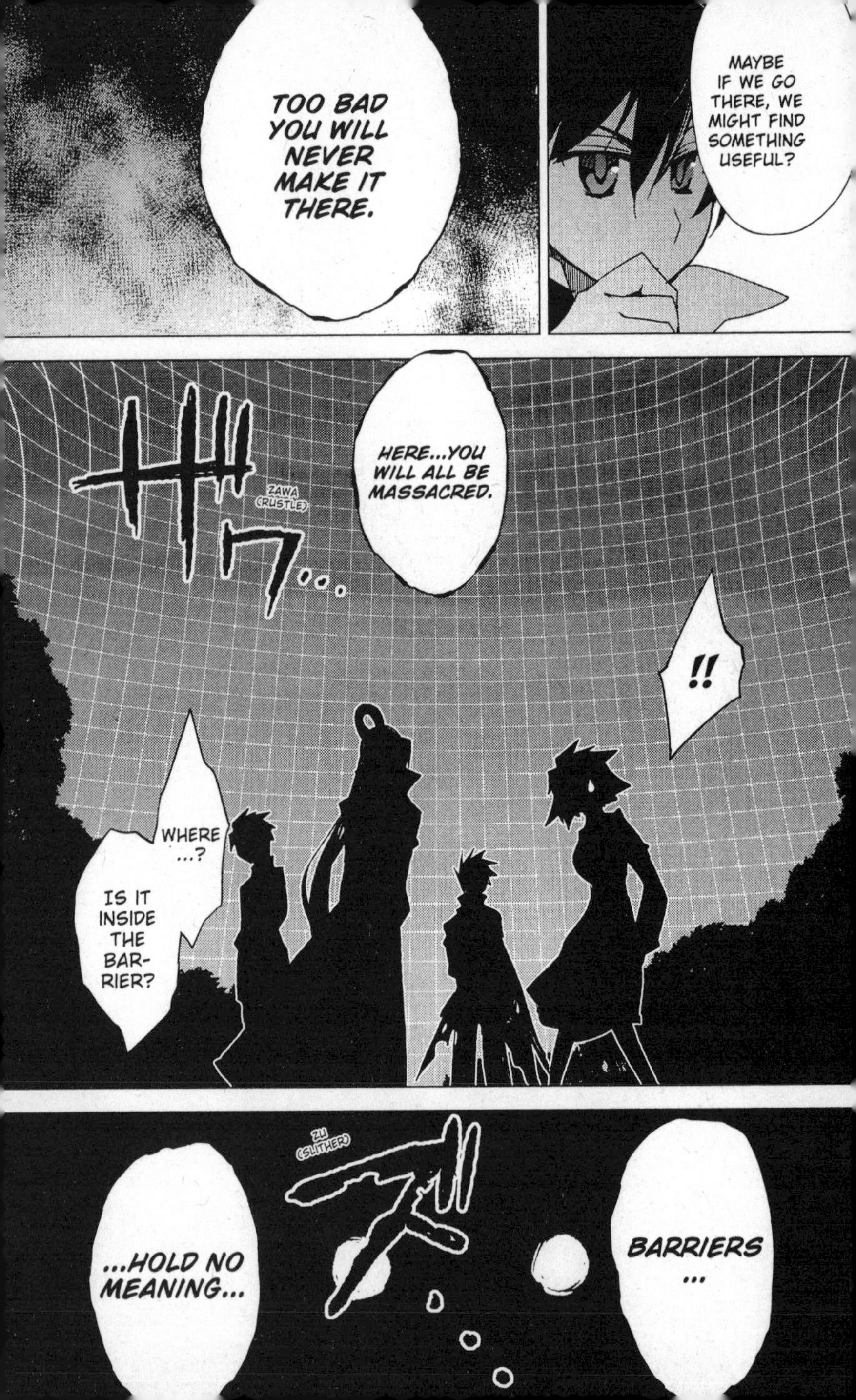
MAYBE IF WE GO THERE, WE MIGHT FIND SOMETHING USEFUL?
TOO BAD YOU WILL NEVER MAKE IT THERE.
HERE...YOU WILL ALL BE MASSACRED.
ZAWA (RUSTLE)
!!
WHERE ...?
IS IT INSIDE THE BAR-RIER?
BARRIERS ...
ZU (SLITHER)
...HOLD NO MEANING...

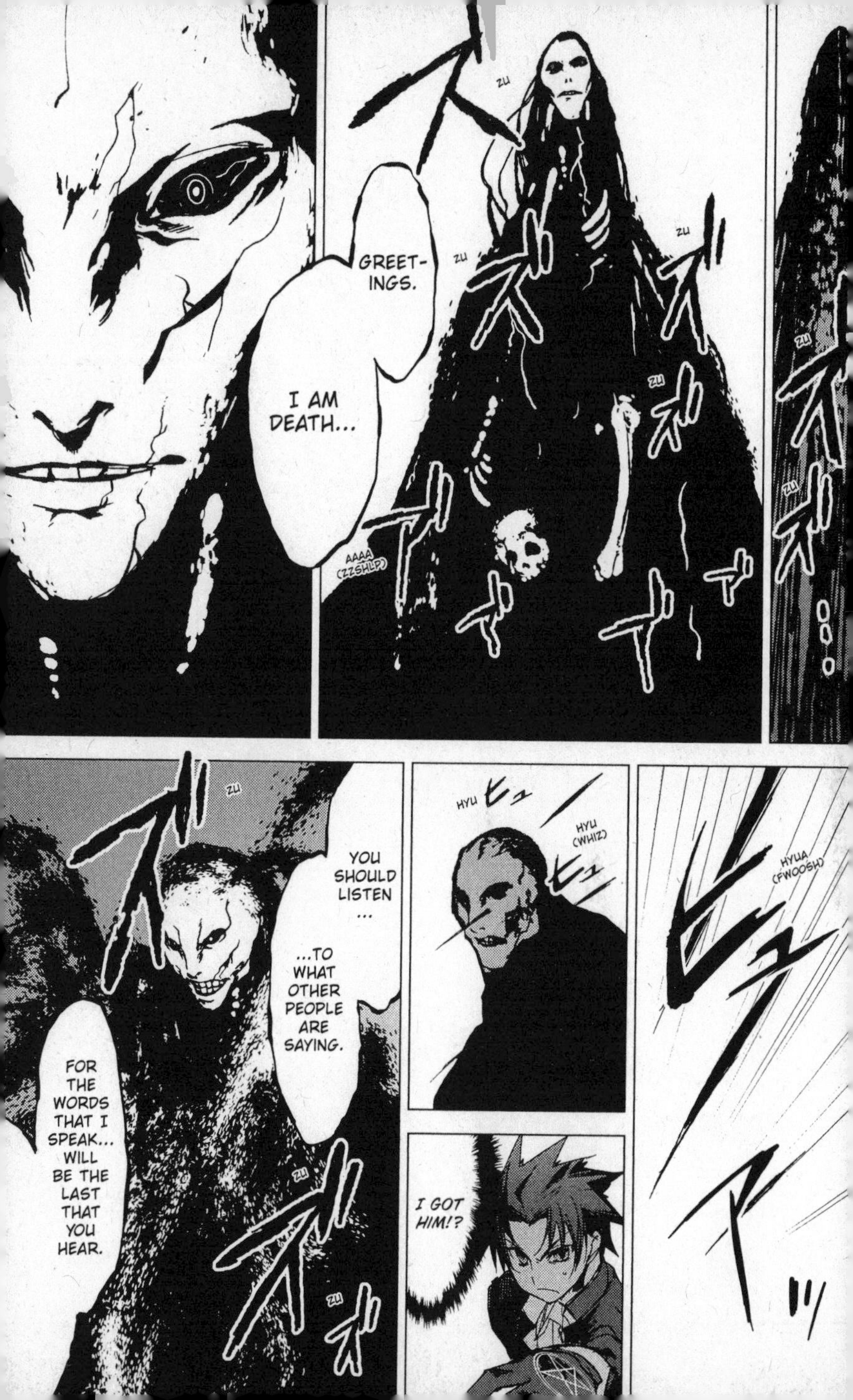
ZU
ZU
ZU
ZU
ZU
ZU
GREET-INGS.
I AM DEATH...
AAAA (ZZSHLP)
HYUA (FWOOSH)
HYU
HYU (WHIZ)
I GOT HIM!?
ZU
YOU SHOULD LISTEN ...
...TO WHAT OTHER PEOPLE ARE SAYING.
FOR THE WORDS THAT I SPEAK... WILL BE THE LAST THAT YOU HEAR.
ZU
ZU

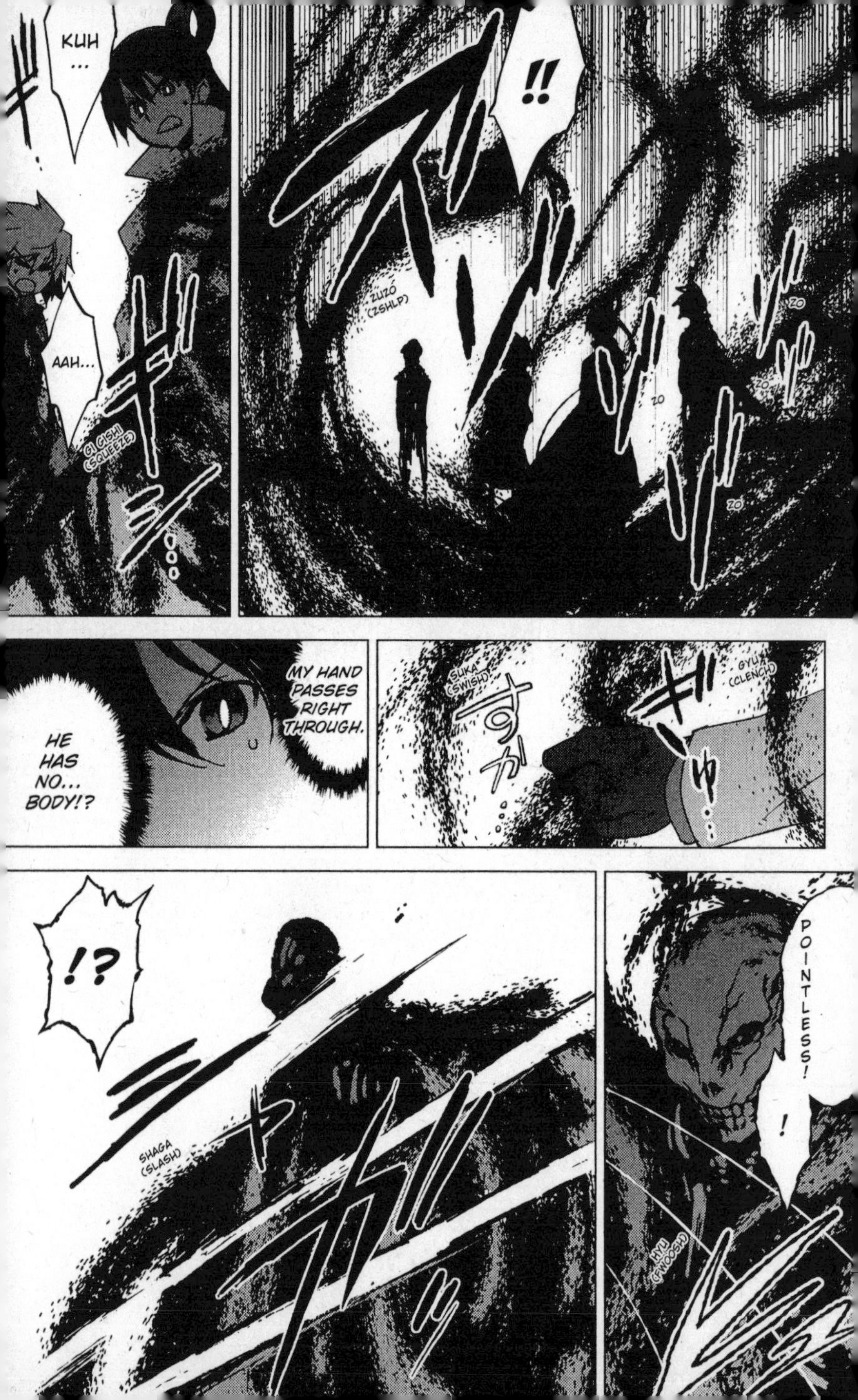
!!
ZUZO (ZSHLP)
ZO
ZO
ZO
ZO
KUH ...
AAH...
GI GISHI (SQUEEZE)
GYU (CLENCH)
SUKA (SWISH)
MY HAND PASSES RIGHT THROUGH.
HE HAS NO... BODY!?
POINTLESS!
!
HYU (FWOOSH)
!?
SHAGA (SLASH)

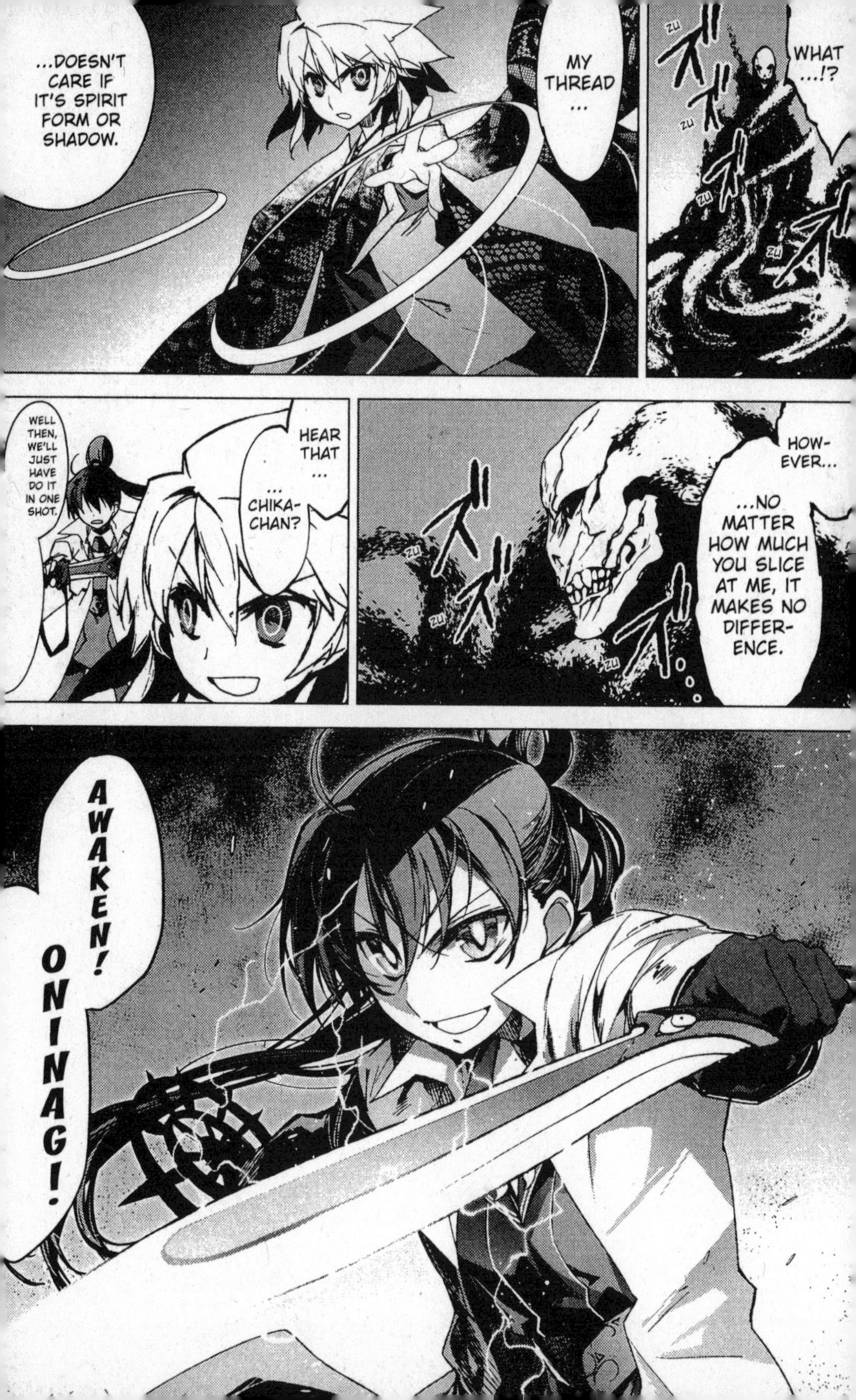
ZU
ZU
ZU
ZU
WHAT ...!?
MY THREAD ...
...DOESN'T CARE IF IT'S SPIRIT FORM OR SHADOW.
HOW-EVER...
...NO MATTER HOW MUCH YOU SLICE AT ME, IT MAKES NO DIFFER-ENCE.
ZU
ZU
ZU
HEAR THAT ...
... CHIKA-CHAN?
WELL THEN, WE'LL JUST HAVE DO IT IN ONE SHOT.
AWAKEN!
ONINAGI!

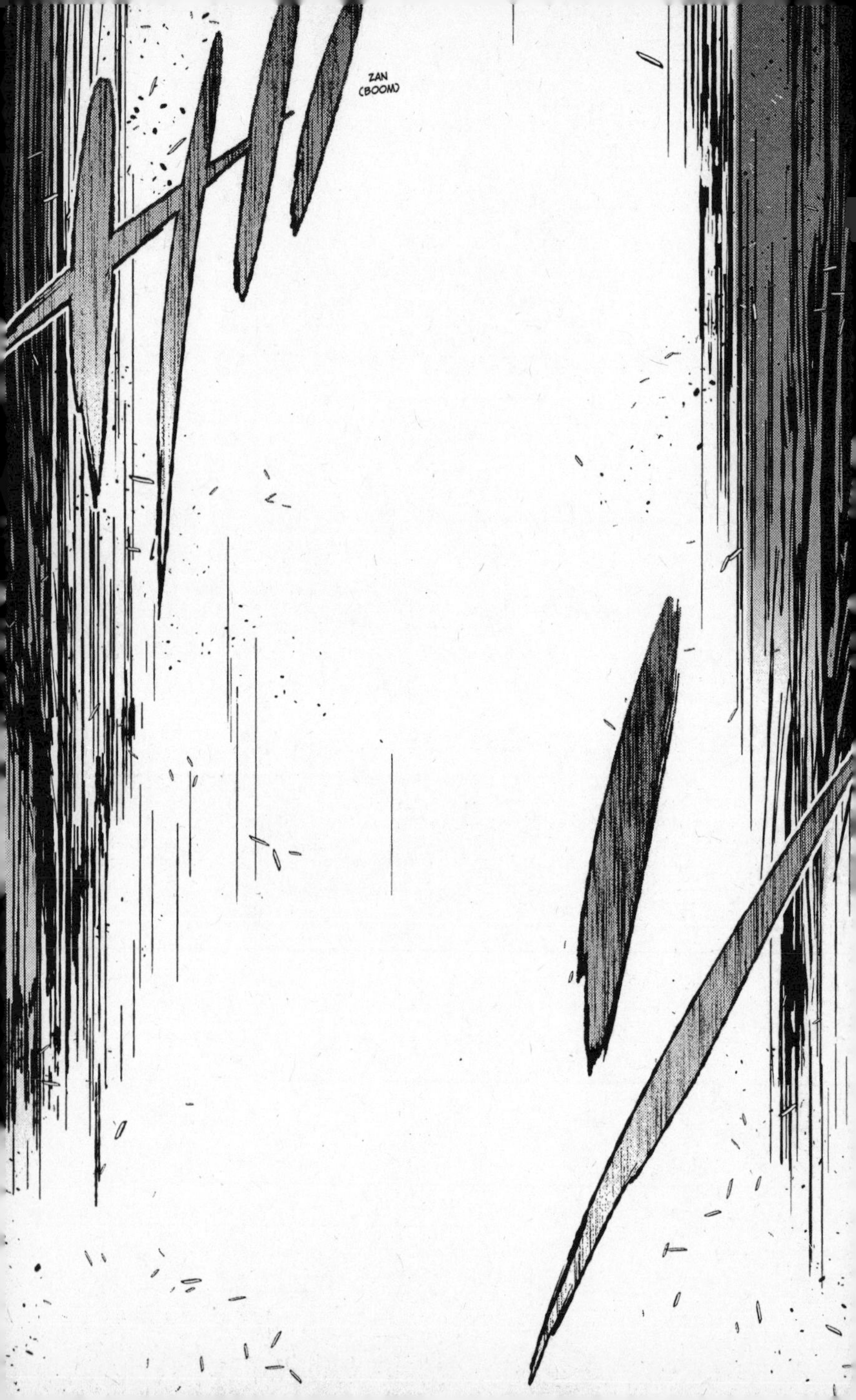
ZAN
(BOOM)

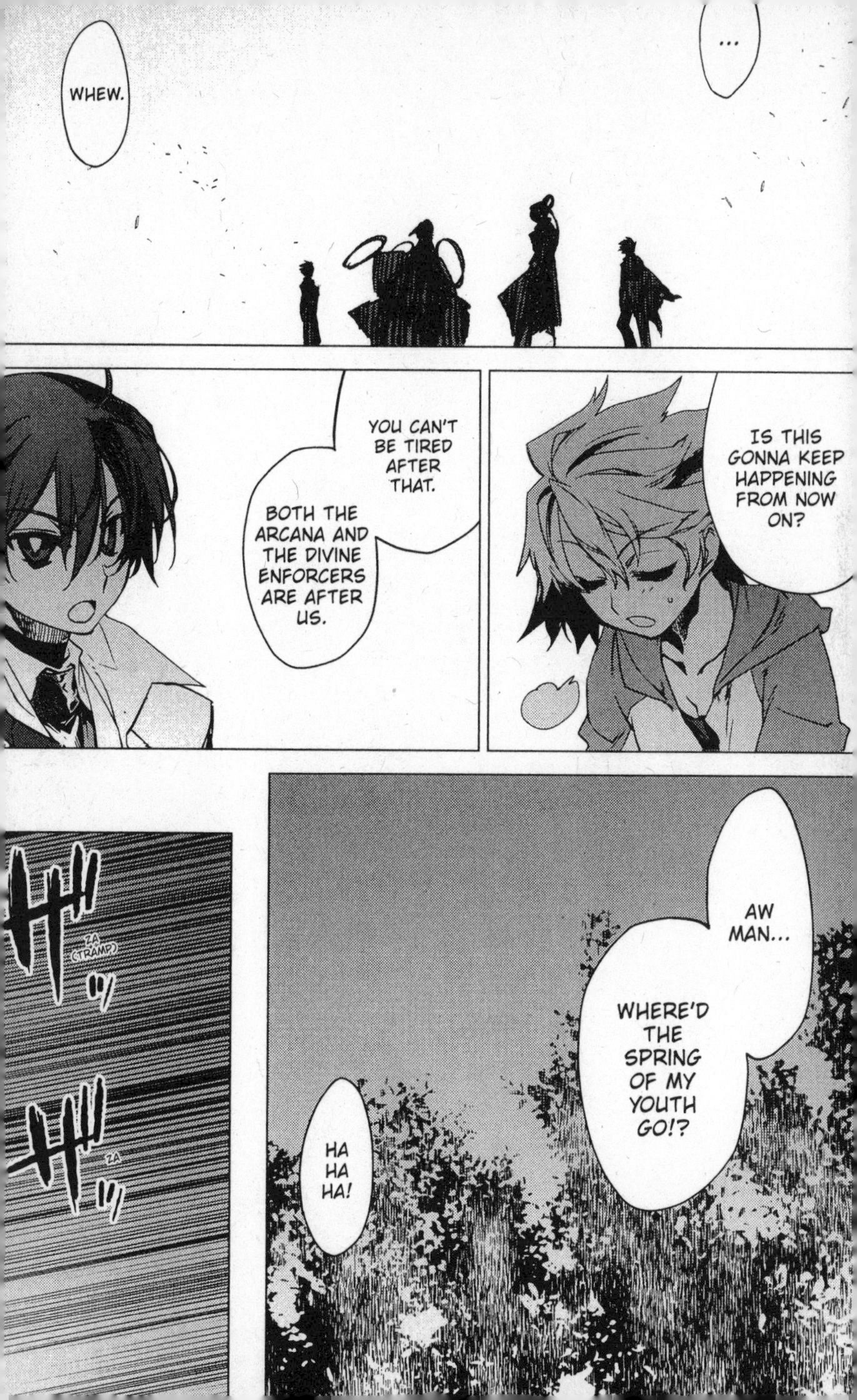
...
WHEW.
IS THIS GONNA KEEP HAPPENING FROM NOW ON?
YOU CAN'T BE TIRED AFTER THAT.
BOTH THE ARCANA AND THE DIVINE ENFORCERS ARE AFTER US.
AW MAN...
WHERE'D THE SPRING OF MY YOUTH GO!?
HA HA HA!
ZA (TRAMP)
ZA

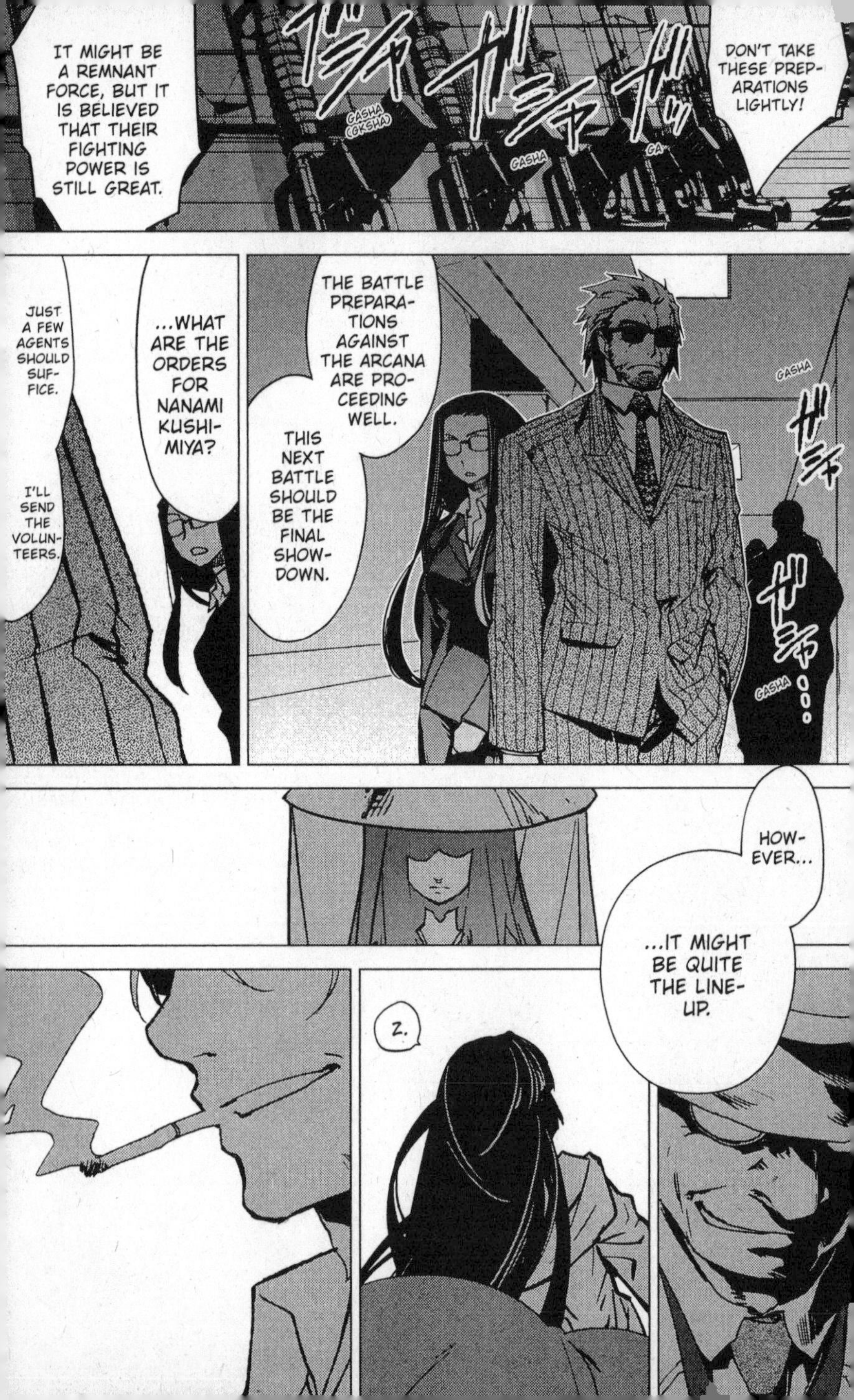

DON'T TAKE THESE PREPARATIONS LIGHTLY!
CA
GASHA
GASHA (GKSHA)
IT MIGHT BE A REMNANT FORCE, BUT IT IS BELIEVED THAT THEIR FIGHTING POWER IS STILL GREAT.
GASHA
GASHA
THE BATTLE PREPARATIONS AGAINST THE ARCANA ARE PROCEEDING WELL.
THIS NEXT BATTLE SHOULD BE THE FINAL SHOWDOWN.
...WHAT ARE THE ORDERS FOR NANAMI KUSHIMIYA?
JUST A FEW AGENTS SHOULD SUFFICE.
I'LL SEND THE VOLUNTEERS.
HOWEVER...
...IT MIGHT BE QUITE THE LINE-UP.
Z.

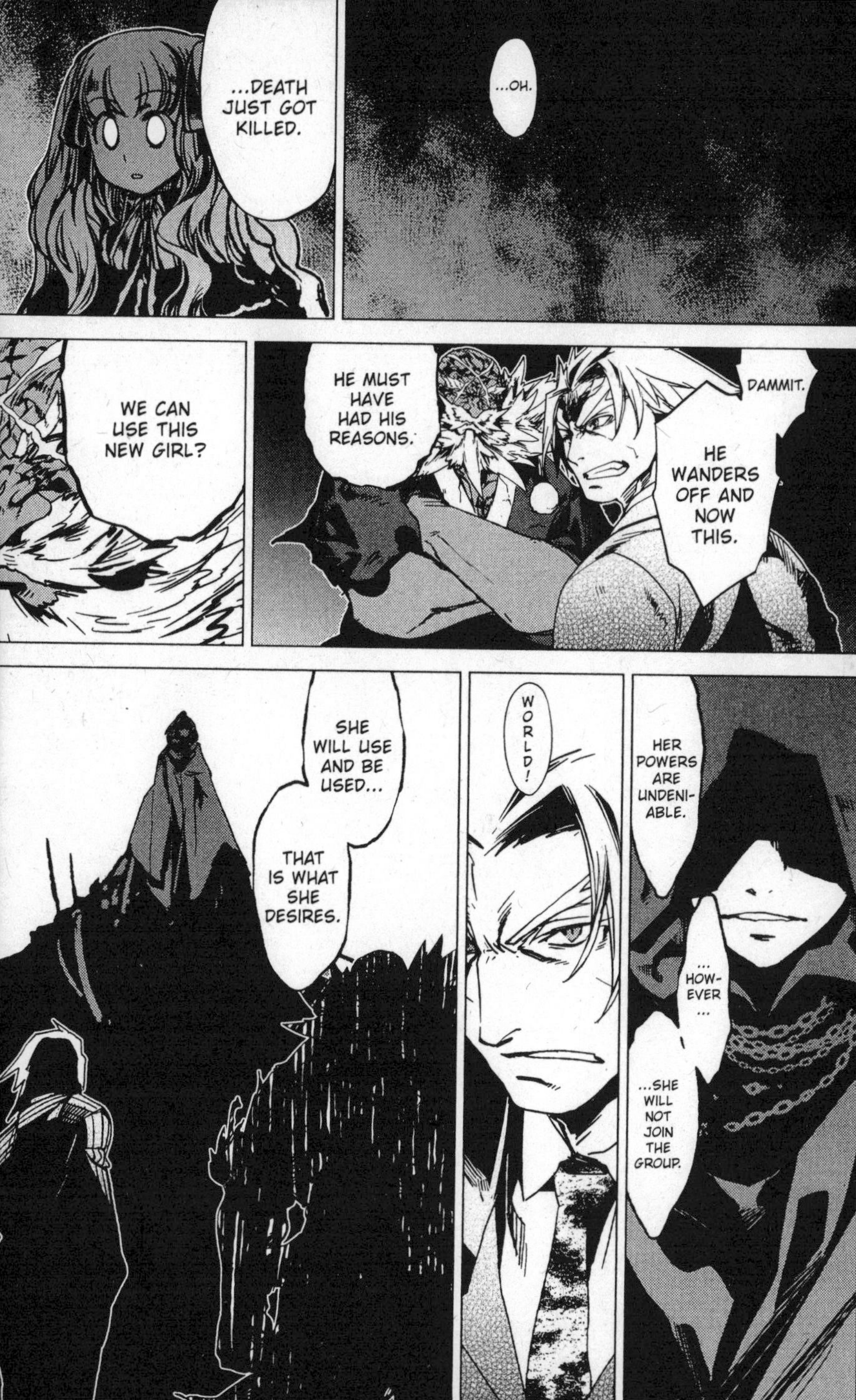
...OH.
...DEATH JUST GOT KILLED.
DAMMIT.
HE WANDERS OFF AND NOW THIS.
HE MUST HAVE HAD HIS REASONS.
WE CAN USE THIS NEW GIRL?
HER POWERS ARE UNDENIABLE.
...HOWEVER...
...SHE WILL NOT JOIN THE GROUP.
WORLD!
SHE WILL USE AND BE USED...
THAT IS WHAT SHE DESIRES.

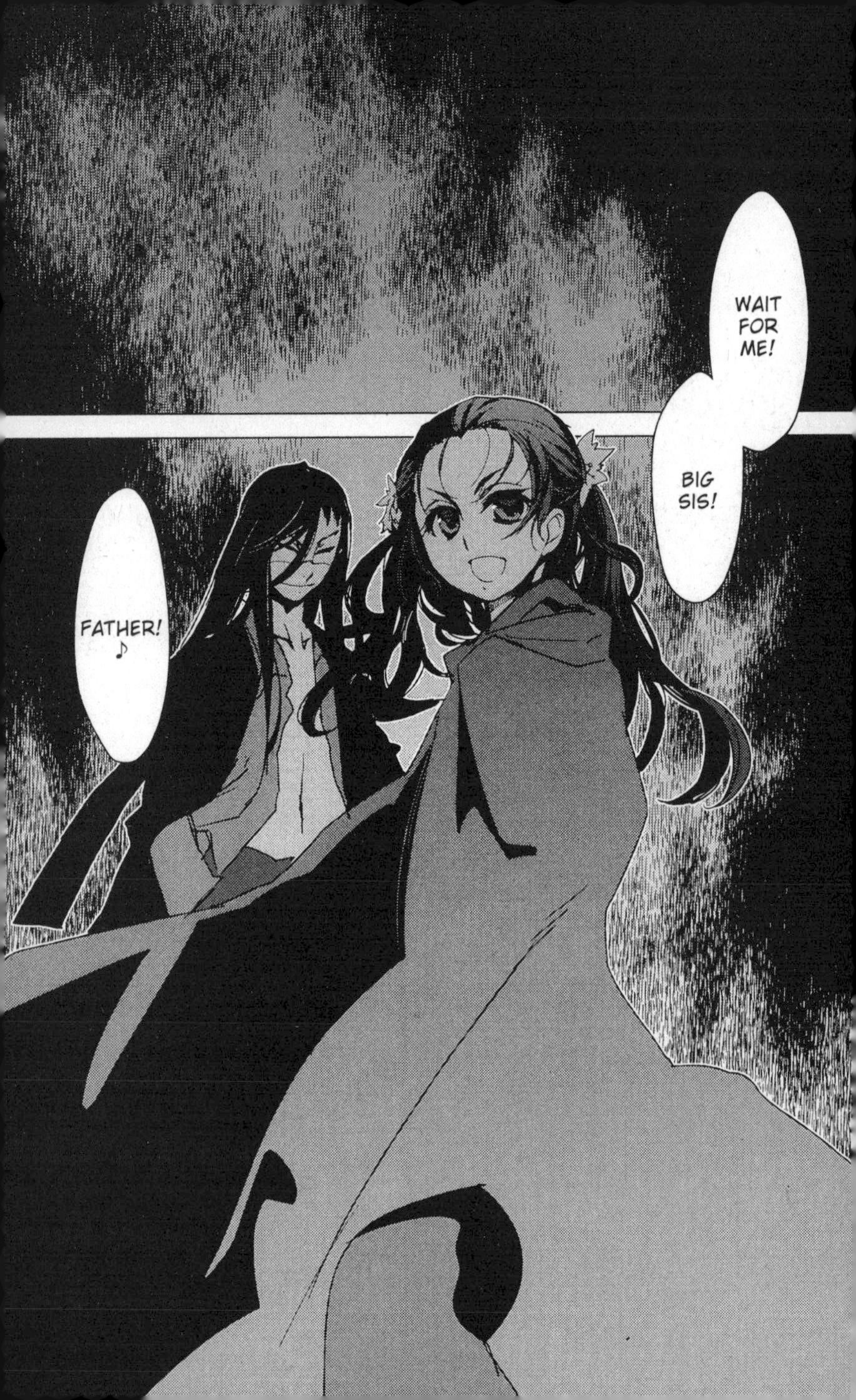
WAIT FOR ME!
BIG SIS!
FATHER! ♪

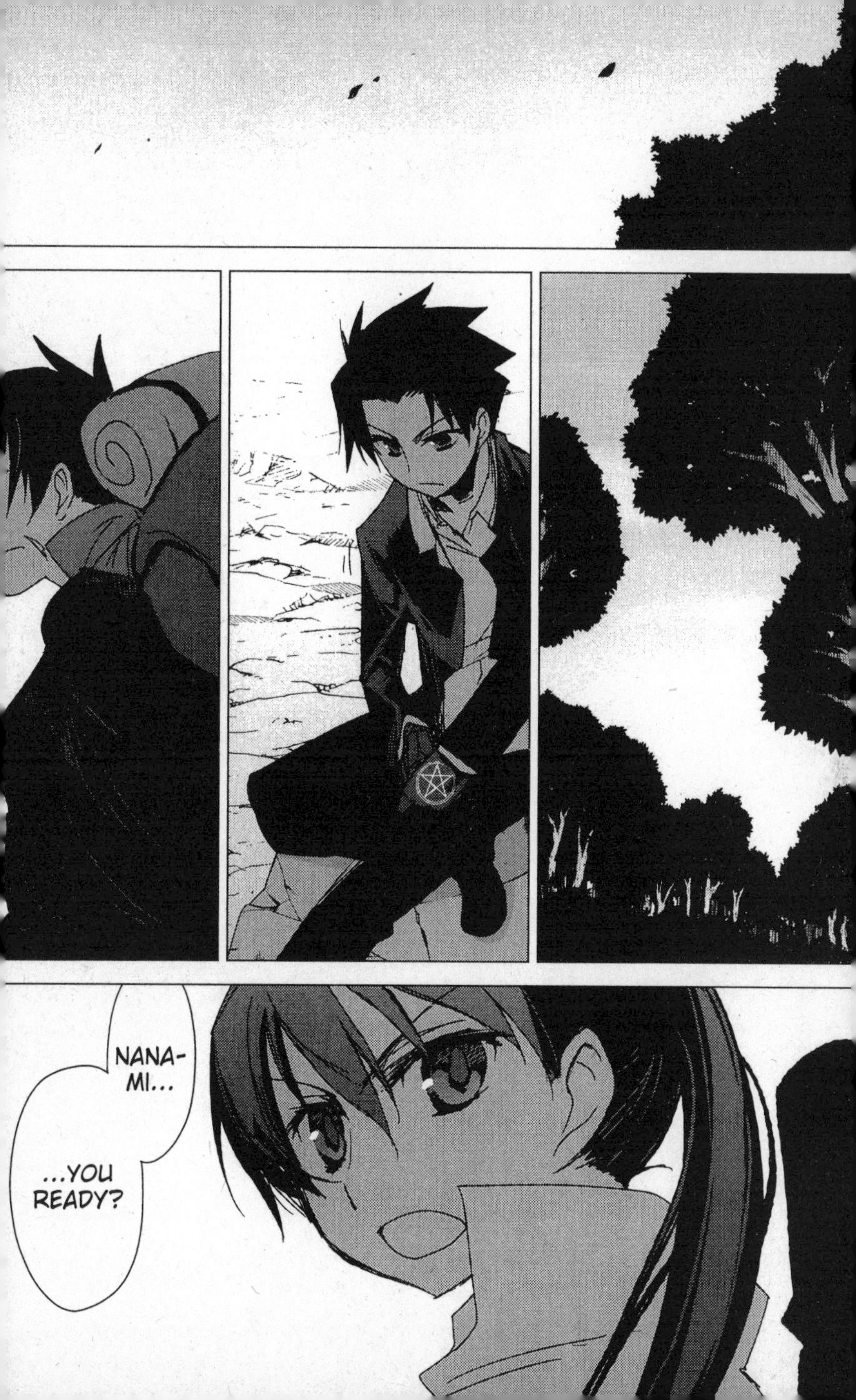
NANA-
MI...
...YOU
READY?

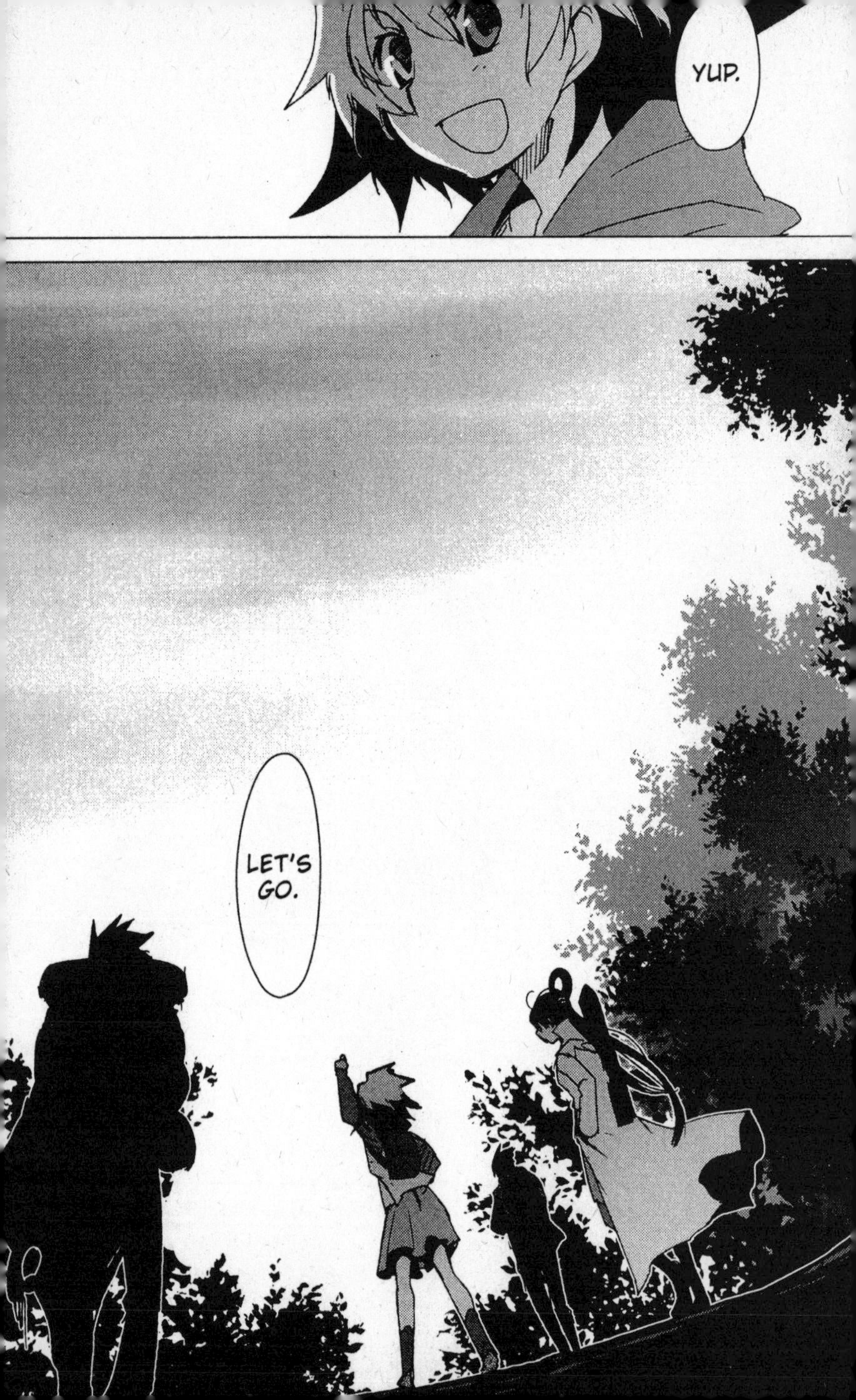
YUP.
LET'S GO.

PREVIEW

HUH ...?
I TOLD YOU BEFORE.

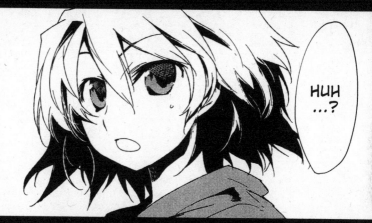

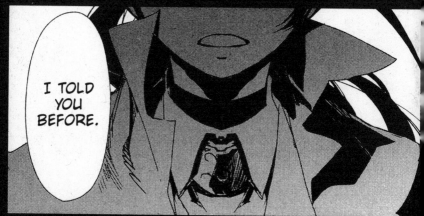

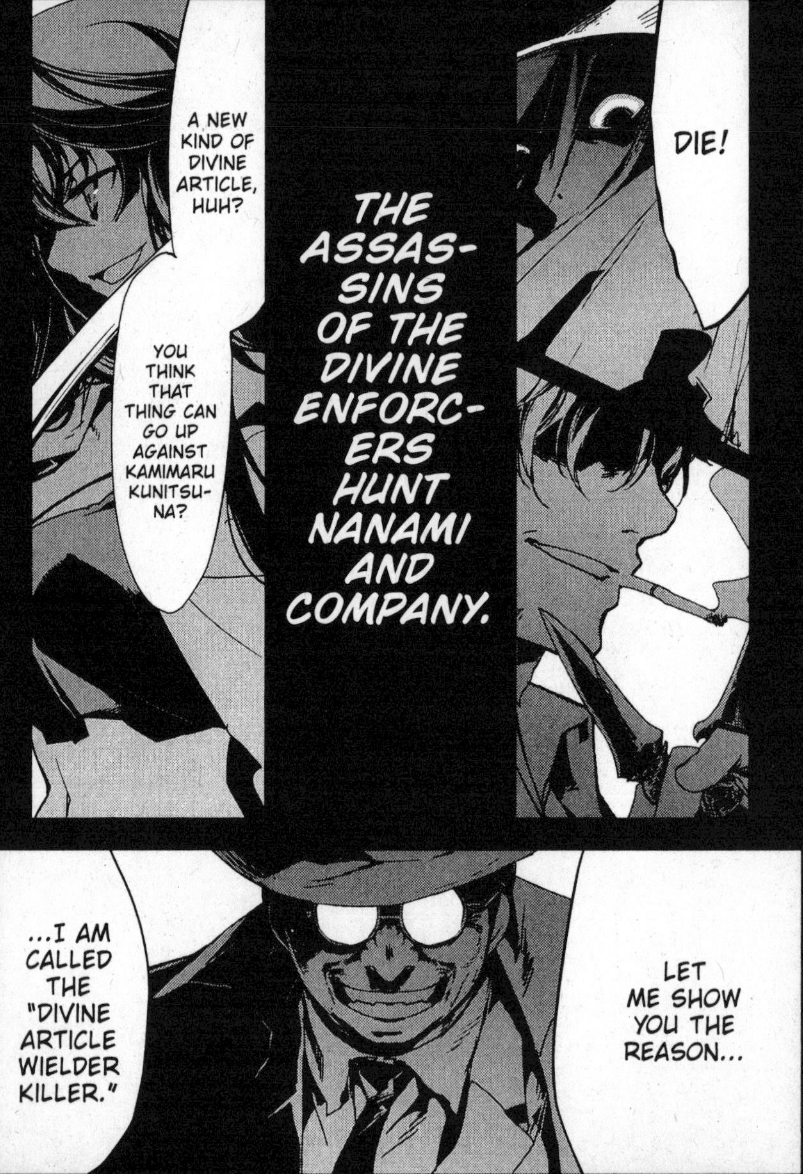
DIE!
THE ASSASSINS OF THE DIVINE ENFORCERS HUNT NANAMI AND COMPANY.
A NEW KIND OF DIVINE ARTICLE, HUH?
YOU THINK THAT THING CAN GO UP AGAINST KAMIMARU KUNITSUNA?
LET ME SHOW YOU THE REASON...
...I AM CALLED THE "DIVINE ARTICLE WIELDER KILLER."

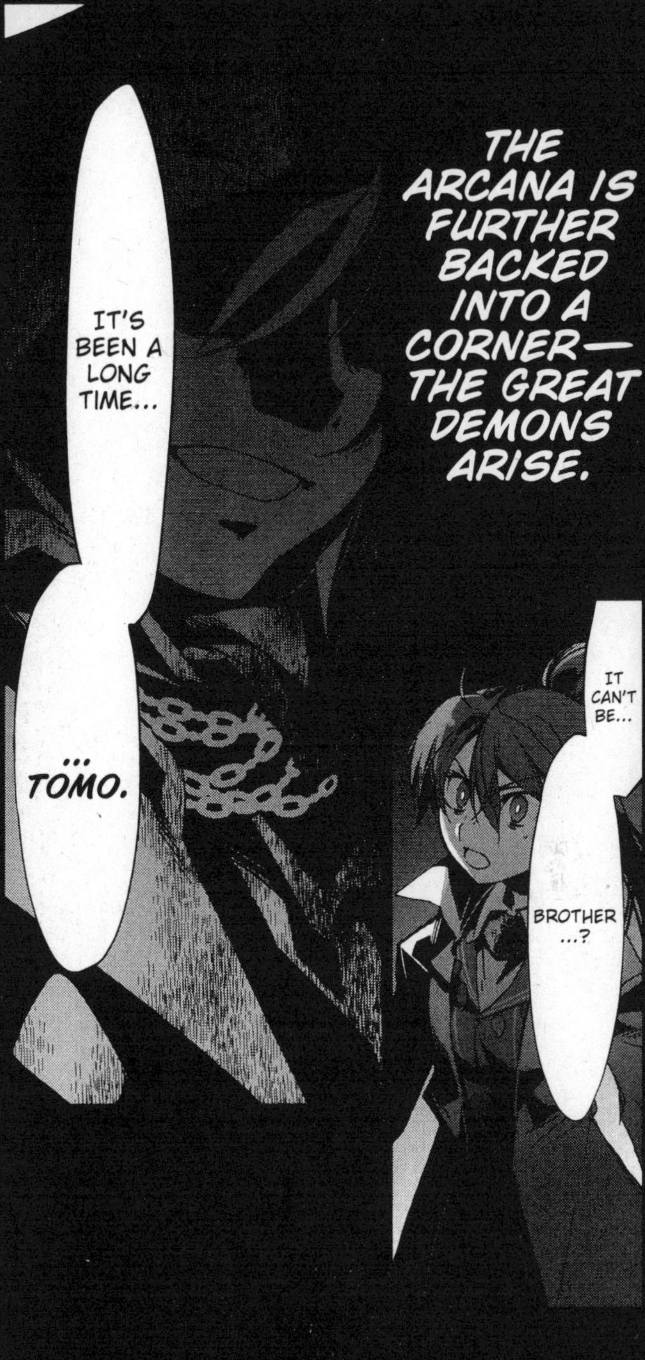
THE ARCANA IS FURTHER BACKED INTO A CORNER—THE GREAT DEMONS ARISE.
IT CAN'T BE...
BROTHER ...?
IT'S BEEN A LONG TIME...
... TOMO.

A MULTITUDE OF STRANGE ROADS WIND TOGETHER...

...AS THE STORY ACCELERATES.

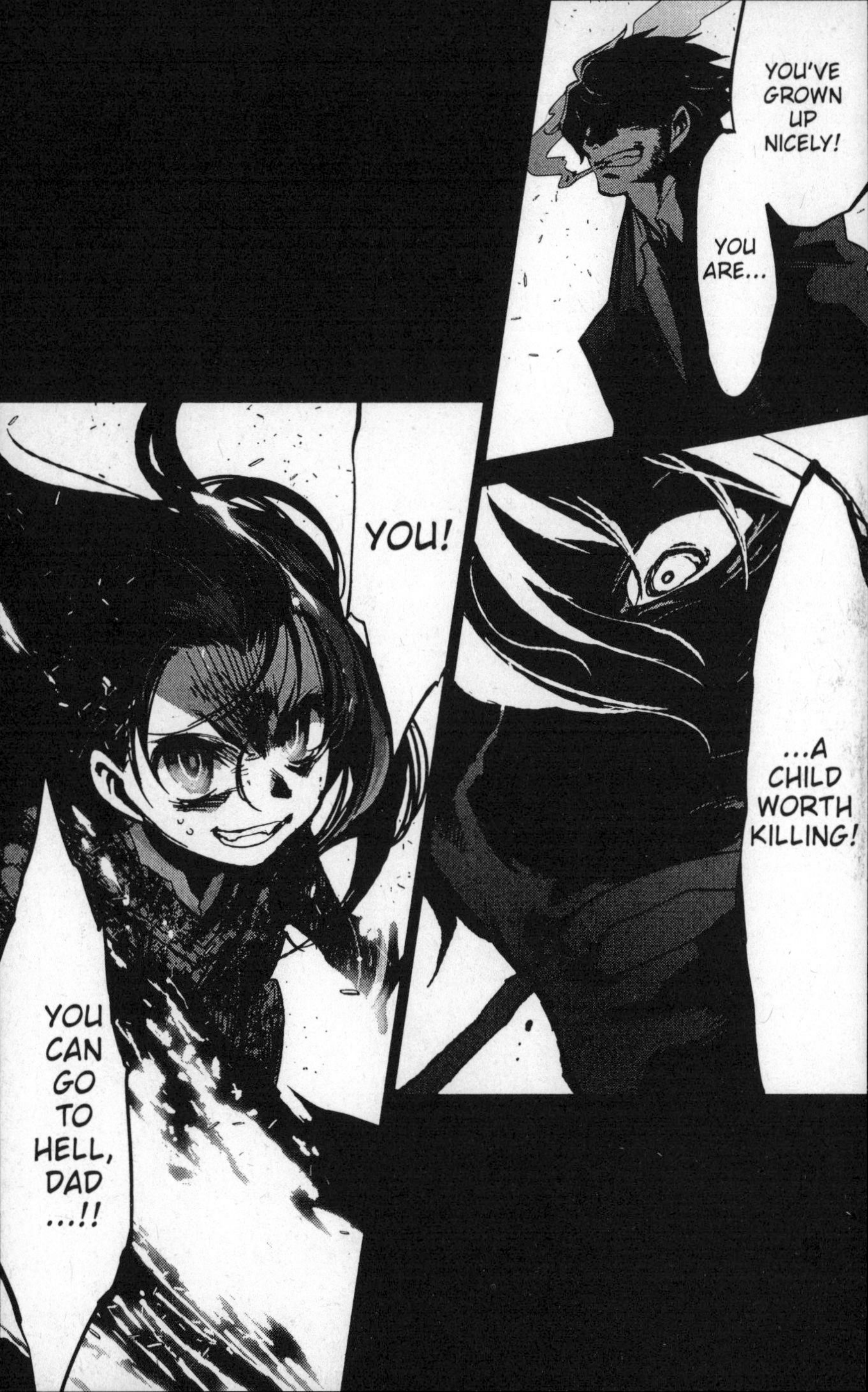
YOU'VE GROWN UP NICELY!
YOU ARE...
...A CHILD WORTH KILLING!
YOU!
YOU CAN GO TO HELL, DAD ...!!

NANAMI'S POWERS BECOME EVER MORE APPARENT—

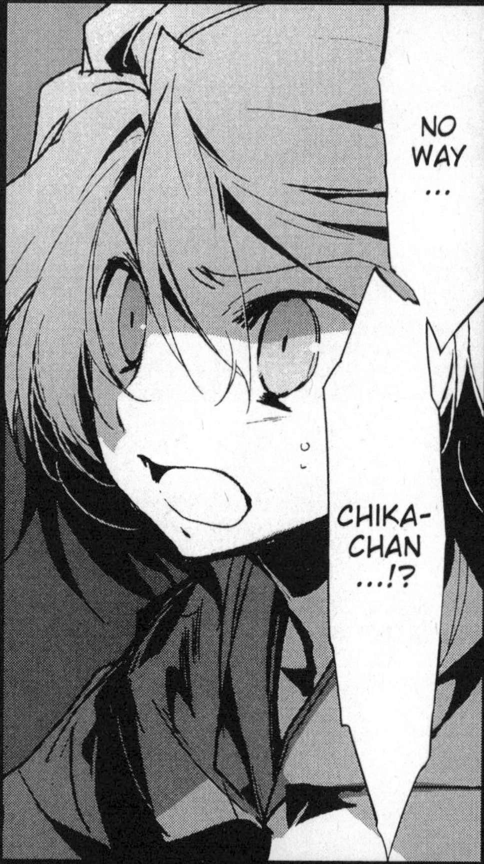
NO WAY ...
CHIKA-CHAN ...!?

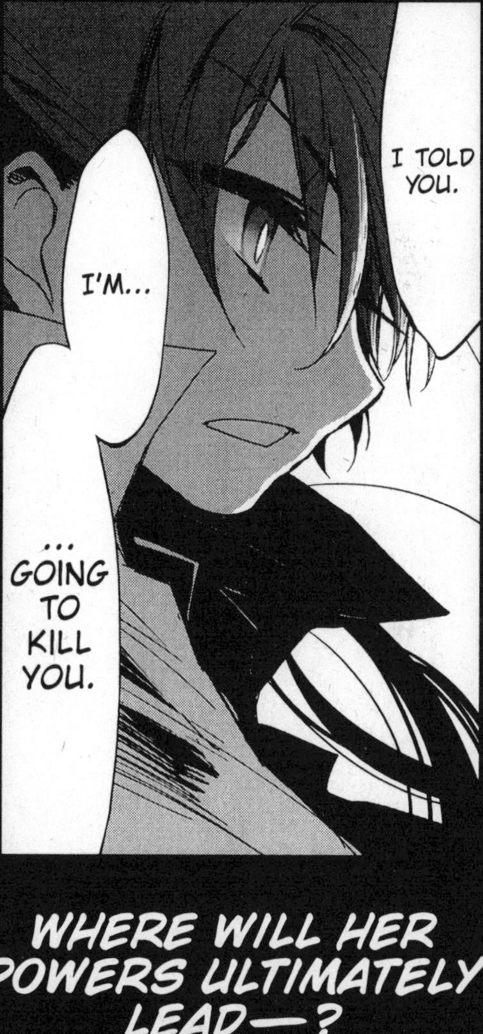
I TOLD YOU.
I'M...
...GOING TO KILL YOU.

WHERE WILL HER POWERS ULTIMATELY LEAD—?

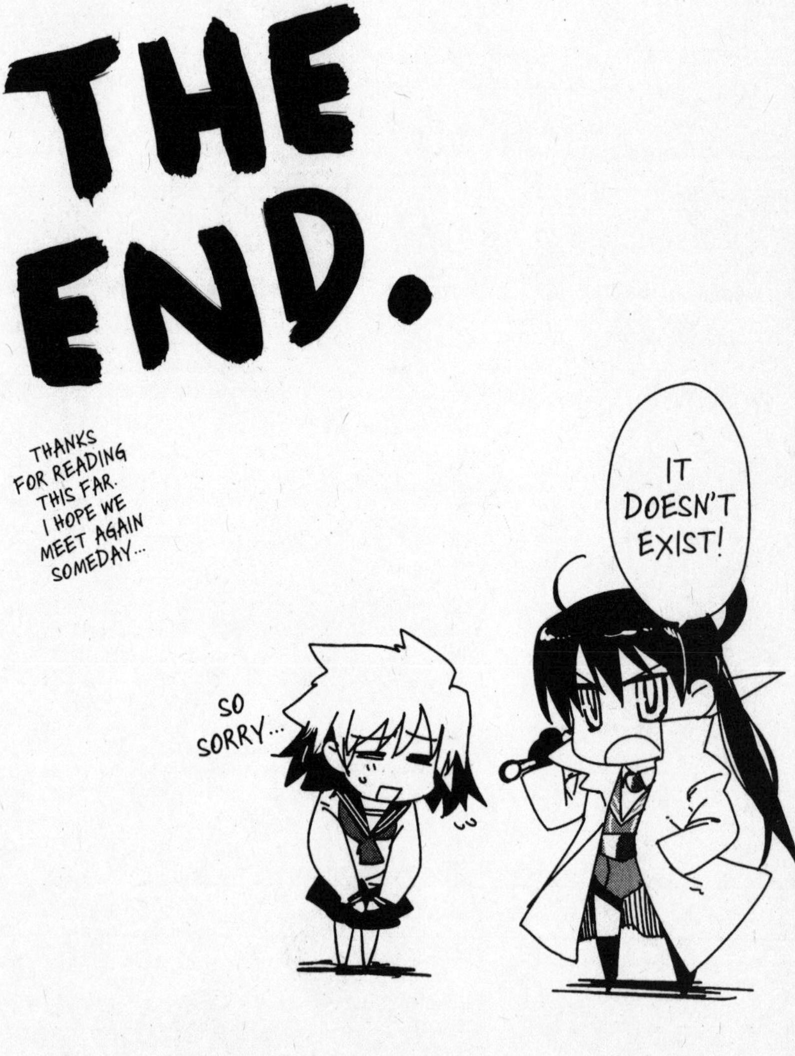
THE END.
IT DOESN'T EXIST!
THANKS FOR READING THIS FAR. I HOPE WE MEET AGAIN SOMEDAY...
SO SORRY...

TRANSLATOR'S NOTES

439523

TITLE
ONINAGI
The *oni* in the title (and the name of the sword) can be
read as "demon."

PAGE 10
Shiki
A demonic being from Japanese folklore.

Shikigami
A familiar-like being from Japanese folklore usually
conjured by a master of Onmyoudou (an *onmyouji*).

PAGE 59
Hiruko
Known as the "leech child," Hiruko was the firstborn
child of central Shinto deities Izanagi and Izanami.
He was born without bones and, as a result of his
deformities, was abandoned by his parents, who cast him
adrift on a river in a reed boat. He came to be known
and worshipped as Ebisu, the god of fishermen, among
other things.

PAGE 83
Flower Garland Sutra
Also known as the Avatamsaka Sutra, this is a metaphor
for becoming a Buddha.

PAGE 108
Oni no Kanbase
The name of Tsurugi's new Divine Article literally means
"Demon Face."

ONINAGI ④

AKIRA ISHIDA

Translation: Kaori Inoue • Lettering: Lys Blakeslee

This book is a work of fiction. Names, characters, places, and incidents are the product of the author's imagination or are used fictitiously. Any resemblance to actual events, locales, or persons, living or dead, is coincidental.

ONINAGI vol. 4 © 2010 Akira Ishida. All rights reserved. First published in Japan in 2010 by HOUBUNSHA Co., Ltd., Tokyo. English translation rights in United States, Canada, and United Kingdom arranged with HOUBUNSHA Co., Ltd. through Tuttle-Mori Agency, Inc., Tokyo.

English translation © 2014 by Hachette Book Group, Inc.

Yen Press
1290 Avenue of the Americas
New York, NY 10104

www.HachetteBookGroup.com
www.YenPress.com

Yen Press is an imprint of Hachette Book Group, Inc. The Yen Press name and logo are trademarks of Hachette Book Group, Inc.

First Yen Press Edition: October 2014

ISBN: 978-0-316-33611-6

10 9 8 7 6 5 4 3 2 1

BVG

Printed in the United States of America